Four Sociological Traditions

SELECTED READINGS

Four Sociological Traditions

SELECTED READINGS

Edited by Randall Collins

Revised and expanded edition of
Three Sociological Traditions: Selected Readings

New York • Oxford
OXFORD UNIVERSITY PRESS
1994

Oxford University Press

Oxford   New York   Toronto
Delhi   Bombay   Calcutta   Madras   Karachi
Kuala Lumpur   Singapore   Hong Kong   Tokyo
Nairobi   Dar es Salaam   Cape Town
Melbourne   Auckland   Madrid

and associated companies in
Berlin   Ibadan

Published by Oxford University Press, Inc.,
198 Madison Avenue, New York, New York 10016-4314

Oxford is a registered trademark of Oxford University Press

Library of Congress Cataloging-In-Publication Data
Four sociological traditions : selected readings /
edited by Randall Collins.
p.   cm.
To be used with: Four sociological traditions / Randall Collins.
Enlarged and updated version of:
Three sociological traditions :
selected readings /
edited by Randall Collins.   1985.
Includes bibliographical references.
ISBN 0-19-508702-X
1. Sociology.   2. Social conflict.
3. Solidarity.   4. Microsociology.
I. Collins, Randall, 1941– .
II. Collins, Randall, 1941–
Four sociological traditions.
III. Three sociological traditions.
HM24.C652   1994 Suppl.
301—dc20   93-23445

9
Printed in the United States of America

PREFACE

Sociology is known for its lack of consensus. Nevertheless, although there is plenty of divisiveness in modern sociology, it is not endless. Amid the countless specialties and viewpoints, there are at least four broad traditions that have developed intellectually and cumulated knowledge within a particular viewpoint over the last century. These four great traditions are the conflict tradition, deriving from Marx, Engels, and Weber; the rational/utilitarian tradition, which began with the English political philosophers and economists such as Locke and Adam Smith, and which has undergone a renaissance in recent decades; the analysis of the ritual and symbolic bases of social solidarity, which I have called the Durkheimian tradition after its greatest exponent; and the microinteractionist tradition that stretches from Cooley and Mead through the symbolic interactionists and ethnomethodologists to current microsociologies.

The following selections trace the four traditions from their classic statements of principles, through succeeding intellectual generations, up to their continuers and developers of today. The traditions are not static; creative new ideas are still emerging from each of them. I hope this explicit tracing of these lineages, along with my companion volume narrating their history, *Four Sociological Traditions*, will lay to rest the popular notion that sociology has gone nowhere and accomplished nothing across the four or five generations it has been alive.

My aim has been to make the classics of sociology, as well as subsequent mileposts of theory, readily accessible in one place, with their major principles clearly focused by the textual selection and by a brief editorial introduction to each. The titles and most of the subheadings, except in the case of the selections from Goffman, Hagstrom, Coleman, Douglas, and Blumer, are the editor's rather than the original authors'.

I would like to thank Ralph Collins, Mark Traugott, and Mary Wagner for assistance with the Hubert and Mauss translation.

San Diego   R.C.
July 1993

CONTENTS

III   THE DURKHEIMIAN TRADITION

IV   THE MICROINTERACTIONIST TRADITION

I THE CONFLICT TRADITION

Some Main Points of the Conflict Tradition

1800–1840	Classical economics: Ricardo		Hegel	
1840–1870	German historical economics *Realpolitik*		Marx and Engels	
1870–1900		Nietzsche	Engels' dialectical materialism	
1900–1920	Weber Michels		Marxist theories of imperialism	Simmel
1920–1940	Mannheim	Lukacs Gramsci	Frankfurt School Marxist sociologists of science	
1940–1960	Hans Gerth, C. Wright Mills Organization theory Stratification theory Political sociology			Functionalist conflict theory: Coser
1960–90	Conflict theory: Dahrendorf Lenski Collins		neo-Marxism neo-Weberianism World systems theory Historical sociology of revolutions, social movements, and the state	
	Gender-stratification theory			

History as Class Struggle [1848]; Materialism and the Theory of Ideology [1846]; The Class Basis of Politics and Revolution [1852]

KARL MARX AND FRIEDRICH ENGELS

• *The roots of modern conflict theory can be traced back to Hegel, Machiavelli, or even further, but for the sociological tradition the founding texts are those of Karl Marx and Friedrich Engels. Not all their works are sociological in the sense that I am concentrating on here (especially the extensive and rather philosophical economics of Marx). Nevertheless, the banner for subsequent conflict theory was first flown in Marx and Engels' phrase from the* Communist Manifesto *(1848): "The history of all hitherto existing society is the history of class struggles."*

The present selections give some of Marx and Engels' key socio-logical principles in relatively pure form: Classes are divided be-tween those who own the property necessary for economic produc-tion and those who own nothing but their own labor and hence must work for the property owners; ideology is shaped by those who control the means of intellectual production; the inner reality of politics is the struggle of different economic class factions over control of the state; political power depends on the material condi-tions that mobilize a class or else keep it split up in isolated fragments unable to formulate their own class interest. The peas-ants, emblematic of the oppressed class under the feudal aristoc-racy, constituted a majority of the population but were unable to mobilize as a unified group; they had no more conscious unity than "potatoes in a sack." In contrast, Marx and Engels expected indus-trial workers to form a victorious class because the growth of large factories was breaking down their isolation and bringing them together. In this way the progress of capitalism was "produc-ing . . . its own grave-diggers." The latter selections, from Marx's The Eighteenth Brumaire of Louis Bonaparte, *describe the process by which the French revolution of 1848, which had overthrown the constitutional monarchy of King Louis Philippe, was itself over-thrown in a* coup d'etat *by Louis Bonaparte, the nephew of the great Napoleon. The account not only shows Marx and Engels' sociological thinking at its most realistic, but also Marx's unparalleled gifts as a dramatic writer reporting on, and stirring up, revolution.*

HISTORY AS CLASS STRUGGLE

The history of all hitherto existing society is the history of class struggles.

Freeman and slave, patrician and plebeian, lord and serf, guild-master and journeyman, in a word, oppressor and oppressed, stood in constant opposition to one another, carried on an uninterrupted, now hidden, now open fight, a fight that each time ended, either in a revolutionary reconstitution of society at large, or in the common ruin of the contending classes.

In the earlier epochs of history, we find almost everywhere a complicated arrangement of society into various orders, a manifold gradation of social rank. In ancient Rome we have patricians, knights, plebeians, slaves; in the Middle Ages, feudal lords, vassals, guild-masters, journeymen, apprentices, serfs; in almost all of these classes, again, subordinate gradations.

The modern bourgeois society that has sprouted from the ruins of feudal society has not done away with class antagonisms. It has but established new classes, new conditions of oppression, new forms of struggle in place of the old ones.

Our epoch, the epoch of the bourgeoisie, possesses, however, this distinctive feature: It has simplified the class antagonisms. Society as a whole is more and more splitting up into two great hostile camps, into two great classes directly facing each other—bourgeoisie and proletariat.

From the serfs of the Middle Ages sprang the chartered burghers of the earliest towns. From these burgesses the first elements of the bourgeoisie were developed.

The discovery of America, the rounding of the Cape, opened up fresh ground for the rising bourgeoisie. The East-Indian and Chinese markets, the colonisation of America, trade with the colonies, the increase in the means of exchange and in commodities generally, gave to commerce, to navigation, to industry, an impulse never before known, and thereby, to the revolutionary element in the tottering feudal society, a rapid development.

The feudal system of industry, in which industrial production was monopolised by closed guilds, now no longer sufficed for the growing wants of the new markets. The manufacturing system took its place. The guild-masters were pushed aside by the manufacturing middle class; division of labour between the different corporate guilds vanished in the face of division of labour in each single workshop.

From Karl Marx and Friedrich Engels, *The Communist Manifesto*, translated by Samuel Moore (London: Swan, 1888); originally published 1848.

Meantime the markets kept ever growing, the demand ever rising. Even manufacture no longer sufficed. Thereupon, steam and machinery revolutionised industrial production. The place of manufacture was taken by the giant, modern industry, the place of the industrial middle class by industrial millionaires, the leaders of whole industrial armies, the modern bourgeois.

Modern industry has established the world market, for which the discovery of America paved the way. This market has given an immense development to commerce, to navigation, to communication by land. This development has, in its turn, reacted on the extension of industry; and in proportion as industry, commerce, navigation, railways extended, in the same proportion the bourgeoisie developed, increased its capital, and pushed into the background every class handed down from the Middle Ages.

We see, therefore, how the modern bourgeoisie is itself the product of a long course of development, of a series of revolutions in the modes of production and of exchange.

Each step in the development of the bourgeoisie was accompanied by a corresponding political advance of that class. An oppressed class under the sway of the feudal nobility, an armed and self-governing association in the medieval commune; here independent urban republic (as in Italy and Germany), there taxable "third estate" of the monarchy (as in France); afterwards, in the period of manufacture proper, serving either the semi-feudal or the absolute monarchy as a counterpoise against the nobility, and, in fact, cornerstone of the great monarchies in general—the bourgeoisie has at last, since the establishment of modern industry and of the world market, conquered for itself, in the modern representative state, exclusive political sway. The executive of the modern state is but a committee for managing the common affairs of the whole bourgeoisie.

The bourgeoisie, historically, has played a most revolutionary part.

The bourgeoisie, wherever it has got the upper hand, has put an end to all feudal, patriarchal, idyllic relations. It has pitilessly torn asunder the motley feudal ties that bound man to his "natural superiors," and has left no other nexus between man and man than naked self-interest, than callous "cash payment." It has drowned the most heavenly ecstasies of religious fervour, of chivalrous enthusiasm, of philistine sentimentalism, in the icy water of egotistical calculation. It has resolved personal worth into exchange value, and in place of the numberless indefeasible chartered freedoms, has set up that single, unconscionable freedom—Free Trade. In one word, for exploitation, veiled by religious and political illusions, it has substituted naked, shameless, direct, brutal exploitation.

The bourgeoisie has stripped of its halo every occupation hitherto honoured and looked up to with reverent awe. It has converted the physician, the lawyer, the priest, the poet, the man of science, into its paid wage labourers.

The bourgeoisie has torn away from the family its sentimental veil, and has reduced the family relation to a mere money relation.

The bourgeoisie has disclosed how it came to pass that the brutal display of vigour in the Middle Ages, which reactionaries so much admire, found its fitting complement in the most slothful indolence. It has been the first to show what man's activity can bring about. It has accomplished wonders far surpassing Egyptian pyramids, Roman aqueducts, and Gothic cathedrals; it has conducted expeditions that put in the shade all former exoduses of nations and crusades.

The bourgeoisie cannot exist without constantly revolutionising the instruments of production, and thereby the relations of production, and with them the whole relations of society. Conservation of the old modes of production in unaltered form was, on the contrary, the first condition of existence for all earlier industrial classes. Constant revolutionising of production, uninterrupted disturbance of all social conditions, everlasting uncertainty and agitation distinguish the bourgeois epoch from all earlier ones. All fixed, fast frozen relations, with their train of ancient and venerable prejudices and opinions, are swept away, all new-formed ones become antiquated before they can ossify. All that is solid melts into air, all that is holy is profaned, and man is at last compelled to face with sober senses his real conditions of life and his relations with his kind.

The need of a constantly expanding market for its products chases the bourgeoisie over the whole surface of the globe. It must nestle everywhere, settle everywhere, establish connections everywhere.

The bourgeoisie has through its exploitation of the world market given a cosmopolitan character to production and consumption in every country. To the great chagrin of reactionaries, it had drawn from under the feet of industry the national ground on which it stood. All old-established national industries have been destroyed or are daily being destroyed. They are dislodged by new industries, whose introduction becomes a life and death question for all civilised nations, by industries that no longer work up indigenous raw material, but raw material drawn from the remotest zones; industries whose products are consumed, not only at home, but in every quarter of the globe. In place of the old wants, satisfied by the production of the country, we find new wants, requiring for their satisfaction the products of distant lands and climes. In place of the old local and national seclusion and self-sufficiency, we have intercourse in every direction, universal inter-dependence of nations. And as in material, so also in intellectual production. The intellectual creations of individual nations become common property. National one-sidedness and narrow-mindedness become more and more impossible, and from the numerous national and local literatures there arises a world literature.

The bourgeoisie, by the rapid improvement of all instruments of production, by the immensely facilitated means of communication, draws all, even the most barbarian, nations into civilisation. The cheap prices of its commodities are the heavy artillery with which it batters down all Chinese walls, with which it forces the barbarians' intensely obstinate hatred of foreigners to capitulate. It compels all nations, on pain of extinction, to adopt the bourgeois mode of production; it compels them to introduce what it calls civilisation into their midst, i.e., to become bourgeois themselves. In one word, it creates a world after its own image.

The bourgeoisie has subjected the country to the rule of the towns. It has created enormous cities, has greatly increased the urban population as compared with the rural, and has thus rescued a considerable part of the population from the idiocy of rural life. Just as it has made the country dependent on the towns, so it has made barbarian and semi-barbarian countries dependent on the civilised ones, nations of peasants on nations of bourgeois, the East on the West.

The bourgeoisie keeps more and more doing away with the scattered state of the population, of the means of production, and of property. It has agglomerated population, centralised means of production, and has concentrated property in a few hands. The necessary consequence of this was political centralisation. Independent, or but loosely connected provinces, with separate interests, laws, governments, and systems of taxation, became lumped together into one nation, with one government, one code of laws, one national class interest, one frontier and one customs tariff.

The bourgeoisie, during its rule of scarce one hundred years, has created more massive and more colossal productive forces than have all preceding generations together. Subjection of nature's forces to man, machinery, application of chemistry to industry and agriculture, steam navigation, railways, electric telegraphs, clearing of whole continents for cultivation, canalisation of rivers, whole populations conjured out of the ground—what earlier century had even a presentiment that such productive forces slumbered in the lap of social labour?

We see then: the means of production and of exchange, on whose foundation the bourgeoisie built itself up, were generated in feudal society. At a certain stage in the development of these means of production and of exchange, the conditions under which feudal society produced and exchanged, the feudal organisation of agriculture and manufacturing industry, in one word, the feudal relations of property became no longer compatible with the already developed productive forces; they became so many fetters. They had to be burst asunder; they were burst asunder.

Into their place stepped free competition, accompanied by a social and political constitution adapted to it, and by the economic and political sway of the bourgeois class.

A similar movement is going on before our own eyes. Modern bourgeois society with its relations of production, of exchange and of property, a society that has conjured up gigantic means of production and of exchange, is like the sorcerer, who is no longer able to control the powers of the nether world whom he has called up by his spells. For many a decade past the history of industry and commerce is but the history of the revolt of modern productive forces against modern conditions of production, against the property relations that are the conditions for the existence of the bourgeoisie and of its rule. It is enough to mention the commercial crises that by their periodical return put the existence of the entire bourgeois society on its trial, each time more threateningly. In these crises a great part not only of the existing products, but also of the previously created productive forces, are periodically destroyed. In these crises there breaks out an epidemic that, in all earlier epochs, would have seemed an absurdity—the epidemic of over-production. Society suddenly finds itself put back into a state of momentary barbarism; it appears as if a famine, a universal war of devastation had cut off the supply of every means of subsistence; industry and commerce seem to be destroyed. And why? Because there is too much civilisation, too much means of subsistence, too much industry, too much commerce. The productive forces at the disposal of society no longer tend to further the development of the conditions of bourgeois property; on the contrary, they have become too powerful for these conditions, by which they are fettered, and so soon as they overcome these fetters, they bring disorder into the whole of bourgeois society, endanger the existence of bourgeois property. The conditions of bourgeois society are too narrow to comprise the wealth created by them. And how does the bourgeoisie get over these crises? On the one hand, by enforced destruction of a mass of productive forces; on the other, by the conquest of new markets, and by the more thorough exploitation of the old ones. That is to say, by paving the way for more extensive and more destructive crises, and by diminishing the means whereby crises are prevented.

The weapons with which the bourgeoisie felled feudalism to the ground are now turned against the bourgeoisie itself.

But not only has the bourgeoisie forged the weapons that bring death to itself; it has also called into existence the men who are to wield those weapons—the modern working class—the proletarians.

In proportion as the bourgeoisie, i.e., capital, is developed, in the same proportion is the proletariat, the modern working class, developed—a class of labourers, who live only so long as they find work, and who find work only so long as their labour increases capital. These labourers, who must sell themselves piecemeal, are a commodity, like every other article of commerce, and are consequently exposed to all the vicissitudes of competition, to all the fluctuations of the market.

Owing to the extensive use of machinery and to division of labour, the work of the proletarians has lost all individual character, and, consequently, all charm for the workman. He becomes an appendage of the machine, and it is only the most simple, most monotonous, and most easily acquired knack, that is required of him. Hence, the cost of production of a workman is restricted, almost entirely, to the means of subsistence that he requires for his maintenance, and for the propagation of his race. But the price of a commodity, and therefore also of labour, is equal to its cost of production. In proportion, therefore, as the repulsiveness of the work increases, the wage decreases. Nay more, in proportion as the use of machinery and division of labour increases, in the same proportion the burden of toil also increases, whether by prolongation of the working hours, by increase of the work exacted in a given time, or by increased speed of the machinery, etc.

Modern industry has converted the little workshop of the patriarchal master into the great factory of the industrial capitalist. Masses of labourers, crowded into the factory, are organised like soldiers. As privates of the industrial army they are placed under the command of a perfect hierarchy of officers and sergeants. Not only are they slaves of the bourgeois class, and of the bourgeois state; they are daily and hourly enslaved by the machine, by the overseer, and, above all, by the individual bourgeois manufacturer himself. The more openly this despotism proclaims gain to be its end and aim, the more petty, the more hateful and the more embittering it is.

The less the skill and exertion of strength implied in manual labour, in other words, the more modern industry becomes developed, the more is the labour of men superseded by that of women. Differences of age and sex have no longer any distinctive social validity for the working class. All are instruments of labour, more or less expensive to use, according to their age and sex.

No sooner is the exploitation of the labourer by the manufacturer, so far at an end, that he receives his wages in cash, than he is set upon by the other portions of the bourgeoisie, the landlord, the shopkeeper, the pawnbroker, etc.

The lower strata of the middle class—the small tradespeople, shopkeepers, and retired tradesmen generally, the handicraftsmen and peasants—all these sink gradually into the proletariat, partly because their diminutive capital does not suffice for the scale on which modern industry is carried on, and is swamped in the competition with the large capitalists, partly because their specialised skill is rendered worthless by new methods of production. Thus the proletariat is recruited from all classes of the population.

The proletariat goes through various stages of development. With its birth begins its struggle with the bourgeoisie. At first the contest is carried on by individual labourers, then by the work people of a factory, then by the operatives of one trade, in one locality, against the individual bourgeois who directly exploits them. They direct their attacks not against the bourgeois conditions of production, but against the instruments of production themselves; they destroy imported wares that compete with their labour, they smash to pieces machinery, they set factories ablaze, they seek to restore by force the vanished status of the workman of the Middle Ages.

At this stage the labourers still form an incoherent mass scattered over the whole country, and broken up by their mutual competition. If anywhere they unite to form more compact bodies, this is not yet the consequence of their own active union, but of the union of the bourgeoisie, which class, in order to attain its own political ends, is compelled to set the whole proletariat in motion, and is moreover yet, for a time, able to do so. At this stage, therefore, the proletarians do not fight their enemies, but the enemies of their enemies, the remnants of absolute monarchy, the landowners, the non-industrial bourgeois, the petty bourgeoisie. Thus the whole historical movement is concentrated in the hands of the bourgeoisie; every victory so obtained is a victory for the bourgeoisie.

But with the development of industry the proletariat not only increases in number; it becomes concentrated in greater masses, its strength grows, and it feels that strength more. The various interests and conditions of life within the ranks of the proletariat are more and more equalised, in proportion as machinery obliterates all distinctions of labour, and nearly everywhere reduces wages to the same low level. The growing competition among the bourgeois, and the resulting commercial crises, make the wages of the workers ever more fluctuating. The unceasing improvement of machinery, ever more rapidly developing, makes their livelihood more and more precarious; the collisions between individual workmen and individual bourgeois take more and more the character of collisions between two classes. Thereupon the workers begin to form combinations (trade unions) against the bourgeois; they club together in order to keep up the rate of wages; they found permanent associations in order to make provision beforehand for these occasional revolts. Here and there the contest breaks out into riots.

Now and then the workers are victorious, but only for a time. The real fruit of their battle lies, not in the immediate result, but in the ever expanding union of the workers. This union is helped on by the improved means of communication that are created by modern industry, and that place the workers of different localities in contact with one another. It was just this contact that was needed to centralise the numerous local struggles, all of the same character, into one national struggle between classes. But every class struggle is a political struggle. And that union, to attain which the burghers of the Middle Ages, with their miserable highways, required centuries, the modern proletarians, thanks to railways, achieve in a few years.

This organisation of the proletarians into a class, and consequently into a political party, is continually being upset again by the competition between the workers themselves. But it ever rises up again, stronger, firmer, mightier. It compels legislative recognition of particular interests of the workers, by taking advantage of the divisions among the bourgeoisie itself. Thus the Ten-Hours Bill in England was carried.

Altogether, collisions between the classes of the old society further in many ways the course of development of the proletariat. The bourgeoisie finds itself involved in a constant battle. At first with the aristocracy; later on, with those portions of the bourgeoisie itself, whose interests have become antagonistic to the progress of industry; at all times with the bourgeoisie of foreign countries. In all these battles it sees itself compelled to appeal to the proletariat, to ask for its help, and thus, to drag it into the political arena. The bourgeoisie itself, therefore, supplies the proletariat with its own elements of political and general education, in other words, it furnishes the proletariat with weapons for fighting the bourgeoisie.

Further, as we have already seen, entire sections of the ruling classes are, by the advance of industry, precipitated into the proletariat, or are at least threatened in their conditions of existence. These also supply the proletariat with fresh elements of enlightenment and progress.

Finally, in times when the class struggle nears the decisive hour, the process of dissolution going on within the ruling class, in fact within the whole range of old society, assumes such a violent, glaring character, that a small section of the ruling class cuts itself adrift, and joins the revolutionary class, the class that holds the future in its hands. Just as, therefore, at an earlier period, a section of the nobility went over to the bourgeoisie, so now a portion of the bourgeoisie goes over to the proletariat, and in particular, a portion of the bourgeois ideologists, who have raised themselves to the level of comprehending theoretically the historical movement as a whole.

Of all the classes that stand face to face with the bourgeoisie to-day, the proletariat alone is a really revolutionary class. The other classes decay and finally disappear in the face of modern industry; the proletariat is its special and essential product.

The lower middle class, the small manufacturer, the shopkeeper, the artisan, the peasant, all these fight against the bourgeoisie, to save from extinction their existence as fractions of the middle class. They are therefore not revolutionary, but conservative. Nay, more, they are reactionary, for they try to roll back the wheel of history. If by chance they are revolutionary, they are so only in view of their impending transfer into the proletariat; they thus defend not their present, but their future interests; they desert their own standpoint to place themselves at that of the proletariat.

The "dangerous class," the social scum, that passively rotting mass thrown off by the lowest layers of old society, may, here and there, be swept into the movement by a proletarian revolution; its conditions of life, however, prepare it far more for the part of a bribed tool of reactionary intrigue.

In the conditions of the proletariat, those of old society at large are already virtually swamped. The proletarian is without property; his relation to his wife and children has no longer anything in common with the bourgeois family relations; modern industrial labour, modern subjection to capital, the same in England as in France, in America as in Germany, has stripped him of every trace of national character. Law, morality, religion, are to him so many bourgeois prejudices, behind which lurk in ambush just as many bourgeois interests.

All the preceding classes that got the upper hand, sought to fortify their already acquired status by subjecting society at large to their conditions of appropriation. The proletarians cannot become masters of the productive forces of society, except by abolishing their own previous mode of appropriation, and thereby also every other previous mode of appropriation. They have nothing of their own to secure and to fortify; their mission is to destroy all previous securities for, and insurances of, individual property.

All previous historical movements were movements of minorities, or in the interest of minorities. The proletarian movement is the self-conscious, independent movement of the immense majority, in the interest of the immense majority. The proletariat, the lowest stratum of our present society, cannot stir, cannot raise itself up, without the whole superincumbent strata of official society being blown to pieces.

Though not in substance, yet in form, the struggle of the proletariat with the bourgeoisie is at first a national struggle. The proletariat of each country must, of course, first of all settle matters with its own bourgeoisie.

In depicting the most general phases of the development of the proletariat, we traced the more or less veiled civil war, raging within existing society, up to the point where that war breaks out into open revolution, and where the violent overthrow of the bourgeoisie lays the foundation for the sway of the proletariat.

Hitherto, every form of society has been based, as we have already seen, on the antagonism of oppressing and oppressed classes. But in order to oppress a class, certain conditions must be assured to it under which it can, at least, continue its slavish existence. The serf, in the period of serfdom, raised himself to membership in the commune, just as the petty bourgeois, under the yoke of feudal absolutism, managed to develop into a bourgeois. The modern labourer, on the contrary, instead of rising with the progress of industry, sinks deeper and deeper below the conditions of existence of his own class. He becomes a pauper, and pauperism develops more rapidly than population and wealth. And here it becomes evident that the bourgeoisie is unfit any longer to be the ruling class in society, and to impose its conditions of existence upon society as an overriding law. It is unfit to rule because it is incompetent to assure an existence to its slave within his slavery, because it cannot help letting him sink into such a state, that it has to feed him, instead of being fed by him. Society can no longer live under this bourgeoisie, in other words, its existence is no longer compatible with society.

The essential condition for the exitence and for the sway of the bourgeois class, is the formation and augmentation of capital; the condition for capital is wage labour. Wage labour rests exclusively on competition between the labourers. The advance of industry, whose involuntary promoter is the bourgeoisie, replaces the isolation of the labourers, due to competition, by their revolutionary combination, due to association. The development of modern industry, therefore, cuts from under its feet the very foundation on which the bourgeoisie produces and appropriates products. What the bourgeoisie therefore produces, above all, are its own grave-diggers. Its fall and the victory of the proletariat are equally inevitable.

MATERIALISM AND THE THEORY OF IDEOLOGY

The premises from which we begin are not arbitrary ones, not dogmas, but real premises from which abstraction can only be made in the imagination. They are the real individuals, their activity and the material conditions under which they live, both those which they find already existing and those produced by their activity. These premises can thus be verified in a purely empirical way.

The first premise of all human history is, of course, the existence of living human individuals. Thus the first fact to be established is the physical organization of these individuals and their consequent relation to the rest of nature. Of course, we cannot here go either into the actual physical nature of man, or into the natural conditions in which man finds himself—geological, orohydrographical, climatic and so on. The writing of history must always set out from these natural bases and their modification in the course of history through the action of man.

Men can be distinguished from animals by consciousness, by religion or anything else you like. They themselves begin to distinguish themselves from animals as soon as they begin to *produce* their means of subsistence, a step

Reprinted from Karl Marx and Friedrich Engels, *The German Ideology* (International Publishers, 1947), 6–7, 13–15, 39–41, reprinted with permission of International Publishers. Originally written in 1846.

which is conditioned by their physical organization. By producing their means of subsistence men are indirectly producing their actual material life.

The way in which men produce their means of subsistence depends first of all on the nature of the actual means they find in existence and have to reproduce. This mode of production must not be considered simply as being the reproduction of the physical existence of the individuals. Rather it is a definite form of activity of these individuals, a definite form of expressing their life, a definite *mode of life* on their part. As individuals express their life, so they are. What they are, therefore, coincides with their production, both with *what* they produce and with *how* they produce. The nature of individuals thus depends on the material conditions determining their production.

The fact is that definite individuals who are productively active in a definite way enter into these definite social and political relations. Empirical observation must in each separate instance bring out empirically, and without any mystification and speculation, the connection of the social and political structure with production. The social structure and the State are continually evolving out of the life-process of definite individuals, but of individuals, not as they may appear in their own or other people's imagination, but as they really are; that is, as they are effective, produce materially, and are active under definite material limits, presuppositions and conditions independent of their will.

The production of ideas, of conceptions, of consciousness, is at first directly interwoven with the material activity and the material intercourse of men, the language of real life. Conceiving, thinking, the mental intercourse of men, appear at this stage as the direct efflux of their material behaviour. The same applies to mental production as expressed in the language of the politics, laws, morality, religion, metaphysics of a people. Men are the producers of their conceptions, ideas, and so on—real, active men, as they are conditioned by a definite development of their productive forces and of the intercourse corresponding to these, up to its furthest forms. Consciousness can never be anything else than conscious existence, and the existence of men is their actual life-process. If in all ideology men and their circumstances appear upside down as in a *camera obscura*, this phenomenon arises just as much from their historical life-process as the inversion of objects on the retina does from their physical life-process.

In direct contrast to German philosophy which descends from heaven to earth, here we ascend from earth to heaven. That is to say, we do not set out from what men say, imagine, conceive, nor from men as narrated, thought of, imagined, conceived, in order to arrive at men in the flesh. We set out from real, active men, and on the basis of their real life-process we demonstrate the development of the ideological reflexes and echoes of this life-process. The phantoms formed in the human brain are also, necessarily, sublimates of their material life-process, which is empirically verifiable and bound to material premises. Morality, religion, metaphysics, all the rest of ideology and their corresponding forms of consciousness, thus no longer retain the semblance of independence. They have no history, no development; but men, developing their material production and their material intercourse, alter, along with this their real existence, their thinking and the products of their thinking. Life is not determined by consciousness, but consciousness by life. In the first method of approach the starting-point is consciousness taken as the living individual; in the second it is the real living individuals themselves, as they are in actual life, and consciousness is considered solely as *their* consciousness.

The ideas of the ruling class are in every epoch the ruling ideas: that is, the class, which is the "ruling material force" of society, is at the same time its ruling intellectual force. The class which has the means of material production at its disposal, has control at the same time over the means of mental production, so that thereby, generally speaking, the ideas of those who lack the means of mental production are subject to it. The ruling ideas are nothing more than the ideal expression of the dominant material relationships, the dominant material relationships grasped as ideas; hence of the relationships which make the one class the ruling one, therefore the ideas of its dominance. The individuals composing the ruling class possess among other things consciousness, and therefore think. In so far, therefore, as they rule as a class and determine the extent and compass of an epoch, it is self-evident that they do this in their whole range, hence among other things rule also as thinkers, as producers of ideas, and regulate the production and distribution of the ideas of their age: thus their ideas are the ruling ideas of the epoch. For instance, in an age and in a country where royal power, aristocracy and bourgeoisie are contending for mastery and where, therefore, mastery is shared, the doctrine of the separation of powers proves to be the dominant idea and is expressed as an "eternal law." The division of labour, which we saw above as one of the chief forces of history up till now, manifests itself also in the ruling class as the division of mental and material labour, so that inside this class one part appears as the thinkers of the class (its active, conceptive ideologists, who make the perfecting of the illusion of the class about itself their chief source of livelihood), while the others' attitude to these ideas and illusions is more passive and receptive, because they are in reality the active members of this class and have less time to make up illusions and ideas about themselves. Within this class this cleavage can even develop into a certain opposition and hostility between the two parts, which, however, in the case of a practical collision, in which the class itself is endangered, automatically comes to nothing, in which case there also vanishes the semblance that the ruling ideas were not the ideas of the ruling class and had a power distinct from the power of this class. The existence of revolutionary ideas in a particular period presupposes the existence of a revolutionary class; about the premises for the latter sufficient has already been said above.

If now in considering the course of history we detach the ideas of the ruling class from the ruling class itself and attribute to them an independent existence, if we confine ourselves to saying that these or those ideas were dominant, without bothering ourselves about the conditions of production and the producers of these ideas, if we then ignore the individuals and world conditions which are the source of the ideas, we can say, for instance, that during the time that the aristocracy was dominant, the concepts honour, loyalty, and so on, were dominant, during the dominance of the bourgeoisie the concepts freedom, equality, etc. The ruling class itself on the whole imagines this to be so. This conception of history, which is common to all historians, particularly since the eighteenth century, will necessarily come up against the phenomenon that increasingly abstract ideas hold sway, that is ideas which increasingly take on the form of universality. For each new class which puts itself in the place of one ruling before it, is compelled, merely in order to carry through its aim, to represent its interest as the common interest of all the members of society, put in an ideal form; it will give its ideas the form of universality, and represent them as the only rational, universally valid ones. The class making a revolution appears from the very start, merely because it is opposed to a *class*, not as a class but as the representative of the whole of society; it appears as the whole mass of society confronting the one ruling class. It can do this because, to start with, its interest really is more connected with the common interest of all other non-ruling classes, because under the pressure of conditions its interest has not yet been able to develop as the particular interest of a particular class. Its victory, therefore, benefits also many individuals of the other classes which are not winning a dominant position, but only in so far as it now puts these individuals in a position to raise themselves into the ruling class. When the French bourgeoisie overthrew the power of the aristocracy, it thereby made it possible for many proletarians to raise themselves above the proletariat, but only in so far as they became bourgeois. Every new class, therefore, achieves its hegemony only on a broader basis than that of the class ruling previously, in return for which the opposition of the non-ruling class against the new ruling class later develops all the more sharply and profoundly. Both these things determine the fact that the struggle to be waged against this new ruling class, in its turn, aims at a more decided and radical negation of the previous conditions of society than could all previous classes which sought to rule.

This whole semblance, that the rule of a certain class is only the rule of certain ideas, comes to a natural end, of course, as soon as society ceases at last to be organized in the form of class-rule, that is to say as soon as it is no longer necessary to represent a particular interest as general or "the general interest" as ruling.

THE CLASS BASIS OF POLITICS AND REVOLUTION

ON THE RECURRENCE OF REVOLUTIONS

France is the land where, more than anywhere else, the historical class struggles were each time fought out to a decision, and where, consequently, the changing political forms within which they move and in which their results are summarized have been stamped in the sharpest outlines. The centre of feudalism in the Middle Ages, the model country of unified monarchy, resting on estates, since the Renaissance, France demolished feudalism in the Great Revolution and established the unalloyed rule of the bourgeoisie in a classical purity unequalled by any other European land. And the struggle of the upward-striving proletariat against the ruling bourgeoisie appeared here in an acute form unknown elsewhere.

It was precisely Marx who had first discovered the great law of motion of history, the law according to which all historical struggles, whether they proceed in the political, religious, philosophical or some other ideological domain, are in fact only the more or less clear expression of struggles of social classes, and that the existence and thereby the collisions, too, between these classes are in turn conditioned by the degree of development of their economic position, by the mode of their production and of their exchange determined by it. This law, which has the same significance for history as the law of the transformation of energy has for natural science—this law gave him here, too, the key to an understanding of the history of the Second French Republic.

· · ·

Hegel remarks somewhere that all facts and personages of great importance in world history occur, as it were, twice. He forgot to add: the first time as tragedy, the second as farce. Caussidière for Danton, Louis Blanc for Robespierre, the *Montagne* of 1848 to 1851 for the *Montagne* of 1793 to 1795, the

From Karl Marx, *The Eighteenth Brumaire of Louis Bonaparte* (International Publishers, 1963) pp. 13–16, 18–19, 23–24, 46–51, 54–55, 61–62, 74–76, 103–105, 120–131. *Reprinted with permission of International Publishers. Originally published in 1852. The first two paragraphs are from Engels' preface to the Third German Edition.*

Nephew for the Uncle. And the same caricature occurs in the circumstances attending the second edition of the eighteenth Brumaire!

Men make their own history, but they do not make it just as they please; they do not make it under circumstances chosen by themselves, but under circumstances directly encountered, given and transmitted from the past. The tradition of all the dead generations weighs like a nightmare on the brain of the living. And just when they seem engaged in revolutionizing themselves and things, in creating something that has never yet existed, precisely in such periods of revolutionary crisis they anxiously conjure up the spirits of the past to their service and borrow from them names, battle cries and costumes in order to present the new scene of world history in this time-honoured disguise and this borrowed language. Thus Luther donned the mask of the Apostle Paul, the Revolution of 1789 to 1814 draped itself alternately as the Roman republic and the Roman empire, and the Revolution of 1848 knew nothing better to do than to parody, now 1789, now the revolutionary tradition of 1793 to 1795. In like manner a beginner who has learnt a new language always translates it back into his mother tongue, but he has assimilated the spirit of the new language and can freely express himself in it only when he finds his way in it without recalling the old and forgets his native tongue in the use of the new.

The social revolution of the nineteenth century cannot draw its poetry from the past, but only from the future. It cannot begin with itself before it has stripped off all superstition in regard to the past. Earlier revolutions required recollections of past world history in order to drug themselves concerning their own content. In order to arrive at its own content, the revolution of the nineteenth century must let the dead bury their dead. There the phrase went beyond the content; here the content goes beyond the phrase.

The February Revolution was a surprise attack, a *taking* of the old society *unawares*, and the people proclaimed this unexpected *stroke* as a deed of world importance, ushering in a new epoch. On December 2 the February Revolution is conjured away by a cardsharper's trick, and what seems overthrown is no longer the monarchy but the liberal concessions that were wrung from it by centuries of struggle. Instead of *society* having conquered a new content for itself, it seems that the *state* only returned to its oldest form, to the shamelessly simple domination of the sabre and the cowl. This is the answer to the *coup de main*[1] of February 1848, given by the *coup de tête*[2] of December

---

[1] *Coup de main*: Unexpected stroke.—*Ed.*
[2] *Coup de tête*: Rash act.—*Ed.*

1851. Easy come, easy go. Meanwhile the interval of time has not passed by unused. During the years 1848 to 1851 French society has made up, and that by an abbreviated because revolutionary method, for the studies and experiences which, in a regular, so to speak, textbook course of development would have had to precede the February Revolution, if it was to be more than a ruffling of the surface. Society now seems to have fallen back behind its point of departure; it has in truth first to create for itself the revolutionary point of departure, the situation, the relations, the conditions under which alone modern revolution becomes serious.

Bourgeois revolutions, like those of the eighteenth century, storm swiftly from success to success; their dramatic effects outdo each other; men and things seem set in sparkling brilliants; ecstasy is the everyday spirit; but they are short-lived; soon they have attained their zenith, and a long crapulent depression lays hold of society before it learns soberly to assimilate the results of its storm-and-stress period. On the other hand, proletarian revolutions, like those of the nineteenth century, criticize themselves constantly, interrupt themselves continually in their own course, come back to the apparently accomplished in order to begin it afresh, deride with unmerciful thoroughness the inadequacies, weaknesses and paltrinesses of their first attempts, seem to throw down their adversary only in order that he may draw new strength from the earth and rise again, more gigantic, before them, recoil ever and anon from the indefinite prodigiousness of their own aims, until a situation has been created which makes all turning back impossible, and the conditions themselves cry out:

> *Hic Rhodus, hic salta!*
> [Get it over with!]

THE DEFEAT OF THE PROLETARIAN INSURRECTION

The *bourgeois monarchy* of Louis Philippe can be followed only by a *bourgeois republic*, that is to say, whereas a limited section of the bourgeoisie ruled in the name of the king, the whole of the bourgeoisie will now rule in the name of the people. The demands of the Paris proletariat replied with the *June Insurrection*, the most colossal event in the history of European civil wars. The bourgeois republic triumphed. On its side stood the aristocracy of finance, the industrial bourgeoisie, the middle class, the petty bourgeois, the army, the *lumpenproletariat* organized as the Mobile Guard, the intellectual lights, the clergy and the rural population. On the side of the Paris proletariat stood none but itself. More than three thousand insurgents were butchered after the victory, and fifteen thousand were transported without trial. With this defeat the proletariat passes into the *background* of the revolutionary stage. It attempts to press forward again on every occasion, as soon as the movement appears to make a fresh start, but with ever decreased expenditure of strength and always slighter results. As soon as one of the social strata situated above it gets into revolutionary ferment, the proletariat enters into an alliance with it and so shares all the defeats that the different parties suffer, one after another. But these subsequent blows become the weaker, the greater the surface of society over which they are distributed. The more important leaders of the proletariat in the Assembly and in the press successively fall victims to the courts, and ever more equivocal figures come to head it. In part it throws itself into *doctrinaire experiments, exchange banks and workers' associations, hence into a movement in which it renounces the revolutionizing of the old world by means of the latter's own great, combined resources, and seeks, rather, to achieve its salvation behind society's back, in private fashion, within its limited conditions of existence, and hence necessarily suffers shipwreck.* It seems to be unable either to rediscover revolutionary greatness in itself or to win new energy from the connections newly entered into, until *all classes* with which it contended in June themselves lie prostrate beside it. But at least it succumbs with the honours of the great, world-historic struggle; not only France, but all Europe trembles at the June earthquake, while the ensuing defeats of the upper classes are so cheaply bought that they require bare-faced exaggeration by the victorious party to be able to pass for events at all, and become the more ignominious the further the defeated party is removed from the proletarian party.

The defeat of the June insurgents, to be sure, had now prepared, had levelled the ground on which the bourgeois republic could be founded and built up, but it had shown at the same time that in Europe the questions at issue are other than that of "republic or monarchy." It had revealed that here *bourgeois republic* signifies the unlimited despotism of one class over other classes.

THE TWO FACTIONS OF THE PARTY OF ORDER: LANDED PROPERTY VERSUS URBAN CAPITAL

Before we pursue parliamentary history further, some remarks are necessary to avoid common misconceptions regarding the whole character of the epoch that lies before us. Looked at with the eyes of democrats, the period of the Legislative National Assembly is concerned with what the period of the Constituent Assembly was concerned with: the simple struggle between republicans and royalists. The movement itself, however, they sum up in the one shibboleth: *"reaction"*—night, in which all cats are grey and which permits them to reel off their night watchman's commonplaces. And, to be sure, at first sight the party of Order, reveals a maze of different royalist factions, which not only intrigue against each other—each seeking to elevate its own pretender to the throne and exclude the pretender of the opposing faction— but also all unite in common hatred of, and common onslaughts on, the "republic." In opposition to this royalist conspiracy the *Montagne*, for its part, appears as the representative of the "republic." The party of Order appears to be perpetually engaged in a "reaction," directed against press, association and the like, neither more nor less than in Prussia, and which, as in Prussia, is carried out in the form of brutal police intervention by the burcaucracy, the *gendarmerie* and the law courts. The *"Montagne,"* for its part, is just as continually occupied in warding off these attacks and thus defending the "eternal rights of man" as every so-called people's party has done, more or less, for a century and a half. If one looks at the situation and the parties more closely, however, this superficial appearance, which veils the *class struggle* and the peculiar physiognomy of this period, disappears.

Legitimists and Orleanists, as we have said, formed the two great factions of the party of Order. Was that which held these factions fast to their pretenders and kept them apart from one another nothing but lily and tricolour, House of Bourbon and House of Orleans, different shades of royalism, was it at all the confession of faith of royalism? Under the Bourbons, *big landed property* had governed, with its priests and lackeys; under the Orleans, high finance, large-scale industry, large-scale trade, that is, *capital*, with its retinue of lawyers, professors and smooth-tongued orators. The Legitimate Monarchy was merely the political expression of the hereditary rule of the lords of the soil, as the July Monarchy was only the political expression of the usurped rule of the bourgeois *parvenus*. What kept the two factions apart, therefore, was not any so-called principles, it was their material conditions of existence, two different kinds of property, it was the old contrast between town and country, the rivalry between capital and landed property. That at the same time old memories, personal enmities, fears and hopes, prejudices and illusions, sympathies and antipathies, convictions, articles of faith and principles bound them to one or the other royal house, who denies this? Upon the different forms of property, upon the social conditions of existence, rises an entire superstructure of dis- tinct and peculiarly formed sentiments, illusions, modes of thought and views of life. The entire class creates and forms them out of its material foundations and out of the corresponding social relations. The single individual, who derives them through tradition and upbringing, may imagine that they form the real motives and the starting point of his activity. While Orleanists and Legitimists, while each faction sought to make itself and the other believe that it was loyalty to their two royal houses which separated them, facts later proved that it was rather their divided interests which forbade the uniting of the two royal houses. And as in private life one differentiates between what a man thinks and says of himself and what he really is and does, so in historical struggles one must distinguish still more the phrases and fancies of parties from their real organism and their real interests, their conception of themselves, from their reality. Orleanists and Legitimists found themselves side by side in the republic, with equal claims. If each side wished to effect the *restoration* of its *own* royal house against the other, that merely signified that each of the *two great interests* into which the *bourgeoisie* is split—landed property and capital—sought to restore its own supremacy and the subordination of the other. We speak of two interests of the bourgeoisie, for large landed property, despite its feudal coquetry and pride of race, has been rendered thoroughly bourgeois by the development of modern society. Thus the Tories in England long imagined that they were enthusiastic about monarchy, the church and the beauties of the old English Constitution, until the day of danger wrung from them the confession that they are enthusiastic only about *ground rent*.

THE SOCIAL-DEMOCRATIC PARTY
OF PETTY BOURGEOIS AND WORKERS

As against the coalesced bourgeoisie, a coalition between petty bourgeois and workers had been formed, the so-called *social-democratic* party. The petty bourgeois saw that they were badly rewarded after the June days of 1848, that their material interests were imperilled and that the democratic guarantees which were to ensure the effectuation of these interests were called in question by the counter-revolution. Accordingly, they came closer to the workers. On the other hand, their parliamentary representation, the *Montagne*, thrust aside during the dictatorship of the bourgeois republicans, had in the last half of the life of the Constituent Assembly reconquered its lost popularity through the struggle with Bonaparte and the royalist ministers. It had concluded an alliance with the socialist leaders. In February 1849, banquets celebrated the reconciliation. A joint program was drafted, joint election committees were set up and joint candidates put forward. From the social demands of the proletariat the revolutionary point was broken off and a democratic turn given to them; from the democratic claims of the petty bourgeoisie the purely political form was stripped off and their socialist point thrust forward. Thus arose the *Social-Democracy*. The new *Montagne*, the result of this combination, contained, apart from some supernumeraries from the working class and some socialist sectarians, the same elements as the old *Montagne*, only numerically stronger. However, in the course of development, it had changed with the class that it represented. The peculiar character of the Social-Democracy is epitomized in the fact that democratic-republican institutions are demanded as a means, not of doing away with two extremes, capital and wage labour, but of weakening their antagonism and transforming it into harmony. However different the means proposed for the attainment of this end may be, however much it may be trimmed with more or less revolutionary notions, the content remains the same. This content is the transformation of society in a democratic way, but a transformation within the bounds of the petty bourgeoisie. Only one must not form the narrow-minded notion that the petty bourgeoisie, on principle, wishes to enforce an egoistic class interest. Rather, it believes that the *special* conditions of its emancipation are the *general* conditions within the frame of which alone modern society can be saved and the class struggle avoided. Just as little must one imagine that the democratic representatives are indeed all shopkeepers or enthusiastic champions of shopkeepers. According to their education and their individual position they may be as far apart as heaven from earth. What makes them representatives of the petty bourgeoisie is the fact that in their minds they do not get beyond the limits which the latter do not get beyond in life, that they are consequently driven, theoretically, to the same problems and solutions to which material interest and social position drive the latter practically. This is, in general, the relationship between the *political* and *literary representatives* of a class and the class they represent.

After the analysis given, it is obvious that if the *Montagne* continually contends with the party of Order for the republic and the so-called rights of man, neither the republic nor the rights of man are its final end, any more than an army which one wants to deprive of its weapons and which resists has taken the field in order to remain in possession of its own weapons.

But the democrat, because he represents the petty bourgeoisie, that is, a *transition class*, in which the interests of two classes are simultaneously mutually blunted, imagines himself elevated above class antagonism generally. The democrats concede that a privileged class confronts them, but they, along with all the rest of the nation, form the *people*. What they represent is the *people's rights*; what interests them is the *people's interests*. Accordingly, when a struggle is impending, they do not need to examine the interests and positions of the different classes. They do not need to weigh their own resources too critically. They have merely to give the signal and the *people*, with all its inexhaustible resources, will fall upon the *oppressors*. Now, if in the performance their interests prove to be uninteresting and their potency impotence, then either the fault lies with pernicious sophists, who split the *indivisible people* into different hostile camps, or the army was too brutalized and blinded to comprehend that the pure aims of democracy are the best thing for it itself, or the whole thing has been wrecked by a detail in its execution, or else an unforeseen accident has this time spoilt the game. In any case, the democrat comes out of the most disgraceful defeat just as immaculate as he was innocent when he went into it, with the newly-won conviction that he is bound to win, not that he himself and his party have to give up the old standpoint, but, on the contrary, that conditions have to ripen to suit him.

THE FIGHT OVER THE STATE APPARATUS

It is immediately obvious that in a country like France, where the executive power commands an army of officials numbering more than half a million individuals and therefore constantly maintains an immense mass of interests and livelihoods in the most absolute dependence; where the state enmeshes, controls, regulates, superintends and tutors civil society from its most comprehensive manifestations of life down to its most insignificant stirrings, from its most general modes of being to the private existence of individuals; where through the most extraordinary centralization this parasitic body acquires a ubiquity, an omniscience, a capacity for accelerated mobility and an elasticity which finds a counterpart only in the helpless dependence, in the loose shapelessness of the actual body politic—it is obvious that in such a country the National Assembly forfeits all real influence when it loses command of the ministerial posts, if it does not at the same time simplify the administration of the state, reduce the army of officials as far as possible and, finally, let civil society and public opinion create organs of their own, independent of the governmental power. But it is precisely with the maintenance of that extensive state machine in its numerous ramifications that the *material interests* of the French bourgeoisie are interwoven in the closest fashion. Here it finds posts for its surplus population and makes up in the form of state salaries for what it cannot pocket in the form of profit, interest, rents and honorariums. On the other hand, its *political interests* compelled it to increase daily the repressive measures and therefore the resources and the personnel of the state power, while at the same time it had to wage an uninterrupted war against public opinion and mistrustfully mutilate, cripple, the independent organs of the social movement, where it did not succeed in amputating them entirely. Thus the French bourgeoisie was compelled by its class position to annihilate, on the one hand, the vital conditions of all parliamentary power, and therefore, likewise, of its own, and to render irresistible, on the other hand, the executive power hostile to it.

BONAPARTE ORGANIZES THE LUMPENPROLETARIAT

As in 1849 so during this year's parliamentary recess, the party of Order had broken up into its separate factions, each occupied with its own Restoration intrigues, which had obtained fresh nutriment through the death of Louis Philippe. The Legitimist king, Henry V, had even nominated a formal ministry which resided in Paris and in which members of the Permanent Commission held seats. Bonaparte, in his turn, was therefore entitled to make tours of the French Departments, and according to the disposition of the town that he favoured with his presence, now more or less covertly, now more or less overtly, to divulge his own restoration plans and canvass votes for himself. On these processions, which the great official *Moniteur* and the little private *Moniteurs* of Bonaparte naturally had to celebrate as triumphal processions, he was constantly accompanied by persons affiliated with the *Society of December 10.* This society dates from the year 1849. On the pretext of founding a benevolent society, the *lumpenproletariat* of Paris had been organized into secret sections, each section being led by Bonapartist agents, with a Bonapartist general at the head of the whole. Alongside decayed *roués* with dubious means of subsistence and of dubious origin, alongside ruined and adventurous offshoots of the bourgeoisie, were vagabonds, discharged soldiers, discharged jailbirds, escaped galley slaves, swindlers, mountebanks, *lazzaroni*, pickpockets, tricksters, gamblers, *maquereaus*, brothel keepers, porters, *literati*, organ-grinders, ragpickers, knife grinders, tinkers, beggars—in short, the whole indefinite, disintegrated mass, thrown hither and thither, which the French term *la bohème*; from this kindred element Bonaparte formed the core of the Society of December 10. A "benevolent society"—in so far as, like Bonaparte, all its members felt the need of benefiting themselves at the expense of the labouring nation. This Bonaparte, who constitutes himself *chief of the lumpenproletariat*, who here alone rediscovers in mass form the interests which he personally pursues, who recognizes in this scum, offal, refuse of all classes the only class upon which he can base himself unconditionally, is the real Bonaparte, the Bonaparte *sans phrase*. An old crafty *roué*, he conceives the historical life of the nations and their performances of state as comedy in the most vulgar sense, as a masquerade where the grand costumes, words and postures merely serve to mask the pettiest knavery. Thus on his expedition to Strasbourg, where a trained Swiss vulture had played the part of the Napoleonic eagle. For his irruption into Boulogne he puts some London lackeys into French uniforms. They represent the army. In his Society of December 10, he assembles ten thousand rascally fellows, who are to play the part of the people, as Nick Bottom that of the lion. At a moment when the bourgeoisie itself played the most complete comedy, but in the most serious manner in the world, without infringing any of the pedantic conditions of French dramatic etiquette, and was itself half deceived, half convinced of the solemnity of its own performance of state, the adventurer, who took the comedy as plain comedy, was bound to win. Only when he has eliminated his solemn opponent, when he himself now takes his imperial role seriously and under the Napoleonic mask imagines he is the real Napoleon, does he become the victim of his own conception of the world, the serious buffoon who no longer takes world history for a comedy but his comedy for world history. What the national *ateliers* were for the socialist workers, what the *Gardes mobiles* were for the bourgeois republicans, the Society of December 10 was for Bonaparte, the party fighting force peculiar to him. On his journeys the detachments of this society packing the railways had to improvise a public for him, stage public enthusiasm, roar *vive l'Empereur*, insult and thrash republicans, of course, under the protection of the police. On his return journeys to Paris they had to form the advance guard, forestall counter-demonstrations or disperse them.

THE ARISTOCRACY OF FINANCE AND THE INDUSTRIAL BOURGEOISIE

[T]he section of the commercial bourgeoisie which had held the lion's share of power under Louis Philippe, namely, the *aristocracy of finance*, had become Bonapartist. Fould represented not only Bonaparte's interests in the *bourse*, he represented at the same time the interests of the *bourse* before Bonaparte. The position of the aristocracy of finance is most strikingly depicted in a passage from its European organ, the London *Economist*. In its number of February 1, 1851, its Paris correspondent writes:

Now we have it stated from numerous quarters that above all things France demands tranquillity. The President declares it in his message to the Legislative Assembly; it is echoed from the tribune; is asserted in the journals; it is announced from the pulpit; *it is demonstrated by the sensitiveness of the public funds at the least prospect of disturbance, and their firmness the instant it is made manifest that the executive is victorious.*

In its issue of November 29, 1851, *The Economist* declares in its own name:

The President is the guardian of order, and is now recognized as such on every Stock Exchange of Europe.

The aristocracy of finance, therefore, condemned the parliamentary struggle of the party of Order with the executive power as a *disturbance of order*, and celebrated every victory of the President over its ostensible representatives as a *victory of order*. By the aristocracy of finance must here be understood not merely the great loan promoters and speculators in public funds, in regard to whom it is immediately obvious that their interests coincide with the interests of the state power. All modern finance, the whole of the banking business, is interwoven in the closest fashion with public credit. A part of their business capital is necessarily invested and put out at interest in quickly convertible public funds. Their deposits, the capital placed at their disposal and distributed by them among merchants and industrialists, are partly derived from the dividends of holders of government securities. If in every epoch the stability of the state power signified Moses and the prophets to the entire money market and to the priests of this money market, why not all the more so today, when every deluge threatens to sweep away the old states, and the old state debts with them?

The *industrial bourgeoisie*, too, in its fanaticism for order, was angered by the squabbles of the parliamentary party of Order with the executive power. After their vote of January 18 on the occasion of Changarnier's dismissal, Thiers, Angles, Sainte-Beuve, and so on, received from their constituents, in precisely the industrial districts, public reproofs in which particularly their coalition with the *Montagne* was scourged as high treason to order. If, as we have seen, the boastful taunts, the petty intrigues which marked the struggle of the party of Order with the President merited no better reception, then, on the other hand, this bourgeois party, which required its representatives to allow the military power to pass from its own parliament to an adventurous pretender without offering resistance, was not even worth the intrigues that were squandered in its interests. It proved that the struggle to maintain its *public* interests, its own *class interests*, its *political power*, only troubled and upset it, as it was a disturbance of private business.

COUP D'ETAT

If ever an event has, well in advance of its coming, cast its shadow before, it was Bonaparte's *coup d'état*. . . . During every parliamentary storm, the Bonapartist journals threatened a *coup d'état*, and the nearer the crisis drew, the louder grew their tone. In the orgies that Bonaparte kept up every night with men and women of the "swell mob," as soon as the hour of midnight approached and copious potations had loosened tongues and fired imaginations, the *coup d'état* was fixed for the following morning. Swords were drawn, glasses clinked, the Representatives were thrown out of the window, the imperial mantle fell upon Bonaparte's shoulders, until the following morning banished the spook once more and astonished Paris learned, from vestals of little reticence and from indiscreet paladins, of the danger it had once again escaped. During the months of September and October rumours of a *coup d'état* followed fast one after the other. Simultaneously, the shadow took on colour, like a variegated daguerreotype. Look up the September and October copies of the organs of the European daily press and you will find, word for word, intimations like the following: "Paris is full of rumours of a *coup d'état*. The capital is to be filled with troops during the night, and the next morning is to bring decrees which will dissolve the National Assembly, declare the Department of the Seine in a state of siege, restore universal suffrage and appeal to the people. Bonaparte is said to be seeking ministers for the execution of these illegal decrees." The letters that bring these tidings always end with the fateful word *"postponed."* The *coup d'état* was ever the fixed idea of Bonaparte. With this idea he had again set foot on French soil. He was so obsessed by it that he continually betrayed it and blurted it out. He was so weak that, just as continually, he gave it up again. The shadow of the *coup d'état* had become so familiar to the Parisians as a spectre that they were not willing to believe in it when it finally appeared in the flesh. What allowed the *coup d'état* to succeed was, therefore, neither the reticent reserve of the chief of the Society of December 10 nor the fact that the National Assembly was caught unawares. If it succeeded, it succeeded despite *his* indiscretion and with *its* foreknowledge, a necessary, inevitable result of antecedent developments.

•   •   •

By splitting up into its hostile factions, the party of Order had long ago forfeited its independent parliamentary majority. It showed now that there was no longer any majority at all in parliament. The National Assembly had become *incapable of transacting business*. Its atomic constituents were no longer held together by any force of cohesion; it had drawn its last breath; it was dead.

Cromwell, when he dissolved the Long Parliament, went alone into its midst, drew out his watch in order that it should not continue to exist a minute after the time limit fixed by him, and drove out each one of the members of parliament with hilariously humourous taunts. Napoleon, smaller than his prototype, at least betook himself on the eighteenth Brumaire to the legislative body and read out to it, though in a faltering voice, its sentence of death.

THE VICTORY OF BUREAUCRACY OVER PARLIAMENT

But if the overthrow of the parliamentary republic contains within itself the germ of the triumph of the proletarian revolution, its immediate and palpable result was *the victory of Bonaparte over parliament, of the executive power over the legislative power, of force without phrases over the force of phrases*. In parliament the nation made its general will the law, that is, it made the law of the ruling class its general will. Before the executive power it renounces all will of its own and submits to the superior command of an alien will, to authority. The executive power, in contrast to the legislative power, expresses the heteronomy of a nation, in contrast to its autonomy. France, therefore, seems to have escaped the despotism of a class only to fall back beneath the despotism of an individual, and, what is more, beneath the authority of an individual without authority. The struggle seems to be settled in such a way that all classes, equally impotent and equally mute, fall on their knees before the rifle butt.

But the revolution is thoroughgoing. It is still journeying through purgatory. It does its work methodically. By December 2, 1851, it had completed one half of its preparatory work; it is now completing the other half. First it perfected the parliamentary power, in order to be able to overthrow it. Now that it has attained this, it perfects the *executive power*, reduces it to its purest expression, isolates it, sets it up against itself as the sole target, in order to concentrate all its forces of destruction against it. And when it has done this second half of its preliminary work, Europe will leap from its seat and exultantly exclaim: Well grubbed, old mole!

This executive power with its enormous bureaucratic and military organization, with its ingenious state machinery, embracing wide strata, with a host of officials numbering half a million, besides an army of another half million, this appalling parasitic body, which enmeshes the body of French society like a net and chokes all its pores, sprang up in the days of the absolute monarchy, with the decay of the feudal system, which it helped to hasten. The seignorial privileges of the landowners and towns became transformed into so many attributes of the state power, the feudal dignitaries into paid officials and the motley pattern of conflicting medieval plenary powers into the regulated plan of a state authority whose work is divided and centralized as in a factory. The first French Revolution, with its task of breaking all separate local, territorial, urban and provincial powers in order to create the civil unity of the nation, was bound to develop what the absolute monarchy had begun: centralization, but at the same time the extent, the attributes and the agents of governmental power. Napoleon perfected this state machinery. The Legitimist Monarchy and the July Monarchy added nothing but a greater division of labour, growing in the same measure as the division of labour within bourgeois society created new groups of interests, and, therefore, new material for state administration. Every *common* interest was straightway severed from society, counterposed to it as a higher, *general* interest, snatched from the activity of society's members themselves and made an object of government activity, from a bridge, a schoolhouse and the communal property of a village community to the railways, the national wealth and the national university of France. Finally, in its struggle against the revolution, the parliamentary republic found itself compelled to strengthen, along with the repressive measures, the resources and centralization of governmental power. All revolutions perfected this machine instead of smashing it. The parties that contended in turn for domination regarded the possession of this huge state edifice as the principal spoils of the victor.

But under the absolute monarchy, during the first Revolution, under Napoleon, bureaucracy was only the means of preparing the class rule of the bourgeoisie. Under the Restoration, under Louis Philippe, under the parliamentary republic, it was the instrument of the ruling class, however much it strove for power of its own.

Only under the second Bonaparte does the state seem to have made itself completely independent.

THE DICTATOR AS REPRESENTATIVE OF A
ONCE-REVOLUTIONARY CLASS GONE CONSERVATIVE:
THE PEASANT PROPRIETOR

And yet the state power is not suspended in midair. Bonaparte represents a class, and the most numerous class of French society at that, the *small-holding peasants*.

Just as the Bourbons were the dynasty of big landed property and just as the Orleans were the dynasty of money, so the Bonapartes are the dynasty of the peasants, that is, the mass of the French people. Not the Bonaparte who submitted to the bourgeois parliament, but the Bonaparte who dispersed the bourgeois parliament is the chosen of the peasantry. For three years the towns had succeeded in falsifying the meaning of the election of December 10 and in cheating the peasants out of the restoration of the empire. The election of December 10, 1848, has been consummated only by the *coup d'état* of December 2, 1851.

The small-holding peasants form a vast mass, the members of which live in similar conditions but without entering into manifold relations with one another. Their mode of production isolates them from one another instead of bringing them into mutual intercourse. The isolation is increased by France's bad means of communication and by the poverty of the peasants. Their field of production, the small holding, admits of no division of labour in its cultivation, no application of science and, therefore, no diversity of development, no variety of talent, no wealth of social relationships. Each individual peasant family is almost self-sufficient; it itself directly produces the major part of its consumption and thus acquires its means of life more through exchange with nature than in intercourse with society. A small holding, a peasant and his family; alongside them another small holding, another peasant and another family. A few score of these make up a village, and a few score of villages make up a Department. In this way, the great mass of the French nation is formed by simple addition of homologous magnitudes, much as potatoes in a sack form a sack of potatoes. In so far as millions of families live under economic conditions of existence that separate their mode of life, their interests and their culture from those of the other classes, and put them in hostile opposition to the latter, they form a class. In so far as there is merely a local interconnection among these small-holding peasants, and the identity of their interests begets no community, no national bond and no political organization among them, they do not form a class. They are consequently incapable of enforcing their class interest in their own name, whether through a parliament or through a convention. They cannot represent themselves, they must be represented. Their representative must at the same time appear as their master, as an authority over them, as an unlimited governmental power that protects them against the other classes and sends them rain and sunshine from above. The political influence of the small-holding peasants, therefore, finds its final expression in the executive power subordinating society to itself.

Historical tradition gave rise to the belief of the French peasants in the miracle that a man named Napoleon would bring all the glory back to them. And an individual turned up who gives himself out as the man because he bears the name of Napoleon, in consequence of the *Code Napoléon*, which lays down that *la recherche de la paternité est interdite*.[3] After a vagabondage of twenty years and after a series of grotesque adventures, the legend finds fulfilment and the man becomes Emperor of the French. The fixed idea of the Nephew was realized, because it coincided with the fixed idea of the most numerous class of the French people.

But, it may be objected, what about the peasant risings in half of France, the raids on the peasants by the army, the mass incarceration and transportation of peasants?

Since Louis XIV, France has experienced no similar persecution of the peasants "on account of demagogic practices."

But let there be no misunderstanding. The Bonaparte dynasty represents not the revolutionary, but the conservative peasant; not the peasant that strikes out beyond the condition of his social existence, the small holding, but rather the peasant who wants to consolidate this holding, not the country folk who, linked up with the towns, want to overthrow the old order through their own energies, but on the contrary those who, in stupefied seclusion within this old order, want to see themselves and their small holdings saved and favoured by the ghost of the empire. It represents not the enlightenment, but the superstition of the peasant; not his judgement, but his prejudice; not his future, but his past; not his modern Cevennes, but his modern Vendée.

After the first revolution had transformed the peasants from semi-villeins into freeholders, Napoleon confirmed and regulated the conditions on which they could exploit undisturbed the soil of France which had only just fallen to their lot and slake their youthful passion for property. But what is now causing the ruin of the French peasant is his small holding itself, the division of the land,

[3]Enquiry into paternity is forbidden.—*Ed.*

the form of property which Napoleon consolidated in France. It is precisely the material conditions which made the feudal peasant a small-holding peasant and Napoleon an emperor. Two generations have sufficed to produce the inevitable result: progressive deterioration of agriculture, progressive indebtedness of the agriculturist. The "Napoleonic" form of property, which at the beginning of the nineteenth century was the condition for the liberation and enrichment of the French country folk, has developed in the course of this century into the law of their enslavement and pauperization.

The economic development of small-holding property has radically changed the relation of the peasants to the other classes of society. Under Napoleon, the fragmentation of the land in the countryside supplemented free competition and the beginning of big industry in the towns. The peasant class was the ubiquitous protest against the landed aristocracy which had just been overthrown. The roots that small-holding property struck in French soil deprived feudalism of all nutriment. Its landmarks formed the natural fortifications of the bourgeoisie against any surprise attack on the part of its old overlords. But in the course of the nineteenth century the feudal lords were replaced by urban usurers; the feudal obligation that went with the land was replaced by the mortgage; aristocratic landed property was replaced by bourgeois capital. The small holding of the peasant is now only the pretext that allows the capitalist to draw profits, interest and rent from the soil, while leaving it to the tiller of the soil himself to see how he can extract his wages. The mortgage debt burdening the soil of France imposes on the French peasantry payment of an amount of interest equal to the annual interest on the entire British national debt. Small-holding property, in this enslavement by capital to which its development inevitably pushes forward, has transformed the mass of the French nation into troglodytes.

Besides the mortgage which capital imposes on it, the small holding is burdened by *taxes*. Taxes are the source of life for the bureaucracy, the army, the priests and the court, in short, for the whole apparatus of the executive power. Strong government and heavy taxes are identical. By its very nature, small-holding property forms a suitable basis for an all-powerful and innumerable bureaucracy. It creates a uniform level of relationships and persons over the whole surface of the land. Hence it also permits of uniform action from a supreme centre on all points of this uniform mass. It annihilates the aristocratic intermediate grades between the mass of the people and the state power. On all sides, therefore, it calls forth the direct interference of this state power and the interposition of its immediate organs. Finally, it produces an unemployed surplus population for which there is no place either on the land or in the towns, and which accordingly reaches out for state offices as a sort of respectable alms, and provokes the creation of state posts. By the new markets which he opened at the point of the bayonet, by the plundering of the Continent, Napoleon repaid the compulsory taxes with interest. These taxes were a spur to the industry of the peasant, whereas now they rob his industry of its last resources and complete his inability to resist pauperism. And an enormous bureaucracy, well-gallooned and well-fed, is the *"idée napoléonienne"* which is most congenial of all to the second Bonaparte. How could it be otherwise, seeing that alongside the actual classes of society he is forced to create an artificial caste, for which the maintenance of his regime becomes a bread-and-butter question? Accordingly, one of his first financial operations was the raising of officials' salaries to their old level and the creation of new sinecures.

Lastly, the culminating point of the *"idées napoléoniennes"* is the preponderance of the *army*. The army was the *point d'honneur*[4] of the small-holding peasants, it was they themselves transformed into heroes, defending their new possessions against the outer world, glorifying their recently won nationhood, plundering and revolutionizing the world. The uniform was their own state dress; war was their poetry; the small holding, extended and rounded off in imagination, was their fatherland, and patriotism the ideal form of the sense of property. But the enemies against whom the French peasant has now to defend his property are not the Cossacks; they are the *huissiers*[5] and the tax collectors. The small holding lies no longer in the so-called fatherland, but in the register of mortgages. The army itself is no longer the flower of the peasant youth; it is the swamp-flower of the peasant *lumpenproletariat*. It consists in large measure of *remplaçants*, of substitutes, just as the second Bonaparte is himself only a *remplaçant*, the substitute for Napoleon.

One sees: *all* "idées napoléoniennes" *are ideas of the undeveloped small holding in the freshness of its youth;* for the small holding that has outlived its day they are an absurdity. They are only the hallucinations of its death struggle, words that are transformed into phrases, spirits transformed into ghosts. But the parody of the empire [*des Imperialismus*] was necessary to free the mass of the French nation from the weight of tradition and to work out in pure form the opposition between the state power and society. With the progressive undermining of small-holding property, the state structure erected

[4]Matter of honour, a point of special touch.—*Ed.*
[5]*Huissiers:* Bailiffs.—*Ed.*

upon it collapses. The centralization of the state that modern society requires arises only on the ruins of the military-bureaucratic government machinery which was forged in opposition to feudalism.

The condition of the French peasants provides us with the answer to the riddle of the *general elections of December 20 and 21*, which bore the second Bonaparte up Mount Sinai, not to receive laws, but to give them.

The Origin of Modern Capitalism [1920]

MAX WEBER

• *Max Weber's contributions to conflict theory, as to sociology in general, are voluminous and would require an entire work of their own to excerpt. Weber's main concern throughout his intellectual career, though, was the origins of modern capitalism. There is only one place in his entire works where he summarizes his overall theory: the concluding part of the lectures he gave in the last year of his life, the* General Economic History. *Far less known than* The Protestant Ethic and the Spirit of Capitalism *or indeed than many of his other writings, this work has been a kind of secret handbook of Weber's encompassing vision.*

The portions presented here give Weber's full schema in compressed form. The "rationalized" form that sets off modern capitalism from most other historical types of capitalism is characterized by two points that Marx also stressed: (1) free and propertyless labor *moving in response to the demands of an unrestricted market and (2) the* entrepreneurial organization of capital. *But Weber also insisted that technology and all other factors of production must be* rationalized and calculable *and* centralized in the hands of the entrepreneur. *These characteristics only came into being on the basis of a* calculable law, *which itself was further dependent on earlier parts of the historical chain of causes, including the* bureaucratic state, *which monopolized the professional means of violence, as well as strong pockets of* legal citizenship rights, *which allowed business interests some leverage against the state. There is also a second great branch of causal connections behind modern capitalism, culminating in a* methodical, nondualistic, and universally applicable economic ethic, *which had its origins in the Judaic, Greek, and Christian religions. Weber's more famous Protestant Ethic, the subject of his first notable publication, thus comes into the overall scheme as only a late addition to one of the two long chains of historical conditions that were necessary before modern capitalism could emerge.*

Max Weber, *General Economic History* (New York: Greenberg Publishers, 1927), pp. 275–78, 302, 311–16, 322–26, 332–39, 342–44, 352–56, 365–369. Originally published in 1923, from 1920 lectures.

THE MEANING AND PRESUPPOSITIONS OF
MODERN CAPITALISM

Capitalism is present wherever the industrial provision for the needs of a human group is carried out by the method of enterprise, irrespective of what need is involved. More specifically, a rational capitalistic establishment is one with capital accounting, that is, an establishment which determines its income yielding power by calculation according to the methods of modern bookkeeping and the striking of a balance. The device of the balance was first insisted upon by the Dutch theorist Simon Stevin in the year [1582–Ed.].

It goes without saying that an individual economy may be conducted along capitalistic lines to the most widely varying extent; parts of the economic provision may be organized capitalistically and other parts on the handicraft or the manorial pattern. Thus at a very early time the city of Genoa had a part of its political needs, namely those for the prosecution of war, provided in capitalistic fashion, through stock companies. In the Roman empire, the supply of the population of the capital city with grain was carried out by officials, who however for this purpose, besides control over their subalterns, had the right to command the services of transport organizations; thus the leiturgical or forced contribution type of organization was combined with administration of public resources. Today, in contrast with the greater part of the past, our everyday needs are supplied capitalistically, our political needs however through compulsory contributions, that is, by the performance of political duties of citizenship such as the obligation to military service, jury duty, etc. A whole epoch can be designated as typically capitalistic only as the provision for wants is capitalistically organized to such a predominant degree that if we imagine this form of organization taken away the whole economic system must collapse.

While capitalism of various forms is met with in all periods of history, the provision of the everyday wants by capitalistic methods is characteristic of the occident alone and even here has been the inevitable method only since the middle of the 19th century. Such capitalistic beginnings as are found in earlier centuries were merely anticipatory, and even the somewhat capitalistic establishments of the 16th century may be removed in thought from the economic life of the time without introducing any overwhelming change.

The most general presupposition for the existence of this present-day capitalism is that of rational capital accounting as the norm for all large industrial undertakings which are concerned with provision for everyday wants. Such accounting involves, again, first, the appropriation of all physical means of production—land, apparatus, machinery, tools, and so on, as dis-

posable property of autonomous private industrial enterprises. This is a phenomenon known only to our time, when the army alone forms a universal
exception to it. In the second place, it involves freedom of the market, that
is, the absence of irrational limitations on trading in the market. Such
limitations might be of a class character, if a certain mode of life were
prescribed for a certain class or consumption were standardized along class
lines, or if class monopoly existed, as for example if the townsman were not
allowed to own an estate or the knight or peasant to carry on industry; in
such cases neither a free labor market nor a commodity market exists. Third,
capitalistic accounting presupposes rational technology, that is, one reduced
to calculation to the largest possible degree, which implies mechanization.
This applies to both production and commerce, the outlays for preparing as
well as moving goods.

The fourth characteristic is that of calculable law. The capitalistic form of
industrial organization, if it is to operate rationally, must be able to depend
upon calculable adjudication and administration. Neither in the age of the
Greek city-state (polis) nor in the patrimonial state of Asia nor in western
countries down to the Stuarts was this condition fulfilled. The royal "cheap
justice" with its remissions by royal grace introduced continual disturbances
into the calculations of economic life . . . The fifth feature is free labor.
Persons must be present who are not only legally in the position, but are also
economically compelled, to sell their labor on the market without restriction.
It is in contradiction to the essence of capitalism, and the development of
capitalism is impossible, if such a propertyless stratum is absent, a class compelled to sell its labor services to live; and it is likewise impossible if only
unfree labor is at hand. Rational capitalistic calculation is possible only on the
basis of free labor; only where in consequence of the existence of workers who
in the formal sense voluntarily, but actually under the compulsion of the whip
of hunger, offer themselves, the costs of products may be unambiguously
determined by agreement in advance. The sixth and final condition is the
commercialization of economic life. By this we mean the general use of
commercial instruments to represent share rights in enterprise, and also in
property ownership.

To sum up, it must be possible to conduct the provision for needs exclusively on the basis of market opportunities and the calculation of net income.
The addition of this commercialization to the other characteristics of capitalism involves intensification of the significance of another factor not yet mentioned, namely speculation. Speculation reaches its full significance only from
the moment when property takes on the form of negotiable paper.

THE DEVELOPMENT OF INDUSTRIAL TECHNIQUE

It is not easy to define accurately the concept of the factory. We think at once of the steam engine and the mechanization of work, but the machine had its forerunner in what we call "apparatus"—labor appliances which had to be utilized in the same way as the machine but which as a rule were driven by water power. The distinction is that the apparatus works as the servant of the man while in modern machines the inverse relation holds. The real distinguishing characteristic of the modern factory is in general, however, not the implements of work applied, but the concentration of ownership of workplace, means of work, source of power and raw material in one and the same hand, that of the entrepreneur. This combination was only exceptionally met with before the 18th century. . . .

The decisive impetus toward capitalism could come only from one source, namely a mass market demand, which again could arise only in a small proportion of the luxury industries through the democratization of the demand, especially along the line of production of substitutes for the luxury goods of the upper classes. This phenomenon is characterized by price competition, while the luxury industries working for the court follow the handicraft principle of competition in quality. The first example of the policy of a state organization entering upon price competition is afforded in England at the close of the 15th century, when the effort was made to undersell Flemish wool, an object which was promoted by numerous export prohibitions.

The great price revolution of the 16th and 17th centuries provided a powerful lever for the specifically capitalistic tendencies of seeking profit through cheapening production and lowering the price. This revolution is rightly ascribed to the continuous inflow of precious metals in consequence of the great overseas discoveries. It lasted from the thirties of the 16th century down to the time of the Thirty Years' War, but affected different branches of economic life in quite different ways. In the case of agricultural products an almost universal rise in price set in, making it possible for them to go over to production for the market. It was quite otherwise with the course of prices for industrial products. By and large these remained stable or rose in price relatively little, thus really falling, in comparison with the agricultural products. This relative decline was made possible only through a shift in technology and economics, and exerted a pressure in the direction of increasing profit by repeated cheapening of production. Thus the development did not follow the order that capitalism set in first and the decline in prices followed, but the reverse; first the prices fell relatively and then came capitalism.

The tendency toward rationalizing technology and economic relations with a view to reducing prices in relation to costs, generated in the 17th century a feverish pursuit of invention. All the inventors of the period are dominated by the object of cheapening production; the notion of perpetual motion as a source of energy is only one of many objectives of this quite universal movement. The inventor as a type goes back much farther. But if one scrutinizes the devices of the greatest inventor of precapitalistic times, Leonardo da Vinci—(for experimentation originated in the field of art and not that of science)—one observes that his urge was not that of cheapening production but the rational mastery of technical problems as such. The inventors of the pre-capitalistic age worked empirically; their inventions had more or less the character of accidents. An exception is mining, and in consequence it is the problems of mining in connection with which deliberate technical progress took place.

A positive innovation in connection with invention is the first rational patent law, the English law of 1623, which contains all the essential provisions of a modern statute. Down to that time the exploitation of inventions had been arranged through a special grant in consideration of a payment; in contrast the law of 1623 limits the protection of the invention to 14 years and makes its subsequent utilization by an entrepreneur conditional upon an adequate royalty for the original inventor. Without the stimulus of this patent law the inventions crucial for the development of capitalism in the field of textile industry in the 18th century would not have been possible.

Drawing together once more the distinguishing characteristics of western capitalism and its causes, we find the following factors. First, this institution alone produced a rational organization of labor, which nowhere previously existed. Everywhere and always there has been trade; it can be traced back into the stone age. Likewise we find in the most varied epochs and cultures war finance, state contributions, tax farming, farming of offices, etc., but not a rational organization of labor. Furthermore we find everywhere else a primitive, strictly integrated internal economy such that there is no question of any freedom of economic action between members of the same tribe or clan, associated with absolute freedom of trade externally. Internal and external ethics are distinguished, and in connection with the latter there is complete ruthlessness in financial procedure; nothing can be more rigidly prescribed than the clan economy of China or the caste economy of India, and on the other hand nothing so unscrupulous as the conduct of the Hindu foreign trader. In contrast with this, the second characteristic of western capitalism is a lifting of the barrier between the internal economy and external economy, between internal and external ethics, and the entry of the commercial principle into the internal economy, with the organization of labor on this basis. Finally, the disintegration of primitive economic fixity is also met with elsewhere, as for example in Babylon, but nowhere else do we find the entrepreneur organization of labor as it is known in the western world.

If this development took place only in the occident the reason is to be found in the special features of its general cultural evolution which are peculiar to it. Only the occident knows the state in the modern sense, with a professional administration, specialized officialdom, and law based on the concept of citizenship. Beginnings of this institution in antiquity and in the orient were never able to develop. Only the occident knows rational law, made by jurists and rationally interpreted and applied, and only in the occident is found the concept of citizen (*civis Romanus, citoyen, bourgeois*) because only in the occident again are there cities in the specific sense. Furthermore, only the occident possesses science in the present-day sense of the word. Theology, philosophy, reflection on the ultimate problems of life, were known to the Chinese and the Hindu perhaps even of a depth unreached by the European; but a rational science and in connection with it a rational technology remained unknown to those civilizations. Finally, western civilization is further distinguished from every other by the presence of men with a rational ethic for the conduct of life. Magic and religion are found everywhere; but a religious basis for the ordering of life which consistently followed out must lead to explicit rationalism is again peculiar to western civilization alone.

CITIZENSHIP

In the concept of citizenship (*Bürgertum*) as it is used in social history are bound up three distinct significations. First, citizenship may include certain social categories or classes which have some specific communal or economic interest. As thus defined the class citizen is not unitary; there are greater citizens and lesser citizens; entrepreneurs and hand workers belong to the class. Second, in the political sense, citizenship signifies membership in the state, with its connotation as the holder of certain political rights. Finally, by citizens in the class sense, we understand those strata which are drawn together, in contrast with the bureaucracy or the proletariat and others outside their circle, as "persons of property and culture," entrepreneurs, recipients of funded incomes, and in general all persons of academic culture, a certain class standard of living, and a certain social prestige.

The first of these concepts is economic in character and is peculiar to western civilization. There are and have been everywhere hand laborers and entrepreneurs, but never and nowhere were they included in a unitary social class. The notion of the citizen of the state has its forerunners in antiquity and in the medieval city. Here there were citizens as holders of political rights, while outside of the occident only traces of this relation are met with, as in the Babylonian patriciate and the Josherim, the inhabitants of a city with full legal rights, in the Old Testament. The farther east we go the fewer are these traces; the notion of citizens of the state is unknown to the world of Islam, and to India and China. Finally, the social class signification of citizen as the man of property and culture, or of one or the other, in contrast with the nobility, on the one hand, and the proletariat, on the other, is likewise a specifically modern and western concept, like that of the bourgeoisie. It is true that in antiquity and in the middle ages, citizen was a class concept; membership in specific class groups made the person a citizen. The difference is that in this case the citizen was privileged in a negative as well as a positive sense. In the positive sense in that he only—in the medieval city for example—might pursue certain occupations; negatively in that certain legal requirements were waived, such as the qualification for holding a fief, the qualification for the tourney, and that for membership in the religious community. The citizen in the quality of membership in a class is always a citizen of a particular city, and the city in this sense, has existed only in the western world, or elsewhere, as in the early period in Mesopotamia, only in an incipient stage. . . .

For the fact that this development took place only in the occident there are two reasons. The first is the peculiar character of the organization for defense. The occidental city is in its beginnings first of all a defense group, an organization of those economically competent to bear arms, to equip and train themselves. Whether the military organization is based on the principle of self-equipment or on that of equipment by a military overlord who furnishes horses, arms and provisions, is a distinction quite as fundamental for social history as is the question whether the means of economic production are the property of the worker or of a capitalistic entrepreneur. Everywhere outside the west the development of the city was prevented by the fact that the army of the prince is older than the city. The earliest Chinese epics do not, like the Homeric, speak of the hero who fares forth to battle in his own chariot, but only of the officer as a leader of the men. Likewise in India an army led by officers marched out against Alexander the Great. In the west the army equipped by the war lord, and the separation of soldier from the paraphernalia of war, in a way analogous to the separation of the worker from the means of production, is a product of the modern era, while in Asia it stands at the apex of the historical development. There was no Egyptian or Babylonian-Assyrian army which would have presented a picture similar to that of the Homeric mass army, the feudal army of the west, the city army of the ancient *polis*, or the medieval guild army.

The distinction is based on the fact that in the cultural evolution of Egypt, western Asia, India, and China the question of irrigation was crucial. The water question conditioned the existence of the bureaucracy, the compulsory service of the dependent classes, and the dependence of the subject classes upon the functioning of the bureaucracy of the king. That the king also expressed his power in the form of a military monopoly is the basis of the distinction between the military organization of Asia and that of the west. In the first case the royal official and army officer is from the beginning the central figure of the process, while in the west both were originally absent. The forms of religious brotherhood and self equipment for war made possible the origin and existence of the city. It is true that the beginnings of an analogous development are found in the east. In India we meet with relations which verge upon the establishment of a city in the western sense, namely, the combination of self equipment and legal citizenship; one who could furnish an elephant for the army is in the free city of Vaiçali a full citizen. In ancient Mesopotamia, too, the knights carried on war with each other and established cities with autonomous administration. But in the one case as in the other these beginnings later disappear as the great kingdom arises on the basis of water regulation. Hence only in the west did the development come to complete maturity.

The second obstacle which prevented the development of the city in the orient was formed by ideas and institutions connected with magic. In India the castes were not in a position to form ritualistic communities and hence a city, because they were ceremonially alien to one another. The same facts explained the peculiar position of the Jews in the middle ages. The cathedral and the eucharist were the symbols of the unity of the city, but the Jews were not permitted to pray in the cathedral or take part in the communion and hence were doomed to form diaspora-communes. On the contrary, the consideration which made it natural for cities to develop in the west was in antiquity the extensive freedom of the priesthood, the absence of any monopoly in the hands of the priests over communion with the gods, such as obtained in Asia. In western antiquity the officials of the city performed the rites, and the resultant proprietorship of the *polis* over the things belonging to the gods and the priestly treasures was carried to the point of filling the priestly offices by auction, since no magical limitations stood in the way as in India. For the later period in the west three great facts were crucial. The first was prophecy among the Jews, which destroyed magic within the confines of Judaism; magical procedure remained real but was devilish instead of divine.

The second fact was the pentecostal miracle, the ceremonial adoption into the spirit of Christ which was a decisive factor in the extraordinary spread of the early Christian enthusiasm. The final factor was the day in Antioch (Gal. 2; 11 ff.) when Paul, in opposition to Peter, espoused fellowship with the uncircumcised. The magical barriers between clans, tribes, and peoples, which were still known in the ancient *polis* to a considerable degree, were thus set aside and the establishment of the occidental city was made possible.

.   .   .

The basis of democratization is everywhere purely military in character; it lies in the rise of disciplined infantry, the *hoplites* of antiquity, the guild army in the middle ages. The decisive fact was that military discipline proved its superiority over the battle between heroes. Military discipline meant the triumph of democracy because the community wished and was compelled to secure the co-operation of the non-aristocratic masses and hence put arms, and along with arms political power, into their hands. In addition, the money power plays its role, both in antiquity and in the middle ages.

Parallelism is also manifest in the mode in which democracy establishes itself. Like the state in the beginning, the *popolo* carries on its struggle as a separate group with its own officials. Examples are the Spartan ephors as representatives of the democracy against the kings, and the Roman tribunes of the people, while in the Italian cities of the middle ages the *capitano del popolo*, or *della mercadanzao*, are such officials. It is characteristic of them that they are the first concededly "illegitimate" officials. The consuls of the Italian cities still prefix the *dei gratia* to their titles but the *capitano del popolo* no longer does so. The source of the power of the tribune is illegitimate; he is *sacrocanctus* precisely because he is not a legitimate official and hence is protected only by divine interference, or popular vengeance.

The two courses of development are also equivalent in regard to their purpose. Social and not economic class interests are decisive; it is a question primarily of protection against the aristocratic families. The *popolani* know that they are rich and have fought and won the great wars of the city along with the nobility; they are armed, and hence feel themselves discriminated against and are no longer content with the subordinate class position which they have previously accepted. Similarity exists also, and finally, in the means available to the officials of the separate organization (*Sonderbund*). Everywhere they secure the right of intervention in legal processes in which the plebeians are opposed to the aristocrats. This purpose is served by the right of intercession of the Roman tribune as well as the Florentine *capitano del popolo*, a right which is carried out through appeal or through lynch justice.

The *Sonderbund* sets up the claim that the statutes of the city shall be valid only after they have been ratified by the plebeians, and finally establishes the principle that only that is law which they have determined. The Roman legal principle: *ut quod tributim plebs iussisset populum tenerit* has its counterpart in the Florentine *ordinamenti della giustizia*, and in the exclusion of all non-workers from Lenin's labor dictatorship.

· · ·

Turning to the question as to the consequences of these relations in connection with the evolution of capitalism, we must emphasize the heterogeneity of industry in antiquity and in the middle ages, and the different species of capitalism itself. In the first place, we are met in the most widely separated periods with a multiplicity of non-rational forms of capitalism. These include first capitalistic enterprises for the purpose of tax farming—in the occident as well as in China and western Asia—and for the purpose of financing war, in China and India, in the period of small separate states; second, capitalism in connection with trade speculation, the trader being entirely absent in almost no epoch of history; third, money-lending capitalism, exploiting the necessities of outsiders. All these forms of capitalism relate to spoils, taxes, the pickings of office or official usury, and finally to tribute and actual need. It is noteworthy that in former times officials were financed as Cæsar was by Crassus and endeavored to recoup the sums advanced through misuse of their official position. All this, however, relates to occasional economic activity of an irrational character, while no rational system of labor organization developed out of these arrangements.

Rational capitalism, on the contrary, is organized with a view to market opportunities, hence to economic objectives in the real sense of the word, and the more rational it is the more closely it relates to mass demand and the provision for mass needs. It was reserved to the modern western development after the close of the middle ages to elevate this capitalism into a system, while in all of antiquity there was but one capitalistic class whose rationalism might be compared with that of modern capitalism, namely, the Roman knighthood. When a Greek city required credit or leased public land or let a contract for supplies, it was forced to incite competition among different interlocal capitalists. Rome, in contrast, was in possession of a rational capitalistic class which from the time of the Gracchi played a determining role in the state. The capitalism of this class was entirely relative to state and governmental opportunities, to the leasing of the *ager publicus* or conquered land, and of domain land, or to tax farming and the financing of political adventures and of wars. It influenced the public policy of Rome in

a decisive way at times, although it had to reckon with the constant antagonism of the official nobility.

The capitalism of the late middle ages began to be directed toward market
opportunities, and the contrast between it and the capitalism of antiquity
appears in the development after the cities have lost their freedom. Here again
we find a fundamental distinction in the lines of development as between
antiquity and medieval and modern times. In antiquity the freedom of the
cities was swept away by a bureaucratically organized world empire within
which there was no longer a place for political capitalism. In the beginning
the emperors were forced to resort to the financial power of the knighthood
but we see them progressively emancipate themselves and exclude the knightly
class from the farming of the taxes and hence from the most lucrative source
of wealth—just as the Egyptian kings were able to make the provisions for
political and military requirements in their realms independent of the capitalist powers and reduce the tax farmers to the position of tax officials. In the
imperial period of Rome the leasing of domain land everywhere decreased in
extent in favor of permanent hereditary appropriation. The provision for the
economic needs of the state was taken care of through compulsory contributions and compulsory labor of servile persons instead of competitive contracts.
The various classes of the population became stratified along occupational
lines and the burden of state requirements was imposed on the newly created
groups on the principle of joint liability.

This development means the throttling of ancient capitalism. A conscript
army takes the place of the mercenaries and ships are provided by compulsory
service. The entire harvest of grain, insofar as regions of surplus production
are concerned, is distributed among the cities in accordance with their needs,
with the exclusion of private trade. The building of roads and every other
service which has to be provided for is laid on the shoulders of specific
personal groups who become attached by inheritance to the soil and to their
occupations. At the end the Roman urban communities, acting through their
mayors in a way not very different from the village community through its
common meeting, demand the return of the rich city councilmen on property
grounds, because the population is jointly responsible for the payments and
services due to the state. These services are subject to the principle of the *origo*
which is erected on the pattern of the ἰδία of Ptolemaic Egypt; the compulsory dues of servile persons can only be rendered in their home commune.
After this system became established the political opportunities for securing
gain were closed to capitalism; in the late Roman state, based on compulsory
contributions (*Leiturgiestaat*) there was as little place for capitalism as in the
Egyptian state organized on the basis of compulsory labor service (*Fronstaat*).

Quite different was the fate of the city in the modern era. Here again its autonomy was progressively taken away. The English city of the 17th and 18th centuries had ceased to be anything but a clique of guilds which could lay claim only to financial and social class significance. The German cities of the same period, with the exception of the imperial cities, were merely geographical entities (*Landstadt*) in which everything was ordered from above. In the French cities this development appeared even earlier, while the Spanish cities were deprived of their power by Charles V, in the insurrection of the *communeros*. The Italian cities found themselves in the power of the "signory" and those of Russia never arrived at freedom in the western sense. Everywhere the military, judicial, and industrial authority was taken away from the cities. In form the old rights were as a rule unchanged, but in fact the modern city was deprived of its freedom as effectively as had happened in antiquity with the establishment of the Roman dominion, though in contrast with antiquity they came under the power of competing national states in a condition of perpetual struggle for power in peace or war. This competitive struggle created the largest opportunities for modern western capitalism. The separate states had to compete for mobile capital, which dictated to them the conditions under which it would assist them to power. Out of this alliance of the state with capital, dictated by necessity, arose the national citizen class, the bourgeoisie in the modern sense of the word. Hence it is the closed national state which afforded to capitalism its chance for development—and as long as the national state does not give place to a world empire capitalism also will endure.

THE RATIONAL STATE

The state in the sense of the rational state has existed only in the western world. Under the old regime in China a thin stratum of so-called officials, the mandarins, existed above the unbroken power of the clans and commercial and industrial guilds. The mandarin is primarily a humanistically educated literatus in the possession of a benefice but not in the least degree trained for administration; he knows no jurisprudence but is a fine writer, can make verses, knows the age-old literature of the Chinese and can interpret it. In the way of political service no importance is attached to him. Such an official performs no administrative work himself; administration lies rather in the hands of the chancery officials. The mandarin is continually transferred from one place to another to prevent his obtaining a foothold in his administrative district, and he could never be assigned to his home province. As he does not understand the dialect of his province he cannot communicate with the public. A state with such officials is something different from the occidental state.

In reality everything is based on the magical theory that the virtue of the empress and the merits of the officials, meaning their perfection in literary culture, keeps things in order in normal times. If a drought sets in or any untoward event takes place an edict is promulgated intensifying the examinations in verse-making, or speeding up legal trials in order to quiet the spirits. The empire is an agrarian state; hence the power of the peasant clans who represent nine-tenths of the economic life—the other one-tenth belonging to commercial and trading guild organizations—is entirely unbroken. In essence things are left to take care of themselves. The officials do not rule but only interfere in the event of disturbances or untoward happenings.

Very different is the rational state in which alone modern capitalism can flourish. Its basis is an expert officialdom and rational law. The Chinese state changed over to administration through trained officials in the place of humanistically cultured persons as early as the 7th and 11th centuries but the change could be only temporarily maintained; then the usual eclipse of the moon arrived and arrangements were transformed in reverse order. It cannot be seriously asserted, however, that the spirit of the Chinese people could not tolerate an administration of specialists. Its development, and that of the rational state, was rather prevented by the persistence of reliance upon magic. In consequence of this fact the power of the clans could not be broken, as happened in the occident through the development of the cities and of Christianity.

The rational law of the modern occidental state, on the basis of which the trained official renders his decisions, arose on its formal side, though not as to its content, out of Roman law. The latter was to begin with a product of the Roman city state, which never witnessed the dominion of democracy and its justice in the same form as the Greek city. A Greek heliast court administered a petty justice; the contestants worked upon the judges through pathos, tears, and abusing their opponents. This procedure was also known in Rome in political trials, as the orations of Cicero show, but not in civil trials where the prætor appointed an *iudex* to whom he gave strict instructions as to the conditions requiring a judgment against the accused or the throwing out of the case. Under Justinian the Byzantine bureaucracy brought order and system into this rational law, in consequence of the natural interest of the official in a law which would be systematic and fixed and hence easier to learn.

With the fall of the Roman empire in the west, law came into the hands of the Italian notaries. These, and secondarily the universities, have on their conscience the revival of Roman law. The notaries adhered to the old contractual forms of the Roman empire and re-interpreted them according to the needs of the time. At the same time a systematic legal doctrine was developed in the universities. The essential feature in the development, however, was the rationalization of procedure. As among all primitive peoples the ancient German legal trial was a rigidly formal affair. The party which pronounced wrongly a single word in the formula lost the case, because the formula possessed magical significance and supernatural evils were feared. This magical formalism of the German trial fitted in with the formalism of Roman law. At the same time the French kingdom played a part through the creation of the institution of the representative or advocate whose task it was especially to pronounce the legal formulas correctly, particularly in connection with the canon law. The magnificent administrative organization of the church required fixed forms for its disciplinary ends in relation to the laity and for its own internal discipline. No more than the bourgeoisie could it take up with the Germanic ordeal or judgment of God. The business man could not permit commercial claims to be decided by a competition in reciting formulas, and everywhere secured exemptions from this legalistic contest and from the ordeal. The church also, after hesitating at first, ended by adopting the view that such procedure was heathenish and not to be tolerated, and established the canonical procedure on lines as rational as possible. This two-fold rationalization of procedure from the profane and spiritual sides spread over the western world. . . .

This formalistic law, is however, calculable. In China it may happen that a man who has sold a house to another may later come to him and ask to be taken in because in the meantime he has been impoverished. If the purchaser refuses to heed the ancient Chinese command to help a brother, the spirits will be disturbed; hence the impoverished seller comes into the house as a renter who pays no rent. Capitalism cannot operate on the basis of a law so constituted. What it requires is law which can be counted upon, like a machine; ritualistic-religious and magical considerations must be excluded.

The creation of such a body of law was achieved through the alliance between the modern state and the jurists for the purpose of making good its claims to power. For a time in the 16th century it attempted to work with the humanists, and the first Greek gymnasia were established with the idea that men educated in them would be suitable for state officials; for political contests were carried out to a large extent through the exchange of state papers and only one schooled in Latin and Greek had the necessary equipment. This illusion was short-lived. It was soon found that the products of the gymnasia were not on that account alone equipped for political life, and the jurists were the final resort. In China, where the humanistically cultured mandarin ruled the field, the monarch had no jurists at his disposal, and the struggle among the different philosophical schools as to which of them formed the best statesmen waged to and fro until finally orthodox Confucianism was victorious.

India also had writers but no trained jurists. In contrast the western world had at its disposal a formally organized legal system, the product of the Roman genius, and officials trained in this law were superior to all others as technical administrators. From the standpoint of economic history this fact is significant in that the alliance between the state and formal jurisprudence was indirectly favorable to capitalism.

The Economic Policy of the Rational State

For the state to have an economic policy worthy of the name, that is one which is continuous and consistent, is an institution of exclusively modern origin. The first system which it brought forth is mercantilism, so-called. Before the development of mercantilism there were two widespread commercial policies, namely, the dominance of fiscal interests and of welfare interests the last in the sense of the customary standard of living.

In the east it was essentially ritualistic considerations, including caste and clan organizations, which prevented the development of a deliberate economic policy. . . .

[C]apitalistic development was not an outgrowth of national mercantilism; rather capitalism developed at first in England alongside the fiscal monopoly policy. The course of events was that a stratum of entrepreneurs which had developed in independence of the political administration secured the systematic support of Parliament in the 18th century, after the collapse of the fiscal monopoly policy of the Stuarts. Here for the last time irrational and rational capitalism faced each other in conflict, that is, capitalism in the field of fiscal and colonial privileges and public monopolies, and capitalism oriented in relation to market opportunities which were developed from within by business interests themselves on the basis of saleable services.

THE EVOLUTION OF THE CAPITALISTIC SPIRIT

In the last resort the factor which produced capitalism is the rational permanent enterprise, rational accounting, rational technology and rational law, but again not these alone. Necessary complementary factors were the rational spirit, the rationalization of the conduct of life in general, and a rationalistic economic ethic.

At the beginning of all ethics and the economic relations which result, is traditionalism, the sanctity of tradition, the exclusive reliance upon such trade and industry as have come down from the fathers. This traditionalism survives far down into the present; only a human lifetime in the past it was futile to double the wages of an agricultural laborer in Silesia who mowed a certain tract of land on a contract, in the hope of inducing him to increase his exertions. He would simply have reduced by half the work expended because with this half he would have been able to earn . . . as much as before. . . . This general incapacity and indisposition to depart from the beaten paths is the motive for the maintenance of tradition.

Primitive traditionalism may, however, undergo essential intensification through two circumstances. In the first place, material interests may be tied up with the maintenance of the tradition. When for example in China, the attempt was made to change certain roads or to introduce more rational means or routes of transportation, the perquisites of certain officials were threatened; and the same was the case in the middle ages in the west, and in modern times when railroads were introduced. Such special interests of officials, land-holders and merchants assisted decisively in restricting a tendency toward rationalization. Stronger still is the effect of the stereotyping of trade on magical grounds, the deep repugnance to undertaking any change in the established conduct of life because supernatural evils are feared. Generally some injury to economic privilege is concealed in this opposition, but its effectiveness depends on a general belief in the potency of the magical processes which are feared.

Traditional obstructions are not overcome by the economic impulse alone. The notion that our rationalistic and capitalistic age is characterized by a stronger economic interest than other periods is childish; the moving spirits of modern capitalism are not possessed of a stronger economic impulse than, for example, an oriental trader. The unchaining of the economic interest merely as such has produced only irrational results; such men as Cortez and Pizarro, who were perhaps its strongest embodiment, were far from having an idea of a rationalistic economic life. If the economic impulse in itself is universal, it is an interesting question as to the relations under which it becomes rationalized and rationally tempered in such fashion as to produce rational institutions of the character of capitalistic enterprise.

Originally, two opposite attitudes toward the pursuit of gain exist in combination. Internally, there is attachment to tradition and to the pietistic relations of fellow members of tribe, clan, and house-community, with the exclusion of the unrestricted quest of gain within the circle of those bound together by religious ties; externally, there is absolutely unrestricted play of the gain spirit in economic relations, every foreigner being originally an enemy in relation to whom no ethical restrictions apply; that is, the ethics of internal and external relations are categorically distinct. The course of development involves on the one hand the bringing in of calculation into the traditional brotherhood, displacing the old religious relationship. As soon as accountability is established within the family community, and economic relations are no longer strictly communistic, there is an end of the naive piety and its repression of the economic impulse. This side of the development is especially characteristic in the west. At the same time there is a tempering of the unrestricted quest of gain with the adoption of the economic principle into the internal economy. The result is a regulated economic life with the economic impulse functioning within bounds.

In detail, the course of development has been varied. In India, the restrictions upon gain-seeking apply only to the two uppermost strata, the Brahmins and the Rajputs. A member of these castes is forbidden to practice certain callings. A Brahmin may conduct an eating house, as he alone has clean hands; but he, like the Rajput, would be unclassed if he were to lend money for interest. The latter, however, is permitted to the mercantile castes, and within it we find a degree of unscrupulousness in trade which is unmatched anywhere in the world. Finally, antiquity had only legal limitations on interest, and the proposition *caveat emptor* characterizes Roman economic ethics. Nevertheless no modern capitalism developed there.

· · · ·

. . . Judaism was . . . of notable significance for modern rational capitalism, insofar as it transmitted to Christianity the latter's hostility to magic. Apart from Judaism and Christianity, and two or three oriental sects (one of which is in Japan), there is no religion with the character of outspoken hostility to magic. Probably this hostility arose through the circumstance that what the Israelites found in Canaan was the magic of the agricultural god Baal, while Jahveh was a god of volcanoes, earthquakes, and pestilences. The hostility between the two priesthoods and the victory of the priests of Jahveh discredited the fertility magic of the priests of Baal and stigmatized it with a character of decadence and godlessness. Since Judaism made Christianity possible and gave it the character of a religion essentially free from magic, it rendered an important service from the point of view of economic history. For the dominance of magic outside the sphere in which Christianity has prevailed is one of the most serious obstructions to the rationalization of economic life. Magic involves a stereotyping of technology and economic relations. When attempts were made in China to inaugurate the building of railroads and factories a conflict with geomancy ensued. The latter demanded that in the location of structures on certain mountains, forests, rivers, and cemetery hills, foresight should be exercised in order not to disturb the rest of the spirits.

Similar is the relation to capitalism of the castes in India. Every new technical process which an Indian employs signifies for him first of all that he leaves his caste and falls into another, necessarily lower. Since he believes in the transmigration of souls, the immediate significance of this is that his chance of purification is put off until another re-birth. He will hardly consent to such a change. An additional fact is that every caste makes every other impure. In consequence, workmen who dare not accept a vessel filled with water from each other's hands, cannot be employed together in the same factory room. Not until the present time, after the possession of the country by the English for almost a century, could this obstacle be overcome. Obviously, capitalism could not develop in an economic group thus bound hand and foot by magical beliefs.

In all times there has been but one means of breaking down the power of magic and establishing a rational conduct of life; this means is great rational prophecy. Not every prophecy by any means destroys the power of magic; but it is possible for a prophet who furnishes credentials in the shape of miracles and otherwise, to break down the traditional sacred rules. Prophecies have released the world from magic and in doing so have created the basis for our modern science and technology, and for capitalism. In China such prophecy has been wanting. What prophecy there was has come from the outside as in the case of Lao-Tse and Taoism. India, however, produced a religion of salvation; in contrast with China it has known great prophetic missions. But they were prophecies by example; that is, the typical Hindu prophet, such as Buddha, lives before the world the life which leads to salvation, but does not regard himself as one sent from God to insist upon the obligation to lead it; he takes the position that whoever wishes salvation, as an end freely chosen, should lead the life. However, one may reject salvation, as it is not the destiny of everyone to enter at death into Nirvana, and only philosophers in the strictest sense are prepared by hatred of this world to adopt the stoical resolution and withdraw from life.

The result was that Hindu prophecy was of immediate significance for the intellectual classes. These became forest dwellers and poor monks. For the masses, however, the significance of the founding of a Buddhistic sect was quite different, namely the opportunity of praying to the saints. There came to be holy men who were believed to work miracles, who must be well fed so that they would repay this good deed by guaranteeing a better reincarnation or through granting wealth, long life, and the like, that is, this world's goods. Hence Buddhism in its pure form was restricted to a thin stratum of monks. The laity found no ethical precepts according to which life should be molded; Buddhism indeed had its decalogue, but in distinction from that of the Jews it gave no binding commands but only recommendations. The most important act of service was and remained the physical maintenance of the monks. Such a religious spirit could never be in a position to displace magic but at best could only put another magic in its place.

In contrast with the ascetic religion of salvation of India and its defective action upon the masses, are Judaism and Christianity, which from the beginning have been plebeian religions and have deliberately remained such. The struggle of the ancient church against the Gnostics was nothing else than a struggle against the aristocracy of the intellectuals, such as is common to ascetic religions, with the object of preventing their seizing the leadership in the church. This struggle was crucial for the success of Christianity among the masses, and hence for the fact that magic was suppressed among the general population to the greatest possible extent. True, it has not been possible even down to today to overcome it entirely, but it was reduced to the character of something unholy, something diabolic. . . .

It is also necessary to distinguish between the virtuoso religion of adepts and the religion of the masses. Virtuoso religion is significant for everyday life only as a pattern; its claims are of the highest, but they fail to determine everyday ethics. The relation between the two is different in different religions. In Catholicism, they are brought into harmonious union insofar as the claims of the religious virtuoso are held up alongside the duties of the laymen as *consilia evangelica*. The really complete Christian is the monk; but his mode of life is not required of everyone, although some of his virtues in a qualified form are held up as ideals. The advantage of this combination was that ethics was not split asunder as in Buddhism. After all the distinction between monk ethics and mass ethics meant that the most worthy individuals in the religious sense withdrew from the world and established a separate community.

Christianity was not alone in this phenomenon, which rather recurs frequently in the history of religions, as is shown by the powerful influence of asceticism, which signifies the carrying out of a definite, methodical conduct of life. Asceticism has always worked in this sense. The enormous achievements possible to such an ascetically determined methodical conduct of life are demonstrated by the example of Tibet. The country seems condemned by nature to be an eternal desert; but a community of celibate ascetics has carried out colossal construction works in Lhassa and saturated the country with the religious doctrines of Buddhism. An analogous phenomenon is present in the middle ages in the west. In that epoch the monk is the first human being who lives rationally, who works methodically and by rational means toward a goal, namely the future life. Only for him did the clock strike, only for him were the hours of the day divided—for prayer. The economic life of the monastic communities was also rational.

But the rational mode of life remained restricted to the monastic circles. The Franciscan movement indeed attempted through the institution of the tertiaries to extend it to the laity, but the institution of the confessional was a barrier to such an extension. The church domesticated medieval Europe by means of its system of confession and penance, but for the men of the middle ages the possibility of unburdening themselves through the channel of the confessional, when they had rendered themselves liable to punishment, meant a release from the consciousness of sin which the teachings of the church had called into being. The unity and strength of the methodical conduct of life were thus in fact broken up. In its knowledge of human nature the church did not reckon with the fact that the individual is a closed unitary ethical personality, but steadfastly held to the view that in spite of the warnings of the confessional and of penances, however strong, he would again fall away morally; that is, it shed its grace on the just and the unjust.

The Reformation made a decisive break with this system. The dropping of the *concilia evangelica* by the Lutheran Reformation meant the disappearance of the dualistic ethics, of the distinction between a universally binding morality and a specifically advantageous code for virtuosi. The other-worldly asceticism came to an end. The stern religious characters who had previously gone into monasteries had now to practice their religion in the life of the world. For such an asceticism within the world the ascetic dogmas of protestantism created an adequate ethics. Celibacy was not required, marriage being viewed simply as an institution for the rational bringing up of children. Poverty was not required, but the pursuit of riches must not lead one astray into reckless enjoyment. Thus Sebastian Franck was correct in summing up the spirit of the Reformation in the words, "you think you have escaped from the monastery, but everyone must now be a monk throughout his life."

The wide significance of this transformation of the ascetic ideal can be followed down to the present in the classical lands of protestant ascetic religiosity. It is especially discernible in the import of the religious denominations in America. Although state and church are separated, still, as late as fifteen or twenty years ago no banker or physician took up a residence or established connections without being asked to what religious community he belonged, and his prospects were good or bad according to the character of his answer. Acceptance into a sect was conditioned upon a strict inquiry into one's ethical conduct. Membership in a sect which did not recognize the Jewish distinction between internal and external moral codes guaranteed one's business honor and reliability and this in turn guaranteed success. Hence the principle "honesty is the best policy" and hence among Quakers, Baptists, and Methodists the ceaseless repetition of the proposition based on experience that God would take care of his own. "The Godless cannot trust each other across the road; they turn to us when they want to do business; piety is the surest road to wealth." This is by no means "cant," but a combination of religiosity with consequences which were originally unknown to it and which were never intended.

It is true that the acquisition of wealth, attributed to piety, led to a dilemma, in all respects similar to that into which the medieval monasteries constantly fell; the religious guild led to wealth, wealth to fall from grace, and this again to the necessity of re-constitution. Calvinism sought to avoid this difficulty through the idea that man was only an administrator of what God had given him; it condemned enjoyment, yet permitted no flight from the world but rather regarded working together, with its rational discipline, as the religious task of the individual. Out of this system of thought came our word "calling," which is known only to the languages influenced by the Protestant translations of the Bible. It expresses the value placed upon rational activity carried on according to the rational capitalistic principle, as the fulfillment of a God-given task. Here lay also in the last analysis the basis of the contrast between the Puritans and the Stuarts. The ideas of both were capitalistically directed; but in a characteristic way the Jew was for the Puritan the embodiment of everything repugnant because he devoted himself to irrational and illegal occupations such as war loans, tax farming, and leasing of offices, in the fashion of the court favorite.

This development of the concept of the calling quickly gave to the modern entrepreneur a fabulously clear conscience,—and also industrious workers; he gave to his employees as the wages of their ascetic devotion to the calling and of co-operation in his ruthless exploitation of them through capitalism the prospect of eternal salvation, which in an age when ecclesiastical discipline took control of the whole of life to an extent inconceivable to us now, represented a reality quite different from any it has today. The Catholic and Lutheran churches also recognized and practiced ecclesiastical discipline. But in the Protestant ascetic communities admission to the Lord's Supper was conditioned on ethical fitness, which again was identified with business honor, while into the content of one's faith no one inquired. Such a powerful, unconsciously refined organization for the production of capitalistic individuals has never existed in any other church or religion, and in comparison with it what the Renaissance did for capitalism shrinks into insignificance.

The religious root of modern economic humanity is dead; today the concept of the calling is a *caput mortuum* in the world. Ascetic religiosity has been displaced by a pessimistic though by no means ascetic view of the world, such as that portrayed in Mandeville's Fable of the Bees, which teaches that private vices may under certain conditions be for the good of the public. With the complete disappearance of all the remains of the original enormous religious pathos of the sects, the optimism of the Enlightenment which believed in the harmony of interests, appeared as the heir of Protestant asceticism in the field of economic ideas; it guided the hands of the princes, statesmen, and writers of the later 18th and early 19th century. Economic ethics arose against the background of the ascetic ideal; now it has been stripped of its religious import. It was possible for the working class to accept its lot as long as the promise of eternal happiness could be held out to it. When this consolation fell away it was inevitable that those strains and stresses should appear in economic society which since then have grown so rapidly. This point had been reached at the end of the early period of capitalism, at the beginning of the age of iron, in the 19th century.

Power Divisions as the Basis of Class Conflict [1959]

RALF DAHRENDORF

• *Ralf Dahrendorf's* Class and Class Conflict in Industrial Society *(1959) set off the modern debate over conflict theory. Dahrendorf is known for his polemical attack on functionalist theories of
society, but his work is also a profound—one might say
heretical—revision of the Marxian theory of classes. Dahrendorf
sets out to write Marx's unfinished chapter on classes, of which
only a fragment survives in the posthumous Part 3 of* Capital.
*Marx mistook a historically specific form of class and class con-
flict for the basis of class conflict in general, according to Dahrendorf; Marx had founded class on the ownership or nonownership
of capital, but in fact this was only the specific form that power
took within the society of his time. The more generic division is
between those who have power and those who lack power. Thus,
any formal organization and any society have class divisions and
potential conflicts—between those who give orders and those who
have to take orders. Socialist societies (one might think of modern
Poland) have classes as well as capitalist societies, although they
are not based on ownership of capital. Dahrendorf then proceeds
to lay out a series of hypotheses on the conditions that mobilize or
inhibit the outbreak of overt conflicts among classes.*

MARX'S MODEL

What are the structural conditions of the formation of social classes? For simplicity's sake I shall treat this aspect of Marx's theory of class with reference to
his analysis of capitalist society, since the question remains undecided for the
time being whether this theory can be applied to other types of society at all.

Marx states quite clearly that class conflicts do not originate in differences of
income, or of the sources of income. His classes are not tax classes in the
sense of the Roman censors. Rather, the determinant of classes is "property."
Property, however, must not be understood in terms of purely passive wealth,
but as an effective force of production, as "ownership of means of production"

Reprinted from *Class and Class Conflict in Industrial Society,* pp. 20–23, 64, 71, 125–26, 136–41,
165–88, 200–201, 237–40, by Ralf Dahrendorf, with permission of the publishers, Stanford
University Press. Copyright 1959 by the Board of Trustees of the Leland Stanford Junior University.

and its denial to others. In this sense, the "relations of production," i.e., the authority relations resulting from the distribution of effective property in the realm of (industrial) production, constitute the ultimate determinant of the formation of classes and the development of class conflicts. The capitalists possess factories and machines, and buy the only property of the proletarians, their labor power, in order to produce a surplus value with these means of production and augment their capital.

But our question cannot be answered all that easily. The role of property in Marx's theory of class poses a problem of interpretation, and on this interpretation the validity of Marx's theory of class stands or falls. Does Marx understand, by the relations of property or production, the relations of factual control and subordination in the enterprises of industrial production—or merely the authority relations in so far as they are based on the legal title of property? Does he conceive of property in a loose (sociological) sense—that is, in terms of the exclusiveness of legitimate control (in which the manager also exercises property functions)—or merely as a statutory property right in connection with such control? Is property for Marx a special case of authority—or, vice versa, authority a special case of property? These questions are of considerable significance. If one works with the narrow concept of property, class conflict is the specific characteristic of a form of production which rests on the union of ownership and control. In this case a society in which control is exercised, for example, by state functionaries, has by definition neither classes nor class conflicts. If, on the other hand, one works with the wider concept of property, class structure is determined by the authority structure of the enterprise, and the category of class becomes at least potentially applicable to all "relations of production."

Marx does not always make his answer to our questions entirely clear. But it can be shown that his analyses are essentially based on the narrow, legal concept of property. This procedure, and this procedure only, enables Marx to link his sociology with his philosophy of history—a brilliant attempt, but at the same time a fault that robs his sociological analyses of stringency and conviction, a fault made no more acceptable by the fact that orthodox Marxists have remained faithful to their master in this point to the present day.

The most striking evidence for this interpretation can be found in the preliminary attempts at an analysis of the new form of ownership characteristic of joint-stock companies which Marx presents in Volume III of *Capital*. Marx is here explicitly concerned with the phenomenon that is commonly described today as the separation of ownership and control. He discusses what he calls the "transformation of the really functioning capitalist into a mere director, an administrator of alien capital, and of the owners of capital into mere owners, mere money capitalists." "In joint-stock companies, function is separated from capital ownership; thereby labor is entirely separated from ownership of the means of production, and of surplus labor." Now, hard though it is for ordinary minds to see why this change in the size and legal structure of industrial enterprises should end the conflict between entrepreneurs who can command and workers who have to obey (the conflict that Marx postulates for the "pure" capitalist enterprise), Marx ascribes to the joint-stock company a peculiar place in history. Time and again he describes the joint-stock company as "private production without the control of private property," as "the elimination of capital as private property within the capitalist mode of production itself," and even as the "abolition of the capitalist mode of production within the capitalist mode of production itself." For him, the joint-stock company is "a necessary point on the way to reconverting capital into the property of the producers, this no longer being the private property of individual producers but their associated property, that is, immediate social property." It is a "point on the way to the transformation of all functions in the process of reproduction hitherto connected with capital ownership into mere functions of the associated producers, into social functions." The joint-stock company, in other words, is halfway to the communist—and that means classless—society.

One of the critical pivots of Marx's theory of class is the undisputed identification of economic and political power and authority. Although classes are founded on the "relations of production," that is, the distribution of effective property in the narrow sphere of commodity production, they become socially significant only in the political sphere. But both these spheres are inseparable. "The political power" of a class arises for Marx "from the relations of production." The relations of production are "the final secret, the hidden basis of the whole construction of society"; industrial classes are *eo ipso* also social classes, and industrial class conflict is political class conflict. Nowhere has Marx explicitly discussed the basis of this empirical proposition—nor has he seen sufficiently clearly that it is an empirical proposition rather than a postulate or premise. The thesis that political conditions are determined by industrial conditions seems to stem, for him, from the generalized assertion of an absolute and universal primacy of production over all other structures of economy and society. It is evident that a postulate of this kind requires empirical test; how it fares in this test will have to be shown.

[T]he equalization of status resulting from social developments of the past century has contributed greatly to changing the issues and diminishing the intensity of class conflict. By way of extrapolation—fairly wild extrapolation, I may say—some authors have visualized a state in which there are no classes and no class conflicts, because there is simply nothing to quarrel about. I do not think that such a state is ever likely to occur. But in order to substantiate this opinion, it is necessary to explore the structural limits of equality, that is, to find the points at which even the most fanatic egalitarian comes up against insurmountable realities of social structure. One of these is surely the variety of human desires, ideas, and interests, the elimination of which is neither desirable nor likely. But while this is important, it is not as such an element of social structure. I shall suggest in this study that the fundamental inequality of social structure, and the lasting determinant of social conflict, is the inequality of power and authority which inevitably accompanies social organization.

[I]n post-capitalist as in capitalist industrial enterprises there are some whose task it is to control the actions of others and issue commands, and others who have to allow themselves to be controlled and who have to obey. Today as a hundred years ago there are governments, parliaments, and courts the members of which are entitled to make decisions that affect the lives of many citizens, and there are citizens who can protest and shift their vote but who have to abide by the law. Insofar as either of these relations can be described as one of authority, I would claim that relations of domination and subordination have persisted throughout the changes of the past century. Again, I believe that we can go even further. The authority exercised in both capitalist and post-capitalist society is of the same type; it is, in Weber's terms, "rational authority" based "on the belief in the legality of institutionalized norms and the right of command on the part of those invested with authority by these norms." From this condition many others, including the necessity of bureaucratic administration, follow. But these are based above all on the fundamental social inequality of authority which may be mitigated by its "rational" character, but that nevertheless pervades the structure of all industrial societies and provides both the determinant and the substance of most conflicts and clashes.

SOCIOLOGICAL CRITIQUE OF MARX

Marx succeeded in tracing conflicts that effect change back to patterns of social structure. For him, social conflicts were not random occurrences which forbid explanation and therefore prediction. Rather, he believed these conflicts to be necessary outgrowths of the structure of any given society and, in particular, of capitalist society. It is doubtful whether Marx, by assuming property relations to be the structural origin of conflict, was right in the substance of his analysis. But this does not diminish the analytical achievement of tracing in the structure of a given society the seeds of its supersedure. The idea of a society which produces in its structure the antagonisms that lead to its modification appears an appropriate model for the analysis of change in general.

Secondly, Marx properly assumed the dominance of one particular conflict in any given situation. Whatever criticism may be required of the Marxian theory, any theory of conflict has to operate with something like a two-class model. There are but two contending parties—this is implied in the very concept of conflict. There may be coalitions, of course, as there may be conflicts internal to either of the contenders, and there may be groups that are not drawn into a given dispute; but from the point of view of a given clash of interests, there are never more than two positions that struggle for domination. We can follow Marx in this argument (which, for him, is often more implicit than explicit) even further. If social conflicts effect change, and if they are generated by social structure, then it is reasonable to assume that of the two interests involved in any one conflict, one will be pressing for change, the other one for the *status quo*. This assumption, again, is based on logic as much as on empirical observation. In every conflict, one party attacks and another defends. The defending party wants to retain and secure its position, while the attacking party has to fight it in order to improve its own condition. Once again, it is clear that these statements remain on a high level of formality. They imply no reference to the substance or the origin of conflicting interests. But, again, it will prove useful to have articulated the formal prerequisites of Marx's and, indeed, of any theory of conflict.

With these formal points, however, our agreement with Marx ends. Although the heuristic purpose and general approach of his theory of class can and must be sustained, this is not the case with respect to most other features of this theory. Only by rejecting these can we hope to clear the way for a more useful theory of class conflict in industrial societies.

Property and Social Class: Marx Rejected

For Marx, the determinant of social classes was effective private property in the means of production. In all essential elements, his theory of class is based on this definition of the concept of class. We have seen, meanwhile, that precisely this tie between the concept of class and the possession of, or exclusion from, effective private property limits the applicability of class theory to a relatively short period of European social history. A theory of class based on the division of society into owners and nonowners of means of production loses its analytical value as soon as legal ownership and factual control are separated. For this reason, any effective supersedure of Marx's theory of class has to start at this point. Now, it is one of the central theses of this study that such a supersedure is possible if we replace the possession, or nonpossession, of effective private property by the exercise of, or exclusion from, authority as the criterion of class formation. Renner, Schumpeter, Burnham, Djilas, and others have prepared the ground for this decision; by contrast to most of these we shall not confine the notion of authority to the control of the means of production, but consider it as a type of social relations analytically independent of economic conditions. The authority structure of entire societies as well as particular institutional orders within societies (such as industry) is, in terms of the theory here advanced, the structural determinant of class formation and class conflict. The specific type of change of social structures caused by social classes and their conflicts is ultimately the result of the differential distribution of positions of authority in societies and their institutional orders. Control over the means of production is but a special case of authority, and the connection of control with legal property an incidental phenomenon of the industrializing societies of Europe and the United States. Classes are tied neither to private property nor to industry or economic structures in general, but as an element of social structure and a factor effecting change they are as universal as their determinant, namely, authority and its distribution itself. On the basis of a concept of class defined by relations of authority, a theory can be formulated which accounts for the facts described by Marx as well as for the changed reality of post-capitalist society.

At several points of our investigation it has become apparent how many doubts and objections can be raised against Marx's treatment of the relationship between property and social class. In presenting Marx's theory, in describing the phenomenon of the separation of ownership and control, and in discussing Burnham's inferences from this phenomenon and Djilas's analysis of Communist totalitarianism, we have seen how, by connecting the concept of class with private property (and thereby capitalism), Marx renders this concept fit for inclusion in his philosophical conception of history but unfit for the sociological analysis even of the conflicts with which he was concerned. Marx, too, is concerned with relations of authority; indeed, he explicitly refers to these when he describes class conflicts generated by the structure of the industrial enterprise. But Marx believed that authority and power are factors which can be traced back to a man's share in effective private property. In reality, the opposite is the case. Power and authority are irreducible factors from which the social relations associated with legal private property as well as those associated with communal property can be derived. Burnham, and above all Geiger, have rightly stressed that property is in its sociological aspect in the first place a permission to exclude others from control over an object. It is therefore (Weber) a "chance to find obedience with defined persons for an order" (in this case a prohibition), that is, a form of authority. But property is by no means the only form of authority; it is but one of its numerous types. Whoever tries, therefore, to define authority by property defines the general by the particular—an obvious logical fallacy. Wherever there is property there is authority, but not every form of authority implies property. Authority is the more general social relation.

This formal argument is not, however, the only reason for substituting for Marx's definition of classes by private property one by a man's share in authority; this generalization is necessary, also, for the sake of the empirical applicability of the theory of class. For this purpose, it is moreover necessary to separate radically the concept of authority from its narrow application to the control over economic means of production. Just as property is formally, thus control over the means of production is empirically but a special case of those general relations of authority which, according to our conception, lie at the base of class formation and class conflict. Why this extension is empirically necessary will be shown in detail in the following section of this chapter, where we deal with the relation between industrial and social authority structures. However, this much can be stated even without a more detailed discussion: that a theory of group conflict the central category of which is defined by a man's share in the control of the means of production can apply only to the sphere of industrial production. In any case, its significance for structure change would be even more restricted than is the significance of the theory of class.

To say that classes are based on a man's share in legitimate power is not to formulate an empirical hypothesis. If this were so, it would presuppose an independent definition of the concept of class. It is rather a definition which, in a preliminary way, we can state as follows: classes are social conflict groups the determinant (or *differentia specifica*) of which can be found in the participation in or exclusion from the exercise of authority within any imperatively coordinated association. In this sense, classes differ from other conflict groups which rest on religious, ethnic, or legal differences. In principle, a definition is of course an arbitrary decision. If it is logically unassailable, it cannot be refuted by empirical facts. Yet the definition proposed here is more than a terminological decision without empirical consequences. We shall see that this decision alone opens up many new possibilities for the analysis of social conflicts.

If we define classes by relations of authority, it is *ipso facto* evident that "economic classes," that is, classes within economic organizations, are but a special case of the phenomenon of class. Furthermore, even within the sphere of industrial production it is not really economic factors that give rise to class formation, but a certain type of social relations which we have tried to comprehend in the notion of authority. Classes are neither primarily nor at all economic groupings.

It is less easy to determine the relation between classes as authority groups and the system of social stratification. In the first place, it is important to realize that there is no one-to-one correlation between class structure and social stratification in the sense that classes result from people's place in the hierarchy of stratification. The analyses of class and of social stratification are essentially independent subjects of sociological inquiry. On the other hand, there is between them a significant indirect connection which results from the fact that authority, the determinant of class, is at the same time one of the determinants of social status. It can be demonstrated that there is an empirical tendency for the possession of authority to be accompanied, within certain limits and with significant exceptions, by high income and high prestige, and, conversely, for the exclusion from authority to be accompanied by relatively low income and prestige. Indeed, it is one of the distinguishing features of authority that it can become an instrument for the satisfaction of other desires and needs and for the attainment of directly gratifying social rewards. Thus, there is in most societies a tendential, if not unequivocal, correlation between the distribution of authority and the system of social rewards that underlies stratification. In this sense, but only in this sense, the partial parallelism between the lines of class division and those of social stratification may be an empirical fact. One might go further and regard this parallelism as probable, as it could be argued that a certain correspondence between people's share in authority and in social rewards in general is a functional imperative of relatively stable societies. But no parallelism between structures of class and stratification can be postulated. Classes can be identical with strata, they can unite several strata within them, and their structure can cut right through the hierarchy of stratification.

For purposes of clarity it seemed advisable to state, in the strongest possible terms, the way in which class is independent of property, economic conditions, and social stratification. In the abstract, no qualification need be made to this statement. Fortunately, however, empirical conditions do not usually reproduce the simplicity of our assumptions and theories. Although the idea of property, of the relationships that have to do with production, and of the hierarchy of social stratification is, in each instance, clearly distinct from the idea of class, these factors have a great deal to do with the realities of social class and class conflict. Without doubt, the fact that at the time Marx wrote there were capitalists who simultaneously owned and controlled their enterprises contributed greatly to the formation of classes and the antagonism between them. Similarly, the fact that it is possible to identify the powerful with the wealthy cannot be overlooked in class analysis. While the connection between property and social class is not one of definition or mutual dependence, it is one that affects the empirical course of class conflict. If distinctions of property are superimposed on distinctions of class, class conflict is likely to be more violent than if these two lines of social differentiation diverge. An analogous argument could be made for class and social stratification. In fact, this is one of many points at which Marx has transformed a correct empirical observation into a false and useless assumption by arbitrarily generalizing what was characteristic only of the comparatively short historical period which he lived to see.

Power and Authority

From the point of view of the integration theory of social structure, units of social analysis ("social systems") are essentially voluntary associations of people who share certain values and set up institutions in order to ensure the smooth functioning of cooperation. From the point of view of coercion theory, however, the units of social analysis present an altogether different picture. Here, it is not voluntary cooperation or general consensus but enforced constraint that makes social organizations cohere. In institutional terms, this means that in every social organization some positions are entrusted with a right to exercise control over other positions in order to ensure effective coercion; it means, in other words, that there is a differential distribution of power and authority. One of the central theses of this study consists in the assumption that this differential distribution of authority invariably becomes the determining factor of systematic social conflicts of a type that is germane to class conflicts in the traditional (Marxian) sense of this term. The structural origin of such group conflicts must be sought in the arrangement of social roles endowed with expectations of domination or subjection. Wherever there are such roles, group conflicts of the type in question are to be expected. Differentiation of groups engaged in such conflicts follows the lines of differentiation of roles that are relevant from the point of view of the exercise of authority. Identification of variously equipped authority roles is the first task of conflict analysis; conceptually and empirically all further steps of analysis follow from the investigation of distributions of power and authority.

In conflict analysis we are concerned *inter alia* with the generation of conflict groups by the authority relations obtaining in imperatively coordinated associations. Since imperative coordination, or authority, is a type of social relation present in every conceivable social organization, it will be sufficient to describe such organizations simply as associations. Despite prolonged terminological discussions, no general agreement has been attained by sociologists on the precise meaning of the categories "organization," "association," and "institution." If I am not mistaken in my interpretation of the trend of terminological disputes, it appears justifiable to use the term "association" in such a way as to imply the coordination of organized aggregates of roles by domination and subjection. The state, a church, an enterprise, but also a political party, a trade union, and a chess club are associations in this sense. In all of them, authority relations exist; for all of them, conflict analysis is therefore applicable. If at a later stage we shall suggest restriction to the two great associations of the state and the industrial enterprise, this suggestion is dictated merely by considerations of empirical significance, not logical (or definitional) difference. In looking at social organizations not in terms of their integration and coherence but from the point of view of their structure of coercion and constraint, we regard them as (imperatively coordinated) associations rather than as social systems. Because social organizations are also associations, they generate conflicts of interest and become the birthplace of conflict groups.

I have assumed in the preceding remarks that authority is a characteristic of social organizations as general as society itself. Despite the assertion of Renner—and other modern sociologists—that in some contemporary societies the exercise of authority has been eliminated and replaced by the more anonymous "rule of the law" or other nonauthoritative relations, I should indeed maintain that authority is a universal element of social structure. It is in this sense more general than, for example, property, or even status. With respect to postcapitalist industrial society, I hope to establish this position more unambiguously in the final chapters of this study. Generally speaking, however, the universality of authority relations would seem evident as soon as we describe these relations in a "passive" rather than in an "active" sense. Authority relations exist wherever there are people whose actions are subject to legitimate and sanctioned prescriptions that originate outside them but within social structure. This formulation, by leaving open who exercises what kind of authority, leaves little doubt as to the omnipresence of some kind of authority somehow exercised. For it is evident that there are many forms and types of authority in historical societies. There are differences of a considerable order of magnitude between the relations of the citizen of classical Athens and his slaves, the feudal landlord and his villeins and serfs, the nineteenth-century capitalist and his workers, the secretary of a totalitarian state party and its members, the appointed manager of a modern enterprise and its employees, or the elected prime minister of a democratic country and the electorate. No attempt will be made in this study to develop a typology of authority. But it is assumed throughout that the existence of domination and subjection is a common feature of all possible types of authority and, indeed, of all possible types of association and organization.

In referring to the ugly face of authority as a "zero-sum" concept, Parsons brings out one further aspect of this category which is essential for our considerations. By zero-sum, Parsons evidently means that from the point of view of the disruptive "functions" of authority there are two groups or aggregates of persons, of which one possesses authority to the extent to which the other one is deprived of it. This implies—for us, if not for Parsons—that in terms of the coercion theory of society we can always observe a dichotomy of positions in imperatively coordinated associations with respect to the distribution of authority. Parsons, in his critique of Mills, compares the distribution of authority to the distribution of wealth. It seems to me that this comparison is misleading. However unequally wealth may be distributed, there always is a continuum of possession ranging from the lowest to the highest rank. Wealth is not and cannot be conceived as a zero-sum concept. With respect to authority, however, a clear line can at least in theory be drawn between those who participate in its exercise in given associations and those who are subject to the authoritative commands of others. Our analysis of modern societies in later chapters will show that empirically it is not always easy to identify the border line between domination and subjection. Authority has not remained unaffected by the modern process of division of labor. But even here, groups or aggregates can be identified which do not participate in the exercise of authority other than by complying with given commands or prohibitions. Contrary to all criteria of social stratification, authority does not permit the construction of a scale. So-called hierarchies of authority (as displayed, for example, in organization charts) are in fact hierarchies of the "plus-side" of authority, that is, of the differentiation of domination; but there is, in every association, also a "minus-side" consisting of those who are subjected to authority rather than participate in its exercise.

In two respects this analysis has to be specified, if not supplemented. First, for the individual incumbent of roles, domination in one association does not necessarily involve domination in all others to which he belongs, and subjection, conversely, in one association does not mean subjection in all. The dichotomy of positions of authority holds for specific associations only.

In a democratic state, there are both mere voters and incumbents of positions of authority such as cabinet ministers, representatives, and higher civil servants. But this does not mean that the "mere voter" cannot be incumbent of a position of authority in a different context, say, in an industrial enterprise; conversely, a cabinet minister may be, in his church, a mere member, that is, subject to the authority of others. Although empirically a certain correlation of the authority positions of individuals in different associations seems likely, it is by no means general and is in any case a matter of specific empirical conditions. It is at least possible, if not probable, that if individuals in a given society are ranked according to the sum total of their authority positions in all associations, the resulting pattern will not be a dichotomy but rather like scales of stratification according to income or prestige. For this reason it is necessary to emphasize that in the sociological analysis of group conflict the unit of analysis is always a specific association and the dichotomy of positions within it.

As with respect to the set of roles associated with an individual, total societies, also, do not usually present an unambiguously dichotomic authority structure. There are a large number of imperatively coordinated associations in any given society. Within every one of them we can distinguish the aggregates of those who dominate and those who are subjected. But since domination in industry does not necessarily involve domination in the state, or a church, or other associations, total societies can present the picture of a plurality of competing dominant (and, conversely, subjected) aggregates. This, again, is a problem for the analysis of specific historical societies and must not be confounded with the clearer lines of differentiation within any one association. Within the latter, the distribution of authority always sums up to zero, that is, there always is a division involving domination and subjection.

I have introduced, as a structural determinant of conflict groups, the category of authority as exercised in imperatively coordinated associations. While agreeing with Marx that source and level of income—even socioeconomic status—cannot usefully be conceived as determinants of conflict groups, I have added to this list of erroneous approaches Marx's own in terms of property in the means of production. Authority is both a more general and a more significant social relation. The former has been shown in our critique of Marx; the latter will have to be demonstrated by subsequent considerations and analyses. The concept of authority is used, in this context, in a specific sense. It is differentiated from power by what may roughly be referred to as the element of legitimacy; and it has to be understood throughout in the restricted sense of authority as distributed and exercised in imperatively coordinated associations. While its "disruptive" or conflict-generating consequences are not the only aspect of authority, they are the one relevant in terms of the coercion model of society. Within the frame of reference of this model, (1) the distribution of authority in associations is the ultimate "cause" of the formation of conflict groups, and (2), being dichotomous, it is, in any given association, the cause of the formation of two, and only two, conflict groups.

The first of these statements is logically an assumption, since it underlies scientific theories. It cannot as such be tested by observation; its validity is proven, rather, by its usefulness for purposes of explanation. We shall derive from this assumption certain more specific hypotheses which, if refuted, would take the assumption with them into the waste-paper basket of scientific theories. We assume in this sense that if we manage to identify the incumbents of positions of domination and subjection in any given association, we have identified the contenders of one significant type of conflicts—conflicts which occur in this association at all times.

As to the second statement, the one concerned with the dichotomy of authority positions in imperatively coordinated associations, it is not, I suggest, either an assumption or an empirical hypothesis, but an analytical statement. It follows from and is implicit in the very concept of authority that within specified contexts some have authority and others not. If either nobody or everybody had authority, the concept would lose its meaning. Authority implies both domination and subjection, and it therefore implies the existence of two distinct sets of positions or persons. This is not to say, of course, that there is no difference between those who have a great deal and those who have merely a little authority. Among the positions of domination there may be, and often is, considerable differentiation. But such differentiation, while important for empirical analysis, leaves unaffected the existence of a border line somewhere between those who have whatever little authority and the "outs."

.   .   .

That "the realization of a socialist society" constitutes "the true interest of labor" is indeed an assertion for the (empirical) premises of which "the proof is missing." An assumption of this kind cannot be introduced by way of a postulate. The substance of socially structured "objective" interests can be described only in highly formal terms: they are interests in the maintenance or modification of a *status quo*. Our model of conflict group formation involves the proposition that of the two aggregates of authority positions to be distinguished in every association, one—that of domination—is characterized by an interest in the maintenance of a social structure that for them conveys authority, whereas the other—that of subjection—involves an interest in changing a social condition that deprives its incumbents of authority. The two interests are in conflict.

Max Weber has convincingly demonstrated that the problem of maintaining or changing given structures of authority can be expressed, both conceptually and empirically, in terms of the basis of legitimacy of relations of authority. From our assumption of an at least latent conflict of interests in every imperatively coordinated association, it follows that the legitimacy of authority must always be precarious. There always is one aggregate of positions and their incumbents which represents the institutionalized doubt in the legitimacy of the *status quo* of the distribution of authority. In this sense, the proposition that there are "objective" interests in changing any given structure of authority might also be expressed in terms of the potential illegitimacy of all relations of authority. Empirically, group conflict is probably most easily accessible to analysis if it be understood as a conflict about the legitimacy of relations of authority. In every association, the interests of the ruling group are the values that constitute the ideology of the legitimacy of its rule, whereas the interests of the subjected group constitute a threat to this ideology and the social relations it covers.

Quasi-Groups and Interest Groups: Theoretical Conditions of Conflict Group Formation

We have postulated two conflicting orientations of latent interests as characteristic of the role structure of imperatively coordinated associations. By implication, this means, of course, that the authority positions equipped with expected interests as well as their incumbents have at least one attribute in common. In a significant sense, the occupants of identical authority positions, that is, either of positions of domination or of positions of subjection, find themselves in a common situation. Being united by a common, potentially permanent, characteristic, they are more than mere masses or incoherent quantities. At the same time, the incumbents of like authority positions in an association do not in any sociologically tenable sense constitute a group. Just as all doctors, or all inhabitants of Berlin, do not as such constitute social groups, the occupants of positions with identical latent interests are not a group. For groups, a feeling of belongingness is as constitutive as a minimum of organization; but both are explicitly not demanded by the concept of latent interests. The aggregates of incumbents of positions with identical role interests are at best a potential group. Following M. Ginsberg we shall use for this particular type of social grouping the term *quasi-group*. "Not all collectivities or aggregates form groups. Groups are masses of people in regular contact or communication, and possessing a recognizable structure. There are other aggregates or portions of the community which have no recognizable structure, but whose members have certain interests or modes of behavior in common, which may at any time lead them to form themselves into definite groups. To this category of quasi-groups belong such entities as social classes, which, without being groups, are a recruiting field for groups, and whose members have certain characteristic modes of behavior in common."

.   .   .

In what sense are interest groups, such as political parties, to be regarded as representative of the quasi-groups that can be inferred behind them? Can the same quasi-group become a recruiting field for several interest groups? In principle, the possibility intimated by the latter question has to be answered in the affirmative. From the point of view of conflict theory, competing trade unions of, say, Christian and Socialist description originate from the same quasi-group. Empirically, interest groups are always smaller than their recruiting fields, the quasi-groups. They are subsets of the sets constituted by quasi-groups; and the identity of set and subset remains a limiting case. One might compare the relation of the two with that of the members and the voters of one political party. Furthermore, a number of specific intervening variables may disturb the immediacy of the relation between given quasi-groups and interest groups. While quasi-groups, being in the nature of a theoretical construction, are unequivocally defined, organized interest groups may supplement the interests accruing from authority structures by a multitude of other and independent goals and orientations. This is merely another expression for the fact that interest groups are "real phenomena," and that, like all such phenomena, they cannot be completely described by one attribute. Thus, the theory of group conflict involves no statement about the empirical variety of interest groups. It concentrates on one of their aspects: on their function in social conflicts as units of manifest interests which can be explained in terms of latent role interests and their aggregation in quasi-groups. [1]

Quasi-Groups and Interest Groups:
Empirical Conditions of Conflict Group Formation

"It is a matter of no small interest," Ginsberg adds to his definition of quasi-groups, "to determine at what point these looser configurations crystallize into associations." The categories of quasi-group and interest group mark the two

---

[1] To illustrate this rather abstract formulation: for the theory of conflict, socialist parties are of interest not as instruments of workers' education or as clublike associations, but merely as forces in social conflicts. The same party may function in many ways other than as an interest group, but only the latter aspect is in question in the present analysis.

foci of the analysis of conflict group formation, but they do not describe the connecting lines between them. It will now be our task to examine the conditions under which a "class in itself" becomes a "class for itself." Perhaps the negative side of this problem is of even greater importance. We shall want to ascertain the conditions under which the organization of interest groups does not take place despite the presence of quasi-groups of latent interests in an imperatively coordinated association. This is evidently a matter of ascertaining possible intervening variables which we shall comprehend under the collective term of "structural conditions of organization."

In dealing with the empirical process of development of classes Marx has touched upon this problem at many points. Among these there is one which is particularly illuminating for our present context. At the end of his essay on the 18th of Brumaire of Louis Bonaparte, Marx is dealing with "the most numerous class of French society, the small independent peasants." Marx states, to begin with, that these peasants, by virtue of their situation, their conditions of existence, their way of life, and their (latent) interests, constitute a "class," namely, a quasi-group. One would therefore expect a political organization or interest group to grow out of their midst. However, precisely this did not happen. In so far as the identity of the (latent) interests of the peasants "does not produce a community, national association and political organization, they do not constitute a class." In explaining this surprising fact, Marx refers to conditions of the kind of the intervening variables in question here: "The small independent peasants constitute an enormous mass, the members of which live in the same situation but do not enter into manifold relations with each other. Their mode of production isolates them from each other instead of bringing them into mutual intercourse. This isolation is strengthened by the bad state of French means of communication and by the poverty of the peasants . . . Every single peasant family is almost self-sufficient . . . and thus gains its material of life more in exchange with nature than in intercourse with society." The brilliant conclusion Marx draws from this analysis—namely, that Louis Bonaparte is trying to justify his claim for power by reference to this quasi-group of peasants whose interests are condemned to latency—will concern us less here than the problem impressively demonstrated by it. Under certain conditions, quasi-groups may persist as such without interest groups emerging from them. What are these conditions, and under which conditions do interest groups come to be formed?

It is a commonplace that groups cannot exist without members and, in that sense, without a personnel. Moreover, since we have postulated the presence of a personnel in the quasi-groups from which interest groups emerge, this condition does not at first sight appear to be a genuine intervening variable. It is, indeed, not the total membership of an interest group which is in question here, but that sector of the membership which can be described as the leading group or cadre. For an organized interest group to emerge from a quasi-group, there have to be certain persons who make this organization their business, who carry it out practically and take the lead. Every party needs its founders. The availability of founders in this sense, however, is by no means given in our model nor can it be. It is an additional empirical condition of conflict group formation. As such it is a necessary, although not sufficient, condition of organization. To stipulate a leading group as a prerequisite of the organization of interest groups must not be misunderstood to mean that conflict groups are based on the goals and actions of a handful of leaders. The availability of possible organizers, founders, and leaders is essentially a technical prerequisite which must be satisfied for unorganized quasi-groups to be transformed into organized interest groups. The organizers are one of the ferments, not the starting point or cause of organization. That without them organization is impossible has been demonstrated convincingly—in so far as it is not self-evident—by Marx at the place in the "18th Brumaire" quoted above, and above all in the "Communist Manifesto."

Marx has realized, also, that the creation of a charter is not an automatic process. Malinowski defines the charter of an organization as the "system of values for the pursuit of which human beings organize." In the particular case of conflict groups these values consist of what we have called "manifest interests." While latent interests are nonpsychological orientations implicit in the social structure of roles and positions, manifest interests are articulate, formulated (or at least formulable) programs. They entail specific claims related to given structures of authority. The articulation and codification of such interests is again a process that presupposes certain conditions. Either there must be a person or circle of persons who take on themselves the task of articulation and codification, or, alternatively, an "ideology," a system of ideas, must be available which in a given case is capable of serving as a program or charter of groups. As evidence for the first, it seems sufficient to refer to the role of the political ideologist Marx for the organization of the socialist movement; as evidence of the latter alternative, to the role of a certain interpretation of Calvinism for early English capitalists. Ideologies understood as articulated and codified manifest interests are again but a technical condition of organization. Ideologies do not create conflict groups or cause conflict groups to emerge. Yet they are indispensable as obstetricians of conflict groups, and in this sense as an intervening variable.

Even if we are given not only quasi-groups with common latent interests, but leaders and ideologies as well—if, in other words, the technical conditions of organization are present—it is still not justified to make the empirical inference that interest groups will be formed. A second category of prerequisites which have to be satisfied for organization to be possible will be described here as the *political conditions of organization*. The totalitarian state is probably the most unambiguous illustration of a social situation in which these conditions are not fulfilled, and in which therefore at least oppositional interest groups cannot emerge despite the presence of quasi-groups and latent interests.[2] Where a plurality of conflicting parties is not permitted and their emergence suppressed by the absence of freedom of coalition and by police force, conflict groups cannot organize themselves even if all other conditions of their organization are present. The study of the possibilities and actual types of group conflict under such conditions is a problem of sociological analysis of the highest importance. There is a starting point, here, of the analysis not only of "underground movements" and the development of revolutions, but more generally of structure and dynamics of totalitarian states. But this type of problem can be merely intimated here, since we are for the time being concerned with formulating the general structural conditions of organization. We can maintain that the political permissibility of organization is one of the additional intervening prerequisites of conflict group formation.

Apart from technical and political conditions, some, in the narrow sense, *social conditions of organization* are of importance for the formation of interest groups. Among these we find the condition of communication between the "members" of quasi-groups emphasized by Marx in the case of French peasants. If an aggregate within an association can be described as a community of latent interests, is also provided with the technical and political possibilities of organization, but is so scattered topologically or ecologically that a regular connection among the members of the aggregate does not exist and can be established only with great difficulty, then the formation of an organized interest group is empirically most unlikely. However, important as this premise of organization is, the generalization seems tenable that its significance is steadily diminishing in industrial societies with a highly developed system of means of communication. In advanced industrial societies this condition may be assumed to be generally given; it enters, therefore, into the analysis of conflict group formation as a constant.

This is not the case, however, with another social condition of organization

[2]Technically similar conditions obtain in many preindustrial societies. In terms of the political conditions of organization the restriction of this study to industrial societies can be well illustrated. In all preindustrial societies group conflict is seriously impeded by the absence of certain political conditions (the political "citizenship rights"). It would be a matter for separate analysis to investigate forms of group conflict in these societies.

the implications of which will occupy us a good deal more. Empirically, the formation of organized interest groups is possible only if recruitment to quasi-groups follows a structural pattern rather than chance. By this condition, the group described by Marx as *lumpenproletariat* is excluded from conflict group formation. Persons who attain positions relevant for conflict analysis not by the normal process of the allocation of social positions in a social structure, but by peculiar, structurally random personal circumstances, appear generally unsuited for the organization of conflict groups. Thus the lowest stratum of industrial societies is frequently recruited in manifold but structurally irrelevant ways: by delinquency, extreme lack of talent, personal mishaps, physical or psychological instability, and so on. In this case, the condition of structural recruitment is not satisfied, and conflict group formation cannot be expected.

From the empirical conditions of the organization of conflict groups thus briefly sketched, we can, by way of generalization, derive a number of social constellations which are unfavorable if not prohibitive for conflict group formation and group conflict. Here, again, I shall confine myself to giving an indication. One constellation resisting conflict group formation, namely, that of the totalitarian state, is directly given in the formulated conditions. A second important constellation can be defined by combining several of the factors mentioned. If imperatively coordinated associations are either themselves just emerging or subject to radical change, the probability is small that the quasi-groups derived from their authority structure will lead to coherent forms of organization. Examples for this may be seen in the early stages of industrial development, or in societies immediately after social revolutions (such as the Soviet Union in the 1920's). In both cases authority structures, latent interests, and quasi-groups are present. But in both cases it seems reasonable to assume that the absence of leaders and ideologies as well as the still unpatterned and unnormalized recruitment to the relevant positions stand in the way of conflict group formation. In this sense, it seems feasible to attempt to reformulate Marx's problem of the gradual formation of classes in the course of industrialization.

The empirical conditions of organization have been described here as prerequisites of conflict group formation. However, their effect goes beyond the process of emergence of conflict groups. These factors are relevant, also, as variables affecting organized interest groups. They must then be understood, of course, as continua which permit gradations. A relative lack of technical, political, and social conditions of organization can hamper organized interest groups in their operation, and it can, indeed—which is apparent in the case of the political conditions—result in their disintegration.

Subjected conflict groups must therefore not be visualized as essentially unorganized masses without effective force. In analogy to the characteristics of ruling groups we can state (a) that they do not necessarily comprise the majority of the members of an association, (b) that their members are not necessarily connected by "properties" or a "culture" beyond the interests that bind them into groups, and (c) that their existence is always related to particular associations, so that one society may display several subjected conflict groups. Beyond these, one distinguishing feature of subjected groups must be emphasized. The Marxian expression "suppressed classes" might appear to mean that any such group is characterized by the attributes which Marx ascribed to, or found present in, the proletariat of his time. However, this implication is by no means intended here. "Pauperism," "slavery," absolute exclusion from the wealth and liberty of society is a possible but unnecessary attribute of the incumbents of roles of subjection. Here, again, the connection is indeterminate, that is, variable, and its particular pattern can be established only by empirical observation and for particular associations. It is not only conceivable that members of the subjected group of one association belong to the dominating group of another association, it is above all possible that "suppressed classes" enjoy, despite their exclusion from legitimate power, an (absolutely) high measure of social rewards without this fact impeding their organization as interest groups or their participation in group conflicts. Even a "bourgeoisified proletariat" can function as a subjected conflict group, for conflict groups and group conflicts are solely based on the one criterion of participation in or exclusion from the exercise of authority in imperatively coordinated associations. Difficult as it may be for minds schooled in Marx to separate the category of "suppressed class" from the ideas of poverty and exploitation, a well-formulated theory of group conflict requires the radical separation of these spheres.

The Theory of Social Classes and Class Conflict

1. The approach of this study has to be understood in terms of two premises— one formal, one substantive—which, although they are of a meta-theoretical or methodological nature, provide the necessary frame of reference of its elements.

1.1. The heuristic purpose of the approach proposed in the present study is the explanation of structure changes in terms of group conflict. This purpose is therefore neither purely descriptive nor related to problems of integration and coherence in or of society.

1.2. In order to do justice to this heuristic purpose it is necessary to visualize society in terms of the coercion theory of social structure, that is, change and conflict have to be assumed as ubiquitous, all elements of social structure have to be related to instability and change, and unity and coherence have to be understood as resulting from coercion and constraint.

2. Within this frame of reference, the theory of social classes and class conflict involves a number of concepts to be defined.

2.1. "*Authority* is the probability that a command with a given specific content will be obeyed by a given group of persons" (Weber).

2.1.1. By *domination* shall be understood the possession of authority, that is, the right to issue authoritative commands.

2.1.2. By *subjection* shall be understood the exclusion from authority, that is, the duty to obey authoritative commands.

2.2. "An association shall be called *imperatively coordinated association* insofar as its members are, by virtue of a prevailing order, subject to authority relations" (Weber).

2.3 Orientations of behavior which are inherent in social positions without necessarily being conscious to their incumbents (role expectations), and which oppose two aggregates of positions in any imperatively coordinated association, shall be called *latent interests*.

2.4. *Quasi-group* shall mean any collectivity of individuals sharing positions with identical latent interests without having organized themselves as such.

2.5. *Manifest interests* shall mean orientations of behavior which are articulate and conscious to individuals, and which oppose collectivities of individuals in any imperatively coordinated association.

2.6. *Interest group* shall mean any organized collectivity of individuals sharing manifest interests.

2.7. By *social class* shall be understood such organized or unorganized collectivities of individuals as share manifest or latent interests arising from and related to the authority structure of imperatively coordinated associations. It follows from the definitions of latent and manifest interests that social classes are always conflict groups.

2.8. Any antagonistic relationship between organized collectivities of individuals that can be explained in terms of patterns of social structure (and is not, therefore, sociologically random) shall be called *group conflict*.

2.9. *Class conflict* shall mean any group conflict that arises from and is related to the authority structure of imperatively coordinated associations.

2.10. Any deviation of the values (normative structure) or institutions (factual structure) of a unit of social analysis at a given point of time $(T + n)$ from those of a preceding point of time (T) shall be called *structure change*, insofar as it involves the incumbents of positions of domination.

2.10.1. By *radicalness of structure change* shall be understood the significance of consequences and ramifications of structure change.

2.10.2 By *suddenness of structure change* shall be understood the extent to which incumbents of positions of domination are replaced.

3. The formation of conflict groups of the class type follows a pattern that can be described in terms of a model involving the following partly analytical, partly hypothetical steps:

3.1. In any imperatively coordinated association, two, and only two, aggregates of positions may be distinguished, that is, positions of domination and positions of subjection.

3.2. Each of these aggregates is characterized by common latent interests; the collectivities of individuals corresponding to them constitute quasi-groups.

3.3. Latent interests are articulated into manifest interests; and the quasi-groups become the recruiting fields of organized interest groups of the class type.

3.3.1. Articulation of manifest interests and organization of interest groups can be prevented by the intervention of empirically variable conditions of organization.

3.3.2. Among the conditions of organization, technical conditions (personnel, charter), political conditions (freedom of coalition), and social conditions (communication, patterned recruitment) can be distinguished. To these, certain nonstructural psychological conditions (internalization of role interests) may be added.

4. The course of group conflict of the class type also follows a pattern that can be described in terms of a model involving both analytical and hypothetical elements.

4.1. Once the formation of conflict groups of the class type is complete, they stand, within given associations, in a relation of group conflict (class conflict).

4.1.1. The intensity of class conflict varies on a scale (from 0 to 1) according to the operation of certain factors.

4.1.1.1. The intensity of class conflict decreases to the extent that the conditions of class organization are present.

4.1.1.2. The intensity of class conflict decreases to the extent that class conflicts in different associations are dissociated (and not superimposed).

4.1.1.3. The intensity of class conflict decreases to the extent that different group conflicts in the same society are dissociated (and not superimposed).

4.1.1.4. The intensity of class conflict decreases to the extent that the distribution of authority and the distribution of rewards and facilities in an association are dissociated (and not superimposed).

4.1.1.5. The intensity of class conflict decreases to the extent that classes are open (and not closed).

4.1.2. The violence of class conflict varies on a scale (from 0 to 1) according to the operation of certain factors.

4.1.2.1. The violence of class conflict decreases to the extent that the conditions of class organization are present.

4.1.2.2. The violence of class conflict decreases if absolute deprivation of rewards and facilities on the part of a subjected class gives way to relative deprivation.

4.1.2.3. The violence of class conflict decreases to the extent that class conflict is effectively regulated.

4.2. Group conflict of the class type effects structure changes in the associations in which it occurs.

4.2.1. The radicalness of structure change co-varies with the intensity of class conflict.

4.2.2. The suddenness of structure change co-varies with the violence of class conflict.

A Theory of Inequality [1966]

GERHARD E. LENSKI

● *Gerhard Lenski's* Power and Privilege *(1966) was the first systematic triumph for conflict sociology. For decades American sociologists of various persuasions had been posturing about making sociology into a science, but there remained a dearth of genuine theories that actually explained anything. Lenski presented not only a generalized explanatory theory, but also a conflict theory, of a central social phenomenon: the degree of inequality or equality in the distribution of wealth within a society. True to the best scientific method, Lenski made comparisons among the relevant empirical cases: in this instance, the entire range of human societies. Lenski's categorization of types of societies has become classic: hunting-and-gathering, primitive horticulture, advanced horticulture, agrarian, and industrial. It is based on basic productive technologies, and captures far more of the relevant dimensions of historical difference among societies than Marx's alleged stages: "primitive communism" (a confused, early view of the anthropological evidence that mixed hunting-and-gathering and horticultural—that is, tribal, generally stateless—societies), "slavery," "feudalism" (both of which were mainly agrarian in Lenski's sense), and finally "capitalism" (a subtype within industrial societies). On this basis, Lenski lays down several basic laws of distribution: The amount of inequality grows with the size of the economic surplus in society, but also with (and under certain conditions is overridden by) the concentration of political power. The last factor parallels Dahrendorf's emphasis on power as a determining factor in class conflicts.*

The starting point in every sociological discussion of the nature of man is the deceptively simple assertion that *man is a social being obliged by nature to live with others as a member of society*. On this proposition at least, radicals and conservatives agree, and this serves as the *first postulate* in our general theory.

From Gerhard E. Lenski, *Power and Privilege. A Theory of Social Stratification.* New York: McGraw-Hill, 1966, pp. 25–32, 44–52, 63–65, 74–76, 102–6, 308–18, 435–37. Copyright 1966 by Gerhard Lenski. Reprinted by permission of the author.

To say that man is a social being is not to deny that a few individuals withdraw from society and live as hermits. The human race could not survive on this basis, however, since its chief weapon in the struggle for existence has always been culture, and culture is uniquely a social product. Social life is essential not only for the survival of the species but also for the maximum satisfaction of human needs and desires. Through cooperative activity men can satisfy many needs and desires which could never be met otherwise and can satisfy most other needs much more efficiently, that is, with greater return for less effort or other investment.

If our first postulate is relatively noncontroversial, the same cannot be said of the second. It takes us directly into the realm of one of the bitterest disputes between radicals and conservatives—the dispute concerning the origin of evil. As noted in the last chapter, the radical view of man and society steadily gained in popularity and intellectual respectability after the English revolution of the seventeenth century. In an era of European growth and expansion, this optimistic view, which postulated society as the source of evil, found increasing acceptance, especially among intellectuals. Since the rise of Nazism and the outbreak of World War II, however, the trend has been halted and, for the first time in roughly three centuries, the pendulum seems to be moving in the opposite direction. On every hand the evidence mounts that the evil in men's actions is rooted more deeply than radical theorists had supposed. Neither the French Revolution nor the Russian produced the utopias that were promised despite revolutionary institutional change. Though the patterns of men's lives have been changed greatly by the social and technological revolutions of modern times, egoism, selfishness, and cruelty continue to loom large.

Paralleling the argument from modern history is that from contemporary psychology, where current theory and research undermine our faith in the natural goodness of man no less than do political events. Recent research reveals the human infant as an extremely self-centered creature, motivated solely by his own needs and desires. If we rid ourselves of the romantic aura which surrounds babies in our society, we discover that they are totally involved in reducing the various tensions created by their biological nature and the environment. Their early actions are simply trial-and-error probings to discover methods of reducing or relieving these tensions.

In time, of course, the normal child learns to take the wishes of others into account. But this does not mean that he is any less motivated to maximize his own satisfactions. Rather, it means that he has learned that the attainment of his own goals is inextricably linked with the interests of others. For example, a boy who acquires a taste for baseball soon finds that he can satisfy this taste only by cooperating with others who share his enthusiasm. Because he cooperates with them and obeys the rules of the game we should not assume that he is no longer seeking to maximize his own satisfactions. On the contrary, we can be sure he is!

Children's games afford far more insights into the nature of social organization than is usually recognized. In particular, they demonstrate the process by which institutions with their elements of cooperation and morality and their concepts of right and justice can emerge from the actions of an originally unorganized aggregation of individuals each selfishly seeking to maximize his own personal satisfactions. To achieve this maximization individuals are forced to work (and play) together, but they find that this can be rewarding only if the activity takes place within the framework of a system of rules which, above all else, protects the cooperative activity itself. This can only be done if certain basic rights are guaranteed to all of the essential participants; for example, each boy is guaranteed his turn at bat. This may seem to entail some sacrifice on the part of the stronger or abler participants, but really it does not, since the only alternative is the cessation of the cooperative activity and all its benefits. Thus, for them, as for the other participants, adherence to the rules can be accounted for merely as a form of *enlightened self-interest*.

Many years ago William Graham Sumner coined the phrase "antagonistic cooperation" to call attention to this paradoxical feature of human life. As he pointed out, men are "brought into association and held there by compulsion"—the compulsion of self-interest. He declared that "it is quite as wrong to assume mutual good-will as the basis of human cooperation as it would be to suppose its existence between the bee and the clover or the rhinoceros and the tick bird." In his opinion, "most cooperation has in it . . . suppressed antagonisms that are overborne by practical advantage." While he may have overstated the case somewhat, it is especially applicable in the case of those forms of social organization which are so large and complex that they embrace total strangers.

If one is fond of paradox and irony, one might go further and argue that cooperation itself is one of the basic sources of conflict in human life. If man were a solitary species, with each individual living apart from all the rest except for mating, as is the case with certain animals, there would be far less conflict among men. If each produced only for himself and there were no division of labor and exchange of goods, one of the major sources of human strife would be eliminated. By contrast, when men join forces in a cooperative enterprise, whether it be a family or total society, both the opportunity and the motivation for conflict are greatly increased. This is an aspect of the social scene which most conservative theorists have neglected.

We cannot argue, however, that simple self-interest, enlightened or otherwise, is the only motivating force in human affairs. When we take an objective view, we recognize that the problem is more complicated than this. Self-sacrifice *is* an observable reality no less than self-seeking: parents *do* sacrifice for their children and soldiers for their buddies.

From the moral standpoint, these forms of action are highly commendable. Nevertheless, as some of the more insightful observers of the human scene have pointed out, such actions involve a strong element of self-seeking. Jesus pointed this out to his followers at one point where he said, "If you love only those who love you, what credit is that to you? Even tax collectors do that." Many actions appear as sacrifices only when the larger context is ignored. Seen in context, such actions appear as parts of a mutually beneficial system of exchanged favors.

Whatever else is true of this kind of sacrificial action, it is not disinterested. Such actions are seldom taken on behalf of strangers, nor do we expect it. Rather, they presuppose the existence of highly valued and rewarding interpersonal ties between the parties involved. For lack of a better term, we might call this pattern of action "partisan self-sacrifice" and the interests served by it "partisan group interests" to differentiate it from the disinterested pattern of self-sacrifice involved in truly altruistic action.

There is one other aspect of this matter deserving note. Groups which generate sacrificial action by their members in their relations with one another typically foster a very different pattern of action in relations with outsiders. In fact, it sometimes seems that the stronger the sacrificial tendencies in *intragroup* relations, the weaker such tendencies in *intergroup* relations. This means that our *judgments about the frequency and importance of sacrificial action in human life are a function of the social level on which we focus*. If we make the family or some other primary group the object of our analysis, we are far more likely to be impressed by the evidences of self-sacrifice than if we examine a large and complex nation. When we view human action in this broader perspective, as we shall in this volume, we soon discover that these groups which generate so much sacrificial action in their internal relations are often capable of the most ruthless pursuit of their partisan group interests when dealing with outsiders, even though the latter are members of the same society.

Another questionable form of self-sacrifice is the practice of *noblesse oblige*. The well-to-do in some societies accept certain obligations, such as charity, almsgiving and public service, which yield no obvious returns for themselves. Again, however, the element of self-interest intrudes. For the very wealthy, philanthropy costs relatively little but usually yields substantial dividends. It is one of the few trustworthy routes to honor and prestige, and for those who have everything else, this can be important. . . . Also, as the Lynds demonstrated in their famous study of Middletown, philanthropy can be made to pay handsome political and economic dividends. This is not to say that all charitable actions are prompted by self-interest but only that the element of self-interest is not incompatible with philanthropy. A more serious question which must be directed at charitable action concerns its relative importance in the total economy. Charitable donations usually represent only a small fraction of all expenditures; like icing on a cake, their visibility is no measure of their substance.

Lest it seem that all human action is motivated solely by self-interest, it must be affirmed that some is clearly motivated by a genuine concern for others, with no overtones of self-interest. Clearly there are forces in human experience which are capable of evoking the response of *unselfish or altruistic love*. However, since in most persons this pattern of response has only a limited development, altruistic action is most likely to occur in the minor events of daily life where little is at stake. Apparently many men develop a genuine desire to be generous and kind in their dealings with others but find it "impossible" to act in this way when much is at stake. Thus altruistic action is concentrated on the level of lesser events and decisions, and is infrequent on the level of major social decisions. In fact, it appears that one can state as a generalization that *the frequency of altruistic action varies inversely with the magnitude of the values involved*.

This is not to say that men are immoral when major values are at stake. Rather, it points to the need to differentiate between two kinds of morality, *pragmatic morality* and *ideal morality*. Pragmatic morality is the basis of all popular moral codes, and is based on the recognition that men need one another, and therefore condemns many kinds of harmful actions, especially those which threaten to undermine the social order. Ideal morality, by contrast, has never been accepted as the basis of any popular moral code, since it not only condemns harmful actions but requires that men love others as they love themselves and without regard to possible rewards.

This does not mean that altruism, or unselfish love, is of little or no importance. It is extremely important from both the psychological and moral standpoints, and human existence would be much poorer and harsher if it were absent. It is not, however, a major determinant of the distribution of power and privilege.

Thus, when one surveys the human scene, one is forced to conclude that *when men are confronted with important decisions where they are obliged to choose between their own, or their group's, interests and the interests of others, they nearly always choose the former*—though often seeking to hide this fact from themselves and others. This is the *second postulate* in our theory. As is evident, it leans far in the direction of the conservative position with its skeptical view of the innate goodness of man.

Before leaving this controversial postulate, it may be well to point out that the exchange system and the division of labor in all the more complex societies serve as veils which largely hide this ugly truth. In complex societies men seldom see the consequences of their own economic and political actions. Rather, they observe the workings of the impersonal market system, which favors some and penalizes others. Success or failure thus appears to result from impersonal forces, or forces so complex that the influence of any single individual becomes negligible. This helps to foster the myth that man is by nature good and kind.

The *third postulate* in our theory pertains to the objects of men's strivings. Some, such as the air we breathe, are readily available to all, but most are not. *Most are in short supply*—that is, the demand for them exceeds the available supply.

This is a normal feature of the world of nature. Though we often speak of nature's bounty, the fact remains that all living things have a reproductive capacity which, in view of the limited supply of food and other resources, makes it inevitable that large numbers will die well before the end of their normal life span and most of the others live close to the margin of subsistence.

To some extent man has been able to free himself from these difficulties. Thousands of years ago he learned to increase his food supply and, more recently, he has learned to control reproduction. Yet while man enjoys certain advantages when compared with other living things, he also suffers from certain disadvantages. Unlike the various plants and animals, *man has an insatiable appetite for goods and services*. No matter how much he produces and consumes, he always desires more. This is true chiefly because the goods and services he consumes have a *status value* as well as a utilitarian value. If automobiles were simply a means of transportation, a society able to control its reproduction could eventually satisfy this demand. However, automobiles are also status symbols; hence there is no limit to the demand for their improvement and for the goods and services utilized in their production. The very nature of status striving makes it inevitable that the demand will exceed the supply: those of lower status constantly strive to equal those of higher status and those of higher status always seek to preserve the difference. Given these conditions, satiation is impossible no matter how much man increases production or restricts population increase.

If our first three postulates are correct, that is, if man is a social being, and if most of his important actions are motivated by self-interest or partisan group interest, and if many or most of the objects of his striving are in short supply, then it follows logically that *a struggle for rewards will be present in every human society.* This struggle need not always assume violent forms. On the contrary, it can be carried on within the framework of some system of rules. However, the absence of violence does not mean that the struggle is any less real or serious for the parties involved.

TWO LAWS OF DISTRIBUTION

When one seeks to build a theory of distribution on the postulates about the nature of man and society set forth in the last chapter, one soon discovers that these lead to a curious, but important, *dualism.* If those postulates are sound, one would predict that almost all the products of men's labors will be distributed on the basis of two seemingly contradictory principles, *need* and *power.*

In our discussion of the nature of man, it was postulated that where important decisions are involved, most human action is motivated either by self-interest or by partisan group interests. This suggests that power alone governs the distribution of rewards. This cannot be the case, however, since we also postulated that most of these essentially selfish interests can be satisfied only by the establishment of cooperative relations with others. Cooperation is absolutely essential both for survival and for the efficient attainment of most other goals. In other words, men's selfish interests compel them to remain members of society and to share in the division of labor.

If these two postulates are correct, then it follows that *men will share the product of their labors to the extent required to insure the survival and continued productivity of those others whose actions are necessary or beneficial to themselves.* This might well be called the first law of distribution, since the survival of mankind as a species depends on compliance with it.

This first law, however, does not cover the entire problem. It says nothing about how any *surplus,* that is, goods and services over and above the minimum required to keep producers alive and productive, which men may be able to produce will be distributed. This leads to what may be called the second law of distribution. If we assume that in important decisions human action is motivated almost entirely by self-interest or partisan group interests, and if we assume that many of the things men most desire are in short supply, then, as noted before, this surplus will inevitably give rise to conflicts and struggles aimed at its control. If, following Weber, we define power as the probability of persons or groups carrying out their will even when opposed by others, then it follows that *power will determine the distribution of nearly all of the surplus possessed by a society.* The qualification "nearly all" takes account of the very limited influence of altruistic action which our earlier analysis of the nature of man leads us to expect.

This second law points the way to another very important relationship, that between our two chief variables, power and privilege. If privilege is defined as possession or control of a portion of the surplus produced by a society, then it follows that *privilege is largely a function of power, and to a very limited degree, a function of altruism.* This means that to explain most of the distribution of privilege in a society, we have but to determine the distribution of power.

To state the matter this way suggests that the task of explaining the distribution of privilege is simple. Unfortunately, this is not the case since there are many forms of power and they spring from many sources. Nevertheless, the establishment of this key relationship reduces the problem to more manageable proportions, since it concentrates attention on one key variable, power. Thus if we can establish the pattern of its distribution in a given society, we have largely established the pattern for the distribution of privilege, and if we can discover the causes of a given distribution of power we have also discovered the causes of the distribution of privilege linked with it.

To put the matter this way is to invite the question of how the third basic element in every distributive system, *prestige*, is related to power and privilege. It would be nice if one could say that prestige is a simple function of privilege, but unfortunately this does not seem to be the case. Without going into a complex analysis of the matter at this point, the best that can be said is that empirical evidence strongly suggests that *prestige is largely, though not solely, a function of power and privilege, at least in those societies where there is a substantial surplus.* If this is true, it follows that even though the subject of prestige is not often mentioned in this volume, its pattern of distribution and its causes can largely be deduced from discussion of the distribution of power and privilege and their causes in those societies where there is an appreciable surplus.

Graphically, the relationship between these three variables, as set forth in the propositions above, can be depicted in this way:

The solid lines indicate major sources of influence, the dashed lines secondary sources.

To make this diagram complete, one other dashed line should probably be added, indicating some feedback from prestige to power. Thus a more accurate representation of the relationships would look like this:

Power is the key variable in the triad from the causal and explanatory standpoint. Hence, it is with this variable that we shall be primarily concerned in the analysis which follows.

THE VARIABLE ASPECTS OF DISTRIBUTIVE SYSTEMS

As the statement of the two laws indicates, the second law does not have any effect on the distributive process until the conditions specified in the first have been satisfied. Until the necessities of life have been made available to enough productive, mutually interdependent members of the group, there is no surplus to be fought over and distributed on the basis of power. Thus, as a first hypothesis we would be led to predict that *in the simplest societies, or those which are technologically most primitive, the goods and services available will be distributed wholly, or largely, on the basis of need.*

As the productivity of societies increases, the possibility of producing a surplus steadily increases, though it should be noted that the existence of a surplus is not a function of technological advance alone. Even though we cannot say that the surplus available to a society increases proportionately with advances in the level of technology, such advances increase the probability that there will be a surplus and also that there will be a sizable surplus. Hence, as a second hypothesis we are led to predict that *with technological advance, an increasing proportion of the goods and services available to a society will be distributed on the basis of power.*

It should also be noted that classifying societies on the basis of the nature of their technology does not imply that all those in a single category have *identi-*

cal distributive systems any more than that all oligopolistic markets function the same way. Obviously there are variations within each societal type just as within each type of market, and an effort will be made to identify and account for the more important of them. However, these may be thought of as *second-order variations*, which are best dealt with after the first-order variations have been established and the internal uniformities associated with them clearly delineated.

In dealing with these second-order variations we shall sometimes have to rely on inductive logic to establish both causal and descriptive generalizations. However, this will not always be the case. Sometimes deductive logic can be employed. For example, if the size of a society's surplus affects the nature of its distributive system, and if the size of the surplus depends to some degree on the nature of the physical environment, then we should predict that *differences in the physical environment will lead to secondary differences in distributive systems*. More specifically, the richer the environment, the larger the surplus and the greater the importance of power in the distributive process.

There are also reasons for predicting that the influence of environmental differences will be greater in primitive societies than in those which are technologically more advanced. To begin with, technological advance makes possible the geographical expansion of societies, and the larger the territory occupied by a society, the less the probability that the total environment will be extremely favorable or unfavorable and the greater the probability that it will include a mixture of favorable and unfavorable land. Hence, environmental variation should be less among the larger, technologically advanced societies than among the smaller, more primitive. In addition, technological advance frequently means the development of alternative solutions to the various problems of production. Technologically advanced societies, therefore, should be less hampered by environmental limitations than primitive societies are, and thus *environmental variation should have less effect on the level of productivity in advanced societies than in primitive*.

Another important source of secondary variation has been identified by Stanislaw Andrzejewski in his important but neglected book, *Military Organization and Society*. As he has shown, both deductive logic and empirical data indicate that *the degree of inequality in societies of a given level of technological development tends to vary inversely with what he calls "the military participation ratio,"* that is *the proportion of the adult male population utilized in military operations*. Where most adult males are utilized for such purposes, the degree of inequality tends to be less than in those in which military needs are supplied by a small force of military specialists. Thus, this factor can also be used to explain some of the secondary variations which are found among societies of the same technological type.

FORCE AND ITS TRANSFORMATION

As a starting point, it may be well to return briefly to one of the postulates introduced in the last chapter. There it was assumed that survival is the chief goal of the great majority of men. If this is so, then it follows that *the ability to take life is the most effective form of power*. In other words, more men will respond more readily to the threat of the use of *force* than to any other. In effect, it constitutes the final court of appeals in human affairs; there is no appeal from force in a given situation except the exercise of superior force. Hence force stands in the same relationship to other forms of power as trumps to the other suits in the game of bridge, and those who can exercise the greatest force are like those who control trumps.

This fact has been recognized by countless observers of the human scene in every age. As Pascal put it, "Not being able to make that which is just strong, man has made that which is strong just." Cicero made the same point when he said, "Laws are dumb in the midst of arms," and Hobbes asserted that "Covenants without the sword are but words, and of no strength to secure a man at all."

This principle is also recognized by the leaders of nations, the practical men of affairs. Every sovereign state restricts, and where possible prohibits, the independent exercise of force by its subjects. States may be tolerant of many things, but never of the growth of independent military organizations within their territories. The reason is obvious: any government which cannot suppress each and every forceful challenge to its authority is overthrown. Force is the foundation of sovereignty.

If force is the foundation of political sovereignty, it is also the foundation of the distributive system in every society where there is a surplus to be divided. Where coercive power is weak, challenges inevitably occur, and the system is eventually destroyed and replaced by another based more firmly on force. Men struggling over control of the surplus of a society will not accept defeat so long as there is a higher court of appeals to which they may take their case with some likelihood of success and profit to themselves.

The principle involved here is essentially the same as the principle of escalation with which modern military men are so concerned. Small wars based on small weapons inevitably grow into more deadly wars utilizing more deadly weapons if, by advancing the level of conflict, one of the parties anticipates turning defeat into victory. Similarly, in the case of conflicts within societies, the parties involved are always motivated to take the issue to the final court of appeals so long as there is the likelihood of benefiting by it. While men will not resort to armed revolution for trivial gains, when control over the entire surplus of a society is involved, the prospect is more enticing. The attractiveness varies directly with the weakness of the current regime.

Nevertheless, as Edmund Burke, the famed English conservative, recognized, "The use of force alone is but temporary. It may subdue for a moment; but it does not remove the necessity of subduing again: and a nation is not governed, which is perpetually to be conquered." Though force is the most effective instrument for seizing power in a society, and though it always remains the foundation of any system of inequality, it is not the most effective instrument for retaining and exploiting a position of power and deriving the maximum benefits from it. Therefore, regardless of the objectives of a new regime, once organized opposition has been destroyed it is to its advantage to make increasing use of other techniques and instruments of control, and to allow force to recede into the background to be used only when other techniques fail.

If the new elite has materialistic goals and is concerned solely with self-aggrandizement, it soon discovers that the rule of might is both inefficient and costly. So long as it relies on force, much of the profit is consumed by the costs of coercion. If the population obeys only out of fear of physical violence, a large portion of the time, energy, and wealth of the elite are invariably consumed in the effort to keep it under control and separate the producers from the product of their labors. Even worse, honor, which normally ranks high in the scale of human values, is denied to those who rule by force alone.

If materialistic elites have strong motives for shifting from the rule of might to the rule of right, ideologically motivated elites have even stronger. If the visions and ideals which led them to undertake the terrible risks and hardships of revolution are ever to be fulfilled, the voluntary cooperation of the population is essential, and this cannot be obtained by force. Force is, at best, the means to an end. That end, the establishment of a new social order, can never be fully attained until most members of society freely accept it as their own. The purpose of the revolution is to destroy the old elite and their institutions, which prevent the fulfillment of this dream. Once they are destroyed, an ideological elite strives to rule by persuasion. Thus *those who seize power by force find it advantageous to legitimize their rule once effective organized opposition is eliminated.* Force can no longer continue to play the role it did. It can no longer function as the private resource of a special segment of the population. Rather it must be transformed into a public resource used in the defense of law and order.

This may seem to be the equivalent of saying that those who have at great risk to themselves displaced the old elite must now give up all they have won. Actually, however, this is not at all necessary since, with a limited exercise of intelligence, force can be transformed into authority, and might into right.

There are various means by which this transformation can be effected. To begin with, by virtue of its coercive power, a new elite is in a good position to rewrite the law of the land as it sees fit. This affords them a unique opportunity, since by its very nature law is identified with justice and the rule of right. Since legal statutes are stated in general and impersonal terms, they appear to support abstract principles of justice rather than the special interests of particular men or classes of men. The fact that laws exist prior to the events to which they are applied suggests an objective impartiality which also contributes to their acceptance. Yet laws can always be written in such a way that they favor some particular segment of society. Anatole France saw this clearly when he wrote, "The law in its majestic equality forbids the rich as well as the poor to sleep under bridges, to beg in the street, and to steal bread."

As should be evident, those in the employ of the elite are rewarded in proportion to the value of their services to the elite, and the scarcity of the supply of replacements. Contrary to such functionalist theorists as Kingsley Davis and Wilbert Moore, these roles are not rewarded in proportion to their contribution to the common good. It is the needs of the elite, not the needs of the total society, which determine the demand curve for such services. *The distribution of rewards in a society is a function of the distribution of power, not of system needs.* This is inevitable in such imperfect systems as human societies.

Every system of power and privilege also sets in motion a deadly *struggle for survival among the offspring of the common people*, except in those societies which are able to control reproduction or in which there is a temporary shortage of population such as may be created by major plagues, famines, or other disasters. Unhappily, mankind has always been able to produce more offspring than society can maintain, especially when the economic surplus is skimmed off by a privileged elite. Usually there has not been land enough for every farmer's son to farm, nor farmers enough for every farmer's daughter to marry. Hence some of the common people of almost every generation have been reduced to the status of beggars, criminals, and prostitutes. Such persons have usually had short lives, since at this level the competition for survival is intense. From the standpoint of the elite, the struggles which developed among the common people have been a matter of little concern, since human fecundity always insured an ample supply of qualified producers. In fact, these struggles probably served the interests of the elite by diverting attention from their own exploitative role, thus affording them a considerable measure of security against popular protest and revolution.

CLASSES

[P]ower takes many forms and these cannot always be reduced to a meaningful common denominator. An individual may have large property holdings without occupying a correspondingly important and powerful office and vice versa. Similarly, an individual may occupy an important and powerful role in one institutional system but not in others.

In view of this, it is clear that the term "class" should not be defined too narrowly. More can be gained by defining the term broadly and then distinguishing carefully between different kinds of classes. Therefore, we might best define a class as *an aggregation of persons in a society who stand in a similar position with respect to some form of power, privilege, or prestige.*

This is *not* to say that all types of classes are equally important for theoretical and analytical purposes. On the contrary, if our goal is to answer the question of "who gets what and why?" and if our analysis of the last two chapters has any validity at all, *power* classes must be our chief concern. The distribution of privilege and prestige seem largely determined by the distribution of power, at least in those societies in which a significant surplus is produced.

In the last chapter we also saw that power manifests itself in two basic forms, force and institutionalized power. The latter, in turn, can be subdivided into the power of position and the power of property. Building on this, a power class may be defined as *an aggregation of persons in a society who stand in a similar position with respect to force or some specific form of institutionalized power. . . .* Though the definition does not say so explicitly, *the members of every power class share certain common interests with one another, and these shared interests constitute a potential basis for hostility toward other classes.* This follows as a logical corollary of the fact that what unites the members of a class is their common possession, control, or utilization of something which affects their chances of fulfilling their wishes and desires. Given our earlier assumptions about the nature of man, it follows that all members of a given class have a vested interest in protecting or increasing the value of their common resource and in reducing the value of competitive resources which constitute the bases of other classes.

This is not to say that the members of a class always have a conscious awareness of their common interest, much less that they act collectively on the basis of it. Nor are they always consciously or overtly hostile to members of other classes. These are possibilities which may be realized, but there is nothing inevitable about them.

CITIZENSHIP: A POTENTIALLY UNIQUE RESOURCE

In an earlier period the rights of citizenship were reserved for the few and citizenship, like other resources, did divide men into classes. Sometimes citizenship divided the members of societies into citizens and noncitizens, other times into first- and second-class citizens. This traditional pattern can be seen in the early history of this country, when the population was divided into enfranchised citizens, unenfranchised freemen, and slaves. Each stood in a different relation to the state, with enfranchised citizens in the most favored position and slaves in the least.

Today slavery has disappeared in advanced industrial societies and the right of franchise has been extended to include nearly all adults. As a result, citizenship tends to be a resource which all share alike.

Since citizenship is shared by all, one might suppose that it no longer has any special relevance for the student of stratification. This is not the case, however. Citizenship continues to figure prominently in the distributive process. Those who lack other kinds of resources, together with those who, for ideological reasons, believe in social equality, have combined to fight for the enhancement of the value of citizenship at the expense of those resources which generate inequality. This struggle is evident in recent controversies involving the issue of property rights versus human rights. Those who advocate the primacy of human rights over property rights typically advocate the enlargement of the rights of citizenship at the expense of the traditional rights of property. Their opponents take the opposite position. Thus the struggle becomes not merely a struggle between classes, but also a struggle between class systems and thus between differing principles of stratification.

Historically oriented students of stratification will recognize that the modern era is not completely unique in this, since in preindustrial societies the less powerful classes often fought the more powerful classes in the same way, and not without some success. At the very least, they often succeeded in establishing certain uniform legal rights, including the right to a public trial based on an established body of law. Sometimes they were even able to establish the right of all men to protection from extortionary and irregular taxation and other abuses. To be sure, men of property and position usually fought to prevent such rights from being established and to undermine them if they were. Usually they were successful in these efforts. Only in the more advanced industrial societies of the modern era, however, is citizenship simultaneously a resource of *major* importance and one shared by all.

In many ways this centuries-old effort to enhance the value of common citizenship can be viewed as an attempt to reestablish the ascendancy of *need* over *power* as the dominant principle of distribution. As noted in the last chapter, in those societies which are technologically most primitive, need, rather than power, is the chief determinant of "who gets what." With technological advance and the growing capacity to produce a surplus, power became the chief determinant. Today, an organized effort is being made to restore the importance of need. Ironically, however, it appears that this reversal can occur only if the advocates of need can mobilize more power than the advocates of power. This is because advanced industrial societies, unlike primitive hunting and gathering societies, have a surplus and thus their distributive pattern is not dictated by economic necessity. Thus one is led to the conclusion that if need should ever be restored to the position of dominance, it would not rest on the same foundation as that on which it rested in technologically primitive societies.

The Dynamics of Distributive Systems

On the basis of the postulates set forth . . .one would predict that *the degree of inequality in distributive systems will vary directly with the size of a society's surplus*. Some modification of this general pattern could develop, however, when conditions permit persons who individually lack power to combine and organize, and thus to develop a collective counterbalance to those with greater individual power. Such developments seem most probable in democratic nations with an egalitarian or socialist ideology.

EQUALITY IN SOCIETIES WITH NO SURPLUS

Of all the various characteristics shared by hunting and gathering societies, the one of key importance for students of stratification is the absence of any appreciable economic surplus. According to the first and second laws of distribution . . .men are free to monopolize or expropriate only that portion of the product of the group which is not required to sustain the producers. If this is true, and if hunting and gathering societies are incapable of producing any appreciable economic surplus, then our theory leads us to predict that there will be relative equality in these societies, at least with respect to the distribution of goods and services.

The facts support this prediction. If any single feature of the life of hunting and gathering societies has impressed itself upon observers, it is the relative equality of the members. In fact, many untrained observers have reported perfect equality in certain of these societies. While the more careful observations of trained observers force us to reject these extreme claims, the fact remains that the distributive process in hunting and gathering societies is radically different from that in industrial societies such as our own, or the agrarian societies from which industrial societies have so recently emerged.

The Andaman Islanders provide a good illustration of a relatively pure and uncontaminated hunting and gathering society, and one which has not developed even the more rudimentary forms of horticulture. In writing of their economic life, Radcliffe-Brown reports that "it approaches to a sort of communism." Land, the basic resource of the group, is communally owned, thus insuring equal access to the necessities of life. While the produce of the land and all portable property are privately owned, the Andamanese have customs which offset the usual effects of private ownership. For example, though all food is private property, "everyone who has food is expected . . . to give to those who have none." The result is that "practically all of the food obtained is evenly distributed through the whole camp, the only inequality being that the younger men do not fare so well as their elders." In the case of other forms of privately owned property, an egalitarian distribution is assured by the Andamanese custom of exchanging presents. This practice, when combined with the tradition of according honor to persons who are generous with their possessions, insures near equality in the distribution of goods. In such a society a man stands to gain more by sharing than by hoarding.

While no one hunting and gathering society is completely representative of all, a person familiar with the distribution of goods in Andamanese society is not likely to be greatly surprised by what he finds in most of the others. In those societies, too, one finds a close approximation to equality in the distribution of goods. This is usually achieved, as among the Andamenese, by the communal ownership of land and by some type of institutionalized redistributive process. Often there is some limited inequality, with certain segments of the population faring a bit better than others. In the case of the Andamanese the old men enjoy some advantage over the younger. Among the Siriono, the senior wife in a polygynous family and her children are reported to fare somewhat better than the junior wife and hers. In some societies men fare better than women. These differences, however, represent little more than secondary variations on the basic theme of substantial equality.

The distribution of prestige is a very different matter from the distribution of goods. Here there is no problem of short supply, and inequality does not threaten the group's chances of survival. As a consequence, the unequal distribution of honor tends to be the rule rather than the exception in hunting and gathering societies, just as our theory would lead us to expect. However, for reasons which will become evident shortly, the degree of prestige inequality falls far short of that with which members of more advanced societies are familiar.

Once again we may turn to Andamanese society as one which is reasonably typical, at least in the more basic aspects of the matter. Radcliffe-Brown, the leading authority on these people, reports that honor and respect are accorded to three kinds of people: (1) older people, (2) people endowed with supernatural powers, and (3) people with certain valued personal qualities, notably, "skill in hunting and warfare, generosity and kindness, and freedom fiom bad temper." Though it is not completely clear from Radcliffe-Brown's account, there is some indication that men are more likely than women to be highly honored.

Such inequality might properly be called "functional inequality." In other words, the benefits and honors enjoyed by the few represent *a return for services rendered to the many under conditions free from any form of social coercion or man-made shortage*. This can be seen most clearly in the case of an individual who is honored for his skill in hunting and for his generosity. The less able members of the group reward such a person with prestige and influence in exchange for a share in the game he kills. By this spontaneous and uncoerced exchange, those who are generously endowed by nature with talent and energy are stimulated to produce more, and those who are not have greater assurance of obtaining the necessities of life. The alternative would be deprivation, suffering, and possible death for the less able, and, for the more able, surfeit of food and loss of prestige and the respect of others. Thus, *potentially disastrous inequalities in subsistence are transformed into inequalities in prestige and influence, a much safer and more satisfying arrangement*.

One may question whether *all* the inequality in honor and influence in Andamanese and similar societies results in genuine gains for the less favored. For example, are the services of most primitive medicine men of real value to others? This leads into an area of possible disagreement. One observer may feel that the peace of mind a skillful shaman creates for his patients justifies the prestige he receives, while another may not. In this situation it may be wiser to rely on the natives' judgment of the matter and differentiate between functional and nonfunctional inequality on the basis of the relative freedom of the individuals involved. If the exchange is free of man-made coercive elements, then it is reasonable to view such inequality as is generated as functional. If one takes this approach, it is clear that most of the inequality evident in primitive hunting and gathering groups is of just this type.

In hunting and gathering societies, prestige usually goes hand in hand with political influence. The reasons for this are not hard to find. Government by coercion is an impossibility in these societies. The leader of the group is not supported by a force of specialists in violence who are dependent on his favor and therefore motivated to follow his orders. All men are trained and equipped for fighting and the same weapons and training are available to all. The only differences among them are those inherent in the physical constitutions and personalities of the individuals and, while a single man who is unusually well endowed by nature may be the equal, or even the master, of two less favorably endowed men, he is not likely to be able to coerce or defend himself against three who join forces against him. Furthermore, dissatisfied followers may always desert their leader and attach themselves to another band. It follows, therefore, that government must be by persuasion. This means that in any situation in which there is no one obviously correct course of action, effective leadership is possible only if a majority of the population is predisposed to follow the direction of certain individuals and to reject that of others. In short, the limited political development of these societies creates a situation in which honor and respect are necessary prerequisites to political influence.

The same conditions which make honor and respect necessary qualifications for political influence also serve to limit the extent of political inequality possible. The extremes of political domination and subordination are impossible in a society where men must govern by persuasion.

REVERSAL OF A BASIC TREND

[T]he appearance of mature industrial societies marks the first significant reversal in the age-old evolutionary trend toward ever increasing inequality.

The evidence supporting these assertions takes several basic forms. To begin with, a comparison of the political systems of agrarian and industrial societies makes it clear that political power is much more concentrated in the former. In agrarian societies, the powers of government were nearly always vested in the hands of the few; the great majority were wholly excluded from the political process. In industrial societies this is a minority pattern, limited only to those societies in the earlier stages of industrialization and to those ruled by totalitarian parties. In the majority of industrial societies, all adult citizens not only enjoy voting privileges but, far more important, the right to organize politically to promote their own special interests or beliefs, even when these are in opposition to the interests or beliefs of those in power. While this does not mean that all inequalities in political power are eliminated or the democratic millennium ushered in, it does mean a significant reduction in political inequality and a substantial diffusion of political power, both of which are readily evident when these societies are compared with agrarian. This can be seen most clearly in the case of the Scandinavian democracies, where Socialist Parties have been the dominant political force in recent decades, but the pattern is also evident in countries such as the United States and France, where the political influence of the lower classes has not been nearly so great. It should also be noted that even in some of those industrial societies where democracy was not permitted, as in post-Stalinist Russia or Peron's Argentina, the political elite used much of its power to promote programs designed to benefit the lower classes, a practice virtually unknown in agrarian societies.

A second indication of declining inequalities can be found in data on the distribution of income. Earlier we saw evidence which indicated that in agrarian societies the top 1 or 2 per cent of the population, usually received *not less than half* of the total income of the nation. In the case of industrial societies the comparable figure is substantially less. According to official governmental reports, the top 2 per cent of the population of democratic nations receives about 10 per cent of the total personal cash income after taxes. For example, British figures for 1954 indicate that the top 2 per cent received 8.5 per cent of the total income after taxes; Swedish figures for 1950 show the top 1.8 per cent received 9.9 per cent before taxes; Danish figures for 1949 show the top 1.1 per cent received 10.3 per cent *before taxes*; United States figures for 1958 show the top 1.3 per cent received 8.1 per cent, and the top 2.3 per cent received 11.6 per cent, *before taxes*.

These figures cannot, of course, be taken at face value. As a number of recent writers have pointed out, they do not include many billions of dollars of income, sometimes because of fraud and evasion by taxpayers, but more often because the tax statutes do not define certain forms of income as income. . . . Taking the higher estimate for underreporting by the upper-income group, that is, $15 billion, we arrive at the conclusion that, before taxes, 15.5 per cent of the personal income of the American people went to the top 2.3 per cent.

Even this figure, however, is far short of the 50 per cent estimated to be the elite's share of the gross national product in agrarian societies. This difference arises, in part, because the revenues of government are included in agrarian societies but not in industrial. On first inspection this may seem both arbitrary and unjust. Actually it is neither. In agrarian societies government functions almost entirely, as we have seen, as an instrument of, by, and for the few. In modern industrial societies, this is no longer the case. While it is true that the upper classes still benefit disproportionately from the actions of government in every industrial society, it is also true that the masses of ordinary citizens benefit to an extent undreamed of in the agrarian societies of the past, or even in those which still survive.

It is impossible to determine with any precision what percentage of the benefits of government go to the top 2 per cent of the population and what percentage to the remainder in industrial societies. However, even if one were to assume that they went *entirely* to the elite, the total would still fall short of the agrarian figure of 50 per cent. . . . [W]hile it may not be possible to determine precisely what percentage of the gross national product is enjoyed by the top 2 per cent in mature industrial societies, it is safe to conclude that the percentage is considerably less than in agrarian. In fact, it is probably no more than half so large, and quite possibly less than that.

Since the foregoing estimates are all based on data from democratic nations, one may properly ask whether the situation in totalitarian states is not different. This question is not easily answered owing to the paucity of trustworthy quantitative data. However, such as we have indicates that in the Soviet Union, at least, income inequality is substantially less than in the United States. . . . Thus, it appears that the Soviet Union provides no exception to the conclusion about the historic decline in income inequality formulated on the basis of data from democratic nations.

CAUSES OF THE REVERSAL

From the theoretical standpoint, the decline in political and economic inequality associated with the emergence of industrial societies is extremely important. This constitutes a reversal in a major historical trend, and the reasons for this reversal are by no means obvious. On the contrary, given the increased productivity of industrial societies and the growth in the powers of the state, one would normally predict even greater inequality than in agrarian societies. The fact that the opposite occurred indicates either that one or more of the basic postulates with which we began is in error, or that other factors are at work which were not taken into account (or, at least, not sufficiently) in our original, highly general formulation. The evidence, as I shall show, favors the latter interpretation, indicating again the serious difficulties which attend any effort to develop a general theory by purely deductive means.

Among the factors not considered in our earlier assumptions about the nature of man and society, was the relationship between technological and cultural complexity on the one hand, and administrative efficiency on the other. In modern industrial societies, technology in particular, and culture in general, are far more complex than in even the most advanced agrarian societies. In fact, they are so complex that it is no longer possible for those in positions of high command to begin to understand the work of all those beneath them. In effect, there is a growing "ignorance" on the part of those in positions of command. This is not to say that those in authority in industrial societies are less intelligent or knowledgeable than their counterparts in agrarian societies, but rather that they are masters of *a smaller proportion* of what they need to know to maintain effective control over those beneath them. Thus, because of the many gaps in their knowledge, they are often compelled either to issue commands based on insufficient information, or to leave matters to the discretion of their subordinates, thus opening the door to encroachments on their prerogatives. In the former case, authority is preserved, but at the expense of efficiency and productivity, while in the latter case a measure of authority is sacrificed to increase efficiency and productivity. In short, *the relationship between productivity and authority appears to be curvilinear in industrial societies, at least up to the present time*. Thus, unless political authorities are willing and able to sacrifice productivity, it is unlikely that they will be able to rely on the technique of command to the extent their agrarian counterparts did. However, - to the degree that they delegate authority or rely on market mechanisms, they facilitate the diffusion of power and privilege.

A second factor which seems to have contributed to the reversal in the historic trend toward greater inequality is *the rapidity and magnitude of the increases in productivity*. In societies in which the gross national product and per capita income are rapidly rising, and promise to continue rising, elites find themselves in the paradoxical situation in which they can maximize their *net* input of rewards by responding to pressures from below and making certain concessions. By granting the lower classes some share in the economic surplus, they can reduce worker hostility and the accompanying losses from strikes, slowdowns, and industrial sabotage. In an expanding economy, an elite can make economic concessions in *relative* terms without necessarily suffering any loss in *absolute* terms. In fact, if the concessions are not too large, and the rate of the economy's growth is great enough, relative losses can even be accompanied by *substantial* absolute gains. For example, an elite would enjoy a substantially greater income if it took 40 per cent of the gross national product in a $100 billion economy, than if it stubbornly fought to maintain a 50 per cent share and thereby held the economy at the $50 billion level. *If we assume that the majority of men would willingly make modest relative concessions for the sake of substantial absolute gains, and if we also assume that leading members of the elites in industrial societies have an awareness of the benefits they can obtain from concessions, then we can only predict they will make them.*

A willingness to make concessions may also be encouraged by the principle of marginal utility. This principle serves as a reminder that the first million dollars normally has greater value to a man than any subsequent million he may acquire. In societies with very productive economies, many members of the elite may be prepared to make some *economic* concessions in order to maximize other kinds of rewards, such as safety, respect, and leisure. In other words, after a certain level of wealth has been attained, elites may prefer to sacrifice a portion of the economic surplus in order to reduce hostility and the dangers of revolution, and to win for themselves a greater measure of respect and affection. Or, they may find it impossible to maintain tight control over political and economic organizations and at the same time enjoy the benefits of leisure, and so permit a portion of the economic surplus to pass into other hands. In short, *because elites have multiple goals, and are not concerned with maximizing material rewards alone, they may be willing to make certain economic concessions in a highly productive and expanding economy.*

Yet another factor which has played a role in reducing inequality is the development of new and highly effective methods of birth control. In the past, the natural tendency of the human race to multiply usually had the effect of offsetting whatever economic gains might otherwise have resulted from technological advance. Numbers tended to increase up to the carrying power of the economy *except as limited by the development of tyrannical political systems which diverted the "economic surplus" to the elite at the expense of further population increase.* One consequence, of course, was the large and wretched class of expendables, whose very presence served to prevent any substantial long-run improvement in the lot of the peasants and artisans with whom they constantly competed for employment.

Today the situation is rapidly changing, and promises to change even more in the future. For the first time in history, mankind has found safe, simple, and effective means of controlling population growth. In societies where these have been most widely used, the rate of population growth has been slowed to the point where real and substantial gains in per capita income have been achieved in a fairly short time, thus reducing the intensity of the competitive pressures. Now, for almost the first time in centuries, the lower classes are able to bargain for wages in markets no longer perennially glutted with labor. This development has almost certainly contributed to the decline in inequality.

Another factor that has probably contributed to the decline in inequality is the great expansion in human knowledge. In the past, the dominant class chiefly needed unskilled labor, and thanks to human fecundity, this was always plentiful. This put the vast majority of men in a poor bargaining position, and hence the price of labor was minimal. Today, in the more advanced industrial societies, the situation is radically changed. Because of the great functional utility of so much of the new knowledge, a host of occupational specialists have appeared who are not interchangeable to any great degree. This introduces into the labor market certain rigidities which favor the sellers of labor, especially in an era in which the demand for technical skills is rapidly rising. Furthermore, even if the dominant classes could obtain the necessary labor for a subsistence wage, it is doubtful that this would prove expedient. The efficiency of work requiring mental effort or alertness can be seriously reduced when those performing it are not physically fit. Two men working at 50 per cent efficiency in this situation are not the equal of one man working at top efficiency, as in work requiring brute strength alone. Moreover expensive machines and tight production schedules are vulnerable to the mistakes of inattentive workers to a degree that is not characteristic of agrarian societies. These factors all prevent the dominant classes from driving the wages of this increasingly numerous segment of the population down to the subsistence level, and prevent the system from reaching the level of economic inequality that is found in agrarian societies, both past and present.

The egalitarian trend in modern industrial societies is evident in the *political* area no less than in the economic. In many respects the trend toward greater political equality is more surprising than the corresponding economic trend, because the struggle for political power is essentially a zero-sum "game," i.e., gains by one party necessarily entail corresponding losses by opponents. The struggle for privilege, on the other hand, is a positive-sum "game," thanks to the constantly rising level of productivity. Thus in the political realm the privileged classes cannot accept losses in relative terms and still realize absolute gains.

All the reasons for the spread of democratic government are still not completely understood. Obviously, it has not been dictated by economic necessity, as shown by the vigor of a number of nondemocratic, totalitarian nations. On the other hand, the relative frequency of democratic government in industrial states and its virtual absence in agrarian, strongly indicate some connection. Specifically, this suggests that industrialization creates conditions favorable to the growth of democracy, but does not make it inevitable.

One favorable condition is the spread of literacy and the extension of education. An illiterate peasantry lacking access to mass media of information is in a poor position to participate in the political process; a literate middle and working class with many media of information available is much more favorably situated. Advances in the level of living have a similar effect. Peasants and artisans living at, or near, the subsistence level cannot afford the luxury of sustained political activity; workers in an industrial society have more leisure, energy, and money to devote to this. Still another factor favoring the growth of democracy is the modern pattern of warfare which involves the entire population to an extent unknown in agrarian societies. As many observers have noted, the traditional distinction between the military and civilian segments of the population has been almost obliterated, and military men have come to regard urban centers of production as prime military targets. If Andrzejewski and other writers are correct, this trend should have an egalitarian influence, since inequality tends to be most pronounced where military activities are limited to the few.

More important than any of these, however, has been the rise and spread of *the new democratic ideology* which asserts that the state belongs to the people. This ideology is not simply a reflection of changing economic conditions, though, as we have seen, it has been affected by them. Rather, the historical record indicates it had its origin in religious and philosophical developments of the seventeenth century and spread rather widely in the eighteenth century in countries which were still thoroughly agrarian in character, for example, the United States and France. In fact, there appears to be as much justification for the thesis that this new ideology contributed to the emergence of industrial societies as for the converse.

In any case, this new ideology became an important force in the political life of industrial societies. It captured the imagination of all kinds of men, even some of the political elite, thus making the traditional monopoly of political power increasingly untenable. As the democratic ideology spread, those who governed had to make substantial concessions in order to avoid massive challenges to their power—challenges which would have been costly to resist, and might even have led to their overthrow. The idea that the state should be the servant of all the people continues to be a major force in the modern era, mobilizing the egoistic impulses of the disadvantaged classes in an idealistic cause, thereby uniting morality and egoism in a manner reminiscent of their union under the banner of "the divine right of kings," but with the opposite effect.

Wherever democratic theory has become institutionalized, a dramatic new possibility has arisen: *now the many can combine against the few, and even though individually the many are weaker, in combination they may be as strong or stronger.* With this development, the door is opened to a host of revolutionary developments in the distributive realm.

THE GENERAL THEORY REEXAMINED

In the light of the evidence presented . . .one can give an essentially affirmative answer to the basic question of the validity of the general theory presented in the introductory chapters. The most basic characteristics of distributive systems do appear to be shaped by the interaction of those *constant elements* in the human situation which we identified earlier and the *variable element of technology*. As hypothesized, the influence of these factors appears to be mediated by a series of social organizational factors whose variation is greatly influenced by prior variations in technology. It was this systematic covariation, of course, which made possible the development of the societal typology, which proved so valuable.

The high degree of support for the theory was not completely unexpected because of the manner in which the theory was constructed. Despite some appearances to the contrary, the theory presented in the early chapters was not a simple exercise in deductive logic. Rather, it represented the end product of an already extensive process of both induction and deduction. In a sense, the theory was designed to fit the facts, or at least those facts with which I was familiar when I began writing this volume. However, the theory with which I began writing was not the same that I had taught ten years previously. On the contrary, over the course of that decade I constantly shifted and modified my theoretical position to try to get a better fit between theory and data. In the process I found myself shifting from what was basically a functionalist position to what I have called a synthetic or synthesizing position. In other words, I found an increasing need to incorporate hypotheses and postulates which had little or no part in the functionalist tradition, yet without wholly abandoning the latter.

In the light of the evidence set forth . . . it appears that the general theory corresponds reasonably well with the evidence, but the correspondence is not perfect and certain modifications and changes are necessary. To begin with, our survey of advanced horticultural and agrarian societies indicates that the relationship between technology and political organization is not so simple as anticipated. In these societies one finds significant variations in level of political development associated with apparently limited variations in technology. This suggests that we must think of the level of technological advance either as a *necessary*, but not *sufficient*, cause of political advance, or as the generator of a "threshold effect," whereby a limited advance in technology causes (or makes possible) a major advance in political organization. Perhaps both apply. In any case, it is clear that at certain levels of technological development, a considerable degree of variation in political development becomes possible.

This has significant consequences for the distributive process because the level of political development is clearly a major determinant of the character of distributive systems.

A second modification which is indicated is a distinction at the analytical level between the concepts "technology" and "economy." In retrospect, it appears that these two terms were often used interchangeably in the preceding chapters. In the majority of instances this caused no great difficulty because differences in economy, i.e., the economic organization of a society, usually parallel differences in technology, that is, the cultural means by which a society relates to its environment. Thus, a hunting and gathering technology is accompanied by a hunting and gathering economy. Difficulties arise, however, in the case of societal types standing on comparable levels of technological development, as in the case of agrarian and maritime societies. Here, the same elements of technology appear to be available to both, but certain elements are emphasized in one and neglected in the other. The reasons for this reflect, in part at least, the influence of environmental factors, though other factors are probably also at work. Economic variations which occur independently of technological variations appear to have effects on distributive systems comparable to those produced by political variations. Hence, we might more accurately portray the links in the causal chain as follows:[1]

In addition, of course, there are elements of feedback operating, which further complicates relations.

In addition to demonstrating the importance of technology and social organization in the shaping of distributive systems, our findings also demonstrate the influence of other factors. . . . Two of these stand out because of their widespread importance: (1) *variations in ideology*, and (2) *variations in the personal attributes of political leaders*.

Ideology seems to have its greatest impact in the more advanced societies. Ideological variations of great magnitude and importance for distributive systems presuppose the existence of specialists in ideology, supported by appropriate religious and political institutions. These developments seem to have their

[1] The symbols X, Y, and Z are included as a reminder that our theory assumes that other factors exercise an influence at each point in the causal chain.

beginnings in advanced horticultural societies, while coming to full flower
only in industrial societies.

The importance of ideology was seen most clearly in the somewhat unexpected halting, and possible reversal, of the trend toward increasing social
inequality, so pronounced in the evolution from hunting and gathering to
agrarian societies. . . . [I]t was predicted that the degree of inequality in distributive systems would vary directly with the size of a society's surplus. This
was qualified in tentative fashion to make allowance for the possibility that
persons who lacked power individually might, through organization, develop a
measure of countervailing power; and it was "predicted" (not without some
awareness of the facts) that this would be most likely in democratic nations
with an egalitarian or socialistic ideology. Though it was not possible to
develop any quantitative measure of overall inequality, the evidence which we
reviewed strongly suggests that the average level of inequality in the most
advanced industrial societies is no greater than that in the average advanced
agrarian society, and probably less. Graphically, the evolutionary pattern appears to resemble the pattern in Figure 1.

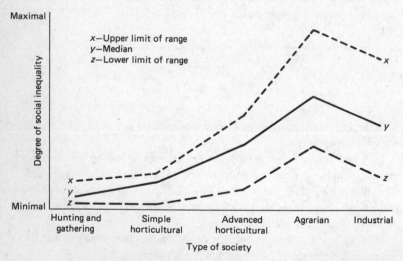

Figure 1   Degree of social inequality by type of society.

A Conflict Theory of Stratification [1975]

RANDALL COLLINS

• Conflict Sociology *was written to show that a general conflict theory could be created beyond the political differences that divided Marxists from Weberians and other factions within sociology. Sociological research had accumulated a great deal of knowledge about stratification and about formal organizations, two topics that provide the backbone for virtually every substantive field within sociology; furthermore, both stratification and organizations can be explained as struggles for dominance whose outcomes are determined by the lineup of resources on a few dimensions. Collins pointed out that if conflict theory is build up from the microlevel, then Durkheim's theory of rituals and Goffman's model of frontstages and backstages can contribute key pieces to the puzzle. Dominant classes create a frontstage ideology or culture, while subordinated classes form their resistance as a backstage culture. Cross-cutting this vertical dimension of class struggle are variations along a dimension of ritual density, which determines the extent to which groups conform to traditional symbols, or instead are composed of cosmopolitan individualists. Knowing where any particular person fits into the possible combinations of these stratifying conditions makes it possible to explain the individual outlooks and behaviors that add up to the larger social structure.*

Any coherent theory of stratification is impressive. Stratification touches so many features of social life—wealth, politics, careers, families, clubs, communities, lifestyles—that any model tying these together is bound to occupy a prominent place in the conceptual landscape of sociology. This is true even if the theories do not really work. Social life has so far proven too complicated to be reduced to a single order. But even though the great theoretical models of stratification are failures, their hulks remain in full view, too massive to be dismantled, too central to be forgotten.

Two great rival systems, Marxism and functionalism, have been with us in articulate form for over a century now. A third model, Max Weber's, has

Reprinted from Randall Collins, *Conflict Sociology: Toward an Explanatory Science* (Academic Press, 1975) pp. 1975, pp. 49, 57–65, 67–77, 86–88 with permission.

been used primarily as an antisystem, a vantage point from which to survey the failings of the others. This has left us in something of an impasse in building a more powerful explanatory system. The classical Marxian model, for all the importance of the economic divisions on which it focuses, ultimately assumed a monocausal explanation for a multicausal world. The result has been either the untenable strategy of explaining all other conditions as correlates of economic ones, or the unfruitful one of leaving them unexplained entirely. The traditional Marxian model founders in the face of ethnic, racial, and religious divisions, political parties that do not coincide with economic groupings, organizational factions in the modern corporation and state, the complex linkages of friendship groups in the community, as well as the phenomenon of social mobility. These matters can, of course, be discussed in a Marxist perspective, but tend to be explained away rather than to be explained systematically.

Put schematically, Marx's sociology states:

1. Historically, particular forms of property (slavery, feudal landholding, capital) are upheld by the coercive power of the state; hence classes formed by property divisions (slaves and slave-owners, serfs and lords, capitalists and workers) are the opposing agents in the struggle for political power—the underpinning of their means of livelihood.
2. Material contributions determine the extent to which social classes can organize effectively to fight for their interests; such conditions of mobilization are a set of intervening variables between class and political power.
3. Other material conditions—the means of mental production—determine which interests will be able to articulate their ideas and hence to dominate the ideological realm.

In all of these spheres, Marx was primarily interested in the determinants of political power, and only indirectly in what may be called a "theory of stratification." The same principles imply, however:

1. The material circumstances of making a living are the main determinant of one's style of life; since property relations are crucial for distinguishing ways of supporting oneself, class cultures and behaviors divide up along opposing lines of control over, or lack of, property.
2. The material conditions for mobilization as a coherent, intercommunicating group also vary among social classes; by implication, another major difference among class lifestyles stems from the differing organization of their communities and their differing experience with the means of social communication.

3. Classes differ in their control of the means of mental production; this produces yet another difference in class cultures—some are more articulated symbolically than others, and some have the symbolic structures of another class imposed upon them from outside.

These Marxian principles, with certain modifications, provide the basis for a conflict theory of stratification. Weber may be seen as developing this line of analysis: adding complexity to Marx's view of conflict, showing that the conditions involved in mobilization and "mental production" are analytically distinct from property, revising the fundamentals of conflict, and adding another major set of resources. Again making principles more explicit than they are in the original presentation, we may summarize Weber as showing several different forms of property conflict coexisting in the same society, and hence, by implication, the existence of multiple class divisions; elaborating the principles of organizational intercommunication and control in their own right, thereby adding a theory of organization and yet another sphere of interest conflict, this time intraorganizational factions; emphasizing that the violent coercion of the state is analytically prior to the economy, and thus transferring the center of attention to the control of the material means of violence.

Weber also opens up yet another area of resources in these struggles for control, what might be called the "means of emotional production." It is these that underlie the power of religion and make it an important ally of the state; that transform classes into status groups, and do the same to territorial communities under particular circumstances (ethnicity); and that make "legitimacy" a crucial focus for efforts at domination. Here, Weber comes to an insight parallel to those of Durkheim, Freud, and Nietzsche: not only that man is an animal with strong emotional desires and susceptibilities, but that particular forms of social interaction designed to arouse emotions operate to create strongly held beliefs and a sense of solidarity within the community constituted by participation in these rituals. I have put this formulation in a much more Durkheimian fashion than Weber himself, for Durkheim's analysis of rituals can be incorporated at this point to show the mechanisms by which emotional bonds are created. There involves especially the emotional contagion that results from physical copresence, the focusing of attention on a common object, and the coordination of common actions or gestures. To invoke Durkheim also enables me to bring in the work of Goffman (1956, 1967), which carries on his microlevel analysis of social rituals, with an emphasis on the materials and techniques of stage-setting that determine the effectiveness of appeals for emotional solidarity.

Durkheim and Goffman are to be seen as amplifying our knowledge of the mechanisms of emotional production, but within the framework of Weber's conflict theory. For Weber retains a crucial emphasis: the creation of emotional solidarity does not supplant conflict, but is one of the main weapons used in conflict. Emotional rituals can be used for domination within a group or organization; they are a vehicle by which alliances are formed in the struggle against other groups; and they can be used to impose a hierarchy of status prestige in which some groups dominate others by providing an ideal to emulate under inferior conditions. Weber's theory of religion incorporates all of these aspects of domination through the manipulation of emotional solidarity, and thereby provides an archetype for the various forms of community stratification. Caste, ethnic group, feudal Estate *(Stand)*, educational–cultural group, or class "respectability" lines are all forms of stratified solidarities, depending on varying distributions of the resources for emotional production. The basic dynamics are captured in the hierarchy implicit in any religion between ritual leaders, ritual followers, and nonmembers of the community.

From this analytical version of Weber, incorporating the relevant principles of Marx, Durkheim, and Goffman, we can move into an explicit theory of stratification. It should be apparent that there are innumerable possible types of stratified societies; our aim is not to classify them, but to state the set of causal principles that go into various empirical combinations. Our emphasis is on the cutting tools of a theory, whatever the complexity of their application in the historical world.

For conflict theory, the basic insight is that human beings are sociable but conflict-prone animals. Why is there conflict? Above all else, there is conflict because violent coercion is always a potential resource, and it is a zero-sum sort. This does not imply anything about the inherence of drives to dominate; what we do know firmly is that being coerced is an intrinsically unpleasant experience, and hence that any use of coercion, even by a small minority, calls forth conflict in the form of antagonism to being dominated. Add to this the fact that coercive power, especially as represented in the state, can be used to bring one economic goods and emotional gratification—and to deny them to others—and we can see that the availability of coercion as a resource ramifies conflicts throughout the entire society. The simultaneous existence of emotional bases for solidarity—which may well be the basis of cooperation, as Durkheim emphasized—only adds group divisions and tactical resources to be used in these conflicts.

The same argument may be transposed into the realm of social phenomenology. Every individual maximizes one's subjective status according to the resources available to oneself and to one's rivals. This is a general principle that will make sense out of the variety of evidence. By this I mean that one's subjective experience of reality is the nexus of social motivation; that everyone constructs one's own world with oneself in it; but this reality construction is done primarily by communication, real or imaginary, with other people; and hence people hold the keys to each other's identities. These propositions will come as no surprise to readers of George Herbert Mead or Erving Goffman. Add to this an emphasis from conflict theories: that each individual is basically pursuing his or her own interests and that there are many situations, notably ones where power is involved, in which those interests are inherently antagonistic. The basic argument, then, has three strands: that people live in self-constructed subjective worlds; that others pull many of the strings that control one's subjective experience; and that there are frequent conflicts over control. Life is basically a struggle for status in which no one can afford to be oblivious to the power of others around him. If we assume that everyone uses what resources are available to have others aid him or her in putting on the best possible face under the circumstances, we have a guiding principle to make sense out of the myriad variations of stratification.[1]

The general principles of conflict analysis may be applied to any empirical area. (1) Think through abstract formulations to a sample of the typical real-life interactions involved. Think of people as animals maneuvering for advantage, susceptible to emotional appeals, but steering a self-interested course toward satisfactions and away from dissatisfactions. (2) Look for the material arrangements that affect interaction: the physical places, the modes of communication, the supply of weapons, devices for staging one's public impression, tools, and goods. Assess the relative resources available to each individual: their potential for physical coercion, their access to other persons with whom to negotiate, their sexual attractiveness, their store of cultural devices for invoking emotional solidarity, as well as the physical arrangements just mentioned. (3) Apply the general hypothesis that inequalities in resources result in efforts by the dominant party to take advantage of the situation; this need not involve conscious calculation, but a basic propensity of feeling one's way toward the areas of greatest immediate reward, like flowers turning to the light. Social structures are to be explained in terms of the behavior following from various lineups of resources, social change from shifts in resources resulting from previous conflicts. (4)

[1]The proposition that individuals *maximize* their subjective status appears to contradict March and Simon's (1958) organizational principle that people operate by *satisficing*—setting minimal levels of payoff in each area of concern, and then troubleshooting where crises arise. The contradiction is only apparent. Satisficing refers to a strategy for dealing with the *cognitive* problem produced by inherent limits on the human capacity for processing information. The principle of maximizing subjective status is a *motivational* principle, telling us what are the goals of behavior. Any analysis of cognitive strategies is incomplete without some motivational principle such as the latter to tell us what are the purposes of action, and what areas of concern are most emphasized. In other words, it is one thing to predict what goals someone will pursue, another to predict what strategies one will use in pursuing them, given the inability to see very far into the future or deal with very many things at once.

Ideals and beliefs likewise are to be explained in terms of the interests which have the resources to make their viewpoint prevail. (5) Compare empirical cases; test hypotheses by looking for the conditions under which certain things occur versus the conditions under which other things occur. Think causally; look for generalizations. Be awake to multiple causes—the resources for conflict are complex.

Nowhere can these principles be better exemplified than on the materials of stratification. Especially in modern societies, we must separate out multiple spheres of social interaction and multiple causes in each one. These influences may be reduced to order through the principles of conflict theory. We can make a fair prediction of what sort of status shell each individual constructs around oneself if we know how one deals with people in earning a living; how one gets along in the household in which one lives; how one relates to the population of the larger community, especially as determined by its political structures; and the ways in which one associates with friends and recreational companions. The conventional variables of survey research are all reflected in this list: occupation, parental occupation, education, ethnicity, age, and sex are cryptic references to how one's associations are structured at work, in the household, and in community and recreational groups. In each sphere, we look for the actual pattern of personal interaction, the resources available to persons in different positions, and how these affect the line of attack they take for furthering their personal status. The ideals and beliefs of persons in different positions thus emerge as personal ideologies, furthering their dominance or serving for their psychological protection.

I begin with occupational situations, as the most pervasively influential of all stratification variables. They are analyzed into several causal dimensions, elaborating a modified version of Marx, Weber, and Durkeim. Other stratified milieux are treated in terms of other resources for organizing social communities; here we find parallel applications of conflict principles as well as interaction with the occupational realm. The sum of these stratified milieux makes up the concrete social position of any individual.

Occupational Influences on Class Cultures

Occupations are the way people keep themselves alive. This is the reason for their fundamental importance. Occupations shape the differences among people, however, not merely by the fact that work is essential for survival, but because people relate to each other in different ways in this inescapable area of their lives. Occupations are the major basis of class cultures; these cultures, in turn, along with material resources for inter-communication, are the mechanisms that organize classes as communities, i.e., as kind of status group. The first process is dealt with here and the second takes up a later part of this chapter. The complexity of a system of class cultures depends on how many dimensions of difference we can locate among occupations. In order of importance, these are dominance relationships, position in a network of communication, and some additional variables, including the physical nature of the work and the amount of wealth it produces.

Dominance Relationships

Undoubtedly, the most crucial difference among work situations is the power relations involved (the ways that people give or take orders). Occupational classes are essentially power classes within the realm of work. In stating this, I am accepting Ralf Dahrendorf's (1959) modification of Marx. Marx took property as the power relation par excellence. The dividing line between possessors and nonpossessors of property marked the crucial breaks in the class structure; changes among different sorts of property—slaves, land, industrial capital— made the difference among historical eras. But, although property classes might be the sharpest social distinctions in certain periods, the twentieth century has shown that other types of power can be equally important. In capitalist societies, the salaried managerial employee has remained socially distinct from the manual worker, although a strictly Marxist interpretation would put both of them in the working class. In socialist countries where conventional property classes do not exist, the same sorts of social distinctions and conflicts of interest appear among various levels of the occupational hierarchy. As Dahrendorf points out, Marx mistook an historically limited form of power for power relations in general; his theory of class divisions and class conflict can be made useful for a wider range of situations if we seek its more abstract form.

Max Weber (1968:53) defined power as the ability to secure compliance against someone's will to do otherwise. This is not the only possible use of the word "power," but it is the most useful one if we are looking for ways to explain people's outlooks. There is power like the engineer's over inanimate objects; there is power like the scholar's over ideas and words; there is the power of the planner to affect future events. But, since persons encountering persons is the whole observable referent of "social causation," a social power that will directly affect someone's behavior is that of a person giving orders to another. It affects the behavior of the person who gives orders, for he or she must take a certain bearing, think certain thoughts, and speak certain formulas. It affects the persons who must listen to orders, even though they may not accept too many of them or carry them out, for they accept at least one thing—to put up with

standing before someone who is giving him or her orders and with deferring to
that person at least for the moment. One animal cows another to its heels: that is
the archetypal situation of organizational life and the shaper of classes and
cultures.

The situations in which authority is acted out are the key experiences of
occupational life. Since one cannot avoid having an occupation or being cared
for by someone who does, it influences everyone. On this basis, three main
classes can be distinguished: those who take orders from few or none, but give
orders to many; those who must defer to some people, but can command others;
and those who are order-takers only. The readily understood continuum from
upper class through middle class to working class corresponds to this dimension.
This is especially clear if we note how the middle-class—working-class break is
commonly assigned: not so much on the basis of the cleanliness of the work, or
of the income derived from it; certainly not, today, on the basis of property
distinctions; but on the basis of where one stands when orders are given.

Upper middle class and lower middle class correspond to relative positions
within the middle group, based on the ratio of order-giving to order-taking.
Lower class can be distinguished from working class as a marginal group who
work only occasionally and at the most menial positions. Farmers and farm
laborers can be fitted into this categorization at a variety of middle-class and
working-class levels. Prosperous farmers are similar to other businessmen; tenant farmers and laborers are not unlike the urban working class, with differences
attributable to the different community structure rather than to occupational
conditions per se. The power situation is similar, too, if one understands that
the people who give orders are not necessarily all in the same organization and
that one need not be an actual employee to be a subordinate; the small farmer or
businessman meets the banker with much the same face as the foreman meets
his supervisor. There are some differences too, of course. First, I want to show
that the most powerful effects on a man's behavior are the sheer volume of
occupational deference he gives and gets. Then I will show how some different
types of situations at about the same class level can add variations on the pattern.

Dahrendorf's (1959) revision of Marx converges here with Weber's emphasis
on power relations. It should be noted that this formulation brings us into the
universe of Durkheimian sociology as well, at least in its Goffmanian variant. If
the successful application of power is a matter of personal bearing (in which
sanctions are implied but not called upon), Goffman's analysis of the ritual
dramatization of status provides us with detailed evidence on the mechanism. In
a sense, the apocryphal Weberian principle of the "means of emotional production" applies not only in the realm of community formation but in the heart of
the occupational relationship. Hence, it happens that Weber's historical sum-

mary of the religious propensities of various classes epitomizes later evidence on class cultures.

Networks of Occupational Communication

Another dimension of occupational cultures comes from the sheer volume and diversity of personal contacts. The politician must see diverse audiences and the king receive the awe of crowds, whereas the tenant farmer and the servant rarely see outsiders, and the workman regularly deals with few besides his boss and a little-changing circle of friends and family. The greater cosmopolitanism of the higher occupational levels is one key to their outlooks. Cosmopolitanism is generally correlated with power because power is essentially the capacity to keep up relations with a fairly large number of persons in such a way as to draw others to back one up against whoever he happens to be with at the moment. But communications are also a separate variable, as we can see in the case of occupations that have greater contacts than power, such as salespeople, enter-tainers, intellectuals, and professionals generally. This variable accounts for horizontal variants within classes, and for their complex internal hierarchies (e.g., within professions or in the intellectual world) that stratify whole sectors over and above their actual order-giving power.

This dimension has its classic theoretical antecedants. Marx's (1963: 123–124) principle of class mobilization by differential control of the means of transportation and communication applies not only to politics but to the differ-entiation of class cultures themselves. Weber's extensions of this principle to the internal structure of organizations reinforces the implication, for organizational evidence not only documents the crucial distinctions in outlook and power derived from control over information and communications but provides a look from a different angle at the *empirically* same phenomenon of occupational stratification. Durkheim's model of ritual interactions and their effects on the "collective conscience" provides a finer specification of the mechanisms in-volved. In the *Division of Labor in Society*, Durkheim shows that the content of social beliefs, and especially the pressure for group conformity and respect for symbols, varies with the intensity and diversity of social contacts. In *The Elemen-tary Forms of the Religious Life*, Durkheim examines the mechanisms at the high-intensity end of the continuum and shows that the highly reified concep-tion of collective symbols, and the intense loyalties to the immediate group, are produced by ceremonial interactions within a group of unchanging characters, in a situation of close physical proximity and highly concentrated attention. By abstraction, we can see that not only entire historical eras but particularly occupational milieu vary along these dimensions and hence produce different sorts of cultural objects and personal loyalties. Weber's distinction between bureaucratic and patrimonial cultures captures this dimension, with its different centers of loyalty and standards of ethics; the bureaucratic and entrepreneurial sectors of the modern occupational world represent these variations across the dimension of class power.[2]

A Summary of Class Cultures

The "upper class" is a way of talking about people who command large numbers of men and women and defer very little to anyone. There are many ways people have gotten into this enviable position. Leaders of conquering armies, and their heirs, have been the commanders throughout most of history; some of them still survive on their landed estates in Latin America and Southeast Asia. Being at or near the head of a government is another way, and being one of the most powerful businessmen in an industrial society is yet another. In practice, business power has tended to mean involving oneself especially in financial matters; mere operating heads of firms have led a precarious existence independent of the financial community.

Max Weber (1968: 472–477) summarized the religious propensities of well-established elites of these sorts; it epitomizes their outlook in general (cf. Baltzell, 1958; McArthur, 1955). The military nobility throughout history has upheld some code of honor, couched in whatever religious terms were convenient. Such classes have at all times used religions for political and military purposes, assimilating them to the ceremonious formalities of their relations with underlings generally. The more bureaucratic elites—the Chinese mandarins, the Catholic officials of the Middle Ages, the office-aristocracy of post-Renaissance Germany, France, and England—have been scrupulously orthodox, usually in some worldly religious philosophy, while maintaining that rites and traditions are good for domesticating the masses. Business elites fit into this pattern too, with certain variations depending essentially on just how elite business is in the context of the particular society. The merchant princes of Medieval Europe and of the Middle East have generally affected a worldly, ostentatious, ritualistic religion, not unlike the military and political elites.

[2]Patrimonial organization, most characteristic of traditional societies, centers around families, patrons and their clients, and other personalistic networks. The emphasis is on traditional rituals that demonstrate the emotional bonds among persons; the world is divided into those whom one can trust because of strongly legitimated personal connections, and the rest of the world from whom nothing is to be expected that cannot be exacted by cold-blooded bargaining or force. In modern bureaucratic organization, by contrast, personal ties are weaker, less ritualized and emotionally demonstrative; in their place is the allegiance to a set of abstract rules and positions. The different class cultures in patrimonial and bureaucratic organizations are accordingly affected. Patrimonial elites are more ceremonious and personalistic. Bureaucratic elites emphasize a colder set of ideals.

Something like this in its modern secular version can be found in the ritualistic social life of well-established industrial and financial upper classes which emerged by the twentieth century in England, the United States, and France. The significant exceptions are those businessmen, usually in the first generation of grand entrepreneurship, who have a more pious, inward and moralistic religion. But this seems to be the result of their middle-class origins rather than of their upper-class destination. Those who live most of their lives in the atmosphere of command tend to fall into the typical pattern.

What causes the upper-class outlook?—primarily, the experience of being continually in command. Getting deference is a matter of bearing; it depends on expecting obedience and treating disobedience as unthinkable. Upper-class assuredness, cool composure, unconscious arrogance is the result. The upper class are arbiters; they are the court of last resort, at least as long as they can convince other people of it. The resulting attitude is one of deliberateness and finality. The upper-class person is the one most committed to his or her organization, for he or she gets the most rewards from it, and it is in the organization's name that one gives orders and receives deference. Moreover, he or she *is* the organization more than anyone else; the network of authority that links subordinates together would not be knit at all if he or she did not knit it, much as an army is destroyed not so much because of casualties but because the general cannot keep its pieces together. Whether the images of organization are religious, political, or secular, the upper class is the strongest believer in them. Their philosophies are, nevertheless, worldly in practice; they have nothing to gain from fundamental changes and no basic failures or lacks to make them humble or fanatical. [3]

All this follows from giving many orders and taking few. Some side effects come from the upper classes' social contacts and wealth. Upper-class persons are on top of the largest organizational networks of communications. This is more or less true by definition, since power over people is precisely this sort of manipulation of human networks. This means the upper-class person is necessarily sociable. At the same time, we have seen that he or she is awesome, self-important, deliberate, and dignified. The result is highly formalized codes of etiquette, ways in which potentates can deal with others without letting down the facades of their positions. The emphasis on forms for their own sake and the concern for tradition reinforce each other here. The possession of the largest available wealth—which usually goes along with high power, since power can procure almost anything—makes it possible for upper-class people to put on a

[3]Modern evidence show that the higher one's social status, the more one participates in organized religious activities, but the less emotionally absorbing it is for one (Demerath, 1965).

very elaborate show of themselves. Expensive tastes in clothes, buildings, food, and other paraphernalia become part of the expected stage setting of power. Another side result of the ideal of generosity to those in need which leavens upper-class arrogance, at least in principle. This fits in with a paternalistic rationalization for their dominance, representing an investment in ceremonial leadership of the community which has comparatively low material costs and high returns in status, and additional insurance for their power.

The more consistently a person experiences situations of unmitigated defer-ence, the more sharply this general outlook appears. Secure business tycoons, like hereditary monarchs, experience more of this in their lifetime than insecure politicians in a competitive democracy. The more a person associates with others, whether family or friends who have experienced only the same situa-tions, the stronger the culture. Weber (1968: 932–948) suggested that times of rapid change in power relations tend to break down upper-class culture into its basic elements—which are the sheer capacity to awe others, the energy to command, the self-identification with the organization's ideological reflection. With the passage of time, there appear the refined manners, the self-contained air, the elaboration of complex systems of mutual recognition through signals of material tastes.

A second major class consists of the functionaries, the middle classes who defer to some and exact deference from others. Actually the term "middle class" loosely covers a variety of situations. Just as "upper class," defined in terms of getting much deference and giving little, includes isolated country squires and industrial overlords of small towns as well as busy emperors and financiers, the "middle class" category contains persons who are highly placed in administrative hierarchies, as well as clerks and supervisors at the very lowest level of com-mand. We are dealing with a continuum here. At one end is the upper middle class, the functionaries who deal only with other functionaries, or the nominally independent larger businessmen and professionals who depend on good rela-tions with bankers, clients, suppliers, and associates. At the other end is the lower middle class of first line supervisors who give orders only to those who give orders to no one at all—that is to say, those who face the sharpest class boundary in power relations.

The lower middle class is the most distinctive type. Weber (1968: 481–484) summarized its religious outlook as ascetic, moralistic, community-oriented, respectable, and hard working.[4] In the premodern societies Weber was review-ing, this class consisted primarily of independent artisans like the small shop-

---

[4]See also Vidich and Bensman (1968), Gans (1967), and general summaries of class differences from community studies in Kahl (1957) and from survey studies in Glen and Alston (1968).

keepers and craftsmen among whom Christianity originated in the cities of the Roman Empire. The same general traits can be found in the modern petite bourgeoisie of minor clerical employees, small businessmen, and independent skilled workers. Weber explained the outlook mainly from the nature of the work situation in which success seems possible through constant self-discipline. No doubt the nearby bad example of working-class hedonism has something to do with the vehemence with which lower-middle-class persons drive themselves to keep up their respectability.

The causal conditions can be seen more clearly if we consider interpersonal relations. The petit bourgeois has a stake in a system of organizational power, however tenuously. Particularly if one is a low-level employee of a larger organization, one has a reason to feel superior to at least some people, provided that one takes responsibility for one's role. In compensation for the deference one must give to superiors, for whom he or she carries out essentially menial and repetitive tasks, one can exact deference from a class of subordinates who have no power at all. But the last are outside the realm of power and hence have no reason to identify with it; the petit bourgeois thus has the hardest struggle in day-to-day class war. Least sure of one's own authority and most pressed to stay on the top side of the sharpest division among power classes, he or she identifies with the values of the organization and of respectability and authority in the most rigid way. The rule-bound "bureaucratic personality" is the functionary with minor authority exercised for all it is worth, oblivious to the larger purposes of organizational coordination visible only to those with less specific responsibilities. Essentially the same pattern is found among small businessmen and minor professionals struggling to set themselves off from a clientele that may be only slightly poorer than themselves. The lesser range of contacts and more meager incomes of the lower middle class, compared to the upper class, accounts for its lack of cosmopolitanism, subtle manners, and refined tastes.

The higher levels of the middle class range in culture between the lower-middle class's rigid and tasteless respectability and the complacent gentility of the upper class (Seeley et al, 1956). In general, all of the middle class is set off from those below by their intermediate position in the communications network of the larger society; the working class makes up a set of little enclaves in the larger community; while the upper class occupies the central links. The lower middle class is just within the circle of these wider linkages; higher levels of the middle class become successively more organizationally conscious, more cosmopolitan, more involved in formalized sociability and community affairs. There also tends to be a continuum of tastes and manners from the crude pleasures and crude asceticism of the lower middle class through the progressively more expensive tastes and subtle manners that the upper middle class borrows from the elite.

Those who hold relatively steady jobs at the bottom of the economy have yet another occupational culture.[5] They are almost exclusively subordinates. Since they do not give orders to anyone in the name of the organization, they do not identify with the organization. Often they identify against it, if only in diffuse apathy to the ideals put forth by their superiors. Working-class culture is localistic, cynical, and oriented toward the immediate present. Lacking an active position in the channels of organizational communication and recognizing that their superiors use control of information to justify and manipulate their dominance over them, workers see the world from an aggressively personal point of view.

The abstract rhetoric of their more cosmopolitan superiors is distrusted. The only accurate information is about what known individuals are doing. The viewpoint of workers is largely confined to what is physically present to themselves and their immediate circle of acquaintance. Thus, we find that workers tend to confine their social relations to their own family and groups of childhood friends. The middle-class cosmopolitanism expressed in joining political, social, and charitable organizations is largely absent in the working classes, as is the pattern of sociability in which strangers are invited to the home for dinner or parties found commonly in the upper- and upper-middle classes. Working-class values, like those of everyone else, emphasize the virtues of their own life situations: in this case, physical toughness, loyalty to friends, courage and wariness toward strangers and superiors. As Bennett Berger has remarked, values are usually self-congratulatory.

The ethos is one that regards life as hard and unpredictable, with little long-range planning possible. One should be prepared to seize the opportunity to enjoy oneself when possible and to endure the inevitable periods of deprivation. In all these respects, industrial working-class culture is similar to the culture of peasants and farm laborers. Weber characterizes both groups, historically, as essentially worldly in their religious attitudes. Moralistic and ascetic religions have never been strong in either group, and the religions that do flourish are those that celebrate the periodic events of life with boisterous festivals. Religion, here, has a magic tone including faith-healing, future-predicting, luck-bringing, and other uses of religious ceremonies for worldly ends and emotional release. Rural pagan

---

[5]See Kahl (1957), Glen and Alston (1968), Gans (1962), Rainwater et al (1962), and Weber (1968: 468–472, 484–486). There tends to be an antiworking-class bias in the literature, presented as it is by middle-class researchers; the data are usually presented so as to characterize working people as parochial, authoritarian, uncultivated, materialistic, and lacking in moral virtues, self-discipline, and foresight. Without romanticizing manual workers, it should be pointed out that the same data can support value judgments of a very different sort: working people are more loyal to their friends, more physically courageous, more capable of enjoying themselves when the opportunity arises (instead of "delaying gratification"), less prone to abstract moralizing, and more realistic (although less informed) about the larger world than much of the middle class with its naïve faith in official definitions of work and politics.

religions, with their annual festivals and fertility rites and the celebrations in-volved in marriages and funeral wakes, have their equivalent in the industrial class's entertainment of violent (or at least highly active) sports and periodic drinking bouts punctuated with fights. Unlike the moralistic lower middle class, and also unlike the sophisticatedly public-image-conscious upper- and upper middle classes, the working-class male culture is explicitly interested in sex, with a rigid dual standard of male control over wives, sisters, and daughters, and free male access to prostitutes and unattached women. The emotional tone is rela-tively uninhibited, whether in fighting or celebrating. Work is regarded as an unavoidable evil.

Lower-class culture, finally, is built on the world view of persons with little stable attachments to the major organizations—transient workers at menial jobs, the chronically unemployed, beggars, outcasts, and derelicts (Roach and Gursslin, 1967; Liebow, 1967). Indeed, it has been widely debated whether or not the lower-class ethos can be referred to as a culture at all, since a prime feature of lower-class life is the lack of strong interpersonal ties and stable groups which might sustain and pass on a culture. If we avoid the terminological aspects of this problem, we can characterize the lower-class outlook. It is essen-tially amoral and individualistic, an attitude of every man for himself. Rules of honesty, suppression of violent impulses, or restrictions on extreme forms of self-indulgence such as alcoholism or narcotic addiction, have little or no force in social aggregates that do not form coherent groups. Weber's (1968: 486) histori-cal survey reflects this best in the situation of slaves, whom he characterizes as religiously disinclined except for short-lived waves of chiliastic beliefs, of fanta-sies and emotional panics about the imminent destruction of the social order.

Clearly enough, these class cultures (upper class, middle class, working class, lower class) are ideal types, guideposts along a continuum. Even this is too simple, as there are several different dimensions along which people's occupa-tional experiences can vary. We are dealing with individuals, each of whom may have his or her own situation; "classes" is just a convenient way of talking. The major occupational distinctions involve the sheer amount of time spent in getting and giving deference, and the sheer amount of communicativeness involved. The former makes one dignified and arrogant, respectable and compli-ant, or cynical and defensive, depending on whether one mostly gives orders, takes and gives, or only takes. The latter makes one cosmopolitan and ceremoni-ous, or localistic and unrefined. A third major variable is income: The more one has of it the more one is likely to be concerned about the refinements that can be bought with it. It is also important because it tends to determine who can associate with whom, and thus tends to knit together class cultures through associational groups.

One can conceive of various mixtures of these traits, along with further variations. For example, the more coercion there is involved in exacting deference, the more sharply the pattern of dignity, respectability, or defensiveness appears at the three main class levels, respectively. This explains some of the difference in tone between traditional societies with their omnipresent military force, and most industrial societies, in which overt coercion has generally declined.

Some Formal Principles

There are a number of different determinants of occupational class cultures. The available evidence, especially from community studies, tends to lump them together and to confuse them with other variables from the realm of status group organization. For the sake of clarity, I will state them here as formal propositions, beginning with some general postulates.

Postulates

I. Each individual constructs one's own subjective reality.

II. Individual cognition is constructed from social communications.

III. Individuals have power over each other's subjective reality (from I and II).

IV. Each individual attempts to maximize one's subjective status to the degree allowed by the resources available to oneself and to others whom one contacts.

V. Each individual values highest what one is best at, and attempts to act it out and communicate about it as much as possible.

VI. Each individual seeks social contacts which give one greatest subjective status, and avoids those in which one has lowest status (from III, IV, and V).

VII. Where individuals' resources differ, social contacts involve inequalities in power to define subjective reality.

VIII. Situations in which differential power is exercised, and withdrawal is not immediately possible, implicitly involve conflict (from IV and VI).

Propositions

1.0 Experiences of giving and taking orders are the main determinants of individual outlooks and behaviors.

1.1 The more one gives orders, the more one is proud, self-assured, formal, and identifies with the organizational ideals in whose name one justifies the orders.

1.2 The more one takes orders, the more one is subservient, fatalistic, alienated from organizational ideals, externally conforming, distrustful of others, concerned with extrinsic rewards, and amoral.

1.3 The more one interacts with others in egalitarian exchanges, the more one is informal, friendly, and tends to accept others' ideals.

1.4 The more one *both* gives and takes orders, the more one combines both formality, self-assurance, and organizational identification with subservience and external conformity; one is little concerned with the long-range or abstract purposes of the organization in whose name one is given orders, but strongly identifies with one's own short-term order-giving rationale; one attempts to transform order-taking situations into orders that one passes on to others.

   1.1, 1.2, and 1.4 are summaries of the occupational and organizational literature, giving us ideal types of upper-class, working-class, and middle-class attitudes. 1.3 is suggested by less explicit studies of middle-managers or professionals interacting among themselves; it is probably also borne out by cooperative activities in relatively unstratified tribal societies. Notice that a large number of different outcomes are possible for different individuals. Not only can one have different mixtures of order-giving and order-taking (thus giving us upper middle class, lower middle class, upper working class, etc.), with different amounts of egalitarian exchanges mixed in; but the sheer amount of *time* one spends doing these things can vary. (That is, both the proportion of order-giving and -taking, and the absolute amount of each, can vary.) Individuals like college students may have to take orders from their teachers at exam time, but the alienation is relatively slight because these situations happen so episodically. Where students have to do class drills daily, the amount of alienation is much greater.

1.5 The more coercion is used in backing up orders, the more accentuated are the effects in 1.1, 1.2, and 1.4.

   The egalitarian situation referred to in 1.3 is known in the organizational literature as a type of normative control. Another form of normative control is to offer opportunities to become an order-giver oneself:

1.6 The more one believes in the future possibility of being in a position as order-giver or order-taker, the more one takes on the attitudes of that position.

This is the well-known principle of anticipatory socialization (Merton, 1968: 316–325). It also works in retrospect; attitudes carry over from the past:

1.7 The more one remembers being in a position as order-giver or order-taker, the more one retains the attitudes of that period.

Since people tend to believe what is most pleasant for them (Postulate IV), downwardly mobile individuals retain old attitudes longer than upwardly mobile ones (Wilensky and Edwards, 1959). Eventually, we should be able to set a time period on these effects (all other influences, such as friendship ties, being equal). I would suggest two years is enough to assimilate anyone to any occupational change that involves taking on a new power position, even moving over the line of class deference from order-taker to order-giver; we might call this the "sell-out span". For shifting friends, the period of attitude change might be much shorter.

1.8 The more physical exertion and danger involved in the work (whether manual labor or fighting), the more one values toughness, courage, and action.

This proposition is based on the emphasis on physical toughness in working-class culture; but it is borne out also in upper-class culture in the era of the military aristocracy, and even in middle-class culture in organizations like the army. It also explains rural–urban and patrimonial–bureaucratic differences in the propensity to use violence (Gastil, 1971; Whitt et al., 1972). The converse might be called the "effeteness principle." Both sides of it follow from Postulate V. Incidentally, situations of physical activity lead to a high value on toughness and hence a considerable use of coercion in backing up orders; the chain ends (via 1.5) by accentuating the cultural differences given in 1.1, 1.2, and 1.4, as in the sharp class distinctions and powerful latent antagonisms of patrimonial societies.

2.0 The amount and structure of social communications make up a second set of determinants of individual outlooks and behaviors.

2.1 *Mutual Surveillance.* The more one is in the physical presence of other people, the more one accepts the culture of the group and the more one expects precise conformity in others. Conversely, the less one is around others, the more one's attitudes are explicitly individualistic and self-centered.

2.2 *Cosmopolitanism.* The greater the diversity of communications one is involved in, the more one develops abstract, relativistic ideas and the habit of thinking in terms of long-range consequences. Conversely, the less the variety of communications, the more one thinks in terms of particular persons and things, short-term contingencies, and an alien and uncontrollable world surrounding familiar local circles.

These two principles divide the Durkheimian notion of social density into several variables.[6] The first has a great many ramifications, from differences in childrearing where surveillance is much or little available, to differences in the ethos of communities both within our own society and throughout history. It can crosscut all the authority variables (1.1–1.8), although part of the difference in occupational cultures are due to the lower experience of surveillance and the higher diversity of contacts at the higher occupational levels.[7]

It also helps explain the cultures of two occupational "classes" not given earlier. One of these is the lower-class culture of individuals who work only episodically, and that at the most menial levels of order-taking; their culture, accordingly, is an extreme form of amoral individualism, deriving from a combination of low authority, low surveillance, and low cosmopolitanism. The other occupational "class" consists of many artists, intellectuals, and other lone wolfs who relate to others as equals or even (with enough money or fame) as order-givers. Their culture is highly self-centered and nonconformist but couched in terms of (at least imaginary) control over the social world, a kind of creative megalomania. Intellectuals, whether personally isolated or not, are relatively high in terms of communications of a very complex sort, which thereby become a major standard of value for them (by Postulate V).[8] Thus intellectuals tend to be high on 2.2 but low on 2.1 (since intellectual pursuits usually require working alone), hence the culture of either arrogance or informality, individualism, and relativism.

High diversity of communications (2.2) can result from encountering or corresponding with a great many different kinds of people, which is the most common meaning of "cosmopolitan"; or from constantly being given new messages from the people one sees repeatedly. High-level executives and members of the intellectual professions experience a great deal of the latter, even if they operate within a relatively homogeneous network of acquaintance. The effects are about the same in either case: the aspect of upper-middle-class and upper-class culture that makes people sophisticated, thinking in terms of abstractions

[6]For the sake of completeness, principles analogous to 1.6 and 1.7 should be added to 2.1, 2.2, and 3.0, since memory and anticipation effects may occur here too, although probably with relatively little additional explanatory power.

[7]Evidence that the closeness of surveillance and the diversity of contacts are both correlated with authority levels, and also contribute *independently* to class attitudes and behaviors, is found in Kohn and Schooler (1969), Pearlin and Kohn (1966), and Hagedorn and Labovitz (1968).

[8]If he or she is at all successful, an intellectual cannot really be too isolated. For getting into the center of a network of intensively felt, if slowly moving, communications is what intellectual success is all about.

and long-term consequences. This variable (2.2), together with 1.1, helps explain why there have been a number of different upper-class cultures throughout history. The relatively isolated rural landowner or even the patrimonial king, for all the deference he got, operated in nothing like the communications network of the modern business executive or politician.

The difference between patrimonial and bureaucratic social organization can also be explained in terms of these variables. Patrimonial organizations have high surveillance but low diversity of contacts; the resulting outlook, which Weber (1968: 212–254) characterized as *traditional legitimacy*, emphasizes personal relationships, a purely local concern, and a surrounding world that is regarded as permanent and beyond human control.[9] Bureaucratic organizations tend to reduce direct surveillance and to increase diversity of communications, especially by adding written messages to personal contacts. Weber termed the legitimating world view *rational–legal*: the notion that arrangements are not only abstract and impersonal but deliberately enacted by human beings. In modern America, there are few truly patrimonial organizations left (especially with the separation of the work place from the family), but the sphere of small or entrepreneurial business provides a similar contrast to bureaucratic organizations. In the former, persons are more likely to be authoritarian, inflexible, and unreceptive to change–differences that can be pinned down to the greater prevalence of diverse communications in bureaucratic organizations (Kohn, 1971).[10]

3.0 Authority and social density are experienced in a number of different spheres of life: work, politics, home, sociable recreation, and moving about the geographic community. The individual's outlook is produced by the linear sum of all of these experiences.

Ethnic groups are simply the results of a particular combination of very general stratification processes. Weber (1958b; 1968:385–398, 932–938) first

---

[9] This reified world view is what has been measured under the rubric of "authoritarian personality." See Gabennesch (1972), where it is interpreted as the result of a situation of low cosmopolitanism rather than as a personality trait. The effects of such conditions on *political* tolerance, however, have been misinterpreted with the usual antiworking-class bias of American sociologists. Many of the indicators of authoritarian attitudes refer to preferences for strict childrearing practices and sexual moralities, which tap stratification within the home and community rather than within the sphere of economic class conflicts. In the latter sphere, working-class people are more likely to have a conspiratorial view of the world than members of the higher classes; but, whereas the latter *prefer* inequality of political influence, it is the former who are more attached to the ideal of democratic pluralism (Form and Rytina, 1969). The effects of self-interest here are obvious.

[10] The differences are consistent across a great many measures, although the effects are relatively small. This seems to be due to the fact that for most workers, bureaucratic organizations *also* tend to have a rather high degree of surveillance. Kohn is characterizing lower-middle and middle-class occupations especially; in those bureaucratic occupations with greater freedom (professional and higher managerial), we might expect more striking differences.

sketched out the interrelations among occupational class, political power, and status communities along these lines: The sharpest distinction among stratified cultural communities occurs where initial cultural distinctions derive from different community forms, economic distinctions become superimposed, and the dominant group enjoys stable political resources. This was the basis of the legally defined estates of Medieval Europe; Bendix (1956) has shown how the continuation of such corporate distinctions in nineteenth-century Russia kept occupational classes maximally distinct as status communities, while the political shifts producing an ideology of individualism in England and America tended to reduce the salience of class-based status groups. The Indian caste system was built up by a long-term continuation of these conditions, building on even sharper cultural distinctions between horticultural tribes and civilized conquerors. Toward the other end of the continuum, where resources are more fluid and the population more generally mobilized, cultural communities are more ephemeral and tend to be based on short-term class relations, like the claims to family descent embodied in America in the Social Register.

In terms of stratification principles previously set forth, ethnicity derives originally from the cultures of communities with particular occupational, political, household, and recreational structures (variables $1.1-2.2$, operative in all of these realms). These produce the initial distinctions; migration or conquest shifts the lineup of variables affecting the mobilization of such communities vis-à-vis each other, because each originally geographically distinct group is drawn together by its possession of a common culture, and because its internal coherence is a powerful weapon to use in struggling with other groups over power and economic position. These noncultural goals of the conflict became mediated by cultural organization that need not in principle coincide with current class lines, and the economic and political antagonisms serve to reinforce these lines of associational inclusion and exclusion.

Education as Pseudoethnicity. Education shows up in all the surveys as an independent contributor to cultural distinctions. This has mostly been taken as a brute fact, without explaining how it fits with the rest of the processes of stratification. We can see a more general pattern, however, if we treat it as a subcase of ethnic stratification—or, to be more precise, a subcase of the same processes that also produce ethnicity.

Education socializes people into a particular kind of culture, working best on those who already have acquired the general orientation in their families. Schools everywhere are established originally to pass on a particular form of religion or elite class culture, and are expanded in the interests of political indoctrination or ethnic hegemony. In these situations, education is nothing more than ethnic or class culture, although it can be taught to those who are not born into it. But long-standing and internally complex school systems bring about some goal displacement, changing the culture into something specifically scholastic; insofar as it goes on to provide the cultural identity for its graduates, it has an independent effect on class and status group cultures. We have been so concerned to determine whether or not schooling can provide social mobility apart from family origins that we fail to notice how the educated class itself is a kind of surrogate ethnic group, setting up job requirements in its own favor and discriminating against those who do not use its vocabulary and do not refer to the same literary classics or technicist ideals (Collins, 1971; Bourdieu and Passeron, 1970).

The same principles apply to the Confucian education of dynastic China, the Christian gentleman of traditional Europe, or the Communist theocracy of the Soviet states. The rhetoric of technocracy prominent in so many places today is not essentially different, except that it reflects much more bureaucratic school and work organizations, in which the legitimating ideology is influenced by middle-level specialists defending the autonomy of their positions; what one learns in school, even today, is not so much real technical skills (which are almost always learned on the job) as it is an esoteric rhetoric to keep outsiders at arms length (Collins, 1971).

A society with a large educational system, then, is different from other stratification systems only in how certain variables are arranged, and not in the basic processes of stratification. The interaction of status group cultures with occupational classes and political power is the main dynamic of stratification in all societies; whether status groups are organized around families, ethnic communities, or education is a set of variations on a common theme.

Conclusion

The possible influences on an individual's behavior are fairly diverse. In a society like modern America where political domination is loose and the number of different organizations and group settings very large, the range of contacts within one individual's lifetime, or even within a few days, can be extraordinary. We should not be surprised that every individual has something unique. In other societies, the range of diversity has been smaller; perhaps in some cases, maybe of the future, the range may be even greater.

But our purpose here is not to marvel about diversity, but to explain behavior in terms of a combination of some relatively simple principles. The reader might try these on someone they know to see how well that level of subjective reality is explained. An occupational career within the minor bureaucratic ranks of the army; a family background amid the prosperous small farmers of a Northern European village in a country still ruled by a landed aristocracy; the head of a mildly patriarchal household with a stay-at-home wife and submissively ambitious children; a respectable citizen of a small American town and of a complacently humdrum Protestant congregation; friendly contacts largely confined to a circle of kin, themselves from the same European communities and the same lower-middle-class occupations—these experiences shape the strongly held world view of this man of caution, with his respect for authority and his ambitious hopes for his children, inhabiting an ordered and complacent universe and threatened only by youthful cultures whose experiences he has never participated in. This describes the world of an old man. At any point in his life, of course, the set of influences might be somewhat different, and a closer look at these would show what moved him along from moment to moment. The example helps check out the theory in my own mind; an analogous set of explanatory rubrics makes sense of myself. To the extent that sociology becomes a powerful theory, it should illuminate more and more surely the lives we see around us.

REFERENCES

Baltzell, E. Digby. 1958 *An American Business Aristocracy.* New York. Macmillan.

Bendix, Reinhard. 1956. *Work and Authority in Industry.* New York: Wiley.

Bourdieu, Pierre, and Jean-Claude Passeron. 1970/1977. *Reproduction: in Education, Society, and Culture.* Beverly Hills: Sage Publications.

Collins, Randall. 1971 "Functional and Conflict Theories of Educational Stratification." *American Sociological Review* 36: 1002–19.

Dahrendorf, Ralf. 1959. *Class and Class Conflict in Industrial Society.* Stanford: Stanford University Press.

Demerath, N.J., III 1965. *Social Class in American Protestantism.* Chicago: Rand McNally.

Form, William H. and Joan Rytina. 1969. "Ideological beliefs on the distribution of power in the United States." *American Sociological Review* 34: 19–30.

Gabennesch, H. 1972. "Authoritarianism as world view." *American Journal of Sociology* 77:857–75.

Gans, Herbert J. 1967. *The Levittowners.* New York: Random House.

Gastil, R. D. 1971. "Homicide and a regional culture of violence." *American Sociological Review* 36: 412–26.

Glenn, Norval D. and J. P. Alston 1968. "Cultural differences among occupational categories." *American Sociological Review* 33: 365–82.

Hagedorn, R. and S. Labowitz. 1968. "Participation in community associations by occupation." *American Sociological Review* 33: 272–83.

Kahl, Joseph A. 1957. *The American Class Structure.* New York: Holt.

Kohn, Melvin L. 1971. "Bureaucratic Man: a Portrait and an Interpretation." *American Sociological Review* 36: 461–74.

Kohn, Melvin L., and Carmi L. Schooler. 1969. "Class, occupation, and orientation." *American Sociological Review* 34: 659–78.

Liebow, Elliot. 1967. *Tally's Corner*. Boston: Little, Brown.

March, James G., and Herbert A. Simon. 1958. *Organizations*. New York: Wiley.

Marx, Karl. 1963. [original 1852] *The Eighteenth Brumaire of Louis Bonaparte*. New York: International Publishers.

McArthur, C. 1955. "Personality differences between middle and upper classes." *Journal of Abnormal and Social Psychology*. 50: 247–54.

Pearlin, Leonard I. and Melvin L. Kohn. 1966. "Social class, occupation, and parental values: a cross-national study." *American Sociological Review* 31: 466–79.

Rainwater, L., R. P. Coleman, and G. Handel. 1962. *Workingman's Wife*. New York: Macfadden.

Roach, J. L. and O. R. Gersslin. 1967. "An evaluation of the concept 'culture of poverty'." *Social Forces* 45: 384–92.

Seeley, J. R., R. A. Sim, and E. W. Loosley. 1956. *Crestwood Heights*. New York: Basic Books.

Vidich, Arthur J. and Joseph Bensman. 1968. *Small Town in Mass Society*. Princeton: Princeton University Press.

Weber, Max. 1968 (original 1922). *Economy and Society*. Edited by Guenter Roth and Klaus Wittich. New York: Bedminster Press.

Whitt, H. P., C. C. Gordon, and J. R. Hofley. 1972. "Religion, economic development, and lethal aggression." *American Sociological Review* 37: 193–201.

Wilensky, Harold L. and H. Edwards. 1959. "The skidder: ideological adjustments of downwardly mobile workers." *American Sociological Review* 24: 215–31.

II THE RATIONAL/UTILITARIAN TRADITION

Some Main Points of the Rational/Utilitarian Tradition

1690	Locke, social contract	
1720	Mandeville, private vices and public virtue	
1740	Hume Hartley association of ideas	
1760–1780	Adam Smith, moral sympathy	
		laissez-faire economics
1800	Bentham, utilitarian legal reform	
1860	J. S. Mill, utilitarian ethics	
1870–1900	Bradley Moore anti-utilitarian ethics	academic economics general equilibrium
	Durkheim criticizes social contract	
1930	Waller, sex and marriage markets	
1940	game theory	
1950	prisoner's dilemma	
		Downs, economic theory of democracy
	March and Simon, satisficing	
1960	Homans Blau exchange theory	Riker, minimum winning coalition
	Olson, free rider	
		Schelling, coercive coaltions crime and illegal markets
1970	distributive justice	Rawls, theory of justice
	Kahneman and Tversky choice anomalies educational inflation split labor market	Buchanan, public choice
1980	Cook Willer power in exchange networks	state protection rent
	Harrison White, market networks	Hechter Coleman solidarity theory
1990		

Social Exchange among Equals and Unequals [1961]

GEORGE C. HOMANS

• *George Homans launched social exchange theory in the 1950s. Synthesizing several decades of research on small groups, Homans attempted to demonstrate that there is a pattern of individual interactions underlying every social institution. His claim that the rewards and costs experienced by human actors are the basis of all sociological explanations set off the micro-macro debate. In this selection, he shows that the famous "Homans' Law"—interaction increases liking and conformity, provided that it takes place among social equals—can be derived from principles of exchange.*

In my earlier book *The Human Group* I stated the proposition that, other things equal, "persons who interact with one another frequently are more like one another in their activities than they are like other persons with whom they interact less frequently,"[1] and I cited evidence that this was true of at least a few groups. In the present book we have encountered further evidence on the relation between personal similarities, on the one hand, and liking and interaction, on the other. . . . Swedish university students showed some tendency to choose others with scores near or equal to their own as well as others with better scores; and . . . persons with similar backgrounds and hence similar values were particularly apt to reward and like one another.

We have also encountered evidence that the similarity in question is often a similarity in esteem or recognized status: that is, the persons concerned are social equals. By equality we do not mean the equality of all members of a group but equality within layers or strata—the rough equality with one another of members who are at the same time superior or inferior to others. Thus the Swedish students showed some tendency to choose students from their own school within the university—students, that is, whose status was equal to their own in the recognized ranking of schools. And . . . in the study of interaction among American high school students, the students tended to receive most interaction from others who fell within their own or neighboring status-classes.

Finally, we saw . . . that when one man exercises authority over another,

From George C. Homans, *Social Behavior: Its Elementary Forms.* New York: Harcourt, Brace 1961, pp. 316–320, 323–324, 326–327, 331–334. Reprinted by permission.
[1]G. C. Homans *The Human Group,* (New York, 1950), p. 135; see also p. 243.

both parties, besides reaping rewards from the interaction, also incur costs, and that these costs lead them sooner or later to escape to the society of their equals—that is, to the society of people to whom they are neither superior nor inferior in authority. With equals, they are particularly apt to be relaxed and at their ease, and they are particularly apt to seek out their equals on "social" occasions in the special sense of "social," meaning occasions when there is no compelling job to be done.

In the present chapter we shall try to understand that these phenomena are not independent but, on the contrary, are often related to one another so as to form a complex of behavior. We shall try to understand why persons who are similar to one another in some respect are apt also to be social equals; why equals are apt to interact with one another and find one another rewarding when the cost of interacting with superiors or inferiors is high; why these occasions are often "social" occasions; and why equals tend to feel particularly at their ease with one another.

EQUALITY AND INEQUALITY IN PRIMITIVE EXCHANGE

Rather than plunging into equality directly, we shall creep up to it roundabout. Social behavior is an exchange of rewards (and costs) between persons. Sometimes a man has good reason for exchanging with another who is in some sense his superior, and sometimes he has good reason for exchanging with another who is his equal. Both tendencies are always present, and we are now interested in the relation between the two. We also believe that the propositions we put forward hold good of all men everywhere. The kinds of things men find rewarding differ from society to society and from group to group within a society, but propositions about the nature of elementary exchange itself, apart from the kinds of things exchanged, hold good of all men. That in this respect at least human nature is the same the world over is a matter of faith with us. We certainly have not tried to prove that it is so, and the research we have cited comes almost wholly from a single society, that of the United States of America. But because it provides some evidence to justify our faith and also serves as a useful introduction to the nature and consequences of the two tendencies—to exchange with a superior and to exchange with an equal—we shall take a little time to study exchange in so-called primitive societies.

In particular, we shall study the exchange of material goods. Over many centuries modern man has developed institutions, beginning with the market, that have tended to take the exchange of material goods out of the domain of elementary social behavior. He has tried to make this sort of exchange impersonal and has pretty well succeeded. When I go into a drugstore and pay money for toothpaste, the exchange implies almost nothing about, does almost nothing to create, a personal tie between the clerk and myself. The segregation of economic exchange from other social relations is always breaking down, and on some occasions, like the exchange of Christmas presents, a little of the older attitude persists. But on the whole in modern societies the exchange of goods is far more impersonal than it is in primitive ones. There it is Christmas all year long: the exchange of goods always has implications for the personal ties between people, and so we speak of it as gift exchange instead of buying and selling.

The assumptions primitive people make about exchange are well summarized in Marcel Mauss' famous little book, *Essai sur le don*.[2] If Primitive Person gives something to Primitive Other, Other is generally bound to return something of equal value according to the terms of exchange current in the tribe in question. If, indeed, Person covets something that Other owns, he will try, like an "operator" in our own society, to force a gift on Other so that he can establish a claim on him—a phenomenon that the pioneers of North America, who were already accustomed to more impersonal rules of exchange, called "Indian giving." Person is in a good position to force Other to accept the gift, for to refuse it would be a refusal to enter into exchange and thus equivalent to a declaration of hostilities: the man who refuses has deprived the other of what he wants.

Should he accept the gift, Other may try to return an object of slightly greater value—which gives rise in primitive societies to something a little like interest, especially if some time goes by before Other makes the return. But the important point is this: just as failure to accept a gift implies hostility, so taking the gift and making a fair return implies friendship. And more than friendship: it also implies that the exchanges will continue indefinitely, that the two have become trading partners, and that, if either party breaks off the exchange later, he has declared hostilities just as much as if he had refused a gift in the first place. With the primitives as with us, an exchange of rewards between two men leads to their friendship and further interaction. But the primitives have gone further than we have in turning what happens into a set of rules about what ought to happen. Where we have institutionalized the market, they have institutionalized the gift.

Should Other spurn the gift, he admits himself an enemy. Should he take it and make a fair return, he becomes a friend. But what if he takes it and fails to make a return? Since the man that makes a fair return is by that fact the giver's

---

[2]M. Mauss, *The Gift*, I. Cunnison, trans. (Glencoe, Ill., 1954); see also D.L. Oliver, *A Solomon Island Society* (Cambridge, Mass., 1955), pp. 335–448.

social equal—he has demonstrated his ability to provide equally rare and valuable rewards—the man that fails to do so confesses himself neither the giver's enemy nor his friend but his inferior. He loses status relative to the giver. What is more, he may, in becoming an inferior, become also a subordinate: the only way he can pay his debt may be to accept the orders of the giver. . . . Something of the same sort occurs in our own society.

The point is that to take a gift and fail to make a return is to incur cost in the form of social inferiority. The gift may be so valuable, Other may need it so badly, that he may take it, accept the cost, and still feel he has done well. But again he may not, and much will depend on his past history. If up until this time he has been Person's social inferior, he will not feel the cost much. By the rule of status congruence, his inferiority in exchange is in line with his inferiority in other respects, and so he loses no further status. But if he has so far been Person's equal, he will feel the cost much more: he will have come down in the world.

The secondary mechanisms of human behavior ride on the backs of the primary ones. Men learn new kinds of behavior whose rewards depend upon the fact that the old are already recognized. That taking a gift one cannot return from a man hitherto one's equal is to confess one's inferiority to him is not only a generalization about actual behavior; it is also a rule a man can turn to his own advantage. He can now with deliberate intent give others gifts they cannot repay in order to humiliate them and make them his inferiors. The final twist of primitive gift giving is the *potlatch* of the Indians of the Northwest Coast: two men of high status try to snow each other under with gifts; the one whose presents fail to match the other's in value loses face, fiercely resents the victor's triumph, and vows social revenge. But the Northwest Coast only carries to a bizarre extreme what is implicit in all primitive gift giving—and some not so primitive. One has from time to time detected the same overtones in the giving of Christmas gifts in modern North America. After all, the differences between the primitives and ourselves are only matters of degree.

These rules apply not only to gifts of material objects but also to the rendering of services. Anyone who accepts from another a service he cannot repay in kind incurs inferiority as a cost of receiving the service. The esteem he gives the other he forgoes himself. The service may be valuable enough to outweigh the cost and return him a profit, but the cost is there. We already have reason to believe that it may not be the only cost he incurs in interacting with his social superiors. Even an American, at any rate, will often hesitate before he asks a favor or help, of a kind he cannot return, from someone who has hitherto been his equal. In these circumstances a man must be a true Christian who fails to feel or, worse, to show his inferiority if he asks for help or his superiority if he gives it.

EQUALITY AND SIMILARITY

With this introduction we are ready to enter upon our main line of argument, using for supporting evidence the research at the New York State Training School for Girls. . . . It was not just their similarity in values, their liking and doing the same things, that led girls to choose for leisure other girls whose esteem in the larger group was equal to their own. If the commonest explanation was that "she likes the same things I do," the next was that "I can be myself with her." But this very explanation implied that a girl could not be herself with everybody, that with some people she felt under constraint. In interacting with some people she incurred, in our language, costs.

What were these costs and where were they incurred? . . . Persons held in high esteem are also apt to hold high authority, and that persons who submit to authority are apt to incur some costs in doing so. We must now consider in more general terms the costs of inferiority. A person held in high esteem is one that has been accorded social approval by many others; and so if two or more different spheres of activity are open to members of a group, the sphere in which esteem is won—and lost—is the more public one, the one in which the larger number of members is brought together. At Hudson this was the sphere of living and working, in cottages and shops. Here a few girls won high esteem by providing services much in demand by many others, but here too, by the same token, the girls that did not win much esteem found their inadequacies shown up. The process that put some up put others down: one man's superiority implies another's inferiority. No doubt the girls were glad to get the services of their superiors, but the price they paid was a tacit confession of their own inferiority.

The girls of high esteem, moreover, in whom others could find little to criticize, felt free in the course of exercising their authority to criticize others. And even if a girl of lesser rank managed to escape criticism and live up to some of the public norms of the group, she was likely to find the effort painful. Whatever offsetting advantages she got from living and working with the rest, her conspicuous inadequacy, the criticism she received, and the strain of measuring up to group standards were costs to her, costs that tended to increase as the working day went on, until she was ready to escape. In the nature of the case she could best escape by leaving the public sphere for the private sphere of leisure and by associating at leisure with her social equals. For the girls below *her* had just as much reason for wanting to escape from her as she had for wanting to escape from those above. The only girls left were her equals, but equals are people who emit equally valuable activities. Accordingly they can exchange rewards on even terms and thus escape the costs of inferiority. Her equals could not make a girl feel inferior—nor could she make them feel so. Only with them, therefore, could she relax and "be herself," free of judging or being judged, and only them could she really "like" in the American sense of liking; for "liking" implies an absence of constraint, and constraint is rarely absent from our relations with superiors.

.   .   .

We have explained the tendency for people to interact with their equals by showing why an inferior has some reason *not* to interact with a superior, especially when at leisure. But . . . a superior also has reason to avoid an inferior under the same circumstances: the avoidance may be mutual. And again status congruence comes in to strengthen the tendency. For once the equation between social equality and interaction during leisure gets established as a recognized social fact, then a man who associates with his inferior under these conditions tends to suggest to his companions that he is not really the other's superior but only his equal after all. By the rule of status congruence he tends to cast doubt on his own superior status, and thus, as we know so well, our pretended superiors often try to avoid being seen with us on "social" occasions. Alas! that the laws of elementary social behavior should be the laws of snobbery—but they are.

On the other hand, a man whose superior status is so firmly established that he need not worry about it, a man who has reached the condition we call social certitude, may allow his inferiors "social" access to him. His status is congruent on so many counts that he can afford to let it be incongruent on this one. Association with him can bring up the apparent status of others and thus reward them, and accordingly he has gained a new way of earning their esteem to add to those he commands already. But note that we have now argued ourselves into assuming two contradictory tendencies: both a tendency for inferiors to avoid interaction with superiors and for them to seek it. Which tendency gets the better of the other seems to depend on the degree to which the relative status of the two parties is established and unshakable.

The association between social equality and interaction on what Americans call "social" occasions—spending leisure time, going to parties, or eating in company—is a conspicuous feature of status, class, and caste system in all times and places. The explanation of the phenomena is not simply that people similar in status are apt also to be similar in other respects, and so apt to reward one another. This plays its part, but it does not altogether account for the prominence of the fact that the interaction is "social." Status is won or inherited in the more public sphere of activity, the sphere in which rather large numbers of people are related to one another, the sphere, like making a living, in which very valuable rewards are to be gained. Because the rewards are high, people will pay highly for them. They will be ready to accept them from others at the cost, for instance, of confessed inferiority to the others. But the more such rewards they get, the less their value becomes and the higher their cost. The time when the profit men get from transactions of this kind sinks toward zero is apt, in the nature of the case, to be the time when "work," however it be defined, is coming to an end and "social" life beginning. In the nature of the case too, men can escape the costs of associating with their superiors only by seeking out the society of their equals; for their own inferiors have the same reasons for avoiding *them* as they have for avoiding their superiors. What their equals have to offer them in the "social" sphere may not be inherently very valuable, though it becomes relatively valuable to the degree that the higher priorities have already been met, but whatever its value it is at least purchased at low cost. For these reasons social equals are apt to spend some of their time interacting with one another on "social" occasions.

A RESULTANT OF SUPERIORITY AND EQUALITY

In earlier chapters and now in this one we have encountered two tendencies: a tendency for men to express approval of, and to interact often with, others who are in some sense "better" than they, and a tendency for men to like and interact with their equals. It is at least conceivable that under some circumstances, especially when no sharp distinction can be made between "work" and "leisure," the two tendencies might combine to produce a resultant tendency for men to interact with, and express liking for, others who are a little "better" than they are themselves but not much better—to choose "up" but only a little "up."

.   .   .

We have seen that equals tend to like and interact with one another particularly on "social" occasions. But how about people who fall short of complete equality, particularly people who, just because they are nearly equal, find that their status relative to one another is in doubt? Earlier we gave brief consideration to the effects of social certitude and incertitude on the interaction between men, and now we must return to the problem. In this field we possess very few good studies, which gives us all the more reason to consider one whose results were clear-cut even though it is less concerned with elementary social behavior and more concerned with status as formally recognized in society at large than we should like it to be.

The research in question was carried out by Zander, Cohen, and Stotland.[3] In six large American cities the investigators and their associates interviewed three different kinds of professional people concerned with mental health: psychiatrists, psychologists, and social workers. In all, they interviewed about 150 members of each profession. They first asked each subject to assess the authority and influence of members of the other two professions in comparison with his own authority and influence. As we should expect from our general knowledge of American society, all three professions agreed that the psychiatrists, who of course held medical degrees, had more authority and influence than the other two groups—though the psychologists and social workers were not quite as sure about it as the psychiatrists were themselves. As for the relation between psychologists and social workers, these two professions saw themselves as about equal in power.

The investigators then asked each subject to say how much he wanted to be respected and liked by members of the other two professions and to have professional and social contacts with them. In accordance with the higher status of the psychiatrists, the other groups were more likely to express such wishes about psychiatrists than the psychiatrists were to express them about the other groups. And in accordance with their higher recognized authority, the psychiatrists were more ready to complain about the behavior of the other two professions than the other two were to complain about the psychiatrists.

Much more interesting and much closer to elementary social behavior were the differences within each profession. Those psychologists and social workers who saw themselves as having relatively high power expressed less desire for professional or social contact with psychiatrists than did psychologists and social workers who saw themselves as having little power. Among the psychiatrists, on the other hand, the relationship reversed itself, and those psychiatrists who saw themselves as having relatively high power expressed more desire for contact with members of the other professions than did psychiatrists who saw themselves as having little power. We may guess that most of the people who believed they had relatively high or low power must in fact have held high or low status, respectively, within their professions. And then we may say that the people who wanted least contact with the other group were the low-status members of the high-status group (the psychiatrists) and the high-status members of the low-status group (the psychologists and social workers). That is, the persons closest in status wanted least contact. This finding may seem to run counter to our proposition that equals will seek out interaction with one another, but we must

[3]A. Zander, A.R. Cohen, and E. Stotland, "Power and the Relations among Professions," in D. Cartwright, ed., *Studies in Social Power* (Ann Arbor, 1959), pp. 15–34.

remember that we are not concerned with equals here: by the standards of American society psychiatrists in general are accorded higher status than the other two professions. We are concerned instead with people who, though divided by status, were still relatively close to one another.

As we saw earlier, a man established as another's equal hesitates before doing anything that might suggest his inferiority to the other; but a man already established as the other's inferior shows no such hesitation. In the present case, there is no question of absolute equality, yet something of the same sort occurred. In the presence of two broad status-classes, the members of the lower class who stood highest within their class were most anxious to avoid contact with members of the upper class, presumably because such contacts would have given the upper class a chance to remind them of an inferiority they were far from feeling within their own group. If frequent social contacts could have ended, as they do in some cases of social climbing, by winning for a psychologist full acceptance as a member of the upper class, no doubt he would have been more eager to make them. But only a medical degree could make him a psychiatrist, and in these circumstances he had little to gain and much to lose by mere interaction. In the same way, the members of the upper class who stood lowest within their class were most anxious to avoid contacts with members of the lower class, presumably because they might have had a hard time maintaining, over against these others, a superiority they were far from feeling within their own group. But the members of the upper class who were firmly established as high in status and the members of the lower class who were firmly established as low had nothing to lose by the contacts and welcomed them at least as a possibility. These people were more congruent in status than the others, who were either low men in a high group or high men in a low group. We are forcibly reminded of the classic peasant who, because after all "he knows his place," can speak up to the lord of the manor, and of the lord who can be perfectly at ease with "the lower orders" because after all they cannot conceivably unnerve his effortless superiority. It is the *bourgeois*, the man in the middle, who is nervous about his relations with other classes.

Phenomena like this bear a family resemblance to what anthropologists have come to call alternate generations. In some primitive kinship systems, the members of the two generations that are closest to one another, like fathers and sons, are apt to express respect rather than close affection for one another and to avoid one another except when required to work together. But members of alternate generations—that is, generations separated by an intervening one, like grandfathers and grandsons—cannot be rivals and are apt in consequence to express close affection for one another and to interact frequently and easily. In the one case the differences in status are determined by generation and in the other by differences in occupation, but in both cases the persons nearest in status, short of complete equality, are the persons whose relations are most strained.

SUMMARY

Unless all the members of a group are equal, social equality between any two of them implies that the members have previously become differentiated in esteem and then in recognized status. Men win high esteem by providing for many others services that the others cannot return except in the form of esteem and obedience. Though these services are rewarding, they are also costly, one of the costs being the status a man loses by the very fact of giving it to another. But as men get their fill of the rewards by persons of high esteem, other rewards, the rewards of sociability, increase in relative value. Men can best get these rewards outside the public sphere of activity, in which esteem is won and lost, and therefore inside the sphere of "social" life; and they can best get them from people neither superior nor inferior to themselves by the standards of the public sphere. Social equals are people who provide equally valuable services, therefore they can exchange on equal terms; and though the services may not be very valuable in themselves, they at least cost nothing in confessed inferiority. Accordingly a man's social behavior displays two tendencies: a tendency to interact with, and repect, persons in some sense "better" than himself and a tendency to interact with, and like, persons in some sense similar to himself. The two are not independent tendencies but closely dependent on each other. Finally, though equals tend to interact with one another, people who are nearly equal but still different in status—and because nearly equal most in doubt about their relative status—these people may not be ready to test their social standing and so may tend to avoid one another. This means further that the tendency for a man to interact with his "betters" may be especially strong when he is not just a little inferior to them but definitely a good deal inferior.

Bounded Rationality and Satisficing [1958]

JAMES G. MARCH AND HERBERT A. SIMON

• *The theory of bounded rationality is the beginning of the so-called neo-rationalist school which has influenced much of the creative work in the renaissance of utilitarian thinking. Here March and Simon examine the organizational manager and argue that the traditional goal of optimizing results is impossible under conditions of complexity, combined with the limits of human cognitive capacities. The most rational pattern of decision-making is instead satisficing—selecting a few salient problem areas to concentrate upon while allowing routine to prevail elsewhere as long as satisfactory levels are maintained.*

COGNITIVE LIMITS ON RATIONALITY

How does the rationality of "administrative man" compare with that of classical "economic man" or with the rational man of modern statistical decision theory? The rational man of economics and statistical decision theory makes "optimal" choices in a highly specified and clearly defined environment:

1. When we first encounter him in the decision-making situation, he already has laid out before him the whole set of alternatives from which he will choose his action. This set of alternatives is simply "given"; the theory does not tell how it is obtained.

2. To each alternative is attached a set of consequences—the events that will ensue if that particular alternative is chosen. Here the existing theories fall into three categories: (*a*) *Certainty:* theories that assume the decision maker has complete and accurate knowledge of the consequences that will follow on each alternative. (*b*) *Risk:* theories that assume accurate knowledge of a probability distribution of the consequences of each alternative. (*c*) *Uncertainty:* theories that assume that the consequences of each alternative belong to some subset of all possible consequences, but that the decision maker cannot assign definite probabilities to the occurrence of particular consequences.

3. At the outset, the decision maker has a "utility function" or a "preference-

From James G. March and Herbert A. Simon, *Organizations*. New York: Wiley, 1958, pp. 137–141, 169–170. Reprinted by permission of James G. March and Basil Blackwell, Ltd.

ordering" that ranks all sets of consequences from the most preferred to the
least preferred.

4. The decision maker selects the alternative leading to the preferred set of
consequences. In the case of *certainty*, the choice is unambiguous. In the
case of *risk*, rationality is usually defined as the choice of that alternative
for which the expected utility is greatest. Expected utility is defined here as
the average, weighted by the probabilities of occurrence, of the utilities
attached to all possible consequences. In the case of *uncertainty*, the
definition of rationality becomes problematic. One proposal that has had
wide currency is the rule of "minimax risk": consider the worst set of
consequences that may follow from each alternative, then select the alternative whose "worse set of consequences" is preferred to the worst sets
attached to other alternatives. There are other proposals (e.g., the rule of
"minimax regret"), but we shall not discuss them here.

Some Difficulties in the Classical Theory

There are difficulties with this model of rational man. In the first place, only in
the case of certainty does it agree well with common-sense notions of rationality.
In the case of uncertainty, especially, there is little agreement, even among
exponents of statistical decision theory, as to the "correct" definition, or
whether, indeed, the term "correct" has any meaning here.

A second difficulty with existing models of rational man is that it makes three
exceedingly important demands upon the choice-making mechanism. It assumes (1) that all the alternatives of choice are "given"; (2) that all the consequences attached to each alternative are known (in one of the three senses
corresponding to certainty, risk, and uncertainty repectively); (3) that the rational
man has a complete utility-ordering (or cardinal function) for all possible sets of
consequences.

One can hardly take exception to these requirements in a normative model—
a model that tells people how they *ought* to choose. For if the rational man
lacked information, he might have chosen differently "if only he had known."
At best, he is "subjectively" rational, not "objectively" rational. But the notion of
objective rationality assumes there is some objective reality in which the "real"
alternatives, the "real" consequences, and the "real" utilities exist. If this is so, it
is not even clear why the cases of choice under risk and under uncertainty are
admitted as rational. If it is not so, it is not clear why only limitations upon
knowledge of consequences are considered, and why limitations upon knowledge of alternatives and utilities are ignored in the model of rationality.

From a phenomenological viewpoint we can only speak of rationality relative to a frame of reference; and this frame of reference will be determined by the limitations on the rational man's knowledge. We can, of course, introduce the notion of a person observing the choices of a subject, and can speak of the rationality of the subject relative to the frame of reference of the observer. If the subject is a rat and the observer is a man (especially if he is the man who designed the experimental situation), we may regard the man's perception of the situation as objective and the rat's as subjective. (We leave out of account the specific difficulty that the rat presumably knows his own utility function better than the man does.) If, however, both subject and observer are men—and particularly if the situation is a natural one not constructed for experimental purposes by the observer—then it becomes difficult to specify the objective situation. It will be safest, in such situations, to speak of rationality only relative to some specified frame of reference.

The classical organization theory . . . like classical economic theory, failed to make explicit this subjective and relative character of rationality, and in so doing, failed to examine some of its own crucial premises. The organizational and social environment in which the decision maker finds himself determines what consequences he will anticipate, what ones he will not; what alternatives he will consider, what ones he will ignore. In a theory of organization these variables cannot be treated as unexplained independent factors, but must themselves be determined and predicted by the theory.

Routinized and Problem-Solving Responses

The theory of rational choice put forth here incorporates two fundamental characteristics: (1) Choice is always exercised with respect to a limited, approximate, simplified "model" of the real situation. We call the chooser's model his "definition of the situation." (2) The elements of the definition of the situation are not "given"—that is, we do not take these as data of our theory—but are themselves the outcome of psychological and sociological processes, including the chooser's own activities and the activities of others in his environment.

Activity (individual or organizational) can usually be traced back to an environmental stimulus of some sort, e.g., a customer order or a fire gong. The responses to stimuli are of various kinds. At one extreme, a stimulus evokes a response—sometimes very elaborate—that has been developed and learned at some previous time as an appropriate response for a stimulus of this class. This is the "routinized" end of the continuum, where a stimulus calls forth a performance program almost instantaneously.

At the other extreme, a stimulus evokes a larger or smaller amount of problem-solving activity directed toward finding performance activities with which to complete the response. Such activity is distinguished by the fact that it can be dispensed with once the performance program has been learned. Problem-solving activities can generally be identified by the extent to which they involve *search*: search aimed at discovering alternatives of action or consequences of action. "Discovering" alternatives may involve inventing and elaborating whole performance programs where these are not already available in the problem solver's repertory.

When a stimulus is of a kind that has been experienced repeatedly in the past, the response will ordinarily be highly routinized. The stimulus will evoke, with a minimum of problem-solving or other computational activity, a well-structured definition of the situation that will include a repertory of response programs, and programs for selecting an appropriate specific response from the repertory. When a stimulus is relatively novel, it will evoke problem-solving activity aimed initially at constructing a definition of the situation and then at developing one or more appropriate performance programs.

Psychologists (e.g., Wertheimer, Duncker, de Groot, Maier) and observant laymen (e.g.,Poincaré, Hadamard) who have studied creative thinking and problem-solving have been unanimous in ascribing a large role in these phenomena to search processes. Search is partly random, but in effective problem-solving it is not blind. The design of the search process is itself often an object of rational decision. Thus, we may distinguish substantive planning—developing new performance programs—from procedural planning—developing programs for the problem-solving process itself. The response to a particular stimulus may involve more than performance—the stimulus may evoke a spate of problem-solving activity—but the problem-solving activity may itself be routinized to a greater or lesser degree. For example, search processes may be systematized by the use of check lists.

Satisfactory Versus Optimal Standards

What kinds of search and other problem-solving activity are needed to discover an adequate range of alternatives and consequences for choice depends on the criterion applied to the choice. In particular, finding the optimal alternative is a radically different problem from finding a satisfactory alternative. An alternative is *optimal* if: (1) there exists a set of criteria that permits all alternatives to be compared, and (2) the alternative in question is preferred, by these criteria, to all other alternatives. An alternative is *satisfactory* if: (1) there exists a set of criteria that describes minimally satisfactory alternatives, and (2) the alternative in question meets or exceeds all these criteria.

Most human decision-making, whether individual or organizational, is con-

cerned with the discovery and selection of satisfactory alternatives; only in exceptional cases is it concerned with the discovery and selection of optimal alternatives. To optimize requires processes several orders of magnitude more complex
than those required to satisfice. An example is the difference between searching
a haystack to find the *sharpest* needle in it and searching the haystack to find a
needle sharp enough to sew with.

In making choices that meet satisfactory standards, the standards themselves
are part of the definition of the situation. Hence, we need not regard these as
given—any more than the other elements of the definition of the situation—
but may include in the theory the processes through which these standards are
set and modified. The standard-setting process may itself meet standards of
rationality: for example, an "optimizing" rule would be to set the standard at
the level where the marginal improvement in alternatives obtainable by raising
it would be just balanced by the marginal cost of searching for alternatives
meeting the higher standard. Of course, in practice the "marginal improvement" and the "marginal cost" are seldom measured in comparable units, or
with much accuracy. Nevertheless, a similar result would be automatically
attained if the standards were raised whenever alternatives proved easy to
discover, and lowered whenever they were difficult to discover. Under these
circumstances, the alternatives chosen would not be far from the optima, if the
cost of search were taken into consideration. Since human standards tend to
have this characteristic under many conditions, some theorists have sought to
maintain the optimizing model by introducing cost-of-search considerations.
Although we doubt whether this will be a fruitful alternative to the model we
are proposing in very many situations, neither model has been used for predic-
tive purposes often enough to allow a final judgment.

ORGANIZATION STRUCTURE AND THE BOUNDARIES
OF RATIONALITY

It has been the central theme of this chapter that the basic features of organization structure and function derive from the characteristics of human problem-
solving processes and rational human choice. Because of the limits of human
intellective capacities in comparison with the complexities of the problems
that individuals and organizations face, rational behavior calls for simplified
models that capture the main features of a problem without capturing all its
complexities.

The simplifications have a number of characteristic features: (1) Optimizing
is replaced by satisficing—the requirement that satisfactory levels of the criterion variables be attained. (2) Alternatives of action and consequences of action

are discovered sequentially through search processes. (3) Repertories of action programs are developed by organizations and individuals, and these serve as the alternatives of choice in recurrent situations. (4) Each specific action program deals with a restricted range of situations and a restricted range of consequences. (5) Each action program is capable of being executed in semi-independence of the others—they are only loosely coupled together.

Action is goal-oriented and adaptive. But because of its approximating and fragmented character, only a few elements of the system are adaptive at any one time; the remainder are, at least in the short run, "givens." So, for example, an individual or organization may attend to improving a particular program, or to selecting an appropriate program from the existing repertory to meet a particular situation. Seldom can both be attended to simultaneously.

The notion that rational behavior deals with a few components at a time was first developed extensively in connection with economic behavior by John R. Commons, who spoke of "limiting factors" that become the foci of attention and adaptation. Commons' theory was further developed by Chester I. Barnard, who preferred the term "strategic factor."

This "one-thing-at-a-time" or "*ceteris paribus*" approach to adaptive behavior is fundamental to the very existence of something we can call "organization structure." Organization structure consists simply of those aspects of the pattern of behavior in the organization that are relatively stable and that change only slowly. If behavior in organizations is "intendedly rational," we will expect aspects of the behavior to be relatively stable that either (*a*) represent adaptations to relatively stable elements in the environment, of (*b*) are the learning programs that govern the process of adaptation.

An organization is confronted with a problem like that of Archimedes: in order for an organization to behave adaptively, it needs some stable regulations and procedures that it can employ in carrying out its adaptive practices. Thus, at any given time an organization's programs for performing its tasks are part of its structure, but the least stable part. Slightly more stable are the switching rules that determine when it will apply one program, and when another. Still more stable are the procedures it uses for developing, elaborating, instituting, and revising programs.

The matter may be stated differently. If an organization has a repertory of programs, then it is adaptive in the short run insofar as it has procedures for selecting from this repertory a program appropriate to each specific situation that arises. The process used to select an appropriate program is the "fulcrum" on which short-run adaptiveness rests. If, now, the organization has processes for adding to its repertory of programs or for modifying programs in the repertory, these processes become still more basic fulcra for accomplishing longer-run adaptiveness. Short-run adaptiveness corresponds to what we ordinarily call problem-solving, long-run adaptiveness to learning.

There is no reason, of course, why this hierarchy of mechanisms should have only three levels—or any specified number. In fact, the adaptive mechanisms need not be arranged hierarchically. Mechanism A may include mechanism B within its domain of action, and vice versa. However, in general there is much asymmetry in the ordering, so that certain elements in the process that do not often become strategic factors (the "boundaries of rationality") form the stable core of the organization structure.

We can now see the relation between Commons' and Barnard's theories of the "limiting" or "strategic" factor and organization structure. Organization will have structure, as we have defined the term here, insofar as there are boundaries of rationality—insofar as there are elements of the situation that must be or are in fact taken as givens, and that do not enter into rational calculations as potential strategic factors. If there were not boundaries to rationality, or if the boundaries varied in a rapid and unpredictable manner, there could be no stable organization structure.

Coordination [1962]

THOMAS C. SCHELLING

• *The strategy of decision-making has been analyzed since the 1940s by means of game theory. In classical game theory, each player knows what the payoff matrix will be for oneself and for one's counterpart player; what he or she doesn't know is which option the other will choose. In the 1960s, Thomas Schelling pointed out a class of situations which he calls a "coordination game". Here both parties will win if they can come to the same decision, but they know nothing about the range of choices and cannot communicate with each other. Schelling's interest was in showing that some solutions to the coordination game exist even during military combat, and these are important for controlling the threat of nuclear war. His model of tacit coordination has important applications to situations of coercive power, where an authoritarian regime keeps itself in power by preventing the coordination of a coalition among its opponents. Conversely, dictatorships fall at sudden "tipping points" which are analogous to the "bandwagon effect" in crowd behavior or politics.*

When a man loses his wife in a department store without any prior understanding on where to meet if they get separated, the chances are good that they will find each other. It is likely that each will think of some obvious place to meet, so obvious that each will be sure that the other is sure that it is "obvious" to both of them. One does not simply predict where the other will go, since the other will go where he predicts the first to go, which is wherever the first predicts the second to predict the first to go, and so ad infinitum. Not "What would I do if I were she?" but "What would I do if I were she wondering what she would do if she were wondering what I would do if I were she . . . ?" What is necessary is to coordinate predictions, to read the same message in the common situation, to identify the one course of action that their expectations of each other can converge on. They must

Reprinted by permission of the publishers from *The Strategy of Conflict* by Thomas C. Schelling, Cambridge, MA: Harvard University Press, © 1960 by the President and Fellows of Harvard College. pp. 54–60, 72–74, 90–92.

"mutually recognize" some unique signal that coordinates their expectations of each other. We cannot be sure they will meet, nor would all couples read the same signal; but the chances are certainly a great deal better than if they pursued a random course of search.

The reader may try the problem himself with the adjoining map. Two people parachute unexpectedly into the area shown, each with a map and knowing the other has one, but neither knowing where the other has dropped nor able to communicate directly. They must get together quickly to be rescued. Can they study their maps and "coordinate" their behavior? Does the map suggest some particular meeting place so unambiguously that each will be confident that the other reads the same suggestion with confidence?

The writer has tried this and other analogous problems on an unscientific sample of respondents; and the conclusion is that people often can coordinate. The following abstract puzzles are typical of those that can be "solved" by a substantial proportion of those who try. The solutions are, of course, arbitrary to this extent: any solution is "correct" if enough people think so. The reader may

River   Road   Building   Pond

wish to confirm his ability to concert in the following problems with those whose scores are given in a footnote.[1]

1. Name "heads" or "tails." If you and your partner name the same, you both win a prize.
2. Circle one of the numbers listed in the line below. You win if you all succeed in circling the same number.

7   100   13   261   99   555

3. Put a check mark in one of the sixteen squares. You win if you all succeed in checking the same square.

☐ ☐ ☐ ☐

☐ ☐ ☐ ☐

☐ ☐ ☐ ☐

☐ ☐ ☐ ☐

4. You are to meet somebody in New York City. You have not been instructed where to meet; you have no prior understanding with the person on where to meet; and you cannot communicate with each other. You are simply told that you will have to guess where to meet and that he is being told the same thing and that you will just have to try to make your guesses coincide.
5. You were told the date but not the hour of the meeting in No. 4; the two of you must guess the exact minute of the day for meeting. At what time will you appear at the meeting place that you elected in No. 4?
6. Write some positive number. If you all write the same number, you win.
7. Name an amount of money. If you all name the same amount, you can have as much as you named.

<hr>

[1]In the writer's sample, 36 persons concerted on "heads" in problem 1, and only 6 chose "tails." In problem 2, the first three numbers were given 37 votes out of a total of 41; the number 7 led 100 by a slight margin, with 13 in third place. The upper left corner in problem 3 received 24 votes out of a total of 41, and all but 3 of the remainder were distributed in the same diagonal line. Problem 4, which may reflect the location of the sample in New Haven, Connecticut, showed an absolute majority managing to get together at Grand Central Station (information booth), and virtually all of them succeeded in meeting at 12 noon. Problem 6 showed a variety of answers, but two-fifths of all persons succeeded in concerting on the number 1; and in problem 7, out of 41 people, 12 got together on $1,000,000, and only 3 entries consisted of numbers that were not a power of 10; of those 3, 2 were $64 and, in the more up-to-date version, $64,000! Problem 8 caused no difficulty to 36 out of 41, who split the total fifty-fifty. Problem 9 secured a majority of 20 out of 22 for Robinson. An alternative formulation of it, in which Jones and Robinson were tied on the first ballot at 28 votes each, was intended by the author to demonstrate the difficulty of concerting in case of tie; but the respondents surmounted the difficulty and gave Jone 16 out of 18 votes (apparently on the basis of Jones's earlier position on the list), proving the main point but overwhelming the subsidiary point in the process. In the map most nearly like the one reproduced here, 7 out of 8 respondents managed to meet at the bridge.

8. You are to divide $100 into two piles, labeled A and B. Your partner is to divide another $100 into two piles labled A and B. If you allot the same amounts to A and B, repectively, that your partner does, each of you gets $100, if your amounts differ from his, neither of you gets anything.

9. On the first ballot, candidates polled as follows:

Smith	 19	Robinson	 29
Jones	 28	White	 9
Brown	 15		

The second ballot is about to be taken. You have no interest in the outcome, except that you will be rewarded if someone gets a majority on the second ballot and you vote for the one who does. Similarly, all voters are interested only in voting with the majority, and everybody knows that this is everybody's interest. For whom do you vote on the second ballot?

These problems are artificial, but they illustrate the point. People *can* often concert their intentions or expectations with others if each knows that the other is trying to do the same. Most situations—perhaps every situation for people who are practiced at this kind of game—provide some clue for coordinating behavior, some focal point for each person's expectation of what the other expects him to expect to be expected to do. Finding the key, or rather finding *a* key—any key that is mutually recognized as the key becomes *the* key—may depend on imagination more than on logic; it may depend on analogy, precedent, accidental arrangement, symmetry, aesthetic or geometric configuration, casuistic reasoning, and who the parties are and what they know about each other. Whimsy may send the man and his wife to the "lost and found"; or logic may lead each to reflect and to expect the other to reflect on where they would have agreed to meet if they had had a prior agreement to cover the contingency. It is not being asserted that they will always find an obvious answer to the question; but the chances of their doing so are ever so much greater than the bare logic of abstract random probabilities would ever suggest.

A prime characteristic of most of these "solutions" to the problems, that is, of the clues or coordinators or focal points, is some kind of prominence or conspicuousness. But it is a prominence that depends on time and place and who the people are. Ordinary folk lost on a plane circular area may naturally go to the center to meet each other; but only one versed in mathematics would "naturally" expect to meet his partner at the center of gravity of an irregularly shaped area. Equally essential is some kind of uniqueness; the man and his wife cannot meet at the "lost and found" if the store has several. The writer's experiments with alternative maps indicate clearly that a map with many houses and a single crossroads sends people to the crossroads, while one with many crossroads and a single house sends most of them to the house. Partly this may reflect only that uniqueness conveys prominence; but it may be more important that uniqueness avoids ambiguousness. Houses may be intrinsically more prominent than anything else on the map; but if there are three of them, none more prominent than the others, there is but one chance in three of meeting at a house, and the recognition of this fact may lead to the rejection of houses as the "clue."

But in the final analysis we are dealing with imagination as much as with logic; and the logic itself is of a fairly casuistic kind. Poets may do better than logicians at this game, which is perhaps more like "puns and anagrams" than like chess. Logic helps—the large plurality accorded to the number 1 in problem 6 seems to rest on logic—but usually not until imagination has selected some clue to work on from among the concrete details of the situation.

TACIT BARGAINING (DIVERGENT INTERESTS)

A conflict of interest enters our problem if the parachutists dislike walking. With communication, which is not allowed in our problem, they would have argued or bargained over where to meet, each favoring a spot close to himself or a resting place particularly to his liking. In the absence of communication, their overriding interest is to concert ideas; and if a particular spot commands attention as the "obvious" place to meet, the winner of the bargain is simply the one who happens to be closer to it. Even if the one who is farthest from the focal point knows that he is, he cannot withhold his acquiescence and argue for a fairer division of the walking; the "proposal" for the bargain that is provided by the map itself—if, in fact, it provides one—is the only extant offer; and without communication, there is no counterproposal that can be made. The conflict gets reconciled—or perhaps we should say ignored—as a by-product of the dominant need for coordination.

"Win" and "lose" may not be quite accurate, since both may lose by comparison with what they could have agreed on through communication. If the two are actually close together and far from the lone house on the map, they might have eliminated the long walk to the house if they could have identified their locations and concerted explicitly on a place to meet between them. Or it may be that one "wins" while the other loses more than the first wins: if both are on the same side of the house and walk to it, they walk together a greater distance than they needed to, but the closer one may still have come off better than if he had had to argue it out with the other.

This last case illustrates that it may be to the advantage of one to be unable to communicate. There is room here for a motive to destroy communication or to refuse to collaborate in advance on a method of meeting if one is aware of his advantage and confident of the "solution" he forsees. In one variant of the writer's test, A knew where B was, but B had no idea where A was (and each knew how much the other knew). Most of the recipients of the B-type question-naire smugly sat tight, enjoying their ignorance, while virtually all the A-questionnaire respondents grimly acknowledged the inevitable and walked all the way to B. Better still may be to have the power to send but not to receive messages: if one can announce his position and state that his transmitter works but not his receiver, saying that he will wait where he is until the other arrives, the latter has no choice. He can make no effective counteroffer, since no counteroffer could be heard.

. . . .

The writer has tried a sample of conflicting-interest games on a number of people, including games that are biased in favor of one party or the other; and on the whole, the outcome suggests the same conclusion that was reached in the purely cooperative games. All these games require coordination; they also, however, provide several alternative choices over which the two parties' interests differ. Yet, among all the available options, some particular one usually seems to be the focal point for coordinated choice, and the party to whom it is a relatively unfavorable choice quite often takes it simply because he knows that the other will expect him to. The choices that cannot coordinate expectations are not really "available" without communication. The odd characteristic of all these games is that neither rival can gain by outsmarting the other. Each loses unless he does exactly what the other expects him to do. Each party is the prisoner or the beneficiary of their mutual expectations; no one can disavow his own expectation of what the other will expect him to expect to be expected to do. The need for agreement overrules the potential disagreement, and each must concert with the other or lose altogether.

Two opposing forces are at the points marked X and Y in a map similar to the [previous map]. The commander of each force wishes to occupy as much of the area as he can and knows the other does too. But each commander wishes to avoid an armed clash and knows the other does too. Each must send forth his troops with orders to take up a designated line and to fight if opposed. Once the troops are dispatched, the outcome depends only on the lines that the two commanders have ordered their troops to occupy. If the lines overlap, the troops will be assumed to meet and fight, to the disadvantage of both sides. If the troops take up positions that leave any appreciable space unoccupied between them, the situation will be assumed "unstable" and a clash inevitable. Only if the troops are ordered to occupy identical lines or lines that leave virtually no unoccupied space between them will clash be avoided. In that case, each side obtains successfully the area it occupies, the advantage going to the side that has the most valuable area in terms of land and facilities. You command the forces located at the point marked X (Y). Draw on the map the line that you send your troops to occupy.

The ability of the two commanders to recognize the stabilizing power of the river—or, rather, their inability not to recognize it—is substantiated by the evidence that if their survival depended on some agreement about where to stabilize their lines *and communication were not allowed*, they probably could perceive and appreciate the qualities of the river as a focus for their tacit agreement. So the tacit analogy at least demonstrates that the idea of "coordinating expectations" is meaningful rather than mystical.

Perhaps we could push the argument further still. Even in those cases in which the only distinguishing characteristic of a bargaining result is its evident "fairness," by standards that the participants are known to appreciate, we might argue that the moral force of fairness is greatly reinforced by the power of a "fair" result to focus attention, if it fills the vacuum of indeterminacy that would otherwise exist. Similarly, when the pressure of public opinion seems to force the participants to the obviously "fair" or "reasonable" solution, we may exaggerate the "pressure" or at least misunderstand the way it works on the participants unless we give credit to its power to coordinate the participants' expectations. It may, to put it differently, be the power of *suggestion*, working through the mechanism described in this paper, that makes public opinion or precedent or ethical standards so effective. Again, as evidence for this view, we need only to suppose that the participants had to reach ultimate agreement without communicating and visualize public opinion or some prominent ethical standard as providing a strong suggestion analogous to the suggestions contained in our earlier examples. The mediator in problem 7 is a close analogy. Finally, even if it is truly the force of moral responsibility or sensitivity to public opinion that constrains the participants, and not the "signal" they get, we must still look to the source of the public's own opinion; and there, the writer suggests, the need for a simple, qualitative rationale often reflects the mechanism discussed in this paper.

But, if this general line of reasoning is valid, any analysis of explicit bargaining must pay attention to what we might call the "communication" that is inherent in the bargaining situations, the signals that the participants read in the inanimate details of the case. And it means that tacit and explicit bargaining are not thoroughly separate concepts but that the various gradations from tacit bargaining up through types of incompleteness or faulty or limited communication to full communication all show some dependence on the need to coordinate expectations. Hence all show some degree of dependence of the participants themselves on their common inability to keep their eyes off certain outcomes.

This is not necessarily an argument for expecting explicit outcomes as a rule to lean toward exactly those that would have emerged if communication had been impossible; the focal points may certainly be different when speech is allowed, except in some of the artificial cases we have used in our illustrations. But what may be the *main* principle in tacit bargaining apparently may be at least *one* of the important principles in the analysis of explicit bargaining. And, since even much so-called "explicit" bargaining includes maneuver, indirect communication, jockeying for position, or speaking to be overheard, or is confused by a multitude of participants and divergent interests, the need for convergent expectations and the role of signals that have the power to coordinate expectations may be powerful.

Perhaps many kinds of social stability and the formation of interest groups reflect the same dependence on such coordinators as the terrain and the circumstances can provide: the band wagon at political conventions that often converts the slightest sign of plurality into an overwhelming majority; the power of constitutional legitimacy to command popular support in times of anarchy or political vacuum; the legendary power of an old gang leader to bring order into the underworld, simply because obedience depends on the expectation that others will be obedient in punishing disobedience. The often expressed idea of a "rallying point" in social action seems to reflect the same concept. In economics the phenomena of price leadership, various kinds of nonprice competition, and perhaps even price stability itself appear amenable to an analysis that stresses the importance of tacit communication and its dependence on qualitatively identifiable and fairly unambiguous signals that can be read in the situation itself. "Spontaneous" revolt may reflect similar principles: when leaders can easily be destroyed, people require some signal for their coordination, a signal so unmistakably comprehensible and so potent in its suggestion for action that everyone can be sure that everyone else reads the same signal with enough confidence to act on it, thus providing one another with the immunity that goes with action in large numbers. (There is even the possibility that such a signal might be provided from outside, even by an agent whose only claim to leadership was its capacity to signal the instructions required for concerted action.)

. . .

It is usually the essence of mob formation that the potential members have to know not only where and when to meet but just when to act so that they act in concert. Overt leadership solves the problem; but leadership can often be identified and eliminated by the authority trying to prevent mob action. In this case the mob's problem is to act in unison without overt leadership, to find some common signal that makes everyone confident that, if he acts on it, he will not be acting alone. The role of "incidents" can thus be seen as a coordinating role; it is a substitute for overt leadership and communication. Without something like an incident, it may be difficult to get action at all, since immunity requires that all know when to act together. Similarly, the city that provides no "obvious" central point or dramatic site may be one in which mobs find it difficult to congregate spontaneously; there is no place so "obvious" that it is evident to everyone that it is obvious to everyone else. Bandwagon behavior, in the selection of leadership or in voting behavior, may also depend on "mutually perceived" signals, when a part of each person's preference is a desire to be in a majority or, at least, to see some majority coalesce.

Excessively polarized behavior may be the unhappy result of dependence on tacit coordination and maneuver. When whites and Negroes see that an area will "inevitably" become occupied exclusively by Negroes, the "inevitability" is a feature of convergent expectation. [2] What is most directly perceived as inevitable is not the final result but the *expectation* of it, which, in turn, makes the result inevitable. Everyone expects everyone else to expect everyone else to expect the result; and everyone is powerless to deny it. There is no stable focal point except at the extremes. Nobody can expect the tacit process to stop at 10, 30 or 60 per cent; no *particular* percentage commands agreement or provides a rallying point. If tradition suggests 100 per cent, tradition could be contradicted only by explicit agreement; if coordination has to be tacit, compromise may be impossible. People are at the mercy of a faulty communication system that makes it easy to "agree" (tacitly) to move but impossible to agree to stay. Quota systems in housing developments, schools, and so forth, can be viewed as efforts to substitute an explicit game with communication and enforcement for a tacit game that has an undesirably extreme "solution."

The coordination game probably lies behind the stability of institutions and traditions and perhaps the phenomenon of leadership itself. Among the possible sets of rules that might govern a conflict, tradition points to the particular set that everyone can expect everyone else to be conscious of as a conspicuous candidate for adoption; it wins by default over those that cannot readily be identified by tacit consent. The force of many rules of etiquette and social restraint, including some (like the rule against ending a sentence with a preposi-

[2] The phenomenon, called "tipping," is analyzed by M. Grodzins, "Metropolitan Segregation," *Scientific America*, 197:33–41 (October, 1957). A more innocuous example of explosively convergent expectations, based on tacit communication that has an almost electric quality, is the snicker that ignites an outburst of uncontrollable laughter in a nervous crowd. An important example was the collapse of the Batista regime [i.e., the Cuban dictatorship which fell suddenly on New Year's Eve 1958—*Ed.*] or of the Fourth Republic.

tion) that have been divested of their relevance or authority, seems to depend on their having become "solutions" to a coordination game: everyone expects everyone to expect everyone to expect observance, so that nonobservance carries the pain of conspicuousness. Clothing styles and motorcar fads may also reflect a game in which people do not wish to be left out of any majority that forms and are not organized to keep majorities from forming. The concept of *role* in sociology, which explicitly involves the expectations that others have about one's behavior, as well as one's expectations about how others will behave toward him, can in part be interpreted in terms of the stability of "convergent expectations," of the same type that are involved in the coordination game. One is trapped in a particular role, or by another's role, because it is the only role that in the circumstances can be identified by a process of tacit consent.

Public Goods and the Free Rider Problem [1965]

MANCUR OLSON

• *One of the most famous puzzles in modern neo-rationalism is the so-called "free rider problem." Mancur Olson pointed out that for self-interested individuals calculating their own advantages, it is usually not rational to contribute to a group that produces a shared good. It is a more rational choice to let others do the work, while one "free rides" upon their results. How then is it possible that groups—especially large ones—are able to accomplish anything at all? Proposed solutions to the free rider problem have been a favorite topic ever since Olson formulated the issue.*

It is often taken for granted, at least where economic objectives are involved, that groups of individuals with common interests usually attempt to further those common interests. Groups of individuals with common interests are expected to act on behalf of their common interests much as single individuals are often expected to act on behalf of their personal interests. This opinion about group behavior is frequently found not only in popular discussions but also in scholarly writings. Many economists of diverse methodological and ideological traditions have implicitly or explicitly accepted it. This view has, for example, been important in many theories of labor unions, in Marxian theories of class action, in concepts of "countervailing power," and in various discussions of economic institutions. It has, in addition, occupied a prominent place in political science, at least in the United States, where the study of pressure groups has been dominated by a celebrated "group theory" based on the idea that groups will act when necessary to further their common or group goals. Finally, it has played a significant role in many well-known sociological studies.

The view that groups act to serve their interests presumably is based upon the assumption that the individuals in groups act out of self-interest. If individuals in a group altruistically disregarded their personal welfare, it would not be very likely that collectively they would seek some selfish common or group objective. Such altruism, is, however, considered exceptional, and self-interested behavior is usually thought to be the rule, at least when economic issues are at stake; no

Reprinted by permission of the publishers from *The Logic of Collective Action* by Mancur Olson, Cambridge, MA: Harvard University Press, © 1965, 1971 by the President and Fellows of Harvard College. Pp. 1–2, 9–10, 34–35, 50–51.

one is suprised when individual businessmen seek higher profits, when individual workers seek higher wages, or when individual consumers seek lower prices. The idea that groups tend to act in support of their group interests is supposed to follow logically from this widely accepted premise of rational, self-interested behavior. In other words, if the members of some group have a common interest or objective, and if they would all be better off if that objective were achieved, it has been thought to follow logically that the individuals in that group would, if they were rational and self-interested, act to achieve that objective.

But it is *not* in fact true that the idea that groups will act in their self-interest follows logically from the premise of rational and self-interested behavior. It does *not* follow, because all of the individuals in a group would gain if they achieved their group objective, that they would act to achieve that objective, even if they were all rational and self-interested. Indeed, unless the number of individuals in a group is quite small, or unless there is coercion or some other special device to make individuals act in their common interest, *rational, self-interested individuals will not act to achieve their common or group interests*. In other words, even if all of the individuals in a large group are rational and self-interested, and would gain if, as a group, they acted to achieve their common interest or objective, they will still not voluntarily act to achieve that common or group interest. The notion that groups of individuals will act to achieve their common or group interests, far from being a logical implication of the assumption that the individuals in a group will rationally further their individual interests, is in fact inconsistent with that assumption.

If the members of a large group rationally seek to maximize their personal welfare, they will *not* act to advance their common or group objectives unless there is coercion to force them to do so, or unless some separate incentive, distinct from the achievement of the common or group interest, is offered to the members of the group individually on the condition that they help bear the costs or burdens involved in the achievement of the group objectives. Nor will such large groups form organizations to further their common goals in the absence of the coercion or the separate incentives just mentioned. These points hold true even when there is unanimous agreement in a group about the common good and the methods of achieving it.

The widespread view, common throughout the social sciences, that groups tend to further their interests, is accordingly unjustified, at least when it is based, as it usually is, on the (sometimes implicit) assumption that groups act in their self-interest because individuals do. There is paradoxically the logical possibility that groups composed of either altruistic individuals or irrational individuals may sometimes act in their common or group interests. But, as later, empirical parts of this study will attempt to show, this logical possibility is

usually of no practical importance. Thus the customary view that groups of
individuals with common interests tend to further those common interests appears to have little if any merit.

PUBLIC GOODS AND LARGE GROUPS

The combination of individual interests and common interests in an organization
suggests an analogy with a competitive market. The firms in a perfectly competitive industry, for example, have a common interest in a higher price for the
industry's product. Since a uniform price must prevail in such a market, a firm
cannot expect a higher price for itself unless all of the other firms in the industry
also have this higher price. But a firm in a competitive market also has an interest
in selling as much as it can, until the cost of producing another unit exceeds the
price of that unit. In this there is no common interest; each firm's interest is
directly opposed to that of every other firm, for the more other firms sell, the lower
the price and income for any given firm. In short, while all firms have a common
interest in a higher price, they have antagonistic interests where output is concerned. This can be illustrated with a simple supply-and-demand model. For the
sake of a simple argument, assume that a perfectly competitive industry is momentarily in a disequilibrium position, with price exceeding marginal cost for all firms
at their present output. Suppose, too, that all of the adjustments will be made by
the firms already in the industry rather than by new entrants, and that the industry
is on an inelastic portion of its demand curve. Since price exceeds marginal cost
for all firms, output will increase. But as all firms increase production, the price
falls; indeed, since the industry demand curve is by assumption inelastic, the total
revenue of the industry will decline. Apparently each firm finds that with price
exceeding marginal cost, it pays to increase its output, but the result is that each
firm gets a smaller profit. Some economists in an earlier day may have questioned
this result, but the fact that profit-maximizing firms in a perfectly competitive
industry can act contrary to their interests as a group is now widely understood and
accepted. A group of profit-maximizing firms can act to reduce their aggregate
profits because in perfect competition each firm is, by definition, so small that it
can ignore the effect of its output on price. Each firm finds it to its advantage to
increase output to the point where marginal cost equals price and to ignore the
effects of its extra output on the position of the industry. It is true that the net result
is that all firms are worse off, but this does not mean that every firm has not
maximized its profits. If a firm, foreseeing the fall in price resulting from the
increase in industry output, were to restrict its own output, it would lose more
than ever, for its price would fall quite as much in any case and it would have a
smaller output as well. A firm in a perfectly competitive market gets only a small

part of the benefit (or a small share of the industry's extra revenue) resulting from a reduction in that firm's output.

For these reasons it is now generally understood that if the firms in an industry are maximizing profits, the profits for the industry as a whole will be less than they might otherwise be. And almost everyone would agree that this theoretical conclusion fits the facts for markets characterized by pure competition. The important point is that this is true because, though all the firms have a common interest in a higher price for the industry's product, it is in the interest of each firm that the other firms pay the cost—in terms of the necessary reduction in output—needed to obtain a higher price.

About the only thing that keeps prices from falling in accordance with the process just described in perfectly competitve markets is outside intervention. Government price supports, tarrifs, cartel agreements, and the like may keep the firms in a competitive market from acting contrary to their interests. Such aid or intervention is quite common. It is then important to ask how it comes about. How does a competitive industry obtain government assistance in maintaining the price of its product?

Consider a hypothetical, competitive industry, and suppose that most of the producers in that industry desire a tariff, a price-support program, or some other government intervention to increase the price of their product. To obtain any such assistance from the government, the producers in this industry will presumably have to organize a lobbying organization; they will have to become an active pressure group. This lobbying organization may have to conduct a considerable campaign. If significant resistance is encountered, a great amount of money will be required. Public relations experts will be needed to influence the newspapers, and some advertising may be necessary. Professional organizers will probably be needed to organize "spontaneous grass roots" meetings among the distressed producers in the industry, and to get those in the industry to write letters to their congressmen. The campaign for the government assistance will take the time of some of the producers in the industry, as well as their money.

There is a striking parallel between the problem the perfectly competitive industry faces as it strives to obtain government assistance, and the problem it faces in the marketplace when the firms increase output and bring about a fall in price. *Just as it was not rational for a particular producer to restrict his output in order that there might be a higher price for the product of his industry, so it would not be rational for him to sacrifice his time and money to support a lobbying organization to obtain government assistance for the industry. In neither case would it be in the interest of the individual producer to assume any of the costs himself. A lobbying organization, or indeed a labor union or any other organization, working in the interest of a large group of firms or workers in some industry, would get no assistance from the rational, self-interested individuals in that industry.* This would be true even if everyone in the industry were absolutely convinced that the proposed program was in their interest (though in fact some might think otherwise and make the organization's task yet more difficult).

Although the lobbying organization is only one example of the logical analogy between the organization and the market, it is of some practical importance. There are many powerful and well-financed lobbies with mass support in existence now, but these lobbying organizations do not get that support because of their legislative achievements. The most powerful lobbying organizations now obtain their funds and their following for other reasons, as later parts of this study will show.

Some critics may argue that the rational person will, indeed, support a large organization, like a lobbying organization, that works in his interest, because he knows that if he does not, others will not do so either, and then the organization will fail, and he will be without the benefit that the organization could have provided. This argument shows the need for the analogy with the perfectly competitive market. For it would be quite as reasonable to argue that prices will never fall below the levels a monopoly would have charged in a perfectly competitive market, because if one firm increased its output, other firms would also, and the price would fall; but each firm could forsee this, so it would not start a chain of price-destroying increases in ouput. In fact, it does not work out this way in a competitive market; nor in a large organization. When the number of firms involved is large, no one will notice the effect on price if one firm increases its output, and so no one will change his plans because of it. Similarly, in a large organization, the loss of one dues payer will not noticeably increase the burden for any other one dues payer, and so a rational person would not believe that if he were to withdraw from an organization he would drive others to do so.

The forgoing argument must at least have some relevance to economic organizations that are mainly means through which individuals attempt to obtain the same things they obtain through their activities in the market. Labor unions, for example, are organizations through which workers strive to get the same things they get with their individual efforts in the market—higher wages, better working conditions, and the like. It would be strange indeed if the workers did not confront some of the same problems in the union that they meet in the market, since their efforts in both places have some of the same purposes.

However similar the purposes may be, critics may object that attitudes in organizations are not at all like those in markets. In organizations, an emotional or ideological element is often also involved. Does this make the argument offered here practically irrelevant?

A most important type of organization—the national state—will serve to test this objection. Patriotism is probably the strongest noneconomic motive for organizational allegiance in modern times. This age is sometimes called the age of nationalism. Many nations draw additional strength and unity from some powerful ideology, such as democracy or communism, as well as from a common religion, language, or cultural inheritance. The state not only has many such powerful sources of support; it also is very important economically. Almost any government is economically beneficial to its citizens, in that the law and order it provides is a prerequisite of all civilized economic activity. But despite the force of patriotism, the appeal of the national ideology, the bond of a common culture, and the indispensability of the system of law and order, no major state in modern history has been able to support itself through voluntary dues or contributions. Philanthropic contributions are not even a significant source of revenue for most countries. Taxes, *compulsory* payments by definition, are needed. Indeed, as the old saying indicates, their necessity is as certain as death itself.

If the state, with all of the emotional resources at its command, cannot finance its most basic and vital activities without resort to compulsion, it would seem that large private organizations might also have difficulty in getting the individuals in the groups whose interests they attempt to advance to make the necessary contributions voluntarily.

The reason the state cannot survive on voluntary dues or payments, but must rely on taxation, is that the most fundamental services a nation-state provides are, in one important respect, like the higher price in a competitive market: they must be available to everyone if they are available to anyone. The basic and most elementary goods or services provided by government, like defense and police protection, and the system of law and order generally, are such that they go to everyone or practically everyone in the nation. It would obviously not be feasible, if indeed it were possible, to deny the protection provided by the military services, the police, and the courts to those who did not voluntarily pay their share of the costs of government, and taxation is accordingly necessary. The common or collective benefits provided by governments are usually called "public goods" by economists, and the concept of public goods is one of the oldest and most important ideas in the study of public finance. A common, collective, or public good is here defined as any good such that, if any person X_i in a group $X_1, \ldots, X_i, \ldots, X_n$ consumes it, it cannot feasibly be withheld from the others in that group. In other words, those who do not purchase or pay for any of the public or collective good cannot be excluded or kept from sharing in the consumption of the good, as they can where noncollective goods are concerned.

It is of the essence of an organization that it provides an inseparable, generalized benefit. It follows that the provision of public or collective goods is the fundamental function of organizations generally. A state is first of all an organization that provides public goods for its members, the citizens; and other types of organizations similarly provide collective goods for their members.

And just as a state cannot support itself by voluntary contributions, or by selling its basic services on the market, neither can other large organizations support themselves without providing some sanction, or some attraction distinct from the public good itself, that will lead individuals to help bear the burdens of maintaining the organization. The individual member of the typical large organization is in a position analogous to that of the firm in a perfectly competitive market, or the taxpayer in the state: his own efforts will not have a noticeable effect on the situation of his organization, and he can enjoy any improvements brought about by others whether or not he has worked in support of his organization.

SMALL GROUPS

[C]ertain small groups can provide themselves with collective goods without relying on coercion or any positive inducements apart from the collective good itself. This is because in some small groups each of the members, or at least one of them, will find that his personal gain from having the collective good exceeds the total cost of providing some amount of that collective good; there are members who would be better off if the collective good were provided, even if they had to pay the entire cost of providing it themselves, than they would be if it were not provided. In such situations there is a presumption that the collective good will be provided. Such a situation will exist only when the benefit to the group from having the collective good exceeds the total cost by more than it exceeds the gain to one or more individuals in the group. Thus, in a very small group, where each member gets a substantial proportion of the total gain simply because there are few others in the group, a collective good can often be provided by the voluntary, self-interested action of the members of the group. In smaller groups marked by considerable degrees of inequality—that is, in groups of members of unequal "size" or extent of interest in the collective good—there is the greatest likelihood that the collective good will be provided; for the greater the interest in the collective good of any single member, the greater the likelihood that that member will get such a significant proportion of the total benefit from the collective good that he will gain from seeing that the good is provided, even if he has to pay all of the cost himself.

Even in the smallest group, however, the collective good will not ordinarily be provided on an optimal scale. That is to say, the members of the group will not provide as much of the good as it would be in their common interest to provide. Only certain special institutional arrangements will give the individual members an incentive to purchase the amounts of the collective good that would add up to the amount that would be in the best interest of the group as a whole. This tendency toward suboptimality is due to the fact that a collective good is, by definition, such that other individuals in the group cannot be kept from consuming it once any individual in the group has provided it for himself. Since an individual member thus gets only part of the benefit of any expenditure he makes to obtain more of the collective good, he will discontinue his purchase of the collective good before the optimal amount for the group as a whole has been obtained. In addition, the amounts of the collective good that a member of the group receives free from other members will further reduce his incentive to provide more of that good at his own expense. Accordingly, *the larger the group, the farther it will fall short of providing an optimal amount of a collective good*.

This suboptimality or inefficiency will be somewhat less serious in groups composed of members of greatly different size or interest in the collective good. In such unequal groups, on the other hand, there is a tendency toward an arbitrary sharing of the burden of providing the collective good. The largest member, the member who would on his own provide the largest amount of the collective good, bears a disproportionate share of the burden of providing the collective good. The smaller member by definition gets a smaller fraction of the benefit of any amount of the collective good he provides than a larger member, and therefore has less incentive to provide additional amounts of the collective good. Once a smaller member has the amount of the collective good he gets free from the largest member, he has more than he would have purchased for himself, and has no incentive to obtain any of the collective good at his own expense. In small groups with common interests there is accordingly *a surprising tendency for the "exploitation" of the great by the small*.

.   .   .

The analog to atomistic competition in the nonmarket situation is the very large group, which will here be called the "latent" group. It is distinguished by the fact that, if one member does or does not help provide the collective good, no other one member will be significantly affected and therefore none has any reason to react. Thus an individual in a "latent" group, by definition, cannot make a noticeable contribution to any group effort, and since no one in the group will react if he makes no contribution, he has no incentive to contribute. Accordingly, large or "latent" groups have no incentive to act to obtain a collective good because, however valuable the collective good might be to the group as a whole, it does not offer the individual any incentive to pay dues to any organization working in the latent group's interest, or to bear in any other way any of the costs of the necessary collective action.

Only a *separate and "selective" incentive* will stimulate a rational individual in a latent group to act in a group-oriented way. In such circumstances group action can be obtained only through an incentive that operates, not indiscriminately, like the collective good, upon the group as a whole, but rather *selectively* toward the individuals in the group. The incentive must be "selective" so that those who do not join the organization working for the group's interest, or in other ways contribute to the attainment of the group's interest, can be treated differently from those who do. These "selective incentives" can be either negative or positive, in that they can either coerce by punishing those who fail to bear an allocated share of the costs of the group action, or they can be positive inducements offered to those who act in the group interest. A latent group that has been led to act in its group interest, either because of coercion of the individuals in the group or because of positive rewards to those individuals, will here be called a "mobilized" latent group. Large groups are thus called "latent" groups because they have a latent power or capacity for action, but that potential power can be realized or "mobilized" only with the aid of "selective incentives."

The chances for group-oriented action are indeed different in each of the categories just explained. In some cases one may have some expectation that the collective or public good will be provided; in other cases one may be assured that (unless there are selective incentives) it will not; and still other cases could just as easily go either way. In any event, size is one of the determining factors in deciding whether or not it is possible that the voluntary, rational pursuit of individual interest will bring forth group-oriented behavior. Small groups will further their common interests better than large groups.

The Realization of Effective Norms [1990]

JAMES S. COLEMAN

• *James S. Coleman expands the free rider problem into a discussion of the fundamental problem of social order: how can individuals following their self-interest come to establish norms that regulate everyone's behavior? Coleman shows that this can come about only when certain conditions are present: external or collective consequences of individual actions, which create a demand for regulation; but also structures of communication and networks which are sufficiently closed to bring about effective sanctioning. Coleman goes on to show why these conditions may be declining in modern American society, resulting in such phenomena as low levels of voting in public elections, and a decreasing interest of parents in socializing their children. This exemplifies Coleman's concern for bringing fundamental theory to bear upon contemporary social issues.*

EXTERNALITIES OF ACTIONS AND THE DEMAND FOR A NORM

One distinction which is important for the functioning of social systems is that between events that have consequences only for those who control them and events that have external consequences (that is, externalities) for actors who have no control over them. The latter events are intrinsically of interest to actors other than those who control them. When such events are actions, there are two kinds of externalities of actions: When an action benefits others, the action has positive externalities; when an action is harmful to others, the action has negative externalities. If an action benefits some and hurts others, then its externalities are positive for the first set of actors and negative for the second.

. . . .

It is when pairwise exchanges cannot bring about a social optimum that interests in a norm arise. This may be illustrated by . . . describ[ing a] . . . project involving three actors. Each has the alternative of contributing $9 or nothing. For every $3 contributed, the product will be $4. The total product will be divided equally among the three. Table 1 shows the outcomes for each

Reprinted by permission of the publishers from *The Foundations of Social Theory* by James S. Coleman, Cambridge, MA: Harvard University Press, © 1990 by the President and Fellows of Harvard College. pp. 249, 255–56, 269–78, 289–92, 296–99.

Table 1   Payoff matrix for three-person common project.

	A_3			
	Contribute A_2		Not contribute A_2	
	Contribute	Not contribute	Contribute	Not contribute
A_1 Contribute	3, 3, 3	-1, 8, -1	-1, -1, 8	-5, 4, 4
Not contribute	8, -1, -1	4, 4, -5	4, -5, 4	0, 0, 0

combination of actions. Since the situation is symmetric for the three actors, these outcomes can be summarized more compactly, as shown in Table 2.

It is not possible for two of the three actors to exchange control over their actions and gain by so doing. If there are no contributions, giving no net gain or loss to each, and then A_1 exchanges control with A_2, each contributing for the other, they end up losing \$1 while A_3 gains \$8. If A_3 is contributing, A_1 and A_2 each gain \$4 without an exchange. If they exchange control, with each contributing for the other, the gain for each is \$3, making each of them \$1 worse off than they would be without the exchange.

Only if *both* A_2 and A_3 can be induced to change their actions from not contributing to contributing, contingent on A_1's contribution, does it become profitable for A_1 to join in such an arrangement. In such a case the outcome for each changes from no gain to a gain of \$3. Thus a compact among the three is necessary to bring about a gain to each. One form of compact is a norm, by which the right to contribute or not is no longer held by each actor, but for each is held by the other two. It is in this way that it can be said that each comes to have interests in a norm.

.   .   .

In the absence of an externally imposed solution to the public-good problem, some kind of combined action is necessary if a social optimum is to be attained. The combined action can be the mutual transfer of rights that constitutes establishment of a norm; but for the norm to be effective there must also be an effective sanction to enforce it, if any of the actors should give indications that he will not contribute. This in turn depends on the existence of a social relationship between two actors affected by the actions of a third. Figure 1 shows two cases: In part (a) actor A_1's action has an effect on A_2 and A_3 (as shown by the arrows), who have no social relationship with one another. Their social relations

Table 2   Summary of outcomes for three-person common project.

| Number of contributions | Gains or loses to— | |
	Contributors	Noncontributors
0	—	0
1	−5	4
2	−1	8
3	3	—

are with other actors, A_4 and A_5. In part (b) there are the same effects of A_1's actions, but actors A_2 and A_3 have a social relationship (the content of which I will discuss shortly).

In the case depicted in Figure 1(a), any sanction by A_2 or A_3 to direct A_1's action so that it is not inimical to their interests must be applied by either independently. As is shown for the three-actor common project in Table 1, neither can do so: a threat to A_1 by A_2 not to contribute if A_1 fails to contribute hurts A_1 by only \$4, and A_1's not contributing gains him \$5. In contrast, as shown in Figure 1(b), a social relationship between A_2 and A_3 may make it possible to impose a sanction on A_1 through some form of joint action that neither A_2 nor A_3 could impose alone. Similarly, if there exists some social relationship between A_1 and A_2, it may be possible to impose a sanction on A_3, and similarly with a relationship between A_1 and A_3.

But two related questions arise: First, what kind of sanction might be applied which could not be applied by either of the actors separately? Second, what is meant by the unanalyzed term "social relationship"?

There are two aspects of a social relationship that can lead to an effective sanction. One is simply communication that allows the possibility of joint action. If A_2 and A_3 pool their contributions, they together offer a sanction that is effective toward A_1: Their combined contribution makes a difference of \$8 to A_1, and his own failure to contribute benefits him by only \$5. Thus a joint threat by A_2 and A_3 to not contribute is sufficient to bring about a contribution from A_1.

Second, the social relationship between A_2 and A_3 may contain some other possibilities, some interests and control which give one or both actors leverage over the other. . . . Because social relationships consist of obligations and expectations, held either asymmetrically or symmetrically, and because each actor continues to control some events in which the other is interested, there exists inherently in each social relationship leverage which can be used for the pur-

Figure 1 Structures of relations among actors that have differing potentials for the emergence of a norm.

pose of developing sanctions. If, in the case depicted in Figure 1(b), A_2 has obligations toward A_3, then A_2 may pay off a portion of those obligations by sanctioning A_1. But he can do this only if he can threaten A_1 with some event that could make a difference of $5 or more to A_1. A_2's own contribution makes a difference of only $4, which is not enough. A_2 must have some obligation toward A_1 that he can threaten not to honor, if his sanction is to be effective. Even a threat which costs him more than he benefits from A_1's contribution may be viable, because of the compensation he receives from A_3. Or if A_2 has control of some event in which A_3 is interested (which may be nothing more than A_2's approval), A_2 and A_3 can carry out an implicit exchange, in which A_3 incurs the cost of sanctioning A_1 in return for control of the event currently controlled by A_2.

This use of social relationships to facilitate the employment of sanctions constitutes a solution to a general problem, to which I now turn.

The Second-Order Public-Good Problem for Norms

The sanctioning problem has been called the second-order public-good problem or the second-order free-rider problem. The problem can be conceptualized by considering one of Aesop's fables, known as "The Mice in Council." The council meeting was called to discuss a problem faced by the mouse society, that of how to control the cat who was slowly decimating the population. In the terms used in this book, the cat's action was imposing severe externalities on the mice and constituted, in effect, a public bad, creating constant danger for each mouse. This is the first-order public-good (or in this case public-bad) problem.

The second-order public-good problem is indicated in the statement of the wise old mouse who finally rose in the council, after a proposed solution (that a bell be put around the cat's neck to warn of its approach) had been roundly applauded. He suggested that the council consider how the bell was to be fastened about the cat's neck and who would undertake the task. The second-order public-good problem lies in the fact that, just as the cat's action imposes externalities on all, an effective sanctioning of the cat's actions also has externalities (positive in this case) for all those experiencing the benefits of the sanction; yet the benefits to the mouse who would undertake to bell the cat would not be sufficient to overcome the costs.

For the case of the three-actor project shown in Table 1, the first-order public-good problem lies in the fact that each will benefit only from the contribution of others; and the second-order public-good problem is that if A_1 does not contribute, then the sanctioning of A_1 is a public good for A_2 and A_3, but neither receives sufficient benefits from his own sanctioning action to compensate the costs of sanctioning A_1. The problem may not appear to be a serious one for the three-actor common project. The second-order public-good problem for sanctioning one actor's failure to contribute to a three-actor common project is reduced to a two-actor joint project. This may be solved whenever there is the possibility of exchange between the two actors who experience externalities from the third. One can compensate the other for the net costs of applying the sanction (in this case, for instance, the costs to A_2 of sanctioning A_1, less the benefits that A_2 will derive directly from the effects of the sanction). More generally, the second-order public-good problem of sanctioning always involves one actor less than the first-order public-good problem.

The sanctioning problem for the case in Table 1 is shown in Table 3, where it is assumed that A_1 proposes not to contribute and that A_2 and A_3 have contributed. Since A_1 gains \$5 by not contributing (the difference between \$3 and \$8), it will cost A_2 or A_3 (or both together) whatever is equivalent to \$5 for A_1. Making up the \$5 for A_1 is not possible for either A_2 or A_3 to do within the framework of the common project, since either alone can only make a difference of \$4

Table 3   Payoff matrix for two potential sanctioners in three-person common project.

| | | A_3 | |
		Sanction	Not sanction
A_2	Sanction	.5, .5	−2, 3
	Not sanction	3, −2	−1, −1

to A_1 by contributing or not contributing. It is further assumed for Table 3 therefore that A_2 and A_3 each have a relation to A_1 that makes it possible to hurt A_1's interests by \$5 and that the cost of such a sanction is equivalent to \$5 to either A_2 or A_3.

These assumptions make it possible to specify for A_2 and A_3 a set of payoffs for the second-order public-good problem posed by the question of how to sanction A_1. If neither A_2 nor A_3 sanctions, they lose \$1 each (from Table 1). If only A_2 sanctions, it costs him \$5 to induce A_1 to contribute (again, the difference between \$8 and \$3). In that case A_3 gains \$4 (the difference between − \$1 and \$3) and ends up with \$3. Similarly, if only A_3 sanctions, it costs him \$5, and A_2 gains \$4. If both sanction, it costs each \$2.50 and each gains \$4, leaving each with a net of \$1.50 after subtracting the cost of the sanction and thus with \$0.50 for the total project.

There are four points of importance to note about this sanctioning problem. First, the structure of payoffs illustrates the fact that the necessity to employ a sanction is costly to the sanctioners. Even though the right to control A_1's action is held by A_2 and A_3, enforcement of that right is costly. The fact that enforcement is possible, at a cost to A_2 and A_3 less than the benefit they can gain from the effects of the sanction in brining A_1 into line, makes the threat of sanction credible, and the norm viable.

Second, the sanctioning problem involves, as stated earlier, one actor fewer than the original public-good problem. When the original problem involves three actors, the sanctioning problem involves two and can ordinarily be re-solved by exchange. With large numbers of actors, of course, the benefit of this size reduction is small.

Third, the sanctioning problem involves a smaller cost to the actors involved than does the original problem. This can be seen in two ways. The difference between the social optimum of a payoff of \$0.50 each and the outcome of −\$1 that results from each taking his individually optimal action is only \$1.50; this difference is \$3 for the original problem. Also, from A_3's perspective, if he sanctions, the difference that A_2's sanction makes for him is only \$2.50, com-pared to \$4 in the original problem. Thus the sanctioning problem is less costly than the original problem.

Fourth, if the second-order sanction is a positive one, rewarding the sanc-tioner, then even though it is less costly than the first-order sanction, it must be provided whenever the right action (sanctioning the initial offender) is taken; a negative sanction must be applied only when the wrong action is taken. If there develops a norm that one must sanction the violator of the initial norm, then the negative second-order sanction for not applying the first-order sanction must be applied only when that sanctioning norm is violated. This cost reduction to norm beneficiaries may give them an interest in establishing a sanctioning norm.

It is now possible to state the second condition for emergence of an effective norm, the condition under which the demand for an effective norm will be satisfied. Stated simply, this condition is that under which the second-order free-rider problem will be overcome by rational holders of a norm. To put it differently, the condition is that under which beneficiaries of a norm, acting rationally, either will be able to share appropriately the costs of sanctioning the target actors or will be able to generate second-order sanctions among the set of beneficiaries that are sufficient to induce effective sanctions of the target actors by one or more of the beneficiaries. This condition depends on the existence of social relationships among the beneficiaries.

FREE RIDING AND ZEAL

The theory developed in this and preceding chapters can be used to solve an empirical puzzle. It is first necessary to restate the free-rider problem: When a number of self-interested persons are interested in the same outcome, which can only be brought about by effort that is more costly than the benefits it would provide to any of them, then, in the absence of explicit organization, there will be a failure to bring about that outcome, even though an appropriate allocation of effort would bring it about at a cost to each which is less than the benefits each would experience.

The puzzle lies in the fact that there are many empirical situations in which just the opposite of free-rider activity seems to occur, even though the circumstances are those in which free riders would be predicted to abound. That is, there is an outcome in which a number of persons are interested, which requires effort whose costs are not fully compensated by the benefits the outcome will bring to any of the persons. Yet in some such situations what is found is the opposite of free riding, that is, an excess of zeal. In the fever of patriotic zeal during wartime, men will volunteer for military service; in the military they will volunteer for front-line duty; and at the front line they will volunteer for dangerous missions. Even among those who are opposed to violence, there are some who will volunteer for front-line duty in providing medical aid to the wounded. In all of these cases the costs that are borne are extreme, including a greatly increased probability of being killed.

Similarly extreme costs are borne by persons in small groups who engage in militant or even terroristic acts on behalf of what they regard as a public good. Examples include the IRA hunger strikers in Northern Ireland, some of whom fasted until death; Mohandas Gandhi and his followers in India, who endured extreme hardship for a cause; the Red Guards in Italy, who engaged in terrorism designed to bring down the system; activists in the PLO in the Middle East; and leaders and activists in the Solidarity movement in Poland. In all these cases a number of persons experienced extreme costs to bring about a result from which they personally could hardly expect to benefit sufficiently to justify those costs.

Another area where free-rider behavior might be expected but zealous activity is often found instead is in team sports. Since the benefits of winning are experienced by all team members, one would expect, by a free-rider logic, to find little or no activity by team members. Yet both in practice and in games, team members often work harder than do participants in individual sports (such as track and field events). Even if one accepts the caveat that is often introduced in predictions about free-rider activity—that it does not occur in small groups—this does not explain the higher levels of effort in team sports. It would predict equal levels of effort. What seems instead to occur in team sports is some free-rider activity, that is, some greater amount of loafing than occurs in individual sports, but also zealous activity at a greater level than occurs in individual sports. The overall average level of effort is probably higher in team sports than in individual sports.

Rationality of Free Riding and of Zeal

How can the two phenomena, free riding and zeal, coexist? How can similar situations produce free riding and zeal?

The rationality of free riding is straightforward: If a number of persons' interests are satisfied by the same outcome, and if the benefits that each experiences from his own actions that contribute to the outcome are less than the costs of those actions, he will not contribute if he is rational. If others contribute, he will experience the benefits of the outcome without incurring costs. If others do not contribute, his costs will outweigh his benefits. Yet in much the same situation another rationality leads to zealous activity. If a number of persons' interests are satisfied by the same outcome, then each has an incentive to reward the others for working toward that outcome. Each may in fact find it in his interest to establish a norm toward working for that outcome, with negative sanctions for shirking and positive sanctions for working toward the common goal. If the norm and sanctions do become established, then each person has two sources of satisfaction when he works for the outcome: the objective achievement of his interests through the contribution of his actions toward the outcome, and the rewards provided by the others for helping to achieve that outcome. Thus one's efforts directly help to satisfy one's interests (even if not enough to outweigh the costs of those efforts), and they also bring benefits from others for helping to satisfy *their* interests. The combination of these two benefits can be greater than the costs of the effort one expends.

The rationality of free riding and the rationality of zeal arise under the same structure of interests. This is not the structure of interests that characterizes most situations, where the interests of different persons are complementary and are realized through some kind of social exchange. Nor is it a structure in which interests are opposed, so one person's interests are realized at the expense of another's. Rather, it is a structure of common interests; that is, the interests of all (or at least all in the vicinity) are realized by the same outcome (winning a war or a game, or achieving a political or community goal). It is in these sorts of situations that both free riding and zeal can be found.

How can these two rationalities be made consistent in a way that will allow prediction as to when one or the other will prevail? To answer this requires looking at the similarities and the differences between the rationality of free riding and the rationality of zeal. The rationality of zeal has the same incentive that leads to free riding, but with a second incentive superimposed on the first. The second incentive, however, becomes effective only through an intervening action: encouragement of others, or positive sanctions, which may overcome the deficiency of the first incentive. It is this intervening action that makes the difference between the deficient incentive leading to free riding and the excess incentive leading to zeal. Thus the condition under which free riding occurs and the condition under which zeal is exhibited are delineated by the absence or presence of this intervening activity.

What are the conditions under which the intervening activity is present? When this intervening activity, which I have described as encouragement of others, is examined more closely, it can be seen to be one of a general class of activities that are described as sanctions in enforcement of a norm. (There can be, as I will indicate later, encouragement of others' activity in the absence of a norm, but this can be effective only under special circumstances, which I will specify.) That is, the activity is a certain kind of sanction which *encourages* the action rather than *discouraging* it, and the norm is of a certain kind, one which *prescribes* a certain action rather than proscribing it. But to say that a norm arises under those two conditions is to beg half the question. The existence of externalities is a necessary condition for the existence of an effective norm, but not a sufficient one—if it were, free riding would not exist when actors have common interests.

The Closure of Networks and the Emergence of Zeal

An earlier section showed the importance of social structure in supporting the employment of sanctions. It has also been suggested that it is social structure that can transform free ridership into zeal. How this occurs can be understood by examining differences among social networks, as shown in Figure 2. In part (a) of the figure actors A_1, A_2, and A_3 are not part of the same network. Whatever social relations they have are not with each other. In parts (b) and (c) actor A_1 is connected to actors A_2 and A_3. In part (b) actors A_2 and A_3 are not connected, but in part (c) they are.

Suppose some circumstance arises which fits the incentive structure for both free riding and zeal. That is, there is an activity in which the action of each actor benefits all three, although the benefits to each actor of his own action are insufficient to overcome the costs of that action. The common project introduced in Table 1 illustrates such an activity.

In a social structure such as is shown in Figure 2(a), each actor has no possibility of influencing the contribution of either of the others. They have no relations, and thus they cannot provide the encouragement or impose the sanctions that will induce the others to contribute. It would be irrational for any of the three to contribute.

In a social structure such as is shown in Figure 2(b), matters are more problematic. If A_1 proposes not to contribute, but to free ride on the contributions of A_2 and A_3, then A_2 would like to induce him to contribute; and in part (b), unlike part (a), A_2 (and A_3 as well) is in a social-structural position that facilitates this. As shown earlier in connection with Figure 1, however, in some circumstances, A_2 cannot do so if he must compensate A_1 in some common medium of exchange in order to encourage him to contribute. There are, of course, public goods for which inducement by A_2 would be sufficient to lead A_1 to contribute while still providing a net benefit to A_2. (For example, suppose in the three-actor common project A_1's contribution of $9 brought a benefit of $6 to each. Then A_2 could induce A_1 to contribute by offering him any amount

(a)   (b)   (c)

Figure 2 Structures of relations among actors that have differing potentials for the growth of zeal.

more than $3 and would benefit if he offered A_1 any amount less than $6.) It may also be true that A_2 can compensate A_1 with something worth little to him but worth a lot to A_1. A_2 could offer this to A_1 with a net surplus for both parties. For example, if A_2 is highly respected by A_1, then A_2's gratitude to A_1 for contributing may fulfill this condition.

In the social structure shown in Figure 2(c), there is an additional possibility. If a sanctioning of A_1 would cost A_2 (or A_3) more than he would benefit from it, then with this structure the second-order sanctioning problem could be overcome, as described in the discussion concerning Figure 1.

Is There an Excess of Zeal?

The above discussion simply restates the earlier result that closure of social networks can overcome free-rider activity through the creation of norms and sanctioning systems. The discussion does not indicate, however, how the contributions (of money or effort or time) can be *greater* than would occur if the three actors were each engaged in producing a private good. In the common project the norm brought the contributions back to what they would have been if the return had been purely private goods, that is, if each had received $12 for his $9 investment but none from the others' investments. In principle, the existence of a norm with sanctions does what formal organization does in the presence of externalities: It internalizes the externalities.

Social networks, and the norms they facilitate, do more than this, however. Under certain circumstances they generate the excessively zealous activity which indicates not a deficiency of incentives to contribute, but an excess. What leads members of an interconnected group to engage in the opposite of free riding?

Earlier I indicated that if A_2 held something that was worth little to him and much to A_1, he could induce A_1's contribution without loss, even in the social structure of Figure 2(b). And in the social structure of Figure 2(c), there is the additional possibility of gains from A_3's holding something of greater value to A_2 than to himself, which he could use in place of money for the second-order sanctioning of A_2. The relationships of which social structures are composed contain such possibilities in abundance. An expression of encouragement or gratitude for another's action may cost the actor very little but provide a great reward for the other. The shouts of encouragement to an athlete from his teammates may cost them little but provide him with rewards that lead him to work even harder. Or a girl's smiling at the athlete may cost her little but impel him to new heights of determined effort.

When there are such differentials, the social structure does more than merely internalize externalities. The social system has within it a potential, analogous to the potential in an electrical system. That is, when one actor carries out an action, thus experiencing costs, and others receive the benefits, the return that the actor experiences is not merely those benefits transmitted back to him through the social structure but those benefits amplified by this potential that exists in the structure. Thus when an actor's activity levels off at the point where marginal cost equals marginal return, that point is at a higher level because of the amplified returns he has received, which were in turn produced by the potential that exists in the structure. The potential lies in the difference between the cost to the sanctioner, in each of the relations that transmits rewards back to an actor, and the benefits the sanctioner gains through the increased activity of the actor who is being (positively) sanctioned.

The Impact of Social Structure

The networks shown in Figure 2 exhibit two components of a social structure that are important for the existence of norms which can transform a deficiency of incentive into an excess of incentive. The first of these two components is the existence of social relations between an actor and those for whom he generates externalities. Even if those others are disconnected members of an audience witnessing his actions, their connection to him may mean that they can provide rewards, at a cost to themselves that is below their benefit from his actions, that spur him on to greater efforts. It is for this reason that a performing athlete, musician, or actor may experience far greater motivation than will a book author, who cannot see the reactions of his audience.

The second component of a social structure that is important for the existence of norms is exhibited by the difference between parts (b) and (c) of Figure 2. This is the closure of the network, the existence of relations between those who experience externalities from another's action. From the example of the common project in conjunction with Figure 1, it is clear how these relations can make a difference between a system in which there is a deficient incentive to act and thus a suboptimal level of activity, and a system in which there is an excess incentive to act and thus a manifestation of zeal. More generally, closure of the network gives increased potential for amplifying returns to the actor. Thus a system in which others have connections to the actor may exhibit a strong potential that induces higher levels of activity, but a system that in addition has high closure has an extra potential, due to the benefits that each of those who experience externalities of the actor's action receive from one another. There is an amplification that occurs even before the rewards get back to the actor himself.

EMERGENCE OF NORMS ABOUT VOTING

The act of voting poses a deep and serious problem to students of the rational calculus of behavior. If a voter is viewed as a rational actor who has an interest in the outcome of an election, but for whom the act of voting itself constitutes a small cost of time and effort, then the act of voting does not directly follow, even though his interest in the outcome may be very great. Straightforward considerations will lead the voter to recognize that if there are many others voting, his own vote is very unlikely to affect the outcome. The small cost in time and effort that voting will incur must outweigh the very minor chance that the act of voting will bring gain. As a consequence, a reflective voter must conclude, as he is going to the polling place, that whatever impels him there, it is not the impact of his vote on the outcome.

This sort of analysis has been carried out by many students of the rational calculus of voting. . . . The empirical fact to be explained is, of course, that although the above considerations seem reasonable, many persons do vote, even in elections involving great numbers of voters. Indeed, even a weaker prediction from rational considerations, to the effect that whatever the level of voting, it should certainly decline as the number of voters increases, does not seem to hold. This problem is so puzzling that it has been described as the paradox of voting (and has received attention second only to that given Arrow's or Condorcet's paradox). The paradox in this case is not logical, but empirical: Why do so many persons vote when it is clearly irrational to do so?

The problem can be expressed more precisely in simple mathematical form. Suppose a person experiences a certain cost, c, from the act of voting. And suppose he would experience a benefit, b, from the election's having the outcome he prefers. Suppose further that he expects that outcome to occur with probability p if he does not vote and with probability $p + \Delta p$ if he does vote. Then he can calculate the expected return if he does participate and the expected return if he does not. His expected return if he participates is $b(p + \Delta p) - c$. His expected return if he does not participate is bp. If he is rational, in the usual meaning of the term, he will participate if and only if the first of these two expected returns is greater than the second, that is, if $b(p + \Delta p) - c$ is greater than bp. This reduces to $b\Delta p$ is greater than c, or Δp is greater than c/b. That is, he should participate only if the increment in the probability of his desired outcome, due to his vote, is greater than the ratio of the costs of voting to the benefits of the desired outcome.

It is obvious that whenever the number of voters is large, Δp is quite small, so an individual's voting can be explained as rational only if the costs of voting to him (c) are nearly zero or the benefits (b) are enormous. Few political scientists would suggest that either condition is met for most voters, and thus the puzzle of apparently nonrational voting remains.

Various authors have tried to "rationalize" voting in a variety of ways. One is to assume that the act of voting may not only incur some costs, but also bring some benefits. For example, if voting is highly approved by a person's friends and not voting is disapproved of, the outcome of the election does not have to be of interest to the person in order for him to vote, nor does he have to believe that his vote will affect the outcome. In that case, if the psychic benefits he experiences from approval are b^* and the costs he experiences from disapproval are c^*, his expected return from voting is $b(p + \Delta p) - c + b^*$ and from not voting is $bp - c^*$. This changes the inequality that must be satisfied if the person is to vote: $b\Delta p + b^* + c^*$ must be greater than c. This inequality may be fulfilled even if he believes his vote will have no effect on the outcome, that is, even if Δp is zero. All that is necessary is that the sum of the psychic benefits from approval for voting and the psychic costs from disapproval for not voting be greater than the direct costs of participation.

This explanation of voting has certain virtues. One is that it gives rise to differential predictions about whether persons will vote in different circumstances and can thus be empirically supported or disconfirmed. For example, one prediction would be that persons removed from the company of their friends or persons in the company of those who do not express approval for voting and disapproval for not voting will be much less likely to vote than others.

This explanation has certain unsatisfactory aspects as well. A principal one is that it provides no answer to the question of why others express approval for participation and disapproval for nonparticipation. Those others are presumably subject to the same rational considerations, which should lead them not to vote themselves, as well as not to apply sanctions to others for not voting. Thus the above explanation merely pushes the problem back one step: Why should there be expressions of approval of voting and disapproval of not voting on the part of others?

What is necessary is an explanation of voting that is consistent with the one given above, but takes the further step of explaining why others, despite their similar circumstances, express approval and disapproval.

Assume there is a system of actors, each of whom has an interest (which corresponds to b in the above discussion) in the outcome of an election and a negative interest in the act of voting itself (which corresponds to c in the above discussion). The latter may of course be very small relative to the former. Each actor has some small fraction of control over the outcome of the election, through his vote. In such a circumstance each actor's action is of interest to each other actor; that is, the actions have externalities. There will be . . . a demand for a norm to vote. And, according to the principle presented in this chapter, satisfaction of that demand depends on the existence of social relationships among potential beneficiaries of the norm if the second-order free-rider problem is to be overcome. When those conditions are met, there will be a general transfer of rights of control over the action of voting or not voting, by each to all.

The end result of this transfer of rights of control will be a system in which each actor has given up a large portion of rights of control over his own action (that is, voting or not voting) and has gained in return a small portion of rights of control over the action of each of the other actors. This constitutes, as discussed in an earlier section, the emergence of a conjoint norm. Each actor will exercise the rights gained in the direction of others' voting, but he may exercise the remaining control he holds over his own action against his own voting (because of the cost to him). His exercise of rights of control over others' voting can be enforced through the exhibiting of approval or disapproval. If each actor has given up most of the control over his own action to others, then the potential approval for voting and disapproval for not voting may be sufficient to overcome the costs each will incur by voting.

One might argue that this conjoint norm would be restricted to a subgroup within the system whose members all support the same candidate, since votes for an opposition candidate impose negative externalities. Since persons generally associate with those whose political sentiments are like their own, the application of such a norm (that is, sanctions of approval for voting or disapproval for not voting) will be toward inducing voting among those who will vote in the same direction as oneself. In fact, the observation by students of voting that persons under so-called cross-pressure are less likely to vote may result from differential application of the norm. . . . The reduced likelihood of voting among persons who are in surroundings different from those to which their background or interests predispose them may result from reduced application of normative sanctions that would lead to voting.

A further implication may be drawn. Since these normative systems are composed of supporters of each candidate, their strength depends on the degree of closure of each. Unless the social networks that link persons together are somewhat distinct, so there is a correlation between the political preferences of friends, these normative systems cannot function. Thus one prediction based on this theory is that the lower that correlation, so that social networks are largely random with respect to political preference, the lower the proportion of the population voting. By a small additional step, a low correlation between social relations and political preference should lower the rate of voting most for those candidates in a minority position in the system under consideration (for example, a city or town).

The central element of this explanation, which was missing in the earlier one, is the giving up of partial rights of control over one's own action and the receiving of partial rights of control over the actions of others, that is, the emergence of a norm. The end result is that control over the voting of each, which was initially held by each alone, becomes widely distributed over the whole set of actors, who exercise that control in the direction of approval for voting and disapproval for not voting—despite the fact that each has some reluctance to vote himself.

Under What Conditions Will Actors Attempt to Bring About Internalization?

The question to be considered here is why a beneficiary of a norm, or more generally an actor interested in exercising control over another's action, will attempt to establish an internal sanctioning system within a target actor rather than merely using external sanctions as the occasion warrants. The answer is immediately apparent if one takes the perspective of a parent of a small child or that of a police officer coping with crime in a neighborhood. The existence of an internal sanctioning system within the small child or within each person in the neighborhood would make unnecessary the continual external policing of actions. Thus if internalization can be brought about at a sufficiently low cost, it is a more efficient means of social control than is external policing of actions. The question then becomes, just what are the conditions under which creation of an internal sanctioning system is likely to be more efficient than maintaining external policing of actions?

First, internalization becomes increasingly efficient the greater the number of different types of actions that the socializing actor, such as a parent, wants to control using norms. The basic process of creating identification with the socializing agent constitutes in effect a capital cost, and there is an additional marginal cost for each different action that is to be subject to a normative constraint. The capital cost seems to be the larger by far of these two types of costs, so the total cost to the sanctioning agent of subjecting a large number of actions to normative constraints is not much greater than the total cost of doing so for a small number of actions. Thus, for example, once a mother has brought about a condition in which her daughter has internalized the mother's wishes, the mother can extend the number of prescriptions and proscriptions contained in her wishes without incurring great cost.

This implies that authority systems that, like religious orders, aim to penetrate all aspects of the member's or subordinate's life will be more likely to attempt to bring about identification through creation of a new self than will authority systems that attempt to exercise less broad social control. A similar but less obvious prediction is that parents whose desired scope of authority over their children is broad will make more use of internalization than will parents whose desired scope of authority is narrower. More particularly, parents who have an egalitarian ideology about raising children, leading to a laissez-faire parental authority system (few prescriptions and proscriptions), will find it less efficient to bring about identification and instill internalization of norms in a child than will parents whose desired scope of authority is broader and more rigid. Thus children of egalitarian parents should show less internalization of norms, or be more nearly sociopathic, than children of authoritarian parents. This prediction counters the commonsense assumption that "enlightened" parents are both more egalitarian and more likely to use internal sanctions than external ones; that assumption leads to the prediction that the correlation between parental egalitarianism and use of internal sanctions is positive.

A second point is that parents (or other actors) who are in a position to establish an internal sanctioning system do not reap all the benefits from it. Parents must pay the costs of internalization, but others will experience some of the future benefits. It is true that parents experience some benefits during the period the child is at home. Since these are only a fraction of the benefits, however, there is an expected underinvestment in internalization from the perspective of the total set of benefits to others that internalization will bring about (reduced policing and fewer negative externalities). This underinvestment should be especially great for internalization of norms which have least to do with a child's actions in the home and are primarily concerned with actions toward others later in life.

This underinvestment in internalization is comparable to and derives largely from the same interests as business firms' underinvestment in human capital. A firm recovers only a portion of the investment in human capital, depending on the length of tenure of the employee. In the literature on human capital, a distinction is made between specific and general human capital. A firm is able to capture all the benefits of investments in specific human capital (firm-specific knowledge or skills) but not able to capture the benefits of general human capital, which can be used in other firms to which an employee might move. This distinction is similar to the distinction between norms covering a child's actions in the home and norms covering actions outside the home or later in life. The implication of this distinction is that there will be less underinvestment in internalization of a norm prescribing honesty, which is part of the child's actions in the home, than in internalization of a norm prescribing fairness to peers, a trait manifested largely outside the home, on the playground, and in school. There should be even greater underinvestment in internalization of norms proscribing sharp practices, which are exhibited primarily in business later in life.

A further prediction is that underinvestment in internalization of norms should be greater in cultures or settings in which children leave home at a younger age. In such settings a parent, engaging in the socialization of children, will experience a smaller fraction of its total benefits and thus will find the investment in internalization to have a lower payoff. One specific prediction is that in modern societies, where the typical household is two-generational, there should be greater underinvestment than in traditional societies, where there tend to be three-generational households or extended families. A second specific prediction is that an increase in divorce rates should decrease the investment in internalization, and children of divorced parents should show a lower degree of internalization. Either divorced parent expects to spend less time with a child and will thus find it less costly to use external sanctions in cases where, if there were a more extended payoff period, the creation of internal sanctions would be more efficient.

A third point is that parents can increase the return on their investment in internalization of norms by identifying with the child and continuing to inform themselves about the child's actions later in life. Such identification, together with information about the child's actions that accord with a parent's wishes and gain approval from others, can bring satisfaction to the parent and thus make an investment in internalization profitable. This would lead to the prediction that the use of internal rather than external sanctions by a parent will be greater if the parent expects that the future associates of the child will hold the same values as the parent does (for instance, as occurs in a stable society).

A specific prediction that follows from this general point is that persons in America and Europe who grew up in the 1960s and experienced a great gap in values between themselves and their parents can be expected to find identification with their own children as they grow up a less profitable investment, and thus a weaker spur toward increasing the investment in creating internal sanctions in their children.

A fourth point concerns different families in the same society. Some families have a strong interest in their status in the community and see family members' actions, throughout life, as affecting that status. Other families have little status in the community, and thus little to lose by the deviant behavior of family members throughout life. Parents in the latter type of family can be expected to seriously underinvest in creating internal sanctions, and parents in the former type can be expected to invest much more heavily in creating such sanctions. Studies of socialization practices of different social groups are quite consistent with this prediction, showing that the lower the social status, the less internal sanctions are used. Further predictions could be tested as well. Any aspect of social structure which reduces the degree to which the child's later actions will benefit or harm the family's interests (such as residence in a more anonymous urban setting as compared to a small-town setting, or geographic mobility and discontinuity in family life) should weaken the relation between the family's interest in its status and the degree to which socialization practices incorporate internal sanctions. Thus, as these conditions proliferate, families of the same social status will use internal sanctions less often and external sanctions more often; persons in future generations will be decreasingly socialized.

A fifth point makes use of a result from the literature on the economics of agency. The efficiency of supervision (that is, external policing), relative to some incentive system that provides internal policing, is reduced as the actions subject to observation become more costly to observe. Thus a worker in a cottage industry is more likely to be paid by the piece and less likely to have supervision than is a factory worker making the same product, and an outside sales representative is likely to receive a higher fraction of compensation as commissions and have less supervision than is an inside salesperson or sales clerk. This principle leads to the prediction that the trait of honesty, which is often difficult to observe, will be more likely to be internalized than will the trait of cleanliness or orderliness, both of which are more easily observed and thus more readily subject to external sanctions.

These five points concerning conditions which will lead parents to instill internal sanctions rather than using external policing lead to predictions that are not at all trivial. Certain of the predictions, if they are borne out by research, have strong implications for social control in the future, for they point to decreasing levels of internalization of norms among future generations, assuming that the family continues as the principal agency of socialization. This implies that either use of external policing systems will increase or there will be lower levels of social control.[1]

---

[1] These predictions, and the points which generate them, make evident the naiveté of certain assumptions, such as "Increasing levels of education will increase the viability of democracy," or "Increasing enlightenment through education will result in parents raising better-socialized children."

III THE DURKHEIMIAN TRADITION

Some Main Points of the Durkheimian Tradition

	Macro wing		Micro wing
1740–1770	Montesquieu		
1770–1800	Revolutionary *philosophes*		
1800–1830	Saint-Simon		Reactionary defenders of religion: De Bonald, De Maistre
1830–1860	Comte's positivism		
	Utilitarian influence: John Stuart Mill		
1860–1890	Herbert Spencer		Crowd psychologists
			Classicists and anthropologists: Frazer Fustel de Coulanges
1890–1920	Durkheim		Anthropology of rituals: Mauss
1920–1960			Cambridge scholars of classical religion
	Functionalists Merton Parsons	Levi-Strauss's structuralism	British social anthropology: Radcliffe-Brown Lloyd Warner
1960–		Bourdieu's cultural capital theory	Goffman's interaction rituals
			Ritual and stratification: Bernstein Mary Douglas Collins
			Durkheimian sociology of science: Hagstrom Bloor

Precontractual Solidarity [1893]; Social Rituals and Sacred Objects [1912]

EMILE DURKHEIM

• *Emile Durkheim may well be sociology's greatest theorist to date. That is not to say all his theories have always proved right or fruitful; some lineages of his intellectual followers, in my opinion (such as the functionalist and evolutionist traditions), pick up more of the fallacies and ideological elements in Durkheim than his strengths. But Durkheim also provides the classic breakthrough insights of sociology, the great "aha!" experiences: of realization that social order and rational thought itself rest on a nonrational foundation; that this substructure is a flow of emotions determined by the density of social interactions and especially by the tightly focused mutual actions of rituals; that symbols like gods are charged with moral energies by the group whose membership they reflect. Following are some key arguments of Durkheim's relentlessly logical and systematic theoretical analysis.*

THE PRE-CONTRACTUAL BASIS OF SOCIAL SOLIDARITY

[If society were based solely on social contracts] . . . the typical social relation would be the economic, stripped of all regulation and resulting from the entirely free initiative of the parties. In short, society would be solely the stage where individuals exchanged the products of their labor, without any action properly social coming to regulate this exchange.

Is this the character of societies whose unity is produced by the division of labor? If this were so, we could with justice doubt their stability. For if interest relates men, it is never for more than some few moments. It can create only an external link between them. In the fact of exchange, the various agents remain outside of each other, and when the business has been completed, each one retires and is left entirely on his own. Consciences are only superficially in contact; they neither penetrate each other, nor do they adhere. If we look further into the matter, we shall see that this total harmony of interests

Reprinted with permission of the Free Press, a Division of Macmillan, Inc., from Emile Durkheim, *The Division of Labor in Society* (New York: Free Press, 1964), pp. 203–204, 212–214, 275–280, 287–291, 345–350; originally published 1893.

conceals a latent or deferred conflict. For where interest is the only ruling force each individual finds himself in a state of war with every other since nothing comes to mollify the egos, and any truce in this eternal antagonism would not be of long duration. There is nothing less constant than interest. Today, it unites me to you; tomorrow, it will make me your enemy. Such a cause can only give rise to transient relations and passing associations. We now understand how necessary it is to see if this is really the nature of organic solidarity.

To be sure, when men unite in a contract, it is because, through the division of labor, either simple or complex, they need each other. But in order for them to co-operate harmoniously, it is not enough that they enter into a relationship, nor even that they feel the state of mutual dependence in which they find themselves. It is still necessary that the conditions of this co-operation be fixed for the duration of their relations. The rights and duties of each must be defined, not only in view of the situation such as it presents itself at the moment when the contract is made, but with foresight for the circumstances which may arise to modify it. Otherwise, at every instant, there would be conflicts and endless difficulties. We must not forget that, if the division of labor makes interests solidary, it does not confound them; it keeps them distinct and opposite. Even as in the internal workings of the individual organism each organ is in conflict with others while co-operating with them, each of the contractants, while needing the other, seeks to obtain what he needs at the least expense; that is to say, to acquire as many rights as possible in exchange for the smallest possible obligations.

It is necessary therefore to pre-determine the share of each, but this cannot be done according to a preconceived plan. There is nothing in the nature of things from which one can deduce what the obligations of one or the other ought to be until a certain limit is reached. Every determination of this kind can only result in compromise. It is a compromise between the rivalry of interests present and their solidarity. It is a position of equilibrium which can be found only after more or less laborious experiments. But it is quite evident that we can neither begin these experiments over again nor restore this equilibrium at fresh expense every time that we engage in some contractual relation. We lack all ability to do that. It is not at the moment when difficulties surge upon us that we must resolve them, and, moreover, we can neither foresee the variety of possible circumstances in which our contract will involve itself, nor fix in advance with the aid of simple mental calculus what will be in each case the rights and duties of each, save in matters in which we have a very definite experience. Moreover, the material conditions of life oppose themselves to the repetition of such operations. For, at each instant, and often at the most inopportune, we find ourselves contracting, either for something we have bought, or sold, somewhere we are traveling, our hiring of one's services, some acceptance of hostelry, and so on. The greater part of our relations with others is of a contractual nature. If, then, it were necessary each time to begin the struggles anew, to again go through the conferences necessary to establish firmly all the conditions of agreement for the present and the future, we would be put to rout. For all these reasons, if we were linked only by the terms of our contracts, as they are agreed upon, only a precarious solidarity would result.

But contract-law is that which determines the juridical consequences of our acts that we have not determined. It expresses the normal conditions of equilibrium, as they arise from themselves or from the average. A résumé of numerous, varied experiences, what we cannot foresee individually is there provided for, what we cannot regulate is there regulated, and this regulation imposes itself upon us, although it may not be our handiwork, but that of society and tradition. It forces us to assume obligations that we have not contracted for, in the exact sense of the word, since we have not deliberated upon them, nor even, occasionally, had any knowledge about them in advance. Of course, the initial act is always contractual, but there are consequences, sometimes immediate, which run over the limits of the contract. We co-operate because we wish to, but our voluntary co-operation creates duties for us that we did not desire.

.   .   .

A corollary of all that has preceded is that the division of labor can be effectuated only among members of an already constituted society.

In effect, when competition places isolated and estranged individuals in opposition, it can only separate them more. If there is a lot of space at their disposal, they will flee; if they cannot go beyond certain boundaries, they will differentiate themselves, so as to become still more independent. No case can be cited where relations of pure hostility are transformed, without the intervention of any other factor, into social relations. Thus, as among individuals of the same animal or vegetable species, there is generally no bond, the war they wage has no other result than to diversify them, to give birth to dissimilar varieties which grow farther apart. It is this progressive disjunction that Darwin called the law of the divergence of characters. But the division of labor unites at the same time that it opposes; it makes the activities it differentiates converge; it brings together those it separates. Since competition cannot have determined this conciliation, it must have existed before. The individuals among whom the struggle is waged must already be solidary and feel so. That is to say, they must belong to the same society. That is why, where this feeling of solidarity is too feeble to resist the dispersive influence of competition, the latter engenders altogether different effects from the division of labor. In countries where existence is too difficult because of the extreme density of the population, the inhabitants, instead of specializing, retire from society, either permanently or temporarily and leave for other countries.

To represent what the division of labor is suffices to make one understand that it cannot be otherwise. It consists in the sharing of functions up to that time common. But this sharing cannot be executed according to a preconceived plan. We cannot tell in advance where the line of demarcation between tasks will be found once they are separated, for it is not marked so evidently in the nature of things, but depends, on the contrary, upon a multitude of circumstances. The division of labor, then, must come about of itself and progressively. Consequently, under these conditions, for a function to be divided into two exactly complementary parts, as the nature of the division of labor demands, it is indispensable that the two specializing parts be in constant communication during all the time that this dissociation lasts. There is no other means for one to receive all the movement the other abandons, and which they adapt to each other. But in the same way that an animal colony whose members embody a continuity of tissue form one individual, every aggregate of individuals who are in continuous contact form a society. The division of labor can then be produced only in the midst of a pre-existing society. By that, we do not mean to say simply that individuals must adhere materially, but it is still necessary that there be moral links between them. First, material continuity by itself produces links of this kind, provided it is durable. But, moreover, they are directly necessary. If the relations becoming established in the period of groping were not subject to any rule, if no power moderated the conflict of individual interests, there would be chaos from which no new order could emerge. It is thought, it is true, that everything takes place through private conventions freely disputed. Thus, it seems that all social action is absent. But this is to forget that contracts are possible only where a juridical regulation, and, consequently, a society, already exists.

Hence, the claim sometimes advanced that in the division of labor lies the fundamental fact of all social life is wrong. Work is not divided among independent and already differentiated individuals who by uniting and associating bring together their different aptitudes. For it would be a miracle if differences thus born through chance circumstance could unite so perfectly as to form a coherent whole. Far from preceding collective life, they derive from it. They can be produced only in the midst of a society, and under the pressure of social sentiments and social needs. That is what makes them essentially harmonious. There is, then, a social life outside the whole division of labor, but which the latter presupposes. That is, indeed, what we have directly established in showing that there are societies whose cohesion is essentially due to a community of beliefs and sentiments, and it is from these societies that those whose unity is assured by the division of labor have emerged. The conclusions of the preceding book and those which we have just reached can then be used to control and mutually confirm each other. The division of physiological labor is itself submitted to this law; it never appears except in the midst of polycellular masses which are already endowed with a certain cohesion.

For a number of theorists, it is a self-evident truth that all society essentially consists of co-operation. Spencer has said that a society in the scientific sense of the word exists only when to the juxtaposition of individuals co-operation is added. We have just seen that this so-called axiom is contrary to the truth. Rather it is evident, as Auguste Comte points out, "that co-operation, far from having produced society, necessarily supposes, as preamble, its spontaneous existence." What bring men together are mechanical causes and impulsive forces, such as affinity of blood, attachment to the same soil, ancestral worship, community of habits, and so on. It is only when the group has been formed on these bases that co-operation is organized there.

Further, the only co-operation possible in the beginning is so intermittent and feeble that social life, if it had no other source, would be without force and without continuity. With stronger reason, the complex co-operation resulting from the division of labor is an ulterior and derived phenomenon. It results from internal movements which are developed in the midst of the mass, when the latter is constituted. It is true that once it appears it tightens the social bonds and makes a more perfect individuality of society. But this integration supposes another which it replaces. For social units to be able to be differentiated, they must first be attracted or grouped by virtue of the resemblances they present. This process of formation is observed, not only originally, but in each phase of evolution. We know, indeed, that higher societies result from the union of lower societies of the same type. It is necessary first that these latter be mingled in the midst of the same identical collective conscience for the process of differentiation to begin or recommence. It is thus that more complex organisms are formed by the repetition of more simple, similar organisms which are differentiated only if once associated. In short, association and co-operation are two distinct facts, and if the second, when developed, reacts on the first and transforms it, if human societies steadily become groups of co-operators, the duality of the two phenomena does not vanish for all that.

If this important truth has been disregarded by the utilitarians, it is an error rooted in the manner in which they conceive the genesis of society. They suppose originally isolated and independent individuals, who, consequently, enter into relationships only to co-operate, for they have no other reason to clear the space separating them and to associate. But this theory, so widely held, postulates a veritable *creatio ex nihilo*.

It consists, indeed, in deducing society from the individual. But nothing we know authorizes us to believe in the possibility of such spontaneous generation. According to Spencer, for societies to be formed within this hypothesis, it is necessary that primitive units pass from the state of perfect independence to that of mutual dependence. But what can have determined such a complete transformation in them? Is it the prospect of the advantages presented by social life? But they are counterbalanced, perhaps more than counterbalanced, by the loss of independence, for, among individuals born for a free and solitary life, such a sacrifice is most intolerable. Add to this, that in the first social types social life is as absolute as possible, for nowhere is the individual more completely absorbed in the group. How would man, if he were born an individualist, as is supposed, be able to resign himself to an existence clashing violently with his fundamental inclination? How pale the problematical utility of co-operation must appear to him beside such a fall! With autonomous individualities, as are imagined, nothing can emerge save what is individual, and, consequently, co-operation itself, which is a social fact, submissive to social rules, cannot arise. Thus, the psychologist who starts by restricting himself to the ego cannot emerge to find the non-ego.

Collective life is not born from individual life, but it is, on the contrary, the second which is born from the first. It is on this condition alone that one can explain how the personal individuality of social units has been able to be formed and enlarged without disintegrating society. Indeed, as, in this case, it becomes elaborate in the midst of a pre-existing social environment, it necessarily bears its mark. It is made in a manner so as not to ruin this collective order with which it is solidary. It remains adapted to it while detaching itself. It has nothing anti-social about it because it is a product of society. It is not the absolute personality of the monad, which is sufficient unto itself, and could do without the rest of the world, but that of an organ or part of an organ having its determined function, but which cannot, without risking dissolution, separate itself from the rest of the organism. Under these conditions, co-operation becomes not only possible but necessary. Utilitarians thus reverse the natural order of facts, and nothing is more deceiving than this inversion. It is a particular illustration of the general truth that what is first in knowledge is last in reality. Precisely because co-operation is the most recent fact, it strikes sight first. If, then, one clings to appearance, as does common sense, it is inevitable that one see in it the primary fact of moral and social life.

But if it is not all of ethics, it is not necessary to put it outside ethics, as do certain moralists. As the utilitarians, the idealists have it consist exclusively in a system of economic relations, of private arrangements in which egotism is the only active power. In truth, the moral life traverses all the relations which constitute co-operation, since it would not be possible if social sentiments, and, consequently, moral sentiments, did not preside in its elaboration.

TWO FORMS OF COLLECTIVE CONSCIENCE:
CONCRETE AND ABSTRACT

In a small society, since everyone is clearly placed in the same conditions of existence, the collective environment is essentially concrete. It is made up of beings of all sorts who fill the social horizon. The states of conscience representing it then have the same character. First, they are related to precise objects, as this animal, this tree, this plant, this natural force, etc. Then, as everybody is related to these things in the same way, they affect all consciences in the same way. The whole tribe, if it is not too widely extended, enjoys or suffers the same advantages or inconveniences from the sun, rain, heat, or cold, from this river, or that source, etc. The collective impressions resulting from the fusion of all these individual impressions are then determined in form as well as in object, and, consequently, the common conscience has a defined character. But it changes its nature as societies become more voluminous. Because these societies are spread over a vaster surface, the common conscience is itself obliged to rise above all local diversities, to dominate more space, and consequently to become more abstract. For not many general things can be common to all these diverse environments. It is no longer such an animal, but such a species; not this source, but such sources; not this forest, but forest *in abstracto*.

Moreover, because conditions of life are no longer the same everywhere, these common objects, whatever they may be, can no longer determine perfectly identical sentiments everywhere. The collective resultants then no longer have the same sharpness, and the more so in this respect as their component elements are more unlike. The more differences among individual portraits serving to make a composite portrait, the more indecisive the latter is. True it is that local collective consciences can keep their individuality in the midst of the general collective conscience and that, as they comprise less space, they more easily remain concrete. But we know they slowly tend to vanish from the first, in so far as the social segments to which they correspond are effaced.

The fact which perhaps best manifests this increasing tendency of the common conscience is the parallel transcendence of the most essential of its elements, I mean the idea of divinity. In the beginning, the gods are not distinct from the universe, or rather there are no gods, but only sacred beings, without their sacred character being related to any external entity as their source. The animals or plants of the species which serves as a clan-totem are the objects of worship, but that is not because a principle *sui generis* comes to communicate their divine nature to them from without. This nature is intrinsic with them; they are divine in and of themselves. But little by little religious forces are detached from the things of which they were first only the attributes, and become hypostatized. Thus is formed the notion of spirits or gods who, while residing here or there as preferred, nevertheless exist outside of the particular objects to which they are more specifically attached. By that very fact they are less concrete. Whether they multiply or have been led back to some certain unity, they are still immanent in the world. If they are in part separated from things, they are always in space. They remain, then, very near us, constantly fused into our life. The Graeco-Latin polytheism, which is a more elevated and better organized form of animism, marks new progress in the direction of transcendence. The residence of the gods becomes more sharply distinct from that of men. Set upon the mysterious heights of Olympus or dwelling in the recesses of the earth, they personally intervene in human affairs only in somewhat intermittent fashion. But it is only with Christianity that God takes leave of space; his kingdom is no longer of this world. The dissociation of nature and the divine is so complete that it degenerates into antagonism. At the same time, the concept of divinity becomes more general and more abstract, for it is formed, not of sensations, as originally, but of ideas. The God of humanity necessarily is less concrete than the gods of the city or the clan.

Besides, at the same time as religion, the rules of law become universal, as well as those of morality. Linked at first to local circumstances, to particularities, ethnic, climatic, and so on, they free themselves little by little, and with the same stroke become more general. What makes this increase of generality obvious is the uninterrupted decline of formalism. In lower societies, the very external form of conduct is predetermined even to the details. The way in which man must eat, dress in every situation, the gestures he must make, the formulae he must pronounce, are precisely fixed. On the contrary, the further one strays from the point of departure, the more moral and juridical prescriptions lose their sharpness and precision. They rule only the most general forms of conduct, and rule them in a very general manner, saying what must be done, not how it must be done. Now, all that is defined is expressed in a definite form. If collective sentiments had the same determination as formerly, they would not be expressed in a less determined manner. If the concrete details of action and thought were as uniform, they would be as obligatory.

It has often been remarked that civilization has a tendency to become more rational and more logical. The cause is now evident. That alone is rational which is universal. What baffles understanding is the particular and the concrete. Only the general is thought well of. Consequently, the nearer the common conscience is to particular things, the more it bears their imprint, the more unintelligible it also is. That is why primitive civilizations affect us as they do. Being unable to subsume them under logical principles, we succeed in seeing only bizarre and fortuitous combinations of heterogeneous elements. In reality, there is nothing artificial about them. It is necessary only to seek their determining causes in sensations and movements of sensibility, not in concepts. And if this is so, it is because the social environment for which they are made is not sufficiently extended. On the contrary, when civilization is developed over a vaster field of action, when it is applied to more people and things, general ideas necessarily appear and become predominant there. The idea of man, for example, replaces in law, in morality, in religion, that of Roman, which, being more concrete, is more refractory to science. Thus, it is the increase of volume in societies and their greater condensation which explain this great transformation.

But the more general the common conscience becomes, the greater the place it leaves to individual variations. When God is far from things and men, his action is no longer omnipresent, nor ubiquitous. There is nothing fixed save abstract rules which can be freely applied in very different ways. Then they no longer have the same ascendancy nor the same force of resistance. Indeed, if practices and formulae, when they are precise, determine thought and movements with a necessity analogous to that of reflexes, these general principles, on the contrary, can pass into facts only with the aid of intelligence. But, once reflection is awakened, it is not easy to restrain it. When it has taken hold, it develops spontaneously beyond the limits assigned to it. One begins by putting articles of faith beyond discussion; then discussion extends to them. One wishes an explanation of them; one asks their reasons for existing, and, as they submit to this search, they lose a part of their force. For reflective ideas never have the same constraining force as instincts. It is thus that deliberated movements have not the spontaneity of involuntary movements. Because it becomes more rational, the collective conscience becomes less imperative, and for this very reason, it wields less restraint over the free development of individual varieties.

THE SOCIAL NATURE OF THE HUMAN INDIVIDUAL

With societies, individuals are transformed in accordance with the changes produced in the number of social units and their relations.

First, they are made more and more free of the yoke of the organism. An animal is almost completely under the influence of his physical environment; its biological constitution predetermines its existence. Man, on the contrary, is dependent upon social causes. Of course, animals also form societies, but, as they are very restricted, collective life is very simple. They are also stationary because the equilibrium of such small societies is necessarily stable. For these two reasons, it easily fixes itself in the organism. It not only has its roots in the organism, but it is entirely enveloped in it to such a point that it loses its own characteristics. It functions through a system of instincts, of reflexes which are not essentially distinct from those which assure the functioning of organic life. They present, it is true, the particular characteristic of adapting the individual to the social environment, not to the physical environment, and are caused by occurrences of the common life. They are not of different nature, however, from those which, in certain cases, determine without any previous education the necessary movements in locomotion. It is quite otherwise with man, because the societies he forms are much vaster. Even the smallest we know of are more extensive than the majority of animal societies. Being more complex, they also change more, and these two causes together see to it that social life with man is not congealed in a biological form. Even where it is most simple, it clings to its specificity. There are always beliefs and practices common to men which are not inscribed in their tissues. But this character is more manifest as the social mass and density grow. The more people there are in association, and the more they react upon one another, the more also does the product of these reactions pass beyond the bounds of the organism. Man thus finds himself placed under the sway of causes *sui generis* whose relative part in the constitution of human nature becomes ever more considerable.

Moreover, the influence of this factor increases not only in relative value, but also in absolute value. The same cause which increases the importance of the collective environment weakens the organic environment in such a manner as to make it accessible to the action of social causes and to subordinate it to them. Because there are more individuals living together, common life is richer and more varied, but for this variety to be possible, the organic type must be less definite to be able to diversify itself. We have seen, in effect, that the tendencies and aptitudes transmitted by heredity became ever more general and more indeterminate, more refractory consequently, to assuming the form of instincts. Thus, a phenomenon is produced which is exactly the inverse of that which we observe at the beginning of evolution. With animals, the organism assimilates social facts to it, and, stripping them of their special nature, transforms them into biological facts. Social life is materialized. In man, on the contrary, and particularly in higher societies, social causes substitute themselves for organic causes. The organism is spiritualized.

The individual is transformed in accordance with this change in dependence. Since this activity which calls forth the special action of social causes cannot be fixed in the organism, a new life, also *sui generis*, is superimposed upon that of the body. Freer, more complex, more independent of the organs which support it, its distinguishing characteristics become ever more apparent as it progresses and becomes solid. From this description we can recognize the essential traits of psychic life. To be sure, it would be exaggerating to say that psychic life begins only with societies, but certainly it becomes extensive only as societies develop. That is why, as has often been remarked, the progress of conscience is in inverse ratio to that of instinct. Whatever may be said of them, it is not the first which breaks up the second. Instinct, the product of the accumulated experience of generations, has a much greater resistive force to dissolution simply because it becomes conscious. Truly, conscience only invades the ground which instinct has ceased to occupy, or where instinct cannot be established. Conscience does not make instinct recede; it only fills the space instinct leaves free. Moreover, if instinct regresses rather than extends as general life extends, the greater importance of the social factor is the cause of this. Hence, the great difference which separates man from animals, that is, the greater development of his psychic life, comes from his greater sociability. To understand why psychic functions have been carried, from the very beginnings of the human species, to a degree of perfection unknown among animal species, one would first have to know why it is that men, instead of living in solitude or in small bands, were led to form more extensive societies. To put it in terms of the classical definition, if man is a reasonable animal, that is because he is a sociable animal, or at least infinitely more sociable than other animals.

This is not all. In so far as societies do not reach certain dimensions nor a certain degree of concentration, the only psychic life which may be truly developed is that which is common to all the members of the group, which is found identical in each. But, as societies become more vast and, particularly, more condensed, a psychic life of a new sort appears. Individual diversities, at first lost and confused amidst the mass of social likenesses, become disengaged, become conspicuous, and multiply. A multitude of things which use to remain outside consciences because they did not affect the collective being become objects of representations. Whereas individuals used to act only by involving one another, except in cases where their conduct was determined by physical needs, each of them becomes a source of spontaneous activity. Particular personalities become constituted, take conscience of themselves. Moreover, this growth of psychic life in the individual does not obliterate the psychic life of society, but only transforms it. It becomes freer, more extensive, and as it has, after all, no other bases than individual consciences, these extend, become complex, and thus become flexible.

Hence, the cause which called forth the differences separating man from animals is also that which has forced him to elevate himself above himself. The ever growing distance between the savage and the civilized man has no other source. If the faculty of ideation is slowly disengaged from the confused feeling of its origin, if man has learned to formulate concepts and laws, if his spirit has embraced more and more extensive portions of space and time, if, not content with clinging to the past, he has trespassed upon the future, if his emotions and his tendencies, at first simple and not very numerous, have multiplied and diversified, that is because the social milieu has changed without interruption. In effect, unless these transformations were born from nothing, they can have had for causes only the corresponding transformations of surrounding milieux. But, man depends only upon three sorts of milieux: the organism, the external world, society. If one leaves aside the accidental variations due to combinations of heredity,—and their role in human progress is certainly not very considerable,—the organism is not automatically modified; it is necessary that it be impelled by some external cause. As for the physical world, since the beginning of history it has remained sensibly the same, at least if one does not take account of novelties which are of social origin. Consequently, there is only society which has changed enough to be able to explain the parallel changes in individual nature.

It is not, then, audacious to affirm that, from now on, whatever progress is made in psycho-physiology will never represent more than a fraction of psychology, since the major part of psychic phenomena does not come from organic causes. This is what spiritualist philosophers have learned, and the great service that they have rendered science has been to combat the doctrines which reduce psychic life merely to an efflorescence of physical life. They have very justly felt that the first, in its highest manifestations, is much too free and complex to be merely a prolongation of the second. Because it is partly independent of the organism, however, it does not follow that it depends upon no natural cause, and that it must be put outside nature. But all these facts whose explanation we cannot find in the constitution of tissues derive from properties of the social milieu. This hypothesis assumes, at least, very great probability from what has preceded. But the social realm is not less natural than the organic realm. Consequently, because there is a vast region of conscience whose genesis is unintelligible through psycho-physiology alone, we must not conclude that it has been formed of itself and that it is, accordingly, refractory to scientific investigation, but only that it derives from some other positive science which can be called socio-psychology. The phenomena which would constitute its matter are, in effect, of a mixed nature. They have the same essential characters as other psychic facts, but they arise from social causes.

It is not necessary, then, with Spencer, to present social life as a simple resultant of individual natures, since, on the contrary, it is rather the latter which come from the former. Social facts are not the simple development of psychic facts, but the second are in large part only the prolongation of the first in the interior of consciences. This proposition is very important, for the contrary point of view exposes the sociologist, at every moment, to mistaking the cause for the effect, and conversely. For example, if, as often happens, we see in the organization of the family the logically necessary expression of human sentiments inherent in every conscience, we are reversing the true order of facts. On the contrary, it is the social organization of the relations of kinship which has determined the respective sentiments of parents and children. They would have been completely different if the social structure had been different, and the proof of this is, in effect, that paternal love is unknown in a great many societies.[1] One could cite many other examples of the same error.[2] Of course, it is a self-evident truth that there is nothing in social life which is not in individual consciences. Everything that is found in the latter, however, comes from society. The major part of our states of conscience would not have been produced among isolated beings and would have been produced quite otherwise among beings grouped in some other manner. They come, then, not from the psychological nature of man in general, but from the manner in which men once associated mutually affect one another, according as they are more or less numerous, more or less close. Products of group life, it is the nature of the group which alone can explain them. Of course, they would not be possible if individual constitutions did not lend themselves to such action, but individual constitutions are only remote conditions, not determinate causes. Spencer in one place compares the work of the

---

[1] This is the case in societies where the matriarchal family rules.

[2] To cite only one example of this,—religion has been explained by the movements of individual feeling, whereas these movements are only the prolongation in the individual of social states which give birth to religion. We have developed this point further in an article in the *Révue Philosophique*, *Etudes de science sociale*, June, 1886. Cf. *Année Sociologique*, Vol. II, pp. 1–28.

sociologist to the calculation of a mathematician who, from the form of a
certain number of balls, deduces the manner in which they must be combined
in order to keep them in equilibrium. The comparison is inexact and does not
apply to social facts. Here, instead, it is rather the form of all which determines that of the parts. Society does not find the bases on which it rests fully
laid out in consciences; it puts them there itself.[3]

SOCIAL RITUALS AND SACRED OBJECTS

In a general way, it is unquestionable that a society has all that is necessary to
arouse the sensation of the divine in minds, merely by the power that it has
over them; for to its members it is what a god is to his worshippers. In fact, a
god is, first of all, a being whom men think of as superior to themselves, and
upon whom they feel that they depend. Whether it be a conscious personality,
such as Zeus or Jahveh, or merely abstract forces such as those in play in
totemism, the worshipper, in the one case as in the other, believes himself
held to certain manners of acting which are imposed upon him by the nature
of the sacred principle with which he feels that he is in communion. Now
society also gives us the sensation of a perpetual dependence. Since it has a
nature which is peculiar to itself and different from our individual nature, it
pursues ends which are likewise special to it; but, as it cannot attain them
except through our intermediacy, it imperiously demands our aid. It requires
that, forgetful of our own interest, we make ourselves its servitors, and it
submits us to every sort of inconvenience, privation and sacrifice, without
which social life would be impossible. It is because of this that at every instant
we are obliged to submit ourselves to rules of conduct and of thought which
we have neither made nor desired, and which are sometimes even contrary to
our most fundamental inclinations and instincts.

Even if society were unable to obtain these concessions and sacrifices from
us except by a material constraint, it might awaken in us only the idea of a
physical force to which we must give way of necessity, instead of that of a

From Emile Durkheim, *The Elementary Forms of Religious Life* (London:Allen and Unwin, 1915), pp.
236–252, 262–264. Originally published in 1912.

[3]This is a sufficient reply, we believe, to those who think they prove that everything in social life is
individual because society is made up only of individuals. Of course, society has no other substratum, but because individuals form society, new phenomena which are formed by association are
produced, and react upon individual consciences and in large part form them. That is why, although
society may be nothing without individuals, each of them is much more a product of society than he
is its maker.

moral power such as religions adore. But as a matter of fact, the empire which it holds over consciences is due much less to the physical supremacy of which it has the privilege than to the moral authority with which it is invested. If we yield to its orders, it is not merely because it is strong enough to triumph over our resistance; it is primarily because it is the object of a venerable respect.

We say that an object, whether individual or collective, inspires respect when the representation expressing it in the mind is gifted with such a force that it automatically causes or inhibits actions, *without regard for any consideration relative to their useful or injurious effects.* When we obey somebody because of the moral authority which we recognize in him, we follow out his opinions, not because they seem wise, but because a certain sort of physical energy is imminent in the idea that we form of this person, which conquers our will and inclines it in the indicated direction. Respect is the emotion which we experience when we feel this interior and wholly spiritual pressure operating upon us. Then we are not determined by the advantages or inconveniences of the attitude which is prescribed or recommended to us; it is by the way in which we represent to ourselves the person recommending or prescribing it. This is why commands generally take a short, peremptory form leaving no place for hesitation; it is because, in so far as it is a command and goes by its own force, it excludes all idea of deliberation or calculation; it gets its efficacy from the intensity of the mental state in which it is placed. It is this intensity which creates what is called a moral ascendancy.

Now the ways of action to which society is strongly enough attached to impose them upon its members, are, by that very fact, marked with a distinctive sign provocative of respect. Since they are elaborated in common, the vigour with which they have been thought of by each particular mind is retained in all the other minds, and reciprocally. The representations which express them within each of us have an intensity which no purely private states of consciousness could ever attain; for they have the strength of the innumerable individual representations which have served to form each of them. It is society who speaks through the mouths of those who affirm them in our presence; it is society whom we hear in hearing them; and the voice of all has an accent which that of one alone could never have. The very violence with which society reacts, by way of blame or material suppression, against every attempted dissidence, contributes to strengthening its empire by manifesting the common conviction through this burst of ardour. In a word, when something is the object of such a state of opinion, the representation which each individual has of it gains a power of action from its origins and the conditions in which it was born, which even those feel who do not submit themselves to it. It tends to repel the representations which contradict it, and it keeps them at a distance; on the other hand, it commands those acts which will realize it, and it does so, not by a material coercion or by the perspective of something of this sort, but by the simple radiation of the mental energy which it contains. It has an efficacy coming solely from its psychical properties, and it is by just this sign that moral authority is recognized. So opinion, primarily a social thing, is a source of authority, and it might even be asked whether all authority is not the daughter of opinion. It may be objected that science is often the antagonist of opinion, whose errors it combats and rectifies. But it cannot succeed in this task if it does not have sufficient authority, and it can obtain this authority only from opinion itself. If a people did not have faith in science, all the scientific demonstrations in the world would be without any influence whatsoever over their minds. Even to-day, if science happened to resist a very strong current of public opinion, it would risk losing its credit there.

Since it is in spiritual ways that social pressure exercises itself, it could not fail to give men the idea that outside themselves there exist one or several powers, both moral and, at the same time, efficacious, upon which they depend. They must think of these powers, at least in part, as outside themselves, for these address them in a tone of command and sometimes even order them to do violence to their most natural inclinations. It is undoubtedly true that if they were able to see that these influences which they feel emanate from society, then the mythological system of interpretations would never be born. But social action follows ways that are too circuitous and obscure, and employs psychical mechanisms that are too complex to allow the ordinary observer to see when it comes. As long as scientific analysis does not come to teach it to them, men know well that they are acted upon, but they do not know by whom. So they must invent by themselves the idea of these powers with which they feel themselves in connection, and from that, we are able to catch a glimpse of the way by which they were led to represent them under forms that are really foreign to their nature and to transfigure them by thought.

But a god is not merely an authority upon whom we depend; it is a force upon which our strength relies. The man who has obeyed his god and who for this reason, believes the god is with him, approaches the world with confidence and with the feeling of an increased energy. Likewise, social action does not confine itself to demanding sacrifices, privations and efforts from us. For the collective force is not entirely outside of us; it does not act upon us wholly from without; but rather, since society cannot exist except in and through individual consciousness, this force must also penetrate us and organize itself within us; it thus becomes an integral part of our being and by that very fact this is elevated and magnified.

There are occasions when this strengthening and vivifying action of society is especially apparent. In the midst of an assembly animated by a common passion, we become susceptible of acts and sentiments of which we are incapable when reduced to our own forces; and when the assembly is dissolved and when, finding ourselves alone again, we fall back to our ordinary level, we are then able to measure the height to which we have been raised above ourselves. History abounds in examples of this sort. It is enough to think of the night of the Fourth of August, 1789, when an assembly was suddenly led to an act of sacrifice and abnegation which each of its members had refused the day before, and at which they were all surprised the day after. This is why all parties political, economic or confessional, are careful to have periodical reunions where their members may revivify their common faith by manifesting it in common. To strengthen those sentiments which, if left to themselves, would soon weaken, it is sufficient to bring those who hold them together and to put them into closer and more active relations with one another. This is the explanation of the particular attitude of a man speaking to a crowd, at least if he has succeeded in entering into communion with it. His language has a grandiloquence that would be ridiculous in ordinary circumstances; his gestures show a certain domination; his very thought is impatient of all rules, and easily falls into all sorts of excesses. It is because he feels within him an abnormal over-supply of force which overflows and tries to burst out from him; sometimes he even has the feeling that he is dominated by a moral force which is greater than he and of which he is only the interpreter. It is by this trait that we are able to recognize what has often been called the demon of oratorical inspiration. Now this exceptional increase of force is something very real; it comes to him from the very group which he addresses. The sentiments provoked by his words come back to him, but enlarged and amplified, and to this degree they strengthen his own sentiment. The passionate energies he arouses re-echo within him and quicken his vital tone. It is no longer a simple individual who speaks, it is a group incarnate and personified.

Besides these passing and intermittent states, there are other more durable ones, where this strengthening influence of society makes itself felt with greater consequences and frequently even with greater brilliancy. There are periods in history when, under the influence of some great collective shock, social interactions have become much more frequent and active. Men look for each other and assemble together more than ever. That general effervescence results which is characteristic of revolutionary or creative epochs. Now this greater activity results in a general stimulation of individual forces. Men see more and differently now than in normal times. Changes are not merely of shades and degrees; men become different. The passions moving them are of such an intensity that they cannot be satisfied except by violent and unrestrained actions, actions of superhuman heroism or of bloody barbarism. This is what explains the Crusades, for example, or many of the scenes, either sublime or savage, of the French Revolution. Under the influence of the general exaltation, we see the most mediocre and inoffensive bourgeois become either a hero or a butcher. And so clearly are all these mental processes the ones that are also at the root of religion that the individuals themselves have often pictured the pressure before which they thus gave way in a distinctly religious form. The Crusaders believed that they felt God present in the midst of them, enjoining them to go to the conquest of the Holy Land; Joan of Arc believed that she obeyed celestial voices.

But it is not only in exceptional circumstances that this stimulating action of society makes itself felt; there is not, so to speak, a moment in our lives when some current of energy does not come to us from without. The man who has done his duty finds, in the manifestations of every sort expressing the sympathy, esteem or affection which his fellows have for him, a feeling of comfort, of which he does not ordinarily take account, but which sustains him, none the less. The sentiments which society has for him raise the sentiments which he has for himself. Because he is in moral harmony with his comrades, he has more confidence, courage and boldness in action, just like the believer who thinks that he feels the regard of his god turned graciously towards him. It thus produces, as it were, a perpetual sustenance of our moral nature. Since this varies with a multitude of external circumstances, as our relations with the groups about us are more or less active and as these groups themselves vary, we cannot fail to feel that this moral support depends upon an external cause; but we do not perceive where this cause is nor what it is. So we ordinarily think of it under the form of a moral power which, though immanent in us, represents within us something not ourselves: this is the moral conscience, of which, by the way, men have never made even a slightly distinct representation except by the aid of religious symbols.

In addition to these free forces which are constantly coming to renew our own, there are others which are fixed in the methods and traditions which we employ. We speak a language that we did not make; we use instruments that we did not invent; we invoke rights that we did not found; a treasury of knowledge is transmitted to each generation that it did not gather itself, etc. It is to society that we owe these varied benefits of civilization, and if we do not ordinarily see the source from which we get them, we at least know that they are not our own work. Now it is these things that give man his own place among things; a man is a man only because he is civilized. So he could not escape the feeling that outside of him there are active causes from which he gets the characteristic attributes of his nature and which, as benevolent powers, assist him, protect him and assure him of a privileged fate. And of course he must attribute to these powers a dignity corresponding to the great value of the good things he attributes to them.

Thus the environment in which we live seems to us to be peopled with forces that are at once imperious and helpful, august and gracious, and with which we have relations. Since they exercise over us a pressure of which we are conscious, we are forced to localize them outside ourselves, just as we do for the objective causes of our sensations. But the sentiments which they inspire in us differ in nature from those which we have for simple visible objects. As long as these latter are reduced to their empirical characteristics as shown in ordinary experience, and as long as the religious imagination has not metamorphosed them, we entertain for them no feeling which resembles respect, and they contain within them nothing that is able to raise us outside ourselves. Therefore, the representations which express them appear to us to be very different from those aroused in us by collective influences. The two form two distinct and separate mental states in our consciousness, just as do the two forms of life to which they correspond. Consequently, we get the impression that we are in relations with two distinct sorts of reality and that a sharply drawn line of demarcation separates them from each other: on the one hand is the world of profane things, on the other, that of sacred things.

Also, in the present day just as much as in the past, we see society constantly creating sacred things out of ordinary ones. If it happens to fall in love with a man and if it thinks it has found in him the principal aspirations that move it, as well as the means of satisfying them, this man will be raised above the others and, as it were, deified. Opinion will invest him with a majesty exactly analogous to that protecting the gods. This is what has happened to so many sovereigns in whom their age had faith: if they were not made gods, they were at least regarded as direct representatives of the deity. And the fact that it is society alone which is the author of these varieties of apotheosis, is evident since it frequently chances to consecrate men thus who have no right to it from their own merit. The simple deference inspired by men invested with high social functions is not different in nature from religious respect. It is expressed by the same movements: a man keeps at a distance from a high personage; he approaches him only with precautions; in conversing with him, he uses other gestures and language than those used with ordinary mortals. The sentiment felt on these occasions is so closely related to the religious sentiment that many peoples have confounded the two. In order to explain the consideration accorded to princes, nobles and political chiefs, a sacred character has been attributed to them. In Melanesia and Polynesia, for example, it is said that an influential man has *mana*, and that his influence is due to this *mana*. However, it is evident that his situation is due solely to the importance attributed to him by public opinion. Thus the moral power conferred by opinion and that with which sacred beings are invested are at bottom of a single origin and made up of the same elements. That is why a single word is able to designate the two.

In addition to men, society also consecrates things, especially ideas. If a belief is unanimously shared by a people, then, for the reason which we pointed out above, it is forbidden to touch it, that is to say, to deny it or to contest it. Now the prohibition of criticism is an interdiction like the others and proves the presence of something sacred. Even to-day, howsoever great may be the liberty which we accord to others, a man who should totally deny progress or ridicule the human ideal to which modern societies are attached, would produce the effect of a sacrilege. There is at least one principle which those the most devoted to the free examination of everything tend to place above discussion and to regard as untouchable, that is to say, as sacred: this is the very principle of free examination.

This aptitude of society for setting itself up as a god or for creating gods was never more apparent than during the first years of the French Revolution. At this time, in fact, under the influence of the general enthusiasm, things purely laïcal by nature were transformed by public opinion into sacred things: these were the Fatherland, Liberty, Reason. A religion tended to become established which had its dogmas, symbols, altars and feasts. It was to these spontaneous aspirations that the cult of Reason and the Supreme Being attempted to give a sort of official satisfaction. It is true that this religious renovation had only an ephemeral duration. But that was because the patriotic enthusiasm which at first transported the masses soon relaxed. The cause being gone, the effect could not remain. But this experiment, though short-lived, keeps all its sociological interest. It remains true that in one determined case we have seen society and its essential ideas become, directly and with no transfiguration of any sort, the object of a veritable cult.

All these facts allow us to catch glimpses of how the clan was able to awaken within its members the idea that outside of them there exist forces which dominate them and at the same time sustain them, that is to say in fine, religious forces: it is because there is no society with which the primitive is more directly and closely connected. The bonds uniting him to the tribe are much more lax and more feebly felt. Although this is not at all strange or foreign to him, it is with the people of his own clan that he has the greatest number of things in common; it is the action of this group that he feels the most directly; so it is this also which, in preference to all others, should express itself in religious symbols.

But this first explanation has been too general, for it is applicable to every sort of society indifferently, and consequently to every sort of religion. Let us attempt to determine exactly what form this collective action takes in the clan and how it arouses the sensation of sacredness there. For there is no place where it is more easily observable or more apparent in its results.

The life of the Australian societies passes alternately through two distinct phases. Sometimes the population is broken up into little groups who wander about independently of one another, in their various occupations; each family lives by itself, hunting and fishing, and in a word, trying to procure its indispensable food by all the means in its power. Sometimes, on the contrary, the population concentrates and gathers at determined points for a length of time varying from several days to several months. This concentration takes place when a clan or a part of the tribe is summoned to the gathering, and on this occasion they celebrate a religious ceremony, or else hold what is called a corrobbori in the usual ethnological language.

These two phases are contrasted with each other in the sharpest way. In the first, economic activity is the preponderating one, and it is generally of a very mediocre intensity. Gathering the grains or herbs that are necessary for food, or hunting and fishing are not occupations to awaken very lively passions. The dispersed condition in which the society finds itself results in making its life uniform, languishing and dull. But when a corrobbori takes place, everything changes. Since the emotional and passional faculties of the primitive are only imperfectly placed under the control of his reason and will, he easily loses control of himself. Any event of some importance puts him quite outside himself. Does he receive good news? There are at once transports of enthusiasm. In the contrary conditions, he is to be seen running here and there like a madman, giving himself up to all sorts of immoderate movements, crying, shrieking, rolling in the dust, throwing it in every direction, biting himself, brandishing his arms in a furious manner, and so on. The very fact of the concentration acts as an exceptionally powerful stimulant. When they are once come together, a sort of electricity is formed by their collecting which quickly transports them to an extraordinary degree of exaltation. Every sentiment expressed finds a place without resistance in all the minds, which are very open to outside impressions; each re-echoes the others, and is re-echoed by the others. The initial impulse thus proceeds, growing as it goes, as an avalanche grows in its advance. And as such active passions so free from all control could not fail to burst out, on every side one sees nothing but violent

gestures, cries, veritable howls, and deafening noises of every sort, which aid
in intensifying still more the state of mind which they manifest. And since a
collective sentiment cannot express itself collectively except on the condition
of observing a certain order permitting co-operation and movements in unison, these gestures and cries naturally tend to become rhythmic and regular;
hence come songs and dances. But in taking a more regular form, they lose
nothing of their natural violence; a regulated tumult remains tumult. The
human voice is not sufficient for the task; it is reinforced by means of artificial
processes: boomerangs are beaten against each other; bull-roarers are whirled.
It is probable that these instruments, the use of which is so general in the
Australian religious ceremonies, are used primarily to express in a more adequate fashion the agitation felt. But while they express it, they also strengthen
it. This effervescence often reaches such a point that it causes unheard-of
actions. The passions released are of such an impetuosity that they can be
restrained by nothing. They are so far removed from their ordinary conditions
of life, and they are so thoroughly conscious of it, that they feel that they must
set themselves outside of and above their ordinary morals. The sexes unite
contrarily to the rules governing sexual relations. Men exchange wives with
each other. Sometimes even incestuous unions, which in normal times are
thought abominable and are severely punished, are now contracted openly
and with impunity. If we add to all this that the ceremonies generally take
place at night in a darkness pierced here and there by the light of fires, we can
easily imagine what effect such scenes ought to produce on the minds of those
who participate. They produce such a violent super-excitation of the whole
physical and mental life that it cannot be supported very long: the actor taking
the principal part finally falls exhausted on the ground.

·   ·   ·

One can readily conceive how, when arrived at this state of exaltation, a
man does not recognize himself any longer. Feeling himself dominated and
carried away by some sort of an external power which makes him think and
act differently than in normal times, he naturally has the impression of being
himself no longer. It seems to him that he has become a new being: the
decorations he puts on and the masks that cover his face and figure materially
in this interior transformation, and to a still greater extent, they aid in determining its nature. And as at the same time all his companions feel themselves
transformed in the same way and express this sentiment by their cries, their
gestures and their general attitude, everything is just as though he really were
transported into a special world, entirely different from the one where he
ordinarily lives, and into an environment filled with exceptionally intense

forces that take hold of him and metamorphose him. How could such experiences as these, especially when they are repeated every day for weeks, fail to leave in him the conviction that there really exist two heterogeneous and mutually incomparable worlds? One is that where his daily life drags wearily along, but he cannot penetrate into the other without at once entering into relations with extraordinary powers that excite him to the point of frenzy. The first is the profane world, the second, that of sacred things.

So it is in the midst of these effervescent social environments and out of this effervescence itself that the religious idea seems to be born. The theory that this is really its origin is confirmed by the fact that in Australia the really religious activity is almost entirely confined to the moments when these assemblies are held. To be sure, there is no people among whom the great solemnities of the cult are not more or less periodic; but in the more advanced societies, there is not, so to speak, a day when some prayer or offering is not addressed to the gods and some ritual act is not performed. But in Australia, on the contrary, apart from the celebrations of the clan and tribe, the time is nearly all filled with lay and profane occupations. Of course there are prohibitions that should be and are preserved even during these periods of temporal activity; it is never permissible to kill or eat freely of the totemic animal, at least in those parts where the interdiction has retained its original vigour; but almost no positive rites are then celebrated, and there are no ceremonies of any importance. These take place only in the midst of assembled groups. The religious life of the Australian passes through successive phases of complete lull and of superexcitation, and social life oscillates in the same rhythm. This puts clearly into evidence the bond uniting them to one another, but among the peoples called civilized, the relative continuity of the two blurs their relations. It might even be asked whether the violence of this contrast was not necessary to disengage the feeling of sacredness in its first form. By concentrating itself almost entirely in certain determined moments, the collective life has been able to attain its greatest intensity and efficacy, and consequently to give men a more active sentiment of the double existence they lead and of the double nature in which they participate.

But the explanation is still incomplete. We have shown how the clan, by the manner in which it acts upon its members, awakens within them the idea of external forces which dominate them and exalt them; but we must still demand how it happens that these forces are thought of under the form of totems, that is to say, in the shape of an animal or plant.

It is because this animal or plant has given its name to the clan and serves it as emblem. In fact, it is a well-known law that the sentiments aroused in us by something spontaneously attach themselves to the symbol which represents them. For us, black is a sign of mourning; it also suggests sad impressions and ideas. This transference of sentiments comes simply from the fact that the idea of a thing and the idea of its symbol are closely united in our minds; the result is that the emotions provoked by the one extend contagiously to the other. But this contagion, which takes place in every case to a certain degree, is much more complete and more marked when the symbol is something simple, definite and easily representable, while the thing itself, owing to its dimensions, the number of its parts and the complexity of their arrangement, is difficult to hold in the mind. For we are unable to consider an abstract entity, which we can represent only laboriously and confusedly, the source of the strong sentiments which we feel. We cannot explain them to ourselves except by connecting them to some concrete object of whose reality we are vividly aware. Then if the thing itself does not fulfil this condition, it cannot serve as the accepted basis of the sentiments felt, even though it may be what really aroused them. Then some sign takes it place; it is to this that we connect the emotions it excites. It is this which is loved, feared, respected; it is to this that we are grateful; it is for this that we sacrifice ourselves. The soldier who dies for his flag, dies for his country; but as a matter of fact, in his own consciousness, it is the flag that has the first place. It sometimes happens that this even directly determines action. Whether one isolated standard remains in the hands of the enemy or not does not determine the fate of the country, yet the soldier allows himself to be killed to regain it. He loses sight of the fact that the flag is only a sign, and that it has no value in itself, but only brings to mind the reality that it represents; it is treated as if it were this reality itself.

Now the totem is the flag of the clan. It is therefore natural that the impressions aroused by the clan in individual minds—impressions of dependence and of increased vitality—should fix themselves to the idea of the totem rather than that of the clan: for the clan is too complex a reality to be represented clearly in all its complex unity by such rudimentary intelligences. More than that, the primitive does not even see that these impressions come to him from the group. He does not know that the coming together of a number of men associated in the same life results in disengaging new energies, which transform each of them. All that he knows is that he is raised above himself and that he sees a different life from the one he ordinarily leads. However, he must connect these sensations to some external object as their cause. Now what does he see about him? On every side those things which appeal to his senses and strike his imagination are the numerous images of the totem. They are the waninga and the nurtunja, which are symbols of the sacred being. They are churinga and bull-roarers, upon which are generally carved combinations of lines having the same significance. They are the decorations covering the different parts of his body, which are totemic marks. How could this image, repeated everywhere and in all sorts of forms, fail to stand out with exceptional relief in his mind? Placed thus in the centre of the scene, it becomes representative. The sentiments experienced fix themselves upon it, for it is the only concrete object upon which they can fix themselves. It continues to bring them to mind and to evoke them even after the assembly has dissolved, for it survives the assembly, being carved upon the instruments of the cult, upon the sides of rocks, upon bucklers, etc. By it, the emotions experienced are perpetually sustained and revived. Everything happens just as if they inspired them directly. It is still more natural to attribute them to it for, since they are common to the group, they can be associated only with something that is equally common to all. Now the totemic emblem is the only thing satisfying this condition. By definition, it is common to all. During the ceremony, it is the centre of all regards. While generations change, it remains the same; it is the permanent element of the social life. So it is from it that those mysterious forces seem to emanate with which men feel that they are related, and thus they have been led to represent these forces under the form of the animate or inanimate being whose name the clan bears.

In fact, if left to themselves, individual consciousnesses are closed to each other; they can communicate only by means of signs which express their internal states. If the communication established between them is to become a real communion, that is to say, a fusion of all particular sentiments into one common sentiment, the signs expressing them must themselves be fused into one single and unique resultant. It is the appearance of this that informs individuals that they are in harmony and makes them conscious of their moral unity. It is by uttering the same cry, pronouncing the same word, or performing the same gesture in regard to some object that they become and feel themselves to be in unison. It is true that individual representations also cause reactions in the organism that are not without importance; however, they can be thought of apart from these physical reactions which accompany them or follow them, but which do not constitute them. But it is quite another matter with collective representations. They presuppose that minds act and react upon one another; they are the product of these actions and reactions which are themselves possible only through material intermediaries. These latter do not confine themselves to revealing the mental state with which they are associated; they aid in creating it. Individual minds cannot come in contact and communicate with each other except by coming out of themselves; but they cannot do this except by movements. So it is the homogeneity of these movements that gives the group consciousness of itself and consequently makes it exist. When this homogeneity is once established and these movements have once taken a stereotyped form, they serve to symbolize the corresponding representations. But they symbolize them only because they have aided in forming them.

Moreover, without symbols, social sentiments could have only a precarious existence. Though very strong as long as men are together and influence each other reciprocally, they exist only in the form of recollections after the assembly has ended, and when left to themselves, these become feebler and feebler; for since the group is now no longer present and active, individual temperaments easily regain the upper hand. The violent passions which may have been released in the heart of a crowd fall away and are extinguished when this is dissolved, and men ask themselves with astonishment how they could ever have been so carried away from their normal character. But if the movements by which these sentiments are expressed are connected with something that endures, the sentiments themselves become more durable. These other things are constantly bringing them to mind and arousing them; it is as though the cause which excited them in the first place continued to act. Thus these systems of emblems, which are necessary if society is to become conscious of itself, are no less indispensable for assuring the continuation of this consciousness.

So we must refrain from regarding these symbols as simple artifices, as sorts of labels attached to representations already made, in order to make them more manageable: they are an integral part of them. Even the fact that collective sentiments are thus attached to things completely foreign to them is not purely conventional: it illustrates under a conventional form a real characteristic of social facts, that is, their transcendence over individual minds. In fact, it is known that social phenomena are born, not in individuals, but in the group. Whatever part we may take in their origin, each of us receives them from without. So when we represent them to ourselves as emanating from a material object, we do not completely misunderstand their nature. Of course they do not come from the specific thing to which we connect them, but nevertheless, it is true that their origin is outside of us. If the moral force sustaining the believer does not come from the idol he adores or the emblem he venerates, still it is from outside of him, as he is well aware. The objectivity of its symbol only translates its externalness.

Thus social life, in all its aspects and in every period of its history, is made possible only by a vast symbolism. The material emblems and figurative representations with which we are more especially concerned in our present study, are one form of this; but there are many others. Collective sentiments can just as well become incarnate in persons or formulæ: some formulæ are flags, while there are persons, either real or mythical, who are symbols.

The Social Circulation of Sentiments, Magic, and Money [1906–1934]

HENRI HUBERT AND MARCEL MAUSS

• *In the Durkheimian tradition, society and its ritual density charge individuals with their emotional energies and ideas. But how does the individual fit into this? Henri Hubert and Marcel Mauss set out to show how the individual can act alone, independent of society or even against it. In tribal societies, the ritual presence of society is particularly strong; if individual forces can be found even there, their inner power should be revealed most sharply. Hubert and Mauss find the key to individualism in magic, a private appropriation of an emotional force that is, nevertheless, social in its origins. And by a strange dialectic, this appropriation is the beginning of an economy of individual exchanges. For it is magically charged objects (which is to say, those charged with social excitement and belief) that are the early form of money. Even today the money economy is ultimately a circulation of emotions of confidence, of payoffs expected from other people in the future. "J'attends," says Mauss. "I await, I expect: that is the definition of all actions of a collective nature."*

In a considerable group of religious phenomena, the double character of rites and beliefs, as both sacred and social, is not apparent at first glance. Such is magic. In order to generalize and verify the results of our work on sacrifice [Hubert and Mauss, 1899], we needed to assure ourselves that magic does not constitute an exception. Magic presents us with an ensemble of rituals which are as efficacious as sacrifice, but which lack the formal adherence of society. They are practiced outside of society and society keeps its distance from them. Moreover, magic rituals are sacrileges, impieties, or simply secular and technical acts, lacking at first glance the sacred character of the sacrifice. On the other hand, in magic also there are symbolic representations, ranging from gods and

From Henri Hubert and Marcel Mauss, "Introduction a l'analyse de quelques phénomènes religieux," *Revue de l'histoire des religions*, 58 (1906); Marcel Mauss, "Les Origins de la Notion de Monnaie," *Anthropologie* 25 (1914); Marcel Mauss, "Intervention a la suite d'une communication de Francois Simiand, 'La monnaie, realité sociale,' " *Annales Sociologiques* serie D, (1934). Translated by Randall Collins. Citations to Hubert and Mauss's anthropological sources and to most of their polemical opponents have been omitted.

religious representations. Magic has myths whose recitation acts like a charm [Hubert and Mauss, 1904], and notions such as nature, substance, force, *physis* and *dynamis*, whose merits were so little contested that they were admitted into the sciences and technologies. Nevertheless, neither these myths nor these representations explicitly receive the unanimous and necessary accord of society. Nor does the notion of the sacred seem to be a principle for the rites of magic and its accompanying notions and myths. Do magical practices, then, have the same kind of efficacy as technologies, and is the certitude of its notions and myths of the same kind as that of the sciences?

At the time we were posing these questions, the mental operations from which magic derives were regarded as natural sophisms of the human mind. For Frazer and Jevons, the entire mechanism of magic was composed of associations of ideas, analogical reasonings, and false applications of the principle of causality. In this way the English school of anthopologists arrived at results completely opposite those toward which our investigations into religion have led us.

Our inquiry has established that all the elements of magic—magicians, rituals, and magical representations—receive their qualifications from society.

The memoir that we published on "The Origin of Magical Powers in Australian Societies" [Mauss, 1904] has proved precisely this concerning the consciousness [*conscience*] of the magician: the magician is a functionary of society, who often is appointed by it, and who never finds within himself the source of his own power. We have been reproached for having exaggerated the importance of corporations of magicians. But even individual magicians are connected by magical traditions and form associations.

In the first place, the magician does not invent his rituals and representations anew at each step. The efficacy of his gestures and the authority of his ideas are guaranteed by the tradition that he observes. But who says tradition, says society. In the second place, although magic is not public like the ritual of sacrifice, society is no less present. If the magician retires and hides himself, it is from society; and if society drives him away, it is not because he is a matter of indifference to it. Society is afraid of the magician but only because of the powers that it gives to him; he does not act against society except as armed by it.

These powers and qualities, found alike within religion and in magic, all have the same character and proceed from the same general idea. To this notion we have given the name *mana*, borrowed from the Malayo-polynesian tongues; this is how the general idea is designated in Melanesian magic. It is at one and the same time the notion of a power, of a cause, a force, a quality or a substance, even of a milieu. The word *mana* is simultaneously noun, adjective, and verb; it designates attributes, actions, natures, and things. It is applied to the rites, the actors, the materials, and the spirits of magic, as well as to those of religion.

It follows that magical rites and representations have the same social character as sacrifices, and they depend upon a notion identical or analogous to the notion of the sacred. Moreover we began to demonstrate that there are some magical ceremonies in which are produced phenomena of collective psychology from which the notion of *mana* arises.

Since we did not dissimulate that we knew only a few authentic examples of this notion, Jevons has reproached us with founding all of magic upon a principle whose explicit existence is not absolutely universal. Our additional researches permit us to affirm that this notion is widespread, and the number of societies which do not notice it expressly has become more and more restricted.

In Africa, the Bantu, that is to say the largest of the African families, possesses the all but identical notion of *nkissi*. The Ehwe, who are a good part of the Negritos, have the notion of *dzo*. From this fact we conclude for all of Africa that it is necessary to replace the notion of fetish with that of *mana*. In America, we have already noted the Iroquois *orenda*, the Algonquin *manitou*, the Sioux *wakan*, and the *naual* of central Mexico, related to the *nauala* of the Kwakiutl. Our hypothesis on the kinship which connects the notion of *brahman* in Vedic India with that of *mana* was recently accepted by Strauss. Add to these an indefinite number of languages where the same notion is fragmented into several expressions. That which one language says in one word, other languages say in several. It is not even necessary that they express it: the notion of cause is not explicit in the transitive verb, but it is there nevertheless.

To verify the existence of a certain principle of mental operations, it is necessary and sufficient that these operations cannot be explained without it. No one has taken it into his head to contest the universality of the notion of the sacred, yet it would be difficult to cite a word in Sanscrit or Greek that corresponds to the *sacer* of the Latins. In India one says: pure (*medhya*), sacrificial (*yajñiya*), divine (*devya*), terrible (*ghora*); in Greece, holy (*ieros* or *agios*), venerable (*semnos*), just (*thesmos*), respectable (*aidesimos*). Nevertheless, hadn't the Greeks and the Hindus a very strong consciousness of the sacred?

Without being obligatory, the rites of magic are nevertheless social. Properly speaking, obligation is not the distinctive characteristic of social things, acts, and sentiments. For us the illicit act of magic remains social, without there being any contradiction. The act is social because it takes its form from society and it has no reason to exist [*raison d'être*] except by relation with it. Such is the case that Huvelin cites of the sacrificiant who makes a sacrifice to kill his enemy.

Moreover, magic is not necessarily illicit, and in the law, in fact, it can serve the public right just as well as the individual. Thus, in the Australian tribes, threats of spells are for the elders a means to make others respect their discipline. It is not without reason that Frazer relates the powers of magicians to the powers of the king.

Certainly Huvelin is right to show that magic has aided the formation of the techniques of law, as we have supposed magic has done for other techniques [Hubert and Mauss, 1904]. We are in accord with him when he alleges that, in the law, magic has facilitated individual action. Magic has in effect furnished the individual with means to make himself valuable in his own eyes and in the eyes of others, as well as to evade the crowd, to escape from social pressure and routine. In the shelter of magic are possible not only juridical audacities, but also experimental initiatives. Scientists [*savants*] are sons of the magicians.

We have frequently made allusions to the role that the individual plays in magic and to where it places him. Our work has precisely as its object to determine the place of the individual in magic by relation to society.

At the beginning of our studies, we proposed above all to comprehend institutions, that is to say, public rules of action and thought. In the sacrifice, the public character of the institution, collective in action and in symbolic representations, is quite clear. The magic whose acts are as little public as possible furnishes us with an occasion to push further our sociological analysis. It is important to know how and in what measure these facts were social. To put it another way: What is the attitude of the individual in social phenomena? What is the part of the society in the consciousness [*conscience*] of the individual? When individuals assemble, when they conform their gestures to a ritual, and their ideas to a dogma, are they moved by purely individual motives, or by motives whose presence in their consciousness is explained only by the presence of society? Since society is composed of individuals organically assembled, we have to look for that which they bring of themselves and that which they receive from it. We believe we have isolated this process and shown how, in magic, the individual neither thinks nor acts except as directed by tradition; or pushed by a collective suggestion; or certainly at least by a suggestion that he gives himself under the pressure of the collectivity.

Having verified our theory even for the difficult case of magic, where the acts of the individual are as secular and personal as possible, we are quite sure of our principles concerning sacrifice, prayer, and myth. One ought not then to accuse us of contradiction if we sometimes talk of renowned magicians who introduce practices into vogue, or of strong religious personalities who found sects and religions. For it is always society which speaks by their mouths.

THE ORIGINS OF THE NOTION OF MONEY

Money is not a material and physical fact, but essentially a social fact; its value is its power to purchase, and the measure of confidence that one has in it. We are speaking of the origin of a notion, an institution, and a faith.

It is not a question of showing the origin, that is to say an absolute commencement, a birth so to speak out of nothing. Contrary to the received idea, you will see that in effect it is not certain that there have been, among the societies that we know or that we can represent to ourselves by hypothesis, any which were completely unprovided with notions at least analogous to that which we designate today under the name of money. We are not looking for how humanity suddenly hit on the idea of money to which it has previously been a stranger. We are looking for the most primitive, the simplest, better yet the most elementary form, under which the notion of money has presented itself.

I was working, about four years ago, on the beautiful documents that the German missionaries to Togo have published on the Ehwe languages and nations of that region. I was not at all preoccupied at that moment with the question of the origins of money. It was in reading these Ehwe documents, that several chance remarks furnished me with the hypothesis that I am going to present.

I was studying in particular the notion of *dzo*; equivalent to that of *mana*, used among the Ehwe in reference to magical power, substances, and actions. Among the derivates of the radical *dzo*, I found in Westermann's dictionary, the word *dzonu*, (*Zauberding*), magical thing: "all kinds of pearls, or things in form of a pearl, etc." That is one of the names of the cowrey-shells which are so much utilized in the magic and the religion of the Negro nations in general.

Around this fact, other facts crystallized very quickly, and formed a sort of system. Here are some samples:.

The notion of *mana* in Melanesia is directly connected to the notion of money. At the Banks Isles and at Santa Cruz, one calls *rongo* (sacred red), the shell money that also carries the name of *diwarra*. Another example of the notion of magical-religious power is the notion of *manitou* among the Algonquins. Now Father Thavenet says that the pearls of the traders were for the Algonquins the scales of a *manitou* fish. Elsewhere the notion of money is allied to a more precise notion of the sacred. In New Guinea, as in the Bismark archipelago, money kept in the homes of men carries the title of *tambu* [cf. *taboo*].

Elsewhere it is more neatly connected with the notion of the talisman. That is the case particularly in the tribes of North-West America, and especially among the Kwakiutl, where the name of *logwa*, talisman, a supernatural being and object, was the true name of the clans' paraphernalia, emblazoned blankets and coppers; and these were a veritable money used in the course of the potlatches, a series of exchanges from clan to clan. The primitive sense of the word *logwa* is connected to a root *log*, that Boas translated as supernatural power.

In all these cases the religious and magical character of money was strongly charged, and in a number of populations the notion of money was expressly attached through its name to that of magic power.

Since we have pursued our researches, we have found hardly any society, sufficiently close to its origins, where the cult and the magic of stones, of shells, and of precious metals did not give these objects their value. The religious uses of gold in [European] antiquity, the lapidaries that made the tour of the civilizations of the ancient world, the name of the pearl in Arabic, i.e. *baraka* (benediction = good *mana*), all these facts crowd upon us and are too well known for us to insist upon them.

But let us descend lower in the scale of societies. For a long time we have been struck by the importance of crystals and in particular crystals of quartz, in a very large number of societies both extremely primitive and highly civilized. We have already drawn attention to the facts which concern the acquisition of crystals by the Australian magicians [Mauss, 1904]. Isn't it striking that the myth of quartz, of the mountain of quartz as the source of talismans, is found in North-West America almost in the equivalent terms that one finds in Australia?

Moreover, we have in Australia facts which are not only equivalent to a purely magical and religious order, but also to facts which are economic. The commerce in these stones of quartz and other talismans is as well attested as their high value. Thus, among the Aruntas, Spencer and Gillen have established the use of the *lonka-lonka*, large shells procured from the Gulf of Carpentaria, and which are considered descended from thunder. The word *lonka-lonka* is moreover a word which means far, far away.

An even more remarkable fact is that in these same tribes, not only these magical talismans are objects of commerce, but even the sacred emblems of individuals, the *churinga*, are objects of exchange. It is necessary to see not only religious facts but also economic facts in the pilgrimages of which Spencer and Gillen have given us such lively descriptions, with their exchange and commerce of these totemic emblems. These visits involve numerous pretestations: food, enjoyment of women, etc., or presents made for the occasion. But there is also another testimony besides Spencer and Gillen, that of Eylmann, who says expressly and without the shadow of a preconceived idea, that the *churinga*, the sacred objects (which is the sense of the word), serve as a measure of value in these tribes. He tells an anecdote in which his guides, originating from very distant nations, told him spontaneously that this was "the money of the blacks."

Such a translation is, perhaps, the expedient by which the primitive forms of the notion of money can be represented.

Money—whatever definition one adopts—is a value on display, and also a use value that is not fungible, that is permanent, transmissible, that is able to be the object of transactions and usages without deteriorating. At the same time, money is the means to procure other values which are fungible, transitory, goods for consumption and for gifts. No doubt since the most primitive societies, the talisman and its possessor have played this role of objects equally convertable by all, of which the possession conferred to their holder a power which easily became a power of purchasing.

Even beyond this, isn't there something which retains a social nature? Let us take an example. The word *mana* in the Malayo-Polynesian languages dsignates not only the power of magical substances and acts, but also the authority of men. It designates equally well precious objects, the talismans of the tribe, which are known to have been the object of exchanges, battles, and inheritances. There is nothing irrational about this, if we know how to represent to ourselves the spirit in which these institutions functioned. Isn't the purchasing power of money natural, when it is attached to a talisman which can rigorously constrain the subordinates of chiefs, and the clients of magicians to make the presents that they demand? And inversely, isn't it necessary, since the notion of riches emerged in such a vague form, that the riches of the chief and the magician resides above all in the emblems which incarnate their magic powers, in a word their authority, or which symbolize the force of the clan?

[M]oney was not primitively employed to acquire the means of consumption, but to acquire things of luxury, and those of authority over men. The purchasing power of primitive money is above all the prestige that the talisman confers on whoever posseses it, and its use in commanding others.

Isn't that a sentiment which is still very much alive among ourselves? Isn't the true faith that we nourish vis-à-vis gold and all the values that flow from its estimation, in large part the confidence that we have in its power? Doesn't the essence of faith in the value of gold reside in the belief that we can obtain, thanks to it, presents from our contemporaries—in goods or in services—that the state of the market permits us to extract?

.   .   .

This magical power of money, this prestige grows with the exchanges it undergoes.. The famous "wampum" of the Iroquois circulated in the interior of the Five nations and inside the phratries and among the clans. The more it circulated, the higher price it acquired, since each collectivity added a new figure of pearls; sometimes it increased in value even without anyone augmenting the number of figures woven into its pattern. This is the same fact that Malinowski exposed apropos the *kula* commerce in the Trobriand islands. These exotic moneys took on much more value the more they have circulated; in the same fashion that a family jewel augments its value from generation to generation, in the same fashion that an old precious object requires a large potlatch each time it changes hands.

At the bottom, that which we have arrived at is the importance of the notion of awaiting, of anticipation, which is precisely one of the forms of collective thought. Among ourselves, in society, we have to wait upon each other for this or that result; that is the essential form of the community. In our sociological theory we have formerly used the expressions: constraint, force, authority; these concepts have some value, but the notion of collective awaiting is, in my opinion, one of the fundamental notions of social life. I know no other notion which generates both the law and the economy. "I expect", "I await" [*J'attends*]: that is the definition of all actions of a collective nature.

REFERENCES

Hubert, Henri, and Marcel Mauss. "Essai sur la nature et al fonction du sacrifice." *Année Sociologique*, 2 (1899), pp. 2–138.
———. 1904. "Esquisse d'une théorie génerale de la magie." *Année Sociologique* 7 (1904).
Mauss, Marcel. "L'origine des pouvoirs magiques dans les sociétés australiennes." Paris: Ecole Pratique des Hautes Études, 1904.

Kinship as Sexual Property Exchange [1949]

CLAUDE LEVI-STRAUSS

• *The central argument of Claude Lévi-Strauss's great theory of kinship is diffusely spread through the 500 pages of* The Elementary Structures of Kinship *(1949) and is hard to follow or excerpt. The following analytical summary gives its main points, stressing especially its Maussian aspect and its points of linkage with the conflict tradition.*

The *Elementary Structures of Kinship* by no means gives an idealized picture of primitive social life. There are struggles for food, warfare and threats of violent death, quarrels, divorces, and all the other ills of human life in an imperfect world. Lévi-Strauss's view on this is as hard-nosed as the most cynical conflict theorist. The very basis of the kinship system is sexual domination. Males exert property rights over the bodies and labor of females, and exchange them with other males. Lévi-Strauss is thus the prime mover of a modern sociology of sexual stratification, as well as of alliance theory within modern treatments of kinship. To be sure, Lévi-Strauss states his position without regard for the variations in the degrees and kinds of sexual stratification across the whole range of history. But certainly his theory of alliances, augmented with a consideration of variations in other resources and motives for sexual domination, opens the way toward a more refined theory, which does not take male domination as a universal but as a condition that emerges under specific circumstances.

The purposes for which males dominate females in tribal societies are manifold. Aside from sexual gratification, there is also a struggle for food and livelihood itself; women as food providers are a major source of wealth. In the Australian desert, Lévi-Strauss remarks, the bachelor is a poor thing, a creature who barely eaks out his survival without a woman's help. The major value of women is that they determine alliances among groups. Alliances are necessary because of the constant danger of violence. Lévi-Strauss describes the way in which Australians encounter a stranger: They first ascertain his

From Randall Collins, *Sociology Since Midcentury* (New York: Academic Press, 1981), pp. 115–131. Reprinted with permission of Academic Press.

lineage and his marriage ties, because these divide friends from enemies. The man (the sexism is explicit here) without marriage ties is defenseless, thus marriages are the main means of military defense.

Lévi-Strauss continually emphasizes that exchange brings solidarity, and he distinguishes among various types of kinship exchange systems in terms of the amount of solidarity that they bring. But this is not a naïve pan-functionalist argument based on the society's demand for solidarity. Solidarity is important precisely because of the threat of conflict. It is the solidarity of various groups within the society, not of the total social order itself. It is the solidarity of warfare groups, as Lévi-Strauss explicitly remarks (1949/1969:149). Exchange is a crucial weapon of each group, and hence the object of its explicit strategizing.

Lévi-Strauss's most striking point, though, is that exchange both creates solidarity among groups and structures new conflicts among them. Exchange produces conflict itself, and not just in the obvious sense that the structure produced is a lineup of opposing alliances. Exchange also produces strains and potential conflicts within alliances. Gifts give grounds for grievances, if reciprocity is not properly lived up to. The strains in the marriage alliance system are still apparent even today, in our jokes about in-laws, and these were much more serious in societies in which the whole economic and political organization was based on such marriage connections. Many of the fights within tribal societies break out precisely over the way in which rights and gifts due from previous donations are not properly repaid (1949/1969:261). Part of this very instability is due to the fact that gifts are often used as a means of ending a conflict. A murder or an insult might be repaid by the gift of a woman, just as a truce in a feudal war could best be sealed by a diplomatic marriage (1949/1969:113). Marriage, then, is a way of containing quarrels, of keeping them from becoming more serious. This is one reason why tribal marriage ceremonies often involve competitive games or even mock fights (1949/1969:481). The ceremonial carrying-off of the bride is not a survivor of some bygone era of bride-capture, but an indicator of current realities. Lévi-Strauss quotes with approval the phrase "marriage is a socially regulated act of hostility [1949/1969:261]," and sums up his position with a telling remark: "Exchanges are peacefully resolved wars, and wars are the result of unsuccessful transactions [1949/1969:67]."

This interdependence of conflict and exchange is the structural key to historical change. As we shall see, from the existing structure of alliances, the lines of further conflicts and breakdowns of structure are predictable. History is a series of alliance structures, with their strains and conflictual transformations.

THE INCEST TABOO AS EXTERNALLY IMPOSED

The incest taboo itself, by implication, is explainable in these terms. All would agree that the incest taboo is crucial for establishing the larger, non-nuclear networks of society. But Lévi-Strauss's formulation about exchange does not leave us with the usual teleological functionalist explanation of the taboo in terms of its consequences. The logic of Lévi-Strauss's theme of the interdependence of exchange and conflict provides a sequential hypothesis for the creation of the incest taboo.

Men without daughters or sisters cannot get them within the nuclear group, and hence must go outside it to find women. Such situations must have happened often, due to sheer demographic accident. In the absence of exchange relations, raiding for women must have been a source of much warfare, even when there were no other natural scarcities due to an abundance of land. Although Lévi-Strauss does not mention it, the archaeological evidence certainly suggests that primitive humanoids killed one another quite frequently; many of the protohuman species were apparently made extinct in this way.

On the other hand, demographic change would have produced many groups with more than enough females for the men. Men in such groups would have found it advantageous to use this sexual surplus to gain alliances. Thus a gift-economy of women would have arisen. Perhaps the women were given in a purely defensive spirit: instead of being robbed and perhaps killed, better to give the plunder away. The more initiative in doing this, the more goodwill that could be created, and thus alliances would come into being. Eventually the families carrying out this strategy would become more powerful militarily than isolated nuclear families. The exogamous, alliance-making families would sooner or later drive the more traditional groups out of existence.

The incest taboo, then, is not a psychological phenomenon at all, nor is it merely a latently functional practice that first appeared by accident. The incest taboo is imposed from without: It reflects people's recognition that outsiders demand their women and will not allow them to be kept selfishly within the group. It is fear of other people that enforces the feeling that women must not become sexual property in their own families, and it is precisely conflict situations that enforce this feeling.

The theory has the merit of being testable. The larger the network of family-based alliances, the further the incest taboo–exogamy requirement extends among consanguinal relations. In a modern society with a bureaucratic state and impersonal economy, the family is no longer important for alliances; incest taboos shrink back to the minimum level of enforcement, which still requires women to be available in the general sexual marketplace. The mother–son taboo cannot be established in this way, of course, but it is easily explicable in terms of male domination: the father asserting exclusive sexual property rights over his wife against his most immediate male rival. The other incest taboos—on cousins, whole exogamous lineages and groups, and so forth—have narrowed their scope, and perhaps have also been less enforced even where they exist, as modern societies have moved further away from kinship-based economic and political organization. But the mother–son taboo survives, as the strongest and least violated prohibition, precisely because it is not based on exchange.

IDEAL STRATEGIES AND MATERIAL REALITIES

These conflicts are only the first step in human prehistory. They are followed by many more, whose contours are revealed by Lévi-Strauss. But already in the incest model, we can see a key dynamic of Lévi-Strauss's scheme. The demographic realities shift. Some of the proto-human nuclear families had no daughters, some had many. It is precisely this demographic variability that people must take into account in their social arrangements.

Lévi-Strauss has discussed this point intermittently, both in debates over his general method and throughout his writings on kinship and mythology. Lévi-Strauss has been accused of placing too much emphasis on the ideal side of kin structures. It is said that he has failed to attend to the distinction between preferential and prescriptive rules, and has ignored the empirical data of what marriages actually take place, since this data often show the rules being evaded in practice. These criticisms are misplaced.

1. Lévi-Strauss has directly replied that even if only a small percentage of marriages take place according to the kinship rules, this gives a certain tendency to the development of the social structure. Those families that do not or cannot obey the rules act essentially at random, and give rise to no sustained changes; it is those that do obey the rules that make social history (1949/1969:xxx-xxxv).

2. Furthermore, Lévi-Strauss argues that the natives themselves tend to see the rules in the same complex way that he does. Sometimes the rules are ideologies, upheld mainly as claims to prestige, not because they can always be carried out. He even remarks that the formal rules can be a kind of myth. Moreover, the natives can deliberately manipulate and change the rules. Australian tribal elders sit and discuss them at great length, devising possible changes to fit new problems. Lévi-Strauss sees such men as native intellectu-

als, producing deliberate strategies for coordinating pre-existing structures with new demographic problems and political aims (1949/1969:125). In his later reflections on his kinship theory (1962/1966:251), Lévi-Strauss remarks that he should have given even greater emphasis to this conscious creation of rules and myths.

Native intellectuals, in other words, knew what they were doing when they formulated the kinship rules. One can see this as they reformulate the rules to deal with current problems. One can thus infer that similar conscious decision-making went into formulating the earlier rules. We cannot necessarily recover the reasoning directly in the case of strategies that have been in effect for a long time. Kinship strategies are constantly in motion, contrary to the notion that tribal societies are structurally static. It is these new problems and strategies that occupy people's minds. Because of this, the older strategies that are not practically called into question are taken for granted. To focus on one thing necessarily defocuses everything else. Incest taboos would fall into that category, since they are still the fundamental basis of all other kinship alliances, but the reasoning behind them is no longer of interest. They have been thoroughly routinized for tens of thousands of generations.

3. Lévi-Strauss's accounts of the particular kinship patterns found at one point in time are frequently set in terms of their adaptations to changing demographic circumstances. From highly complicated structures, he reconstructs the sequence of changes that must have brought a particular pattern to its condition. The hypothesized causes are sometimes conflicts, sometimes demographic accidents. He mentions that some lineages die out, and that this must happen not infrequently; other groups grow large and split. Such changes have structural consequences to which the rest of the system must adjust. Even in his later work on the structure of myths, Lévi-Strauss applies the same analysis. A tribe might have had three clans, for example: bear—turtle—eagle (in this case reflecting a division among three elements: land—water—sky). If the bear clan dies out, the structural organization of the society can be re-established only by subdividing the larger of the remaining clans. The modern observer would thus find: yellow turtle—grey turtle—eagle (1962/1966:67). Lévi-Strauss comments: "Demographic evolution can shatter the structure but. . . . if the structural orientation survives the shock it has, after each upheaval, several means of reestablishing a system, which may not be identical with the earlier one but is at least formally of the same type [1962/1966:68]."

The basic process, then, is an interplay of raw demographic facts of nature with deliberate human attempts to strategically respond to them; it is this interplay that produces human history and culture. It is, in fact, by knowing this interplay that one can read the code of the myths. Lévi-Strauss remarks that it is precisely this emphasis upon material history that sets his position apart from that of Durkheim: "Although there is undoubtedly a dialectical relation between the social structure and systems of categories, the latter are not an effect or result of the former: each, at the cost of laborious mental adjustments, translates certain historical and local modalities of the relations between man and the world, which form their common substratum [1962/1966:214]."

Lévi-Strauss's full view, then, not only takes account of demographic accidents, but also builds this into the center of his model. We should add that such arguments refer not merely to demography in the narrow sense, but to the full range of conditions in which humanity interacts with the material environment, to "wars, epidemics, and famines [1962/1966:71]." Social structure is generally to be explained, as Lévi-Strauss remarks of a particular instance, "by the combined action of two forces, one of demographic origin which pushes it towards disorganization, and the other of speculative inspiration which pushes it towards a reorganization as closely as possible in line with the earlier state of affairs (1962/1966:71)." Lévi-Strauss is thus not merely paying lip-service to Marxism when he declares that the material infrastructure is basic grounds for all human action, while at the same time stating that his purpose is to contribute to the theory of superstructures. It is fully consistent with the thrust of this approach that we may broaden it further in this direction than Lévi-Strauss himself has done, to take account of variations in the abundance or scarcity of food and natural resources, and in the geographical dispersion or concentration of populations, and build an alliance theory of kinship upon a fuller treatment of these conditions.

Lévi-Strauss, then, is elaborating a Maussian theme. Women are currency in a gift exchange system which is really a system of communications. It is not, as mistakenly interpreted, a group mind talking to itself, even though Lévi-Strauss himself often gives grounds for this impression in his later works. The communications are among specific groups of allies. Mauss (1925/1962) showed that shells passing around a kula ring in symbolic ceremonies make possible mundane economic transactions within the structure of the ring; Lévi-Strauss shows that women passing around a kinship structure make possible political alliances. (One might add that this is an economic structure, too, since not only marriage payments, funeral contributions, and property inheritance pass through this network, but also many other and frequent deliveries of food and goods.) These exchanges are carried out under actual or potential threat of warfare, and its milder conflictual equivalent, the scramble for prestige. Conflicts not only force exchanges, but exchanges also structure conflicts, as Mauss, too, was well aware. Exchanges can contain conflicts and make them milder, but they also produce them in predictable ways.

From a mass of kinship data from many different societies, Lévi-Strauss has tried to reconstruct the basic logic of such alliances and their transformations. Although this project was left incomplete—and still remains so—it is a powerful and at least partially convincing effort. Let us look at its main outlines.

BASIC ELEMENTS: RESIDENCE AND LINEAGE

There are two basic elements of a kinship system. *Residence:* Where do the husband, the wife, and their children live after their marriage? In the tribal societies with which Lévi-Strauss was concerned, the main choices are patrilocal or matrilocal (with avunculocal—residence with the maternal uncle—as a variant on the latter). *Lineage:* What group do the children belong to? Again, for these tribes, the major choice is patrilineal or matrilineal. Bilineality is also a possibility, but an unimportant one in the Lévi-Strauss model: not that it doesn't occur, but that nothing of structural significance can come from it. We might note, in addition, that lineages need not be narrow family chains in the modern sense, but can be organized as entire clans or subclans, or subdivided into elaborate sectional systems, as in many Australian societies.

These basic forms are by no means ideal constructs. Both are grossly behavioral and material; both in fact can be looked on as forms of property. This is obvious in the case of lineage: In a matrilineal system, children inherit not only their names but also their material goods from their mother's family, while in a patrilineal system this property is inherited from the father's family. But the children themselves are property as well: they are usable for exchange, and hence for alliances, and matri–patrilineality tells us which family group gets to use them as such.

Locality of residence is also a form of property: secondarily as property over the children, but primarily as property over the wife. In a patrilocal system, the woman goes to live with her husband and his kin. She is lost from her own family and cut off from its support, and even her children are not her own. This is an extreme form of male domination. In matrilocality (or its variant, avunculocality), the woman stays with her own kinfolk, and the male is the one in the midst of an alien group. Such practices take various forms: sometimes the males only visit their wives for intercourse; sometimes they live there for a period but later return home; sometimes the males actually move in, although this is rare and confined to subservient relations, since it prevents a man from being with his own property in his sister's household. Although matrilocal groups are also dominated by men, the position of women within them is much stronger than in patrilocal ones. In terms of property relations, sexual property in the form of erotic access and labor service of married men from their wives is a good deal weaker in matrilocal than patrilocal arrangements.

In general, one might say that locality is sexual property as daily enacted; lineality is the long-term, macroaspect of sexual property.

On can infer from these circumstances something of the conditions under which these systems are likely to arise. Matrilocal residence is empirically rather rare. From a structural viewpoint, its rarity should not be surprising, since it is just barely one step away from an incest situation, in which no sexual trades and alliances are made at all. Matrilineality, too, is a good deal less common than patrilineality. (And in fact, both are less common statistically than bilineality.) These empirical distributions seem not to be widely known. The impression is often given in comparative surveys of social history that all societies of a primitive horticultural type are matrilineal. This is probably because, as Lévi-Strauss points out, matrilineal societies are more spectacular than patrilineal ones. They have been the subjects of some of the most famous anthropological studies, such as those of Malinowski. Why are they so dramatic? Not only because of the reversal of our familiar modern forms of kinship, but also because their atmosphere tends to be psychologically heavy, full of jealousies, divorces, conflicts, and their religious and symbolic expressions. In fact, matrilineal societies indicate a situation in which the women-giving groups do not give up very much: they strike a hard bargain in the marriage market. It is in effect a sellers' market.

If we ask, then, what causes these patterns, the answer is that matrilineal societies (and matrilocal ones as well, to the extent that we find them) are much more likely than patrilineal and patrilocal ones to exist in a situation of a high degree of warfare. More recent empirical comparisons confirm this judgment (Divale, 1975). An ecological factor also enters in: matrilineal societies are usually ones in which various exogenous groups live very close to each other, so that males are not greatly inconvenienced by their relative separation from their property. Patrilineality and patrilocality, however, fit well with situations where groups are geographically remote: the woman leaves her home once and for all, and there are few occasions for subsequent contact. Lévi-Strauss comments that these systems are best suited to creating long-distance alliances between culturally rather divergent groups (1949/1969:289).

Wars are probably both the cause and the effect of matrilineality, as the structure emerges from a situation of high distrust, and also tends to foster further quarrels. Variations in the scarcity of ecological conditions also enter into these determinations; more recent alliance theories have developed this point (e.g., Harris, 1979:81–84, 96–100).

HARMONIC AND DISHARMONIC SYSTEMS

The key structural difference, in Lévi-Strauss's scheme, is neither lineage nor residence *per se*, but their combination. Either patrilineal–patrilocal or matri-lineal–matrilocal is called *harmonic*; matrilineal–patrilocal or patrilineal–matrilocal is called *disharmonic*. (In practice the second of each pair can be dropped as empirically rare or nonexistent.) In effect, this is the difference between a sexual property system dominated either by takers of wives (a buyer's market), or by the givers of wives (a seller's market). These two situations make possible quite different historical sequences.

THREE MARRIAGE STRATEGIES

Given these property situations, the native policymakers must decide on an optimum strategy for achieving family alliances. Strategies are put into practice by formulating marriage rules, be they preferential or prescribed, closely adhered to or widely violated, as discussed previously. There are three elementary sorts of marriage strategies. Most prominently, these involve cross-cousins: marriages that link a man either to his mother's or to his father's family.

Two of these strategies are asymmetrical:

- Man marries mother's brother's daughter (matrilateral cross-cousin marriage).
- Man marries father's sister's daughter (patrilateral cross-cousin marriage).

There is also a symmetrical form, in which either cross-cousin marriage is permitted. Such symmetrical systems can also work by equivalent rules, which do not specify the actual cross-cousin but someone from an equivalent place in the generational and lineage structure.

Even with the best intentions, of course, such marriages cannot always be made. There may not be any matrilateral cross-cousin in that particular generation, or there may be too many sons or daughters, or too few. All of these are historically specific contingencies through which these systems work themselves out. It is, in fact, these various contingencies, which are bound to come up over and over again across the generations, that prove the relative power of one or another type of marriage strategy.

The core of Lévi-Strauss's model is to work out the logical consequences of these different strategies.

SYMMETRICAL MARRIAGE AND RESTRICTED EXCHANGE

Symmetrical cross-cousin rules bring about a particular kind of social structure. If the rules are followed out consistently, they link the same two families together continuously, with a marriage in each direction, perhaps as often as several times in the same generation. The society is not linked together as a whole, but braided into independent and parallel strands: A⇆B C⇆D. The same result follows from other symmetrical rules that do not necessarily involve cross-cousins, such as those found in societies with dual organization, a division of the tribe into halves, quarters, eighths, and so on, .with specific rules regarding preferred and prohibited marriages among members of these sections.

ASYMMETRICAL MARRIAGE AND GENERALIZED EXCHANGE

If marriage rules specify only one cross-cousin and prohibit the other, the system of exchange does not form braids but a long chain of families. The longest chain occurs if matrilateral cross-cousin marriage is consistently performed; A→B→C→D→. (Eventually the first in the chain also receives a wife by this system: →A.) This is the long cycle. It is simultaneously the most risky, in that there are many places in which the chain can be broken, either by conflict or by demographic accident. On the other hand, there is the most to gain; the widest network of alliances can be forged in this way. As we shall see, it is via this route that important historical changes occur. This form results in each lineage being linked to another, which always gives it wives but never takes any in return, and then of course to a second, to which it is wife-giver but not wife-taker. The structure is a system of permanent debts. It is out of this that the stratification of the system arises.

The other form of asymmetrical cross-cousin marriage, patrilateral, also creates chains. But in this case they are not very long ones. If followed out, each alternating generation receives a wife back for its previous gift to that particular family. The patrilateral strategy results in a discontinuous structure, with all accounts settled every second generation. Less is risked, but less is gained. It constitutes a short cycle.

WHY ONE ROUTE RATHER THAN ANOTHER?

The structural determinant of which way a system will go, Lévi-Strauss argues, is whether it is harmonic or disharmonic. *Disharmonic systems* (which are mostly of the matrilineal–patrilocal form) tend to follow the patrilateral cross-cousin strategy: they opt for a short cycle, and cut their risks. They are, of course, already in a high-conflict situation in their local relations, even within family groups themselves. This may seem sufficient reason for their unwillingness to invest in the long run. It is also possible to see a structural consequence of the patrilateral cross-cousin strategy in this situation: a man's grandchildren come back into his own descent group, and hence male line-ages can be covertly reestablished even though the official connection passes entirely through females (Harris, 1979:182). This amounts to a strategy for preserving some of the power of husbands over their own property, in a situation in which the wive's families otherwise tend to dominate. The strategy boils down to fighting for power within the family, and giving up on the possibility of long-term investments that would strengthen the position of the family as a whole.

Harmonic systems, on the other hand (mainly patrilineal–local), are much more likely to prefer the matrilateral cross-cousin strategy. For a patrilateral strategy here would not only create no more than a short cycle, but would also pass property to grandchildren back into the female's linage. The structural consequences of a patrilateral marriage strategy in a strongly male-dominated system would, paradoxically, undermine control by males (Harris, 1979:182). The matrilateral strategy, then, is much more widespread in these societies, and hence it is in these societies that long cycles of exchange are constituted. (Many patrilineal–patrilocal societies, however, especially in Africa, do not practice cross-cousin marriage at all, and hence fail to create these long alliance chains. Harmonic systems are a precondition, but not a sufficient determinant of this strategy.)

LONG-TERM CHANGES AND THE KINSHIP REVOLUTION

Which path a group starts down is fateful for the future of that society. Societies with symmetrical or short cycle exchanges produce restricted alliance patterns. A good deal of change can occur here, of course. But conflicts, demographic accidents, and environmental pressures, when they change such structures, nevertheless leave them within the orbit of restricted exchange. Particular family alliances come and go, and particular lineages or even ar-rangements of lineages appear and disappear. But the structural peculiarity of these forms is that changes are caught within the walls of a certain social type. Quarrels within a reciprocal exchange system, for example, frequently break out because of what their members think of as breaches of gift obligations. These can result in the groups breaking off contacts or going to war with each other. But the now-isolated groups can only go on to establish new alliances of the same sort with some other group (1949/1969:78–9). The very number of groups can change. Dual systems can become more complex, subdividing into further categories. Australian elders make quite elaborate policy decisions on such matters, creating new exchange rules and new subsections of their tribes to meet the political exigencies of the day. But the structures always change into another version of a restricted exchange system. Moieties may turn into eight-class systems, or sometimes eight-class systems devolve into four or two classes (1949/1969:152). Alliances are patched up, wars arranged, demographic accidents smoothed out. Much changes, but the scale of social organization—especially its form of stratification and its degree of political decentralization—stays the same.

A truly generalized exchange system, though, is unstable in a different way. Because of demographic accident, some groups will have more daughters than others, and they will be able to make more alliances. The returns on these investments take a longer time to materialize, but they are proportionately greater. A family embarked on a positive cycle as giver of wives puts increasing numbers of clients in its debt. In subsequent generations, it has more women coming in, which in turn allows it to get a demographic jump on its rivals in the next cycle. With excess claims on women, privileged families can become polygymous. Since women work, they are an increasing source of direct wealth, while the alliances that they bring make the family increasingly powerful militarily. On the other side, families that get behind in this cycle are likely to become steadily poorer, both demographically and economically. They have fewer women, and these become less desirable for other families as tokens of alliance. Marriages are made on increasingly unequal terms; poorer men marrying upper-lineage women become servitors of the powerful families, while upper-lineage men confine themselves to alliances with other powerful families. Social classes develop, and some groups may even become slaves.

As the system becomes stratified, its forms eventually break down. Exchanges are no longer substantially equal, and additional economic goods are added on as a kind of immediate recompense, through the institution of brideprice. This further exacerbates the stratifying tendencies of the system, because poorer families are less likely to be able to pay the brideprice, hence less likely to be able to produce more daughters. They fall increasingly further behind. Richer families, on the other hand, can afford to pay those prices, and hence increasingly monopolize the marriage (and the political alliance) market. The returns on this, in more daughters and more brideprices, make them richer still. Perhaps the brideprice was even deliberately instituted as a strategy by dominant families for this purpose, a kind of tax they were enforcing by their commanding position on the market.

Finally, both upper and lower classes are motivated to withdraw from the system. The lower-class families can no longer afford to make a marriage in the traditional way; they begin to withdraw among themselves and set up reciprocal exchanges with some other lineage. This at least gets wives for the men, but it seals the family's fate in the overall stratification picture. Upper-class families, on the other hand, are now embarked on an aristocratic scale of living, and on political alliances of major scope. Some are on their way to outright military and political rule. They begin to find their obligations to their lesser kin a drag on their own ambitions. They begin to make short-term alliances outside the kin network entirely, without using marriage politics. In this way, kings eventually arise. Through the feudal tendencies of an unstable system of generalized exchange, the state finally emerges.

THE STRUCTURALIST THEORY OF PREHISTORY

Lévi-Strauss thus allows us to infer the outlines of human history for the last half-million years or so, from the protohuman condition onwards through the emergence of stratified society and the state. The first major event was the development of a strategy of exogamous wife-giving, which enabled some nuclear groups to make alliances and to take an edge in the hostilities that pervaded this period. The incest taboo, as a strategy imposed by the threat of external raiding, eventually became the basis upon which more complex alliance strategies could emerge.

Subsequent history is full of a variety of kinship forms: bilateral and cognate lineages, the so-called "Crow-Omaha" types of purely negative kinship prohibitions, as well as the unilateral forms that Lévi-Strauss concentrated on. These pure unilateral forms may be statistically a minority, but if Lévi-Strauss is right, they are the ones that have an historical logic built into them. Bilateral marriage strategies, cognatic descent, and so forth all tend either to subdivide property, and hence dissipate it, or in effect to randomize and localize alliance patterns. The purer version of restricted exchange and short-cycle generalized exchange stand out with a greater structural elegance. Their histories are structurally more predictable, in that they fall within a given compass, although they are doomed to go around and around the same set of variations. Ironically, it is these pure forms that were especially locked into a kind of historyless eternity: if not strictly without histories, they made a major part of human prehistory into a sort of cyclical universe.

It is the pure form of patrilineal–patrilocal harmonic systems, then, that are the true makers of linear history. That is, they brought about the transformation of relatively egalitarian and small-scale groups into class-stratified societies and into incipient states. This emergence into modern-style history has an almost Marxian dialectic to it. This particular kind of kinship alliance system not only brought about a new society, but also broke down the very system on which it was formerly based. The long chains of matrilateral cross-cousin marriage were eventually repudiated both from below and above. The one structural path out of the cycles of purely kinship-based societies ended by overturning even the most dynamic type of kinship system itself. The first step was to institute a strategy that turned from a series of balanced exchanges to a set of imbalanced exchanges. The imbalanced system finally undermined kinship exchange itself. In its place emerged nonexchange domination: the state.

Is this the only way the state could, or did, come about? We are not sure. Certainly there are competing theories: conquest, hydraulic economies, incipient priesthoods, big-man redistribution systems. The evidence is not really in yet. The Lévi-Strauss theory has mainly been debated in terms of specialized anthropological interests in kinship, and the requisite cross-societal comparisons have not been produced. On the other hand, the rival theories have so far been formulated in general terms, and have not come to grips with the social realities of daily human interaction, and with human strategizing, the way Lévi-Strauss's model does. Surely conquest was often involved in the rise of the states that we know about. But how did the conquerors become organized into a sufficiently large and permanent group to rule, rather than to raid, and for that matter to win, rather than to chip away piecemeal? Again, how did a community become organized to be able to carry out irrigation projects? How could priesthoods break old bonds of religious allegiance and establish new ones? Where did the big man get the wealth to redistribute? Kinship politics was more than likely involved in all of these, and a full model would certainly have to be built up around a structural theory of alliances.

On the face of it, the Lévi-Strauss argument is supported by the existing distribution of kinship structures, which were founded around the world in historical times. Patrilineal–patrilocal systems are found across the major state-building areas of China, India, the Middle East, and Europe. (Exceptions within these areas may help prove the case: If these are the groups that failed to establish strong stratified structures, they would appear to have been held back by their kinship structure.) On the other side, the weakness of state formation in Africa, North America, and Australia fits the model in that these were the areas of bilateral marriage strategies or restricted or randomized exchange systems.

Certainly we know of societies within these large areas that do not follow the hypothesized kinship–state linkage. There were states in central and west Africa, or example, or the Mexican and Andean states, or the North American Indian confederations, that arose in response to European incursions. But a closer look at these may reveal kinship–alliance patterns that approximate those given in the structuralist model. This may be especially likely if we can break that model into a series of variations, predicting partial and weak stratifying tendencies as well as stronger ones. It is also possible, of course, that we will find evidence for other, nonkinship factors, which must be entered into a theory of the state. We may also have to make variant paths within a kinship–alliance theory that have not yet been envisioned: the patrilateral cross-cousin strategy within a harmonic system may not be the only one which has long-term structural consequences. In any case, this line of analysis can only bring an enrichment of our understanding.

A CONTEMPORARY PAYOFF

Finally, we might ask: Why should sociologists be interested in this? One answer is that sociology and anthropology are really the same discipline, and that all of human history and all types of human societies come into the purview of a science· of society. Another answer is that the tide of structuralism now washing over American sociology from the other side of the Atlantic deserves a critical analysis aimed at finding its most valuable elements. But most essentially, I would suggest, there is a theoretical lesson in Lévi-Strauss's effort to explain the long-term patterns of change in "historyless" tribal societies.

Formalized kinship networks are no longer important in modern society, but alliances certainly are. Lévi-Strauss's structuralist version of exchange theory appears a much more promising route to understanding this phenomenon than the individual-level, utilitarian style of exchange theory we have seen so far of the type of Homans, Blau, et al. Neoclassical economics shares the same utilitarian assumptions, and ignores the structural–network side of theory, which is precisely the strength of the Durkheim–Mauss–Lévi-Strauss tradition. The merit of Lévi-Strauss's version is that it concentrates on the structures resulting from exchange, not just the form of bargaining at the individual level, and that it systematically accounts for the histories of various kinds of structures, instead of reducing everything structurally to one ideally open market.

The major elements in Lévi-Strauss, in fact, give us the range of types of economic systems. Restricted exchange is a barter system, in which little is risked, but little gained, while social structure remains fragmented and localized. The generalized exchange strategy works on extending credit, betting on getting it back manyfold in the long run. It is a direct parallel to Schumpeter's definition of capitalism: enterprise carried out with borrowed money. The particular formulations of Lévi-Strauss regarding kinship systems may not be precisely the analogies we need to solve problems in other sociological fields. But Lévi-Strauss's concepts, taken more abstractly, may provide just the right building blocks. We find then in his model, property in both a short-term enacted form and in the long-term form of an exchange strategy for reproducing it. We furthermore understand property as a variable institution, representing varying degrees of compromise among conflicting groups. There are strategies for property-enhancing alliances, which are consciously considered while they are on the forefront of pressing issues, but become taken-for-granted forms of prestige or taboo in their more deeply embedded forms. There are unintended consequences of various strategies as they are carried out over many trials: those that produce merely random shifts, those that lock the structure into endless permutations of a basic pattern, and those that give rise to revolutionary breaks.

These elements, taken more abstractly and reworked as needed, may be just what is wanted for a better theory of the alliances that make up modern politics and international relations, as well as interorganizational ties, business communities, friendship networks, and the intellectual world itself. A tremendous amount of the problems of modern sociology—community and national power structures, business elites, social movements, social mobility—hinge upon a successful theoretical conceptualization of the descriptive materials we have been amassing. Above all, we need to see in general terms the conditions under which these structures appear, give rise to new conflicts, and are transformed either in cyclical or revolutionary directions. Perhaps some Lévi-Strauss of the future will seize on this material and one day give us an elegant model beyond the narrow tribalisms of the ethnographers of modern society.

REFERENCES

Divale, William. 1975. "An explanation of matrilocal residence." In D. Raphael (ed.), *Being Female: Reproduction, Power, and Change*. The Hague: Mouton.
Harris, Marvin. 1979. *Cultural Materialism*. New York: Random House.

Lévi-Strauss, Claude. 1949/1969. *The Elementary Structures of Kinship*. Boston: Beacon Press.

Lévi-Strauss, Claude. 1962/1966. *The Savage Mind*. Chicago: University of Chicago Press.

Mauss, Marcel. 1925/1962. *The Gift*. New York: Norton.

The Nature of Deference and Demeanor [1956]

ERVING GOFFMAN

• *Erving Goffman is not usually thought of as a follower of the Durkheimian tradition. But the early works that made him famous are explicitly built on Durkheim's theory of rituals. Goffman shows that these crucial ceremonials still exist in the little microrituals of everyday life. Because our modern social structure has the crisscrossing complexity of social paths that promotes individualism, the "sacred object" that these rituals create and worship is, appropriately enough, the individual self. Goffman's deference and demeanor rituals also follow the pattern of Mauss's theory that social exchange proceeds from symbolic gifts: in this case, a kind of mutual obeisance among personal cults. Each individual, Goffman says, has become her own god, who nevertheless needs the worship of others to keep up her own reality.*

Under the influence of Durkheim and Radcliffe-Brown, some students of modern society have learned to look for the symbolic meaning of any given social practice and for the contribution of the practice to the integrity and solidarity of the group that employs it. However, in directing their attention away from the individual to the group, these students seem to have neglected a theme that is presented in Durkheim's chapter on the soul.[1] There he suggests that the individual's personality can be seen as one apportionment of the collective *mana*, and that (as he implies in later chapters), the rites performed to representations of the social collectivity will sometimes be performed to the individual himself.

In this paper I want to explore some of the senses in which the person in our urban secular world is allotted a kind of sacredness that is displayed and confirmed by symbolic acts. An attempt will be made to build a conceptual scaffold by stretching and twisting some common anthropological terms. This will be used to support two concepts which I think are central to this

From Erving Goffman, "The Nature of Deference and Demeanor." Reproduced by permission of the American Anthropological Association from *American Anthropologist* 58 (3): 473–499, 1956.
[1]Emile Durkheim, *The Elementary Forms of the Religious Life*, tr. J. W. Swain (Free Press, Glencoe, Ill., 1954), pp. 240–72.

area: deference and demeanor. Through these reformulations I will try to show that a version of Durkheim's social psychology can be effective in modern dress.

Data for the paper are drawn chiefly from a brief observational study of mental patients in a modern research hospital. I use these data on the assumption that a logical place to learn about personal properties is among persons who have been locked up for spectacularly failing to maintain them. Their infractions of propriety occur in the confines of a ward, but the rules broken are quite general ones, leading us outward from the ward to a general study of our Anglo-American society.

INTRODUCTION

A rule of conduct may be defined as a guide for action, recommended not because it is pleasant, cheap, or effective, but because it is suitable or just. Infractions characteristically lead to feelings of uneasiness and to negative social sanctions. Rules of conduct infuse all areas of activity and are upheld in the name and honor of almost everything. Always, however, a grouping of adherents will be involved—if not a corporate social life—providing through this a common sociological theme. Attachment to rules leads to a constancy and patterning of behavior; while this is not the only source of regularity in human affairs it is certainly an important one. Of course, approved guides to conduct tend to be covertly broken, side-stepped, or followed for unapproved reasons, but these alternatives merely add to the occasions in which rules constrain at least the surface of conduct.

Rules of conduct impinge upon the individual in two general ways: directly, as *obligations*, establishing how he is morally constrained to conduct himself; indirectly, as *expectations*, establishing how others are morally bound to act in regard to him. A nurse, for example, has an obligation to follow medical orders in regard to her patients; she has the expectation, on the other hand, that her patients will pliantly co-operate in allowing her to perform these actions upon them. This pliancy, in turn, can be seen as an obligation of the patients in regard to their nurse, and points up the interpersonal, actor-recipient character of many rules: what is one man's obligation will often be another's expectation.

Because obligations involve a constraint to act in a particular way, we sometimes picture them as burdensome or irksome things, to be fulfilled, if at all, by gritting one's teeth in conscious determination. In fact, most actions which are guided by rules of conduct are performed unthinkingly, the questioned actor saying he performs "for no reason" or because he "felt like doing so." Only when his routines are blocked may he discover that his neutral little actions have all along been consonant with the proprieties of his group and that his failure to perform them can become a matter of shame and humiliation. Similarly, he may so take for granted his expectations regarding others that only when things go unexpectedly wrong will he suddenly discover that he has grounds for indignation.

Once it is clear that a person may meet an obligation without feeling it, we can go on to see that an obligation which *is* felt as something that *ought* to be done may strike the obligated person either as a desired thing or as an onerous one, in short, as a pleasant or unpleasant duty. In fact, the same obligation may appear to be a desirable duty at one point and an undesirable one at another, as when a nurse, obliged to administer medication to patients, may be glad of this when attempting to establish social distance from attendants (who in some sense may be considered by nurses to be not "good enough" to engage in such activity), yet burdened by it on occasions when she finds that dosage must be determined on the basis of illegibly written medical orders. Similarly, an expectation may be perceived by the expectant person as a wanted or unwanted thing, as when one person feels he will deservedly be promoted and another feels he will deservedly be fired. In ordinary usage, a rule that strikes the actor or recipient as a personally desirable thing, apart from its propriety, is sometimes called a right or privilege, as it will be here, but these terms have additional implications, suggesting that special class of rules which an individual may invoke but is not required to do so. It should also be noted that an actor's pleasant obligation may constitute a recipient's pleasant expectation, as with the kiss a husband owes his wife when he returns from the office, but that, as the illustration suggests, all kinds of combinations are possible.

When an individual becomes involved in the maintenance of a rule, he tends also to become committed to a particular image of self. In the case of his obligations, he becomes to himself and others the sort of person who follows this particular rule, the sort of person who would naturally be expected to do so. In the case of his expectations, he becomes dependent upon the assumption that others will properly perform such of their obligations as affect him, for their treatment of him will express a conception of him. In establishing himself as the sort of person who treats others in a particular way and is treated by them in a particular way, he must make sure that it will be possible for him to act and be this kind of person. For example, with certain psychiatrists there seems to be a point where the obligation of giving psychotherapy to patients, *their* patients, is transformed into something they must do if they are to retain the image they have come to have of themselves. The effect of this transformation can be seen in the squirming some of them may do in the early phases of their careers when they may find themselves employed to do research, or administer a ward, or give therapy to those who would rather be left alone.

In general then, when a rule of conduct is broken we find that two individuals run the risk of becoming discredited: one with an obligation, who should have governed himself by the rule; the other with an expectation, who should have been treated in a particular way because of this governance. Both actor and recipient are threatened.

An act that is subject to a rule of conduct is, then, a communication, for it represents a way in which selves are confirmed—both the self for which the rule is an obligation and the self for which it is an expectation. An act that is subject to rules of conduct but does not conform to them is also a communication—often even more so—for infractions make news and often in such a way as to disconfirm the selves of the participants. Thus rules of conduct transform both action and inaction into expression, and whether the individual abides by the rules or breaks them, something significant is likely to be communicated. For example, in the wards under study, each research psychiatrist tended to expect his patients to come regularly for their therapeutic hours. When patients fulfilled this obligation, they showed that they appreciated their need for treatment and that their psychiatrist was the sort of person who could establish a "good relation" with patients. When a patient declined to attend his therapeutic hour, others on the ward tended to feel that he was "too sick" to know what was good for him, and that perhaps his psychiatrist was not the sort of person who was good at establishing relationships. Whether patients did or did not attend their hours, something of importance about them and their psychiatrist tended to be communicated to the staff and to other patients on the ward.

In considering the individual's participation in social action, we must understand that in a sense he does not participate as a total person but rather in terms of a special capacity or status; in short, in terms of a special self. For example, patients who happen to be female may be obliged to act shamelessly before doctors who happen to be male, since the medical relation, not the sexual one, is defined as officially relevant. In the research hospital studied, there were both patients and staff who were Negro, but this minority-group status was not one in which these individuals were officially (or even, in the main, unofficially) active. Of course, during face-to-face encounters individuals may participate officially in more than one capacity. Further, some unofficial weight is almost always given to capacities defined as officially irrelevant, and the reputation earned in one capacity will flow over and to a degree determine the reputation the individual earns in his other capacities. But these are questions for more refined analysis.

In dealing with rules of conduct it is convenient to distinguish two classes, symmetrical and asymmetrical. A symmetrical rule is one which leads an individual to have obligations or expectations regarding others that these others have in regard to him. For example, in the two hospital wards, as in most other places in our society, there was an understanding that each individual was not to steal from any other individual, regardless of their respective statuses, and that each individual could similarly expect not to be stolen from by anyone. What we call common courtesies and rules of public order tend to be symmetrical, as are such biblical admonitions as the rule about not coveting one's neighbor's wife. An asymmetrical rule is one that leads others to treat and be treated by an individual differently from the way he treats and is treated by them. For example, doctors give medical orders to nurses, but nurses do not give medical orders to doctors. Similarly, in some hospitals in America nurses stand up when a doctor enters the room, but doctors do not ordinarily stand up when a nurse enters the room.

Students of society have distinguished in several ways among types of rules, as for example, between formal and informal rules; for this paper, however, the important distinction is that between substance and ceremony.[2] A substantive rule is one which guides conduct in regard to matters felt to have significance in their own right, apart from what the infraction or maintenance of the rule expresses about the selves of the persons involved. Thus, when an individual refrains from stealing from others, he upholds a substantive rule which primarily serves to protect the property of these others and only incidentally functions to protect the image they have of themselves as persons with proprietary rights. The expressive implications of substantive rules are officially considered to be secondary; this appearance must be maintained, even though in some special situations everyone may sense that the participants were primarily concerned with expression.

A ceremonial rule is one which guides conduct in matters felt to have secondary or even no significance in their own right, having their primary importance—officially anyway—as a conventionalized means of communication by which the individual expresses his character or conveys his apprecia-

[2] I take this distinction from Durkheim (Emile Durkheim, "The Determination of Moral Facts," *Sociology and Philosophy*, tr. D. F. Pocock, Free Press, Glencoe, Ill., 1953, especially pp. 42–43); see also A. R. Radcliffe-Brown, "Taboo," *Structure and Function in Primitive Society* (Free Press, Glencoe, Ill., 1952, pp. 143–44), and Talcott Parsons, *The Structure of Social Action* (McGraw-Hill, New York, 1937, pp. 430–33); sometimes the dichotomy is phrased in terms of "intrinsic" or "instrumental" versus "expressive" or "ritual."

tion of the other participants in the situation.[3] This usage departs from the everyday one, where "ceremony" tends to imply a highly specified, extended sequence of symbolic action performed by august actors on solemn occasions when religious sentiments are likely to be invoked. In my attempt to stress what is common to such practices as tipping one's hat and coronations, I will perforce ignore the differences among them to an extent that many anthropologists might perhaps consider impracticable.

In all societies, rules of conduct tend to be organized into codes which guarantee that everyone acts appropriately and receives his due. In our society the code which governs substantive rules and substantive expressions comprises our law, morality, and ethics, while the code which governs ceremonial rules and ceremonial expressions is incorporated in what we call etiquette. All of our institutions have both kinds of codes, but in this paper attention will be restricted to the ceremonial one.

The acts or events, that is, the sign-vehicles or tokens which carry ceremonial messages, are remarkably various in character. They may be linguistic, as when an individual makes a statement of praise or depreciation regarding self or other, and does so in a particular language and intonation; gestural, as when the physical bearing of an individual conveys insolence or obsequiousness; spatial, as when an individual precedes another through the door, or sits on his right instead of his left; task-embedded, as when an individual accepts a task graciously and performs it in the presence of others with aplomb and dexterity; part of the communication structure, as when an individual speaks more frequently than the others, or receives more attentiveness than they do. The important point is that ceremonial activity, like substantive activity, is an

---

[3]While the substantive value of ceremonial acts is felt to be quite secondary it may yet be quite appreciable. Wedding gifts in American society provide an example. It is even possible to say in some cases that if a sentiment of a given kind is to be conveyed ceremonially it will be necessary to employ a sign-vehicle which has a given amount of substantive value. Thus in the American lower-middle class, it is understood that a small investment in an engagement ring, as such investments go, may mean that the man places a small value on his fiancee as these things go, even though no one may believe that women and rings are commensurate things. In those cases where it becomes too clear that the substantive value of a ceremonial act is the only concern of the participants, as when a girl or an official receives a substantial gift from someone not interested in proper relations, then the community may respond with a feeling that their symbol system has been abused.

An interesting limiting case of the ceremonial component of activity can be found in the phenomenon of "gallantry," as when a man calmly steps aside to let a strange lady precede him into a lifeboat, or when a swordsman, fighting a duel, courteously picks up his opponent's fallen weapon and proffers it to him. Here an act that is usually a ceremonial gesture of insignificant substantive value is performed under conditions where it is known to have unexpectedly great substantive value. Here, as it were, the forms of ceremony are maintained above and beyond the call of duty.

In general, then, we can say that all ceremonial gestures differ in the degree to which they have substantive value, and that this substantive value may be systematically used as part of the communication value of the act, but that still the ceremonial order is different from the substantive one and is so understood.

analytical element referring to a component or function of action, not to concrete empirical action itself. While some activity that has a ceremonial component does not seem to have an appreciable substantive one, we find that all activity that is primarily substantive in significance will nevertheless carry some ceremonial meaning, provided that its performance is perceived in some way by others. The manner in which the activity is performed, or the momentary interruptions that are allowed so as to exchange minor niceties, will infuse the instrumentally-oriented situation with ceremonial significance.

All of the tokens employed by a given social group for ceremonial purposes may be referred to as its ceremonial idiom. We usually distinguish societies according to the amount of ceremonial that is injected into a given period and kind of interaction, or according to the expansiveness of the forms and the minuteness of their specification; it might be better to distinguish societies according to whether required ceremony is performed as an unpleasant duty or, spontaneously, as an unfelt or pleasant one.

Ceremonial activity seems to contain certain basic components. As suggested, a main object of this paper will be to delineate two of these components, deference and demeanor, and to clarify the distinction between them.

DEFERENCE

By deference I shall refer to that component of activity which functions as a symbolic means by which appreciation is regularly conveyed to a recipient of this recipient, or of something of which this recipient is taken as a symbol, extension, or agent. These marks of devotion represent ways in which an actor celebrates and confirms his relation to a recipient. In some cases, both actor and recipient may not really be individuals at all, as when two ships greet each other with four short whistle blasts when passing. In some cases, the actor is an individual but the recipient is some object or idol, as when a sailor salutes the quarterdeck upon boarding ship, or when a Catholic genuflects to the altar. I shall only be concerned, however, with the kind of deference that occurs when both actor and recipient are individuals, whether or not they are acting on behalf of something other than themselves. Such ceremonial activity is perhaps seen most clearly in the little salutations, compliments, and apologies which punctuate social intercourse, and may be referred to as "status rituals" or "interpersonal rituals." I use the term "ritual" because this activity, however informal and secular, represents a way in which the individual must guard and design the symbolic implications of his acts while in the immediate presence of an object that has a special value for him.

There appear to be two main directions in which the study of deference rituals may go. One is to settle on a given ritual and attempt to discover factors common to all of the social situations in which it is performed, for it is through such an analysis that we can get at the "meaning" of the ritual. The other is to collect all of the rituals that are performed to a given recipient, from whomever the ritual comes. Each of these rituals can then be interpreted for the symbolically expressed meaning that is embodied in it. By piecing together these meanings we can arrive at the conception of the recipient that others are obliged to maintain of him to him.

The individual may desire, earn, and deserve deference, but by and large he is not allowed to give it to himself, being forced to seek it from others. In seeking it from others, he finds he has added reason for seeking them out, and in turn society is given added assurance that its members will enter into interaction and relationships with one another. If the individual could give himself the deference he desired there might be a tendency for society to disintegrate into islands inhabited by solitary cultish men, each in continuous worship at his own shrine.

The appreciation carried by an act of deference implies that the actor possesses a sentiment of regard for the recipient, often involving a general evaluation of the recipient. Regard is something the individual constantly has for others, and knows enough about to feign on occasion; yet in having regard for someone, the individual is unable to specify in detail what in fact he has in mind.

Those who render deference to an individual may feel, of course, that they are doing this merely because he is an instance of a category, or a representative of something, and that they are giving him his due not because of what they think of him "personally" but in spite of it. Some organizations, such as the military, explicitly stress this sort of rationale for according deference, leading to an impersonal bestowal of something that is specifically directed toward the person. By easily showing a regard that he does not have, the actor can feel that he is preserving a kind of inner autonomy, holding off the ceremonial order by the very act of upholding it. And of course in scrupulously observing the proper forms he may find that he is free to insinuate all kinds of disregard by carefully modifying intonation, pronunciation, pacing, and so forth.

In thinking about deference it is common to use as a model the rituals of obeisance, submission, and propitiation that someone under authority gives to someone in authority. Deference comes to be conceived as something a subordinate owes to his superordinate. This is an extremely limiting view of deference on two grounds. First, there are a great many forms of symmetrical deference which social equals owe to one another; in some societies, Tibetan for example, salutations between high-placed equals can become prolonged displays of ritual conduct, exceeding in duration and expansiveness the kind of obeisance a subject may owe his ruler in less ritualized societies. Similarly, there are deference obligations that superordinates owe their subordinates; high priests all over the world seem obliged to respond to offerings with some equivalent of "Bless you, my son." Secondly, the regard in which the actor holds the recipient need not be one of respectful awe; there are other kinds of regard that are regularly expressed through interpersonal rituals also, such as trust, as when an individual welcomes sudden strangers into his house, or capacity-esteem, as when the individual defers to another's technical advice. A sentiment of regard that plays an important role in deference is that of affection and belongingness. We see this in the extreme in the obligation of a newly married man in our society to treat his bride with affectional deference whenever it is possible to twist ordinary behavior into a display of this kind. We find it more commonly, for example, as a component in many farewells where, as in our middle-class society, the actor will be obliged to infuse his voice with sadness and regret, paying deference in this way to the recipient's status as someone whom others can hold dearly. In "progressive" psychiatric establishments, a deferential show of acceptance, affection, and concern may form a constant and significant aspect of the stance taken by staff members when contacting patients. On Ward B, in fact, the two youngest patients seemed to have become so experienced in receiving such offerings, and so doubtful of them, that they would sometimes reply in a mocking way, apparently in an effort to re-establish the interaction on what seemed to these patients to be a more sincere level.

It appears that deference behavior on the whole tends to be honorific and politely toned, conveying appreciation of the recipient that is in many ways more complimentary to the recipient than the actor's true sentiments might warrant. The actor typically gives the recipient the benefit of the doubt, and may even conceal low regard by extra punctiliousness. Thus acts of deference often attest to ideal guide lines to which the actual activity between actor and recipient can now and then be referred. As a last resort, the recipient has a right to make a direct appeal to these honorific definitions of the situation, to press his theoretic claims, but should he be rash enough to do so, it is likely that his relationship to the actor will be modified thereafter. People sense that the recipient ought not to take the actor literally or force his hand, and ought to rest content with the show of appreciation as opposed to a more substantive expression of it. Hence one finds that many automatic acts of deference contain a vestigial meaning, having to do with activity in which no one is any longer engaged and implying an appreciation long since not expected—and yet we know these antique tributes cannot be neglected with impunity.

In addition to a sentiment of regard, acts of deference typically contain a kind of promise, expressing in truncated form the actor's avowal and pledge to treat the recipient in a particular way in the on-coming activity. The pledge affirms that the expectations and obligations of the recipient, both substantive and ceremonial, will be allowed and supported by the actor. Actors thus promise to maintain the conception of self that the recipient has built up from the rules he is involved in. (Perhaps the prototype here is the public act of allegiance by which a subject officially acknowledges his subservience in certain matters to his lord.) Deferential pledges are frequently conveyed through spoken terms of address involving status-identifiers, as when a nurse responds to a rebuke in the operating room with the phrase, "yes, Doctor," signifying by term of address and tone of voice that the criticism has been understood and that, however unpalatable, it has not caused her to rebel. When a putative recipient fails to receive anticipated acts of deference, or when an actor makes clear that he is giving homage with bad grace, the recipient may feel that the state of affairs which he has been taking for granted has become unstable, and that an insubordinate effort may be made by the actor to reallocate tasks, relations, and power. To elicit an established act of deference, even if the actor must first be reminded of his obligations and warned about the consequence of discourtesy, is evidence that if rebellion comes it will come slyly; to be pointedly refused an expected act of deference is often a way of being told that open insurrection has begun.

I have mentioned four very common forms of presentational deference; salutations, invitations, compliments, and minor services. Through all of these the recipient is told that he is not an island unto himself and that others are, or seek to be, involved with him and with his personal private concerns. Taken together, these rituals provide a continuous symbolic tracing of the extent to which the recipient's ego has not been bounded and barricaded in regard to others.

Two main types of deference have been illustrated: presentational rituals through which the actor concretely depicts his appreciation of the recipient; and avoidance rituals, taking the form of proscriptions, interdictions, and taboos, which imply acts the actor must refrain from doing lest he violate the right of the recipient to keep him at a distance. We are familiar with this distinction from Durkheim's classification of ritual into positive and negative rites.[4]

In suggesting that there are things that must be said and done to a recipient, and things that must not be said and done, it should be plain that there is an inherent opposition and conflict between these two forms of deference. To ask

[4]Durkheim, *The Elementary Forms*, p. 299.

after an individual's health, his family's well-being, or the state of his affairs, is to present him with a sign of sympathetic concern; but in a certain way to make this presentation is to invade the individual's personal reserve, as will be made clear if an actor of wrong status asks him these questions, or if a recent event has made such a question painful to answer. As Durkheim suggested, "The human personality is a sacred thing; one dare not violate it nor infringe its bounds, while at the same time the greatest good is in communion with others."[5]

DEMEANOR

It was suggested that the ceremonial component of concrete behavior has at least two basic elements, deference and demeanor. Deference, defined as the appreciation an individual shows of another to that other, whether through avoidance rituals or presentational rituals, has been discussed and demeanor may now be considered.

By demeanor I shall refer to that element of the individual's ceremonial behavior typically conveyed through deportment, dress, and bearing, which serves to express to those in his immediate presence that he is a person of certain desirable or undesirable qualities. In our society, the "well" or "properly" demeaned individual displays such attributes as: discretion and sincerity; modesty in claims regarding self; sportsmanship; command of speech and physical movements; self-control over his emotions, his appetites, and his desires; poise under pressure; and so forth.

When we attempt to analyze the qualities conveyed through demeanor, certain themes become apparent. The well-demeaned individual possesses the attributes popularly associated with "character training" or "socialization," these being implanted when a neophyte of any kind is housebroken. Rightly or wrongly, others tend to use such qualities diagnostically, as evidence of what the actor is generally like at other times and as a performer of other activities. In addition, the properly demeaned individual is someone who has closed off many avenues of perception and penetration that others might take to him, and is therefore unlikely to be contaminated by them. Most importantly, perhaps, good demeanor is what is required of an actor if he is to be transformed into someone who can be relied upon to maintain himself as an interactant, poised for communication, and to act so that others do not endanger themselves by presenting themselves as interactants to him.

It should be noted once again that demeanor involves attributes derived from interpretations others make of the way in which the individual handles

[5]Emile Durkheim, "The Determination of Moral Facts," p. 37.

himself during social intercourse. The individual cannot establish these attributes for his own by verbally avowing that he possesses them, though sometimes he may rashly try to do this. (He can, however, contrive to conduct himself in such a way that others, through their interpretation of his conduct, will impute the kinds of attributes to him he would like others to see in him.) In general, then, through demeanor the individual creates an image of himself, but properly speaking this is not an image that is meant for his own eyes. Of course this should not prevent us from seeing that the individual who acts with good demeanor may do so because he places an appreciable value upon himself, and that he who fails to demean himself properly may be accused of having "no self-respect" or of holding himself too cheaply in his own eyes.

As in the case of deference, an object in the study of demeanor is to collect all the ceremonially relevant acts that a particular individual performs in the presence of each of the several persons with whom he comes in contact, to interpret these acts for the demeanor that is symbolically expressed through them, and then to piece these meanings together into an image of the individual, an image of him in others' eyes.

Rules of demeanor, like rules of deference, can be symmetrical or asymmetrical. Between social equals, symmetrical rules of demeanor seem often to be prescribed. Between unequals many variations can be found. For example, at staff meetings on the psychiatric units of the hospital, medical doctors had the privilege of swearing, changing the topic of conversation, and sitting in undignified positions; attendants, on the other hand, had the right to attend staff meetings and to ask questions during them (in line with the milieu-therapy orientation of these research units) but were implicitly expected to conduct themselves with greater circumspection than was required of doctors. (This was pointed out by a perceptive occupational therapist who claimed she was always reminded that a mild young female psychiatrist was really an M.D. by the fact that this psychiatrist exercised these prerogatives of informal demeanor.) The extreme here perhaps is the master-servant relation as seen in cases where valets and maids are required to perform in a dignified manner services of an undignified kind. Similarly, doctors had the right to saunter into the nurses' station, lounge on the station's dispensing counter, and engage in joking with the nurses; other ranks participated in this informal interaction with doctors, but only after doctors had initiated it.

DEFERENCE AND DEMEANOR

Deference and demeanor are analytical terms; empirically there is much overlapping of the activities to which they refer. An act through which the individ-

ual gives or withholds deference to others typically provides means by which
he expresses the fact that he is a well or badly demeaned individual. Some
aspects of this overlapping may be cited. First, in performing a given act of
presentational deference, as in offering a guest a chair, the actor finds himself
doing something that can be done with smoothness and aplomb, expressing
self-control and poise, or with clumsiness and uncertainty, expressing an ir-
resolute character. This is, as it were, an incidental and adventitious connection between deference and demeanor. It may be illustrated from recent material on doctor-patient relationships, where it is suggested that one complaint a
doctor may have against some of his patients is that they do not bathe before
coming for an examination; while bathing is a way of paying deference to the
doctor it is at the same time a way for the patient to present himself as a clean,
well demeaned person. A further illustration is found in acts such as loud
talking, shouting, or singing, for these acts encroach upon the right of others
to be let alone, while at the same time they illustrate a badly demeaned lack of
control over one's feelings.

The same connection between deference and demeanor has had a bearing
on the ceremonial difficulties associated with intergroup interaction: the gestures of deference expected by members of one society have sometimes been
incompatible with the standards of demeanor maintained by members of
another. For example, during the nineteenth century, diplomatic relations
between Britain and China were embarrassed by the fact that the *Kot'ow*
demanded of visiting ambassadors by the Chinese Emperor was felt by some
British ambassadors to be incompatible with their self-respect.

A second connection between deference and demeanor turns upon the fact
that a willingness to give others their deferential due is one of the qualities
which the individual owes it to others to express through his conduct, just as a
willingness to conduct oneself with good demeanor is in general a way of
showing deference to those present.

In spite of these connections between deference and demeanor, the analytical relation between them is one of "complementarity," not identity. The
image the individual owes to others to maintain of himself is not the same
type of image these others are obliged to maintain of him. Deference images
tend to point to the wider society outside the interaction, to the place the
individual has achieved in the hierarchy of this society. Demeanor images
tend to point to qualities which any social position gives its incumbents a
chance to display during interaction, for these qualities pertain more to the
way in which the individual handles his position than to the rank and place of
that position relative to those possessed by others.

Further, the image of himself the individual owes it to others to maintain through his conduct is a kind of justification and compensation for the image of him that others are obliged to express through their deference to him. Each of the two images in fact may act as a guarantee and check upon the other. In an interchange that can be found in many cultures, the individual defers to guests to show how welcome they are and how highly he regards them; they in turn decline the offering at least once, showing through their demeanor that they are not presumptuous, immodest, or over-eager to receive favor. Similarly, a man starts to rise for a lady, showing respect for her sex; she interrupts and halts his gesture, showing she is not greedy of her rights in this capacity but is ready to define the situation as one between equals. In general, then, by treating others deferentially one gives them an opportunity to handle the indulgence with good demeanor. Through this differentiation in symbolizing function the world tends to be bathed in better images than anyone deserves, for it is practical to signify great appreciation of others by offering them deferential indulgences, knowing that some of these indulgences will be declined as an expression of good demeanor.

There are still other complementary relations between deference and demeanor. If an individual feels he ought to show proper demeanor in order to warrant deferential treatment, then he must be in a position to do so. He must, for example, be able to conceal from others aspects of himself which would make him unworthy in their eyes, and to conceal himself from them when he is in an indignified state, whether of dress, mind, posture, or action. The avoidance rituals which others perform in regard to him give him room to maneuver, enabling him to present only a self that is worthy of deference; at the same time, this avoidance makes it easier for them to assure themselves that the deference they have to show him is warranted.

To show the difference between deference and demeanor, I have pointed out the complementary relation between them, but even this kind of relatedness can be overstressed. The failure of an individual to show proper deference to others does not necessarily free them from the obligation to act with good demeanor in his presence, however disgruntled they may be at having to do this. Similarly, the failure of an individual to conduct himself with proper demeanor does not always relieve those in his presence from treating him with proper deference. It is by separating deference and demeanor that we can appreciate many things about ceremonial life, such as that a group may be noted for excellence in one of these areas while having a bad reputation in the other. Hence we can find a place for arguments such as De Quincey's, that an Englishman shows great self-respect but little respect for others while a Frenchman shows great respect for others but little respect for himself.

We are to see, then, that there are many occasions when it would be improper for an individual to convey about himself what others are ready to convey about him to him, since each of these two images is a warrant and justification for the other, and not a mirror image of it. The Meadian notion that the individual takes toward himself the attitude others take to him seems very much an oversimplification. Rather the individual must rely on others to complete the picture of him of which he himself is allowed to paint only certain parts. Each individual is responsible for the demeanor image of himself and the deference image of others, so that for a complete man to be expressed, individuals must hold hands in a chain of ceremony, each giving deferentially with proper demeanor to the one on the right what will be received deferentially from the one on the left. While it may be true that the individual has a unique self all his own, evidence of this possession is thoroughly a product of joint ceremonial labor, the part expressed through the individual's demeanor being no more significant than the part conveyed by others through their deferential behavior toward him.

CONCLUSIONS

The rules of conduct which bind the actor and the recipient together are the bindings of society. But many of the acts which are guided by these rules occur infrequently or take a long time for their consummation. Opportunities to affirm the moral order and the society could therefore be rare. It is here that ceremonial rules play their social function, for many of the acts which are guided by these rules last but a brief moment, involve no substantive outlay, and can be performed in every social interaction. Whatever the activity and however profanely instrumental, it can afford many opportunities for minor ceremonies as long as other persons are present. Through these observances, guided by ceremonial obligations and expectations, a constant flow of indulgences is spread through society, with others who are present constantly reminding the individual that he must keep himself together as a well demeaned person and affirm the sacred quality of these others. The gestures which we sometimes call empty are perhaps in fact the fullest things of all.

It is therefore important to see that the self is in part a ceremonial thing, a sacred object which must be treated with proper ritual care and in turn must be presented in a proper light to others. As a means through which this self is established, the individual acts with proper demeanor while in contact with others and is treated by others with deference. It is just as important to see that if the individual is to play this kind of sacred game, then the field must be suited to it. The environment must ensure that the individual will not pay too high a price for acting with good demeanor and that deference will be accorded him. Deference and demeanor practices must be institutionalized so that the individual will be able to project a viable, sacred self and stay in the game on a proper ritual basis.

An environment, then, in terms of the ceremonial component of activity, is a place where it is easy or difficult to play the ritual game of having a self. Where ceremonial practices are thoroughly institutionalized, as they were on Ward A, it would appear easy to be a person. Where these practices are not established, as to a degree they were not in Ward B, it would appear difficult to be a person. Why one ward comes to be a place in which it is easy to have a self and another ward comes to be a place where this is difficult depends in part on the type of patient that is recruited and the type of regime the staff attempts to maintain.

One of the bases upon which mental hospitals throughout the world segregate their patients is degree of easily apparent "mental illness." By and large this means that patients are graded according to the degree to which they violate ceremonial rules of social intercourse. There are very good practical reasons for sorting patients into different wards in this way, and in fact that institution is backward where no one bothers to do so. This grading very often means, however, that individuals who are desperately uncivil in some areas of behavior are placed in the intimate company of those who are desperately uncivil in others. Thus, individuals who are the least ready to project a sustainable self are lodged in a milieu where it is practically impossible to do so.

It is in this context that we can reconsider some interesting aspects of the effect of coercion and constraint upon the individual. If an individual is to act with proper demeanor and show proper deference, then it will be necessary for him to have areas of self-determination. He must have an expendable supply of the small indulgences which his society employs in its idiom of regard—such as cigarettes to give, chairs to proffer, food to provide, and so forth. He must have freedom of bodily movement so that it will be possible for him to assume a stance that conveys appropriate respect for others and appropriate demeanor on his own part; a patient strapped to a bed may find it impractical not to befoul himself, let alone to stand in the presence of a lady. He must have a supply of appropriate clean clothing if he is to make the sort of appearance that is expected of a well demeaned person. To look seemly may require a tie, a belt, shoe laces, a mirror, and razor blades—all of which the authorities may deem unwise to give him. He must have access to the eating utensils which his society defines as appropriate ones for use, and may find that meat cannot be circumspectly eaten with a cardboard spoon. And finally, without too much cost to himself he must be able to decline certain kinds of work, now sometimes classified as "industrial therapy," which his social group considers *infra dignitatem*.

When the individual is subject to extreme constraint he is automatically forced from the circle of the proper. The sign vehicles or physical tokens through which the customary ceremonies are performed are unavailable to him. Others may show ceremonial regard for him, but it becomes impossible for him to reciprocate the show or to act in such a way as to make himself worthy of receiving it. The only ceremonial statements that are possible for him are improper ones.

The history of the care of mental cases is the history of constricting devices: constraining gloves, camisoles, floor and seat chains, handcuffs, "biter's mask," wet-packs, supervised toileting, hosing down, institutional clothing, forkless and knifeless eating, and so forth. The use of these devices provides significant data on the ways in which the ceremonial grounds of selfhood can be taken away. By implication we can obtain information from this history about the conditions that must be satisfied if individuals are to have selves. Unfortunately, today there are still mental institutions where the past of other hospitals can be empirically studied now. Students of interpersonal ceremony should seek these institutions out almost as urgently as students of kinship have sought out disappearing cultures.

Throughout this paper I have assumed we can learn about ceremony by studying a contemporary secular situation—that of the individual who has declined to employ the ceremonial idiom of his group in an acceptable manner and has been hospitalized. In a crosscultural view it is convenient to see this as a product of our complex division of labor which brings patients together instead of leaving each in his local circle. Further, this division of labor also brings together those who have the task of caring for these patients.

We are thus led to the special dilemma of the hospital worker: as a member of the wider society he ought to take action against mental patients, who have transgressed the rules of ceremonial order; but his occupational role obliges him to care for and protect these very people. When "milieu therapy" is stressed, these obligations further require him to convey warmth in response to hostility; relatedness in response to alienation.

We have seen that hospital workers must witness improper conduct without applying usual negative sanctions, and yet that they must exercise disrespectful coercion over their patients. A third peculiarity is that staff members may be obliged to render to patients services such as changing socks, tying shoelaces or trimming fingernails, which outside the hospital generally convey elaborate deference. In the hospital setting, such acts are likely to convey something inappropriate since the attendant at the same time exerts certain kinds of power and moral superiority over his charges. A final peculiarity in the cere-monial life of mental hospitals is that individuals collapse as units of minimal ceremonial substance and others learn that what had been taken for granted as ultimate entities are really held together by rules that can be broken with some kind of impunity. Such understanding, like one gained at war or at a kins-man's funeral, is not much talked about but it tends, perhaps, to draw staff and patients together into an unwilling group sharing undesired knowledge.

In summary, then, modern society brings transgressors of the ceremonial order to a single place, along with some ordinary members of society who make their living there. These dwell in a place of unholy acts and unholy understandings, yet some of them retain allegiance to the ceremonial order outside the hospital setting. Somehow ceremonial people must work out mechanisms and techniques for living without certain kinds of ceremony.

In this paper I have suggested that Durkheimian notions about primitive religion can be translated into concepts of deference and demeanor, and that these concepts help us to grasp some aspects of urban secular living. The implication is that in one sense this secular world is not so irreligious as we might think. Many gods have been done away with, but the individual himself stubbornly remains as a deity of considerable importance. He walks with some dignity and is the recipient of many little offerings. He is jealous of the worship due him, yet, approached in the right spirit, he is ready to forgive those who may have offended him. Because of their status relative to his, some persons will find him contaminating while others will find they contami-nate him, in either case finding that they must treat him with ritual care. Perhaps the individual is so viable a god because he can actually understand the ceremonial significance of the way he is treated, and quite on his own can respond dramatically to what is proffered him. In contacts between such deities there is no need for middlemen; each of these gods is able to serve as his own priest.

Social Control in Science [1965]

WARREN O. HAGSTROM

• *Warren O. Hagstrom's* The Scientific Community *(1965) was one of the first works to state a systematic sociological theory of science, and it helped to set off the modern wave of research in the sociology of science. The basic theory, presented here, attempts to show that science is held together by the same mechanism of symbolic gift-exchanges that Marcel Mauss had analyzed as at the foundation of primitive economies. Science is not a collection of self-motivated individuals making discoveries, but a tightly regulated system such as is found wherever "sacred" rather than secular values are at stake.*

A common view of the organization of science, held implicitly or explicitly by most scientists, is that the individual characteristics [of being "self-starting" and "self-controlling"] are sufficient to account for conformity to scientific values and norms. It is often asserted that the scientist does what he wishes to do, attempts to solve problems that are intrinsically interesting and important, and is guided by aesthetic considerations. His social relations with others either interfere with this or are happy, but secondary, consequences of it.

This highly individualistic view is incomplete. It leads to no propositions about the actual scientific community as we know it, except perhaps that the socialization of recruits plays an unusually important part in the community's activities, and the importance of socialization is also consistent with other theoretical approaches. Some facts, which will be presented more fully in succeeding chapters, are inconsistent with the view of the scientist assumed by an individualistic theory. For instance, scientists seek to publish their accomplishments and are greatly disturbed if proper recognition for them is not forthcoming. Moreover, scientists who experience prolonged isolation from their colleagues cease being productive. A more obvious objection to this individualistic approach is that scientists seldom consciously set to work on problems that they know others have solved. If scientists received their major

From Warren O. Hagstrom, *The Scientific Community* (New York: Basic Books, 1965), pp. 11–22, 52. Reprinted by permission of the author.

gratifications from problem-solving alone, the mere fact that others have solved the problem should not deter them from solving it themselves. (Although mountaineers receive egoistic gratifications from being the first to climb a peak, they receive similar gratifications from climbing peaks already climbed: it demonstrates their abilities. Similarly, the egoistic scientist can demonstrate his abilities by solving previously solved problems, yet he seldom chooses to do so, since he also desires social recognition for his discoveries.)

Not only is the extremely individualistic view directly controverted by obvious facts about the scientific community, but there is every theoretical reason to expect this to be so. First, the autonomy of the scientific community cannot be taken for granted; it must be maintained by internal social controls, among other things. Without them, scientists would tend to respond more readily to the goals and standards of nonscientists. Second, communities of autonomous specialists tend to be rigid; they incorporate new goals and standards only with difficulty, for the socialization that produces commitment to norms and values at the highest levels also produces commitment to more specific norms. The scientific training that produces committed scientists also tends to commit them to techniques and particular theories. Since change is intrinsic in any community incorporating scientific values, if science is to thrive, scientists must respond to discoveries by continually changing their goals, techniques, and theories. Third, commitments to norms tend to erode in the absence of reinforcement. Many of the procedures known collectively as the "scientific method" are important only because they make possible communication among scientists. In the absence of sanctions, deviance from such norms would be common.

We may conclude that the socialization of scientists must be supplemented by a dynamic system of social control, if the values and effectiveness of science are to be maintained. Negative arguments are unsatisfying; the best reason for studying social control in science is that it leads one to discover the characteristic tensions within the scientific community, and this endeavor makes meaningful many varieties of scientific behavior that are otherwise unseen or dismissed as idiosyncratic and the consequence of aberrant personalities.

THE SOCIAL RECOGNITION OF DISCOVERY

Manuscripts submitted to scientific periodicals are often called "contributions," and they are, in fact, gifts. Authors do not usually receive royalties or other payments, and their institutions may even be required to aid in the financial support of the periodical. On the other hand, manuscripts for which the scientific authors do receive financial payments, such as textbooks and popularizations, are, if not despised, certainly held in much lower esteem than articles containing original research results.

Gift-giving by scientists is thus similar to one of the most common modes of allocating resources to science, for this often takes the form of gifts from wealthy individuals or organizations. This has been true from the time of Cosimo de Medici to today, the time of the Rockefeller and Ford foundations. The gift status of moneys spent by industrial firms and governments on research is ambiguous; usually money seems to be spent with specific goals in mind, but the vast sums spent on space programs, particle accelerators, radiotelescopes, and so forth often seem like a potlatch by the community of nations. Neil Smelser has suggested that the gift mode of exchange is typical not only of science but of all institutions concerned with the maintenance and transmission of common values, such as the family, religion, and communities.[1]

In general, the acceptance of a gift by an individual or a community implies a recognition of the status of the donor and the existence of certain kinds of reciprocal rights.[2] These reciprocal rights may be to a return gift of the same kind and value, as in many primitive economic systems, or to certain appropriate sentiments of gratitude and deference. In science, the acceptance by scientific journals of contributed manuscripts establishes the donor's status as a scientist—indeed, status as a scientist can be achieved *only* by such gift-giving—and it assures him of prestige within the scientific community. The remainder of this chapter concerns the nature and forms of this allocation of prestige.

The organization of science consists of an exchange of social recognition for information. But, as in all gift-giving, the expectation of return gifts (of recognition) cannot be publicly acknowledged as the motive for making the gift. A gift is supposed to be given, not in the expectation of a return, but as an expression of the sentiment of the donor toward the recipient. Thus, in the kula expeditions of the Melanesians:

> The ceremony of transfer is done with solemnity. The object given is disdained or suspect; it is not accepted until it is thrown on the ground. The donor affects an exaggerated modesty. Solemnly bearing his gift, accompanied by the blowing of a conch-shell, he apologizes for bringing only his leavings and throws the objects at his partner's feet. . . .

[1]Neil J. Smelser, "A Comparative View of Exchange Systems," *Economic Development and Cultural Change*, 7 (1959), 173–182.
[2]Cf. Alvin W. Gouldner, "The Norm of Reciprocity," *American Sociological Review*, 25 (1960), 161–178; and Marcel Mauss, *The Gift: Forms and Functions of Exchange in Primitive Societies* (Glencoe, Ill.: Free Press, 1954), pp. 40 f., 73, *et passim*.

> Pains are taken to show one's freedom and autonomy as well as one's magnanimity, yet all the time one is actuated by the mechanisms of obligation which are resident in the gifts themselves.[3]

Gift-giving is capable of cynical manipulation; if this is publicly expressed, however, the exchange of gifts ceases, perhaps to be succeeded by contractual exchange. Consequently, scientists usually deny that they are strongly motivated by a desire for recognition, or that this desire influences their research decisions.

Nevertheless, the public disavowal of the expectation of recognition in return for scientific contributions should no more be taken to mean that the expectation is absent than the magnanimous front of the kula trader can be taken to mean that he does not expect a return gift. In both instances, this is made clearest when the expected response is not forthcoming. In primitive societies, failure to present return gifts often means warfare.[4] In science, the failure to recognize discovery may give rise, if not to warfare, at least to strong antagonisms and, at times, to intense controversy. A historical summary and analysis of priority controversies has been given by Robert K. Merton,[5] who pointed out that the failure to recognize previous work threatens the system of incentives in science. The pattern is not infrequent today. Of my seventy-nine informants, at least nine admitted to having been involved in questions of disputed priority either as the culprit or the victim.

The desire to obtain social recognition induces the scientist to conform to scientific norms by contributing his discoveries to the larger community. Thomas Sprat, writing near the dawn of modern science, perceived the importance of this: "If neither *Chance*, nor *Friendship*, nor *Treachery* of Servants, have brought such Things out; yet we see *Ostentation* alone to be every day powerful enough to do it. This Desire of Glory, and to be counted Authors, prevails on all. . . ."[6]

Not only does the desire for recognition induce the scientist to communicate his results; it also influences his selection of problems and methods. He will tend to select problems the solution of which will result in greater recognition, and he will tend to select methods that will make his work acceptable to his colleagues.

[3]Mauss, *op. cit.*, p. 21, reporting the work of Malinowski.

[4]Mauss, *op. cit.*, p. 3 *et passim*.

[5]Merton, "Priorities in Scientific Discovery," *American Sociological Review*, 22 (1957), 635–659.

[6]Sprat, *The History of the Royal Society of London* (London, 1673), pp. 74 f. See also Karl Mannheim on the importance of the desire for recognition in science and other cultural pursuits: *Essays on the Sociology of Knowledge* (London: Routledge and Kegan Paul, 1952), ch. VI, especially pp. 239, 242–243, 272.

Another type of sanction is not primarily important in science, although it is often alleged to be. This consists of extrinsic rewards, primarily position and money. It is alleged that scientists publish, select problems, and select methods in order to maximize these rewards. University policies that base advancement and salary on quantity of publication sometimes seem to imply that this is true, that scientists' research contributions are not freely given gifts at all but are, instead, services in return for salary. While it is important for extrinsic rewards to be more or less consistent with recognition, the ideal seems to be that they should follow recognition, and this seems to be the general practice. In any case, an explanation of scientific behavior in terms of extrinsic rewards is weakened by the fact that many scientists in elite positions, whose extrinsic rewards will be unaffected by their behavior, continue to be highly productive and to conform to scientific goals and norms. Furthermore, scientists usually feel that it is degrading and improper to submit manuscripts for publication primarily to gain position without really caring if the work is read by others.

But why should gift-giving be important in science when it is essentially obsolete as a form of exchange in most other areas of modern life, especially the most distinctly "civilized" areas? Gift-giving, because it tends to create particularistic obligations, usually reduces the rationality of economic action. Rationality is maximized when "costs" of alternative courses of action can be assessed, and such costs are usually established in free-market exchanges or in the plans of central directing agencies. When participants are paid a money wage or salary for their efforts, and when this effectively controls their behavior, the system is more flexible than when controls derive from traditional or gift obligations. Why, then, does this frequently inefficient and irrational form of control persist in science? To be sure, it also tends to persist in other professions. Professionals are expected to be motivated by a desire to serve others. For example, physicians do receive a fee for service, yet they are expected to have a "sliding scale" and serve the indigent at reduced fees or for no fees at all. The larger community recognizes two types of public dependence on professions: professional services are regarded as essential, concerned with values that should be realized regardless of a client's ability to pay; and nonprofessionals are unable to evaluate professional services, which makes them vulnerable to exploitation by unqualified persons. The rationale for the norm of service is usually the former type of dependence. In science, for example, the fact that a community has no one willing and able to pay for an important item of useless knowledge is not supposed to interfere with its ability to acquire the knowledge. But the idea of the gift and the norm of service is also related to the dependence of the public that follows from its inability to evaluate services.

The rationality of professional services is not the same as the rationality of the market. In contractual exchanges, when services are rewarded on a direct financial or barter basis, the client abdicates, to a considerable degree, his *moral control* over the producer. In return, the client is freed from personal ties with the producer, and he is able to choose rationally between alternative sources of supply. In the professions, and especially in science, the abdication of moral control would disrupt the system. The producer of professional services must be strongly committed to higher values. He must be responsible for his products, and it is fitting that he not be alienated from them. The scientist, for example, must be concerned with maintaining and correcting existing theories in his field, and his work should be oriented to this end. The exchange of gifts for recognition tends to maintain such orientations. On the one hand, the recipient of the gifts finds it difficult to refuse them (they are "free"), and, on the other, the donor is held responsible for adhering to central norms and values. The maxim, *caveat emptor*, is inapplicable.[7] Furthermore, the donor is not alienated from his gift, but retains a lasting interest in it. It is, in a sense, his property.[8] One indication of this is the frequent practice of eponymy, the affixing of the name of the scientist to all or part of what he has found.[9]

Emphasis on gifts and services occurs frequently in social life, and we can get at the root of this generality by focusing on certain paradoxical elements implicit in the argument presented thus far. It has been argued that scientists are oriented to receiving recognition from colleagues and that this orientation influences their research decisions. Yet evidence that scientists themselves deny this has also been presented. There is a normative component to this denial, one that appears more clearly in analyzing scientific fashions. It is felt that, if a scientist's decisions are influenced by the probability of being recognized, he will tend to deviate from certain central scientific norms—he will fail to be original and critical. Thus, while it is true that scientists are motivated by a desire to obtain social recognition, and while it is true that only work on certain types of problems and with certain techniques will receive

[7]This does not mean that scientists are not supposed to be skeptical; that they should be skeptical about their own work as well as that of their colleagues is one of the more important institutionalized norms of science. Cf. Robert K. Merton, *Social Theory and Social Structure* (Glencoe, Ill.: Free Press, 1949), pp. 315 f. It does mean that unlike the consumer in the free market, the "consumer" of scientific products can hold the producer morally responsible for "defective products."

[8]Cf. Merton, "Priorities in Scientific Discovery," *op. cit.*, pp. 640 f., and *Social Theory and Social Structure, op. cit.*, pp. 312 f. Mauss pointed out that members of some "archaic societies" felt gifts somehow remained part of the donor and that this belief was reinforced by further existential beliefs, e.g., the gift itself possessed the power to harm the recipient if it was not reciprocated. Mauss, *op. cit.*, pp. 41 ff. *et passim*.

[9]Cf. Merton, "Priorities in Scientific Discovery," *op. cit.*, pp. 642–644.

recognition at any particular time, it is also true that, if a scientist were to admit being influenced in his choices of problems and techniques by the probability of being recognized, he would be considered deviant. That is, if scientists conform to norms about problems and techniques as a result of this specific form of social control, they are thereby deviants.

This apparent paradox, that people deviate in the very act of conforming, is common whenever people are expected to be strongly committed to values. In general, *whenever strong commitments to values are expected, the rational calculation of punishments and rewards is regarded as an improper basis for making decisions.* Citizens who refrain from treason merely because it is against the law are, by that fact, of questionable loyalty; parents who refrain from incest merely because of fear of community reaction are, by that fact, unfit for parenthood; and scientists who select problems merely because they feel that in dealing with them they will receive greater recognition from colleagues are, by that fact, not "good" scientists. In all such cases the sanctions are of no obvious value: they evidently do not work for the deviants, and none of those who conform admit to being influenced by them. But this does not mean that the sanctions are of no importance; it does mean that more than overt conformity to norms is demanded, that inner conformity is regarded as equally, or more, important.

Thus, the gift exchange (or the norm of service), as opposed to barter or contractual exchange, is particularly well suited to social systems in which great reliance is placed on the ability of well-socialized persons to operate independently of formal controls. The prolonged and intensive socialization scientists experience is reinforced and complemented by their practice of the exchange of information for recognition. The socialization experience produces scientists who are strongly committed to the values of science and who need the esteem and approval of their peers. The reward of recognition for information reinforces this commitment but also makes it flexible. Recognition is given for kinds of contributions the scientific community finds valuable, and different kinds of contributions will be found valuable at different times.

The scientist's denial of recognition as an important incentive has other consequences related to those already mentioned. When peers exchange gifts, the denial of the expectation of reciprocity in kind implies an expectation of gratitude, a highly diffuse response.[10] It will be shown that this kind of gift

---

[10]As Georg Simmel says, gratitude "establishes the bond of interaction, of the reciprocity of service and return service, even where they are not guaranteed by external coercion." *The Sociology of Georg Simmel*, Kurt Wolff, ed. and trans. (Glencoe, Ill.: Free Press, 1950), p. 387. He goes on to note that persons make great efforts to avoid receiving gifts in order not to make such commitments to others. Something like this may occur in science.

exchange occurs among scientists, although the more important form of scientific contribution is directed to the larger scientific community.[11] In this case the denial of the pursuit of recognition serves to emphasize the universality of scientific standards: it is not a particular group of colleagues at a particular time that should be addressed, but all possible colleagues at all possible periods. These sentiments were expressed with his typical fervor by Johannes Kepler:

> I have robbed the golden vessels of the Egyptians to make out of them a tabernacle for my God, far from the frontiers of Egypt. If you forgive me, I shall rejoice. If you are angry, I shall bear it. Behold, I have cast the dice, and I am writing a book either for my contemporaries, or for posterity. It is all the same to me. It may wait a hundred years for a reader, since God has also waited six thousand years for a witness.[12]

While this orientation is consistent with the scientist's need for autonomy— being dependent on the favors of particular others is terrifying—it also contains a strong element of the tragic. Scientists learn to *expect* injustice, the inequitable allocation of rewards. Occasionally one of them makes this explicit. Max Weber addressed students on "Science as a Vocation" in the following way:

> I know of hardly any career on earth where chance plays such a role. . . . If the young scholar asks for my advice with regard to habilitation, the responsibility of encouraging him can hardly be borne . . . one must ask every . . . man: Do you in all conscience believe that you can stand seeing mediocrity after mediocrity, year after year, climb beyond you, without becoming embittered and without coming to grief? Naturally, one always receives the answer: "Of course, I live only for my calling." Yet, I have found that only a few men could endure this situation without coming to grief.[13]

More common than such an explicit statement is the myth of the hero who is recognized only after his death. This myth is important in science, as in art, because it strengthens universal standards against tendencies to become depen-

---

[11] In other words, the scientific contribution is closely approximated by the sacrificial model of the gift. Cf. Emile Durkheim, *The Elementary Forms of Religious Life*, J. W. Swain, trans. (London: George Allen and Unwin, 1915), pp. 342 f.: "The sacrifice is partially a communion; but it is also, and no less essentially, a gift and an act of renouncement."

[12] Quoted in Arthur Koestler, *The Sleepwalkers* (London: Hutchinson, 1959), pp. 393 f.

[13] Hans H. Gerth and C. Wright Mills, trans. and eds. *From Max Weber: Essays in Sociology* (New York: Oxford University Press, 1946), pp. 132, 134. Weber was partly concerned with the particular aspects of science in German universities, but the entire essay shows that he was also concerned with the more universal aspects of science as a profession.

dent on particular communities. Thus, mathematics has such heroes as Galois, who wrote the major part of his great mathematical opus the night before he was killed in a duel at the age of twenty-one; Abel, who died of tuberculosis as his greatness was coming to be recognized; and Cantor, who died mad, believing his ideas were spurned by others.[14] The stories of Copernicus, receiving his revolutionary book the day he died, and Mendel, rediscovered years after his death, are well known in the larger society, where they perhaps serve a function similar to that performed in science, albeit more general.

SUMMARY

The thesis presented here is that social control in science is exercised in an exchange system, a system wherein gifts of information are exchanged for recognition from scientific colleagues. Because scientists desire recognition, they conform to the goals and norms of the scientific community. Such control reinforces and complements the socialization process in science. It is partly dependent on the socialization of persons to become sensitive to the responses of their colleagues. By rewarding conformity, this exchange system reinforces commitment to the higher goals and norms of the scientific community, and it induces flexibility with regard to specific goals and norms. The very denial by scientists of the importance of recognition as an incentive can be seen to involve commitments to higher norms, including an orientation to a scientific community extending beyond any particular collection of contemporaries.

[14]Cf. Eric T. Bell, *Men of Mathematics* (New York: Simon and Schuster, 1937), for these and others.

Grid and Group [1973]

MARY DOUGLAS

• *In Durkheim's classic formulation, societies vary from the "mechanical solidarity" of tightly integrated, segmented groups, to the "organic solidarity" of social exchange among differentiated individuals. Corresponding to each type of social structure is its characteristic type of culture or mentality—the reified symbols and strong emphasis upon group boundaries which correspond to mechanical solidarity; the abstract principles and fluid boundaries for individual action which go with organic solidarity. Mary Douglas refers to the Durkheimian dimension of social structure as high or low "group", while she expands the model by adding a second, crosscutting dimension, which she calls "grid." The latter is the vertical dimension of social order, varying between high degrees of stratification and internal ranking among a society's members ("high grid"), and low degrees of public ranking ("low grid"). On the resulting four-fold space, Douglas lays out the variations found not only among the different types of tribal societies studied by anthropologists, but also the varied experiences of persons located at different points within modern industrial societies.*

[C]osmology is part of the social bond, according to the following principles. First, any control system, since it has to be made reasonable (be justified, validated or legitimated as Weber put it), must appeal to ultimate principles about the nature of man and of the cosmos. This applies even at the family level. Second, that the control system interacts with the media of control (speech, ritual). Third, that certain consistencies hold between the coding of the medium and the character of the control system. That they should match is a long-run prediction. In a short run the transition process might obscure the match. Our task starts therefore by identifying the control aspects of the cosmology.

Somewhere far away from the level of the English family and home, some machinery is grinding out a set of social pressures. Naked power is decently clothed and made legitimate. Its demand to be made legitimate reaches into the most intimate recesses, even into the dealings the English mother has with her

From Mary Douglas, *Natural Symbols*. Baltimore: Penguin Books, 1973, pp. 80–92. Reprinted with permission of the author.

own child. She learns to assert her control in certain ways and to justify her authority by reference to general principles. The child is thus indoctrinated into the assumptions of his society. His curiosity is checked or roused, his expectations for himself are set in the most hidden way—not by the overt doctrines handed out, but by what is left implicit. Bernstein exposes two implicit world views carried in our styles of speech. He finds them generated in two distinguishable systems of control. To match his exercise, we should look to systems of control and the hidden assumptions which validate them. . . . So, leaving aside speech codes, at this stage I would need to produce a comparison of control systems which will contrast an entirely personal form of relationships, unstructured by fixed principles, with a system equivalent to his positional family. We can concentrate, it seems, upon the interaction of individuals within two social dimensions. One is order, classification, the symbolic system. The other is pressure, the experience of having no option but to consent to the overwhelming demands of other people. Consider order first. Social relations demand that categories be clarified and orientations given. Order is the basic requirement for communication. It could conceivably be possible to compare symbolic systems according to the clarity of definition given to the categories used. There is a hint of such a programme in the first pages of *Primitive Classification*.

> For us, in fact, to classify things is to arrange them in groups which are distinct from each other and are separated by clearly determined lines of demarcation. . . . At the bottom of our conception of class there is the idea of a circumscription with fixed and definite outlines. Now one could almost say that this conception of classification does not go back before Aristotle. . . . Not only has our present notion of classification a history, but this history itself implies a considerable pre-history. It would be impossible to exaggerate, in fact, the state of indistinction from which the human mind developed. Even today a considerable part of our popular literature, our myths, and our religions is based on a fundamental confusion of all images and ideas. They are not separated from each other, as it were, with any clarity. . . . If we descend to the least evolved societies known, those which the Germans call by the rather vague term *Naturvölker*, we shall find an even more general mental confusion
> (Emile Durkheim and Marcel Mauss, *Primitive Classification* 1903: 5–6). transl. London: Cohen & West, [1963]

The authors go on to compare this weakness of definition to the growth of consciousness in the individual from childhood to adulthood: distinctions when they first appear are fragmentary and unstable; only gradually does a steady circumscription of elements of experience lead to classification. However this is not the basis for a comparison of classification systems which I propose to use here. I shall take it as axiomatic that the clarity of bounding of different categories within the total system does not vary, or that, if it does become fuzzy here and rigid there, this is not a difference which I wish to take into account. I shall instead try to compare the overall articulation of the categories which constitute a world view. A classification system can be coherently organized for a small part of experience, and for the rest it can leave the discrete items jangling in disorder. Or it can be highly coherent in the ordering it offers for the whole of experience, but the individuals for whom it is available may enjoy access to another competing and different system, equally coherent in itself, from which they feel free to select segments here and there eclectically, not worrying about the overall lack of coherence. Then there will be conflicts, contradictions, and uncoordinated areas of classification for those people. In effect, loss of coherence results in a narrowing of the total scope of the classification system. We can therefore take the scope and coherent articulation of a system of classification as one social dimension in which any individual must find himself, I shall call it grid.

As Durkheim himself has powerfully argued, any given classification system is itself a product of social relations. Bernstein's example of the positional family shows people putting pressures on one another in terms of classifications. When the pressures are strong and when they uphold a set of classifications, then a process of mutual reinforcement is at work. Such a social system is likely to remain stable, unless counter-pressures develop from outside or unless new knowledge weakens the credibility of the classifications. In either case, the social change will be wrought in the other dimension, that of action or pressure. To draw the dimension of grid vertically up from zero towards more and more comprehensive articulations allows us to consider what absence of classification would mean. The zero would represent a blank, total confusion with no meaning whatever. Rulelessness could be anomy, the suicide's doubt. It could be the mystic's moment of dissociation when all classifications are in abeyance. It could also represent, as the quotation from *Primitive Classification* suggested, the child's first undifferentiated awareness. To distinguish among these possibilities a little, let us separate the publicly accepted classification system from the private one. An increasingly coherent but entirely private system of classification would point away from communication with others, eventually to madness. This world of private thought we draw downwards from zero.

On the horizontal axis, draw pressure, increasing from zero to the right. At zero, no demands are made on the individual. He is free of pressure. This means he is alone. But another case would have to be located on the vertical line. When pressures and counter-pressures completely balance out, the point of indecision would be recorded here. It is the moment before conversion and commitment. Towards the right he is increasingly under the bond of other people. For reasons which will be clear later, I call the tendency towards the maximum personal control the line of group. A child's life starts far along that line (since he is completely controlled by others) and low on the line of grid: as he grows he may be progressively freed from personal pressures and progressively indoctrinated in the prevailing classification system. If he is clever at internalizing the categories and their implications, he can turn them to his own defence against personal tyranny. He can even use them to tyrannize. To allow for this, we can extend the horizontal line from zero to the left. On this side the individual has escaped all pressure from other people. He is exerting pressure on them. Although the public grid of classifications is used by other people to control the individual, he can evade it if ever the insulation breaks down. The mutual reinforcing of grid and group keep the system stable only if it is perfectly insulated. But perfect insulation is rare and there is some scope for change. We have now in hand a device which could consider social change as a dynamic process. We can see the individual under strong pressure to accept a system of classification which degrades him and commits him to a life of servitude. We could assess the other options open to him, and the relative weight of competing pressures. But this is not the exercise I am attempting. Our problem is to find some relation between cosmological ideas and characteristics of social relations. I shall argue that several systems which spread in different patterns across the diagram are liable to develop recognizable trends in the way that the universe is constituted. The first task is to investigate more closely the properties of the chart.

Above the horizontal line is the area of public classification. The social system will always be centred here. Close to the line and below it lie the fringe elements, the marginal sectors of society: the more to the right they are found, the weaker their option not to be exploited by others to the left operating the public system of classifications; towards the left and zero are the voluntary outcastes, tramps, gipsies, rich eccentrics, or others who retain their freedom, at

Grid
System of shared classifications

Ego increasingly
exerting pressure
that controls
other people

Group
ego increasingly
controlled by other
people's pressure

Private system of classification

a cost. This line across the page separates the area of conformity from innovation. Given the way we have defined the vertical dimension we are not suggesting that anyone is dreaming up new conceptual systems from scratch. What is private and innovatory is the way the common cultural categories are articulated. Progress further down that line to greater coherence of the private philosophy depends on an accompanying isolation from social pressures. Beyond a certain point of originality the thinker can give up any reasonable expectation of his ideas being received. This follows from the relation between grid and group above the horizontal line of zero. The framework of institutional life and the distribution of power is the result of a long-term adaptation between social pressures and classification. The big push that changes classification must be big enough to redistribute power as well. To the far right of the fringe area of private thought is socially null. It is under more pressure than it can exert. Far to the left it is in high public esteem: hordes of people to the far right would be applauding each new impulse emanating from the far lower left. It is worth pausing to consider how a person can be located in that quadrant. A musician can innovate, a painter, inventors and writers too. If his idea be ignored, he is still in the right. For most of his long working life the Flemish painter, James Ensor, endured that fate and revenged himself on the public which denied him honour by cruel caricatures. If successful, though, the innovator may see the public system of classification change in his own lifetime. If he wants to stay original, he will have to keep thinking of something new to surprise them with, or devise a technique for maximizing the unexpected, as John Cage has done for his music. To remain free of the public system of classification, the person needs above all not to covet its rewards. Every glance he cocks towards the prize-giving juries makes him vulnerable to their criticisms and liable to be sucked into the general grid. Thus, though it is difficult to stay there, it is possible for people to pass in their lifetimes through different points in the bottom left quadrant.

The bottom right quadrant can be filled for infancy. Here is the personal family in which the child is controlled by being made sensitive to an inventory of his parent's aches and pains: no public system of classification is used to explain the universe and his place in it, but (theoretically at least) he is taught to develop a classificatory system of his own. However, publicly known categories implicitly underline their behaviour and he is quick to deduce them as he grows older. It is surely impossible for an adult to accept heavy social pressure and yet to develop a privately articulated philosophy. If he wishes to have intellectual privacy he must inevitably achieve a solitary state, and so the tendency would be for such a person to move across from right towards the vertical line of no control.

This leads us to considering further the relations between the distribution of power and the coherence of public classifications. It is axiomatic that a steady pattern of control is needed for a coherent system of classification. The more distinguishable places in the control system and the more these are co-ordinated into a lasting hierarchy of responsibilities, the more the public classification system differentiates its categories. So a society spread across the diagram from the highest point mid-way between public grid and group on the right and across to some high point mid-way at the top left is a complex social system. Time depth and corporate institutions are implied in that pattern. Conversely, one political shake-up makes many classifications irrelevant and drags down the coherence of the symbolic system; the expectation of continuing change sets the level lower still. A society that is spread across the diagram at a low level of classification is likely to become one that is continually subject to political upheaval and a changing profile for the distribution of authority. This will be important for our theme.

We should now examine the different ways these dimensions organize our material. Some tribal systems will be spread mostly through the top right hand side of the diagram without showing on the left. A classic instance of high classification which anthropologists would recognize are the Tallensi of the Volta Region of Ghana as described by Meyer Fortes in the colonial period. Here the public system of rights and duties equips each man with a full identity, prescribing for him what and when he eats, how he grooms his hair, how he is buried or born. Most Tallensi, probably all, are under pressure from the others. The chiefs and priests are no exception. The person whose soul is in revolt is regarded as abnormal and needing special ritual curing (Fortes, 1959). In this society piety is the order of the day, piety towards senior kinsmen and piety to the dead, even though the ancestors are seen as aggressive punishers. The only enemy is the rank outsider, bound by no ties of clanship. A few miserable old women outlawed as witches are either hounded from village to village or merely tolerated. Who knows their thoughts? If they are totally mystified by the public grid which rejects them we could locate them below the horizontal line, though far to the right where options are weakest. I will argue later that a social system characterized by high classification would display the same cosmological bias. Strong grid and strong group will tend to a routinized piety towards authority and its symbols; beliefs in a punishing, moral universe, and a category of rejects.

Any bureaucratic system which is sufficiently secure and insulated from criticism will tend to think the same way. This is the monastic life, or the military society. Most clearly it is the stable tribal system discovered by anthropologists in Africa in the colonial era just before and after the Second World War. It is no accident that a functional analysis produced an equilibrium model of primitive society at that time. For the colonial regime itself provided the insulation and protection from the effects of war and famine. It tended to freeze the native social systems into patterns of reinforcement and stability.

However the effect was not the same in Central Africa as it was in Ghana. Here the long nineteenth-century wars with Arabs and other slave-raiders had already broken up the local social structures before the colonial freeze came down. The tribes in the region around Lake Nyasa are very differently character- ized in the writings of the 1950s when labour migration, cash crops, and taxation accelerated the process of change. Here we also find small communi- ties. But as to grid they come much lower on the line of coherent classification than the Tallensi. Their culture promises them contradictory rewards and holds out impossible goals. They believe that it is good to be loyal and obedient and never to split a village into factions. They also believe that the proper ambition of every man is to become head of his own village—impossible without disloy- alty and friction. They put immense pressure on one another and strive inces- santly to define and close the circle of their friends. Accusations of witchcraft are the political idiom of out-casting and re-definition of social boundaries. The broad, normative concept of a human being for whom moral obligations are binding is contrasted with that of the man-eating witch. To convict a rival of witchcraft is to finish him politically. This is the second of the main types of social environment I shall refer to throughout the book. For convenience I shall call it small group. It is a social system which clusters low on the right side of the diagram. Its members know one another and can count their ranks and pros- pects of promotion. They are not conscious of remote control by leaders located far to the left. Hemmed in and face to face, their destiny is in their own hands and they meet it with intrigue and jealousy. The contrast of small group with the previous case of high classification ranges over many aspects. For example, high classification requires a well-defined category of rejects and anomalous persons. But small group broadens the category of potential rejects to include the whole range of acquaintance, male, female, kinsman and unrelated.

The third type to distinguish from these two is the society which spreads widely across our diagram instead of being tidily clustered on the right. The leaders in the small-group case are down in among their community, struggling against their peers. In this third case which I shall call strong grid, the leaders are remote powerful beings, rarely seen face to face. We shall need to deal sepa- rately with the social environment of the leaders and of those who are subject to them.

During the colonial period, for reasons we have suggested, anthropology was much concerned with the properties of corporate groups and with rights and duties transmitted down enduring channels of control. Colonialism itself checked internal evolution and limited tribal political systems to the mere replacement of personnel in a fixed pattern of office. But research in newly independent countries, and above all in newly discovered New Guinea, has focused attention on what is called the network of links a man has to a circle radiating out from himself. In a complex society, networks are the minimum level at which social relations can be investigated. They are the sustaining base line of social ties from which corporate institutions arise. But if corporate organization is so weak that each man has to muster support *ad hoc* for every venture, a system of networks and temporary action-sets may describe the way the whole society functions. . . . I wish to concentrate on one of two possible variations of the network. In the case . . . of the Ndendeule in Tanzania, no person stays in any position of eminence over others, there are no chiefs and there are no effective boundaries to the spread of the open network in all directions. For each man the meanings of society are centred upon himself but the meanings are the same for him as for others. By contrast, in other variants, it is possible for leaders to become effective and to entrench their power in their lifetime at least. Such a leader will gather his own network of allegiances powerfully round himself and create a centre of force for the rest of society. The Big Man system, as it is called in New Guinea, is found all over the world, in Indonesia, among northern Californian Indians, in the Philippines. I take it for my fourth social type, to contrast with the other two patterns. Its interest is the wide spread across the diagram of grid and group at a low level of classification. Success breeds. There are few overriding community interests to check the leader's impetus. The greater his influence, the more support he attracts. A positive feedback propels him further out to the left; it increases the subjection of his followers, so they move to the right. If his success in wealth and war encourages him, he may end by eroding their existing system of obligations and become a law unto himself. Then the inevitable trend would be to lower the level of classification for everyone in his orbit. He has made their lineages and ancestral shrines less meaningful for them than his own favour. The big categories however, solvency, worth, equity, remain as containers into which a changing synthesis of meaning is poured from year to year. However, the leader has to reckon with rivals creeping near to him in eminence. The world of his peers is a sparse and fluctuating scene of coalitions. Each is bent on success. If they are realistic, their followers recognize that right goes with might and line up accordingly. This type of social system in its various stages has now been frequently and well described. There are many more examples from New Guinea. The interesting difference between them is the range within which the competition of Big Men must use existing corporate institutions or can override them and in doing so attaches large parts of the public system of classification to the whims of the Big Men themselves.

We have now distinguished three types of social environment; high classification, small group, strong grid which includes the heroic society of competing
Big Men and that of their followers. The latter come low on the vertical line of
classification because coherence is achieved only at some very general level of
abstraction which is compatible with the syncretizing rivalry of distant giants.
But the spread across the diagram expresses the strong control which these
people experience. Recruited and harnessed to a competition which seems to
hold glittering rewards for all, they find themselves trying to work a complex
system of rules. In the name of the rules the Big Men justify their demands.
Whether it be rules of monetary exchange, debt and credit, or rules of etiquette
and hospitality, the system constitutes an oppressive grid. Londoners too know
what this can mean. As a system of control industrial society is impersonal.
Some more than others feel their lives controlled, not by persons, but by things.
They wander through a forest of regulations, imponderable forces are represented by forms to complete in triplicate, parking meters, inexorable laws. Their
cosmos is dominated by objects of which they and fellow humans are victims.
The essential difference between a cosmos dominated by persons and one dominated by objects is the impossibility of bringing moral pressures to bear upon the
controllers: there is no person-to-person communication with them. Hence the
paradox that some of the people whose metaphysics are most fuzzy and who
respond only to very diffuse symbols—in short, who in their cosmology are most
like pygmies and Arizona peyotists—are those who are much involved in certain
sectors in industrial society. To this paradox I shall return.

For the leaders who have spiralled down far to the left the same impersonal
rules of exchange are made like rungs on a ladder of promotion. The Big Men
live in a world of noble pacts, hard bargains, dastardly betrayals and revenges
Apart from the exotic cases given, there are examples nearer home. Our ancient
Anglo-Saxon vengeance and inheritance laws defined a set of responsible kin
radiating from each particular individual. The Norse sagas expressed a corresponding world view.

With these four social types distinguished it will be possible to show that they
generate distinctive cosmologies. The system of control is validated by a typical
bias in the system of belief. These tendencies are the subject of this book, for
they make their own typical demands on the media of expression and thus
produce natural systems of symbolic behaviour. A brief summary of the types of
belief would go as follows. With high classification, piety and sacralized institutions, strong boundaries between purity and impurity; this is the prototype
original Durkheimian system in which God is Society and Society is God,
where all moral failings are at once sins against religion and the community.
With small group there is less confidence in the power of God to protect the

faithful, a dualist cosmology reckons with the power of demons and their allies; justice is not seen to prevail. Strong grid tends to a pragmatic world view, sin is less understood than shame for loss of personal honour, face or solvency. In the first type a profit and loss calculus applies to the spiritual economy of the whole community; strong grid focuses on the honour of the individual, the number of supporters he can summon up, the control he has over his women folk. Strong grid divides between the heroic society of the Big Men, and the recurrent millennial tendencies of their subjects. Finally the positions near and around zero should be specially noticed. When public classification and pressures are withdrawn or cast aside, the individual left alone with himself develops a distinctive cosmology, benign and unritualistic.

As Durkheim suggested, his experience is the beginning of consciousness, with all the emotional force that that implies. The sense of escape from others and of self-discovery is possible with any shift towards the left of the diagram. Out here, especially below the vertical line, where the individual is articulating his own classificatory system, the thinker does not see his fellow human beings as the principal determinants of social life. Fellow humans do not put their imprint on the world as models of controlling influence. In consequence the cosmos is not anthropomorphic. There is less call for articulate forms of social intercourse and no need for a set of symbols with which to send and receive specific communications. Thus we have already identified one area of the diagram in which there will be less regard for ritual. Furthermore, it suggests another dimension which is not on the diagram, that lying between density and sparsity. When populations are sparse and social relations infrequent, interrupted and irregular, a person does not have the impression of inhabiting a man-dominated world. What preoccupations about his fate he may entertain concern drought, pasture, livestock, movements of game, pests or growth of crops. He is controlled by objects, not persons. Objects do not respond to personal modes of approach. Fellow humans are fellow sufferers.

It is tempting to try to assimilate whole cultures to the general outlook of individuals dropping to near zero. But sparsity conceals too many variables; better to stick to those on the diagram. There is ample material there for explaining the similarity between the world view of pygmies in the Ituri forest and that of certain Londoners deeply implicated in industrial society.

IV THE MICROINTERACTIONIST TRADITION

Some Main Points of the Microinteractionist Tradition

1870–1900	American pragmatists: Peirce, James		German objectivists: Brentano, Meinong
1900–1930	Dewey	Cooley Thomas Mead	Husserl
1930–1960	Symbolic Interactionism: Blumer Theories of deviance, occupations, and professions: Everett Hughes	Schutz	existentialism: Heidegger Sartre
1960–90	Role theory		Ethnomethodology: Garfinkel Conversational analysis Cognitive sociology
		Goffman's frame analysis	

Society Is in the Mind [1902]

CHARLES HORTON COOLEY

• *Charles Horton Cooley is the earliest professional sociologist in the distinctively American tradition of social psychology. In this excerpt from 1902, he attempts to show that social interaction takes place only within each individual's mind, as he or she imagines other people's attitudes and possible responses. "All real persons are imaginery" in a certain sense, according to Cooley; and in a famous conclusion, he asserts: "The imaginations which people have of one another are the* solid facts *of society, and . . . to observe and interpret these must be a chief aim of sociology."*

When left to themselves children continue the joys of sociability by means of an imaginary playmate. Although all must have noticed this who have observed children at all, only close and constant observation will enable one to realize the extent to which it is carried on. It is not an occasional practice, but, rather, a necessary form of thought, flowing from a life in which personal communication is the chief interest and social feeling the stream in which, like boats on a river, most other feelings float. Some children appear to live in personal imaginations almost from the first month; others occupy their minds in early infancy mostly with solitary experiments upon blocks, cards, and other impersonal objects, and their thoughts are doubtless filled with the images of these. But, in either case, after a child learns to talk and the social world in all its wonder and provocation opens on his mind, it floods his imagination so that all his thoughts are conversations. He is never alone. Sometimes the inaudible interlocutor is recognizable as the image of a tangible playmate, sometimes he appears to be purely imaginary. Of course each child has his own peculiarities.

The main point to note here is that these conversations are not occasional and temporary effusions of the imagination, but are the naïve expression of a socialization of the mind that is to be permanent and to underlie all later thinking. The imaginary dialogue passes beyond the thinking aloud of little

From Charles Horton Cooley, *Human Nature and the Social Order* (New York: Scribners', 1902), pp. 88–92, 95–97, 118–28, 143.

children into something more elaborate, reticent, and sophisticated; but it never ceases. Grown people, like children, are usually unconscious of these dialogues; as we get older we cease, for the most part, to carry them on out loud, and some of us practise a good deal of apparently solitary meditation and experiment. But, speaking broadly, it is true of adults as of children, that the mind lives in perpetual conversation. It is one of those things that we seldom notice just because they are so familiar and involuntary; but we can perceive it if we try to. If one suddenly stops and takes note of his thoughts at some time when his mind has been running free, as when he is busy with some simple mechanical work, he will be likely to find them taking the form of vague conversations. This is particularly true when one is somewhat excited with reference to a social situation. If he feels under accusation or suspicion in any way he will probably find himself making a defense, or perhaps a confession, to an imaginary hearer. A guilty man confesses "to get the load off his mind"; that is to say, the excitement of his thought cannot stop there but extends to the connected impulses of expression and creates an intense need to tell somebody. Impulsive people often talk out loud when excited, either "to themselves," as we say when we can see no one else present, or to any one whom they can get to listen. Dreams also consist very largely of imaginary conversations; and, with some people at least, the mind runs in dialogue during the half-waking state before going to sleep. There are many other familiar facts that bear the same interpretation—such, for instance, as that it is much easier for most people to compose in the form of letters or dialogue than in any other; so that literature of this kind has been common in all ages. . . . The fact is that language, developed by the race through personal intercourse and imparted to the individual in the same way, can never be dissociated from personal intercourse in the mind; and since higher thought involves language, it is always a kind of imaginary conversation. The word and the interlocutor are correlative ideas.

It is worth noting here that there is no separation between real and imaginary persons; indeed, to be imagined is to become real, in a social sense, as I shall presently point out. An invisible person may easily be more real to an imaginative mind than a visible one; sensible presence is not necessarily a matter of the first importance. A person can be real to us only in the degree in which we imagine an inner life which exists in us, for the time being, and which we refer to him. The sensible presence is important chiefly in stimulating us to do this. All real persons are imaginary in this sense. If, however, we use imaginary in the sense of illusory, an imagination not corresponding to fact, it is easy to see that visible presence is no bar to illusion. Thus I meet a stranger on the steamboat who corners me and tells me his private history. I care nothing for it, and he half knows that I do not; he uses me only as a lay figure to sustain the agreeable illusion of sympathy, and is talking to an imaginary companion quite as he might if I were elsewhere. So likewise good manners are largely a tribute to imaginary companionship, a make-believe of sympathy which it is agreeable to accept as real, though we may know, when we think, that it is not. To conceive a kindly and approving companion is something that one involuntarily tries to do, in accordance with that instinctive hedonizing inseparable from all wholesome mental processes, and to assist in this by at least a seeming of friendly appreciation is properly regarded as a part of good breeding. To be always sincere would be brutally to destroy this pleasant and mostly harmless figment of the imagination.

Thus the imaginary companionship which a child of three or four years so naïvely creates and expresses is something elementary and almost omnipresent in the thought of a normal person. In fact, thought and personal intercourse may be regarded as merely aspects of the same thing: we call it personal intercourse when the suggestions that keep it going are received through faces or other symbols present to the senses; reflection when the personal suggestions come through memory and are more elaborately worked over in thought. But both are mental, both are personal. Personal images, as they are connected with nearly all our higher thought in its inception, remain inseparable from it in memory. The mind is not a hermit's cell, but a place of hospitality and intercourse. We have no higher life that is really apart from other people. It is by imagining them that our personality is built up; to be without the power of imagining them is to be a low-grade idiot; and in the measure that a mind is lacking in this power it is degenerate. Apart from this mental society there is no wisdom, no power, justice, or right, no higher existence at all. The life of the mind is essentially a life of intercourse.

So far as the study of immediate social relations is concerned the personal idea is the real person. That is to say, it is in this alone that one man exists for another, and acts directly upon his mind. My association with you evidently consists in the relation between my idea of you and the rest of my mind. If there is something in you that is wholly beyond this and makes no impression upon me it has no social reality in this relation. *The immediate social reality is the personal idea*; nothing, it would seem, could be much more obvious than this.

Society, then, in its immediate aspect, *is a relation among personal ideas*. In order to have society it is evidently necessary that persons should get together somewhere; and they get together only as personal ideas in the mind. Where else? What other possible *locus* can be assigned for the real contact of persons, or in what other form can they come in contact except as impressions or ideas formed in this common *locus*? Society exists in my mind as the contact and reciprocal influence of certain ideas named "I," Thomas, Henry, Susan, Bridget, and so on. It exists in your mind as a similar group, and so in every mind. Each person is immediately aware of a particular aspect of society: and so far as he is aware of great social wholes, like a nation or an epoch, it is by embracing in this particular aspect ideas or sentiments which he attributes to his countrymen or contemporaries in their collective aspect. In order to see this it seems to me only necessary to discard vague modes of speech which have no conceptions back of them that will bear scrutiny, and look at the facts as we know them in experience.

Yet most of us, perhaps, will find it hard to assent to the view that the social person is a group of sentiments attached to some symbol or other characteristic element, which keeps them together and from which the whole idea is named. The reason for this reluctance I take to be that we are accustomed to talk and think, so far as we do think in this connection, as if a person were a material rather than a psychical fact. Instead of basing our sociology and ethics upon what a man really is as part of our mental and moral life, he is vaguely and yet grossly regarded as a shadowy material body, a lump of flesh, and not as an ideal thing at all. But surely it is only common sense to hold that the social and moral reality is that which lives in our imaginations and affects our motives. As regards the physical it is only the finer, more plastic and mentally significant aspects of it that imagination is concerned with, and with them chiefly as a nucleus or centre of crystallization for sentiment. Instead of perceiving this we commonly make the physical the dominant factor, and think of the mental and moral only by a vague analogy to it.

Persons and society must, then, be studied primarily in the imagination. It is surely true, *prima facie*, that the best way of observing things is that which is most direct; and I do not see how any one can hold that we know persons directly except as imaginative ideas in the mind. These are perhaps the most vivid things in our experience, and as observable as anything else, though it is a kind of observation in which accuracy has not been systematically cultivated. The observation of the physical aspects, however important, is for social purposes quite subsidiary: there is no way of weighing or measuring men which throws more than a very dim side-light on their personality. The physical factors most significant are those elusive traits of expression already discussed, and in the observation and interpretation of these physical science is only indirectly helpful. What, for instance, could the most elaborate knowledge of his weights and measures, including the anatomy of his brain, tell us of the character of Napoleon? Not enough, I take it, to distinguish him with certainty from an imbecile. Our real knowledge of him is derived from reports of his conversation and manner, from his legislation and military dispositions, from the impression made upon those about him and by them communicated to us, from his portraits and the like; all serving as aids to the imagination in forming a system that we call by his name.

I conclude, therefore, that the imaginations which people have of one another are the *solid facts* of society, and that to observe and interpret these must be a chief aim of sociology. I do not mean merely that society must be studied *by* the imagination—that is true of all investigations in their higher reaches—but that the *object* of study is primarily an imaginative idea or group of ideas in the mind, that we have to imagine imaginations. The intimate grasp of any social fact will be found to require that we divine what men think of one another. Charity, for instance, is not understood without imagining what ideas the giver and recipient have of each other; to grasp homicide we must, for one thing, conceive how the offender thinks of his victim and of the administrators of the law; the relation between the employing and hand-laboring classes is first of all a matter of personal attitude which we must apprehend by sympathy with both, and so on. In other words, we want to get at motives, and motives spring from personal ideas. There is nothing particularly novel in this view; historians, for instance, have always assumed that to understand and interpret personal relations was their main business; but apparently the time is coming when this will have to be done in a more systematic and penetrating manner than in the past. Whatever may justly be urged against the introduction of frivolous and disconnected "personalities" into history, the understanding of persons is the aim of this and all other branches of social study.

It is important to face the question of persons who have no corporeal reality, as for instance the dead, characters of fiction or the drama, ideas of the gods and the like. Are these real people, members of society? I should say that in so far as we imagine them they are. Would it not be absurd to deny social reality to Robert Louis Stevenson, who is so much alive in many minds and so potently affects important phases of thought and conduct? He is certainly more real in this practical sense than most of us who have not yet lost our corporeity, more alive, perhaps, than he was before he lost his own, because of his wider influence. And so Colonel Newcome, or Romola, or Hamlet is real to the imaginative reader with the realest kind of reality, the kind that works directly upon his personal character. And the like is true of the conceptions of supernatural beings handed down by the aid of tradition among all peoples. What, indeed, would society be, or what would any one of us be, if we associated only with corporeal persons and insisted that no one should enter our company who could not show his power to tip the scales and cast a shadow?

On the other hand, a corporeally existent person is not socially real unless he is imagined. If the nobleman thinks of the serf as a mere animal and does not attribute to him a human way of thinking and feeling, the latter is not real to him in the sense of acting personally upon his mind and conscience. And if a man should go into a strange country and hide himself so completely that no one knew he was there, he would evidently have no social existence for the inhabitants.

In saying this I hope I do not seem to question the independent reality of persons or to confuse it with personal ideas. The man is one thing and the various ideas entertained about him are another; but the latter, the personal idea, is the immediate social reality, the thing in which men exist for one another, and work directly upon one another's lives. Thus any study of society that is not supported by a firm grasp of personal ideas is empty and dead— mere doctrine and not knowledge at all.

I believe that the vaguely material notion of personality, which does not confront the social fact at all but assumes it to be the analogue of the physical fact, is a main source of fallacious thinking about ethics, politics, and indeed every aspect of social and personal life. It seems to underlie all four of the ways of conceiving society and the individual alleged in the first chapter to be false. If the person is thought of primarily as a separate material form, in- habited by thoughts and feelings conceived by analogy to be equally separate, then the only way of getting a society is by adding on a new principle of socialism, social faculty, altruism, or the like. But if you start with the idea that the social person is primarily a fact in the mind, and observe him there, you find at once that he has no existence apart from a mental whole of which all personal ideas are members, and which is a particular aspect of society. Every one of these ideas, as we have seen, is the outcome of our experience of all the persons we have known, and is only a special aspect of our general idea of mankind.

To many people it would seem mystical to say that persons, as we know them, are not separable and mutually exclusive, like physical bodies, so that what is part of one cannot be part of another, but that they interpenetrate one another, the same element pertaining to different persons at different times, or even at the same time: yet this is a verifiable and not very abstruse fact. The sentiments which make up the largest and most vivid part of our idea of any person are not, as a rule, peculiarly and exclusively his, but each one may be entertained in conjunction with other persons also. It is, so to speak, at the point of intersection of many personal ideas, and may be reached through any one of them.

As regards one's self in relation to other people, I shall have more to say in a later chapter; but I may say here that there is no view of the self, that will bear examination, which makes it altogether distinct, in our minds, from other persons. If it includes the whole mind, then, of course, it includes all the persons we think of, all the society which lives in our thoughts. If we confine it to a certain part of our thought with which we connect a distinctive emotion or sentiment called self-feeling, as I prefer to do, it still includes the persons with whom we feel most identified. *Self and other do not exist as mutually exclusive social facts,* and phraseology which implies that they do, like the antithesis egoism *versus* altruism, is open to the objection of vagueness, if not of falsity. It seems to me that the classification of impulses as altruistic and egoistic, with or without a third class called, perhaps, ego-altruistic, is empty; and I do not see how any other conclusion can result from a concrete study of the matter. There is no class of altruistic impulses specifically different from other impulses: all our higher, socially developed sentiments are indeterminately personal, and may be associated with self-feeling, or with whatever personal symbol may happen to arouse them. Those feelings which are merely sensual and have not been refined into sentiments by communication and imagination are not so much egoistic as merely animal: they do not pertain to social persons, either first or second, but belong in a lower stratum of thought. Sensuality is not to be confused with the social self. As I shall try to show later we do not think "I" except with reference to a complementary thought of other persons; it is an idea developed by association and communication.

The egoism-altruism way of speaking falsifies the facts at the most vital point possible by assuming that our impulses relating to persons are separable into two classes, the I impulses and the You impulses, in much the same way that physical persons are separable; whereas a primary fact throughout the range of sentiment is a fusion of persons, so that the impulse belongs not to one or the other, but precisely to the common ground that both occupy, to their inter-course or mingling. Thus the sentiment of gratitude does not pertain to me as against you, nor to you as against me, but springs right from our union, and so with all personal sentiment.

According to this view of the matter society is simply the collective aspect of personal thought. Each man's imagination, regarded as a mass of personal impressions worked up into a living, growing whole, is a special phase of society; and Mind or Imagination as a whole, that is human thought con-sidered in the largest way as having a growth and organization extending throughout the ages, is the *locus* of society in the widest possible sense.

Thought as Internalized Conversation [1934]

GEORGE HERBERT MEAD

• *George Herbert Mead was for many years a professor of philosophy at the University of Chicago. His greatest influence was not on philosophy but on the sociologists who came to hear his lectures, among them Herbert Blumer, who developed the ideas of Mead and others into the sociological theory of symbolic interactionism. In this excerpt from Mead's posthumously published lectures, Mead argues that the self is not one's physical body, but, in fact, a complicated set of attitudes that one derives from outside and that can be turned in various directions, both inward and outward. We are multiple selves as we have multiple social relationships, and on these we build yet another degree of multiplicity through reflexive relationships among our own selves. For Mead, the thinking mind is itself social, an internalized conversation among the different parts of the self, the "I," "me," and "generalized other." Symbolism would not be possible without the generalization of perspectives that comes from taking the role of another. "A person who is saying something is saying to himself what he says to others," Mead proposes; "otherwise he does not know what he is talking about."*

We can distinguish very definitely between the self and the body. The body can be there and can operate in a very intelligent fashion without there being a self involved in the experience. The self has the characteristic that it is an object to itself, and that characteristic distinguishes it from other objects and from the body. It is perfectly true that the eye can see the foot, but it does not see the body as a whole. We cannot see our backs; we can feel certain portions of them, if we are agile, but we cannot get an experience of our whole body. There are, of course, experiences which are somewhat vague and difficult of location, but the bodily experiences are for us organized about a self. The foot and hand belong to the self. We can see our feet, especially if we look at them from the wrong end of an opera glass, as strange things which we have

From George Herbert Mead, *Mind, Self, and Society*, edited by Charles W. Morris (University of Chicago Press, 1934), pp. 136–42, 145–62, 175–78. Copyright 1934 by the University of Chicago. Copyright 1962 by Charles W. Morris. Reprinted with permission of University of Chicago Press.

seeks an audience, has to pour himself out to somebody. In reflective intelligence one thinks to act, and to act solely so that this action remains a part of a social process. Thinking becomes preparatory to social action. The very process of thinking is, of course, simply an inner conversation that goes on, but it is a conversation of gestures which in its completion implies the expression of that which one thinks to an audience. One separates the significance of what he is saying to others from the actual speech and gets it ready before saying it. He thinks it out, and perhaps writes it in the form of a book; but it is still a part of social intercourse in which one is addressing other persons and at the same time addressing one's self, and in which one controls the address to other persons by the response made to one's own gesture. That the person should be responding to himself is necessary to the self, and it is this sort of social conduct which provides behavior within which that self appears. I know of no other form of behavior than the linguistic in which the individual is an object to himself, and, so far as I can see, the individual is not a self in the reflexive sense unless he is an object to himself. It is this fact that gives a critical importance to communication, since this is a type of behavior in which the individual does so respond to himself.

We realize in everyday conduct and experience that an individual does not mean a great deal of what he is doing and saying. We frequently say that such an individual is not himself. We come away from an interview with a realization that we have left out important things, that there are parts of the self that did not get into what was said. What determines the amount of the self that gets into communication is the social experience itself. Of course, a good deal of the self does not need to get expression. We carry on a whole series of different relationships to different people. We are one thing to one man and another thing to another. There are parts of the self which exist only for the self in relationship to itself. We divide ourselves up in all sorts of different selves with reference to our acquaintances. We discuss politics with one and religion with another. There are all sorts of different selves answering to all sorts of different social reactions. It is the social process itself that is responsible for the appearance of the self; it is not there as a self apart from this type of experience.

The peculiar character possessed by our human social environment belongs to it by virtue of the peculiar character of human social activity; and that character, as we have seen, is to be found in the process of communication, and more particularly in the triadic relation on which the existence of meaning is based: the relation of the gesture of one organism to the adjustive response made to it by another organism, in its indicative capacity as pointing to the

difficulty in recognizing as our own. The parts of the body are quite distinguishable from the self. We can lose parts of the body without any serious invasion of the self. The mere ability to experience different parts of the body is not different from the experience of a table. The table presents a different feel from what the hand does when one hand feels another, but it is an experience of something with which we come definitely into contact. The body does not experience itself as a whole, in the sense in which the self in some way enters into the experience of the self.

It is the characteristic of the self as an object to itself that I want to bring out. This characteristic is represented in the word "self," which is a reflexive, and indicates that which can be both subject and object. This type of object is essentially different from other objects, and in the past it has been distinguished as conscious, a term which indicates an experience with, an experience of, one's self. It was assumed that consciousness in some way carried this capacity of being an object to itself. In giving a behavioristic statement of consciousness we have to look for some sort of experience in which the physical organism can become an object to itself. [1]

When one is running to get away from someone who is chasing him, he is entirely occupied in this action, and his experience may be swallowed up in the objects about him, so that he has, at the time being, no consciousness of self at all. We must be, of course, very completely occupied to have that take place, but we can, I think, recognize that sort of a possible experience in which the self does not enter. . . . In such instances there is a contrast between an experience that is absolutely wound up in outside activity in which the self as an object does not enter, and an activity of memory and imagination in which the self is the principal object. The self is then entirely distinguishable from an organism that is surrounded by things and acts with reference to things, including parts of its own body. These latter may be objects like other objects, but they are just objects out there in the field, and they do not involve a self that is an object to the organism. This is, I think, frequently overlooked. It is that fact which makes our anthropomorphic reconstructions of animal life so fallacious. How can an individual get outside himself (experientially) in such a way as to become an object to himself? This is the essential psychological problem of selfhood or of self-consciousness; and its solution is to be found by referring to the process of social conduct or activity in which

[1] Man's behavior is such in his social group that he is able to become an object to himself, a fact which constitutes him a more advanced product of evolutionary development than are the lower animals. Fundamentally it is this social fact—and not his alleged possession of a soul or mind with which he, as an individual, has been mysteriously and supernaturally endowed, and with which the lower animals have not been endowed—that differentiates him from them.

the given person or individual is implicated. The apparatus of reason would not be complete unless it swept itself into its own analysis of the field of experience; or unless the individual brought himself into the same experiential field as that of the other individual selves in relation to whom he acts in any given social situation. Reason cannot become impersonal unless it takes an objective, non-affective attitude toward itself; otherwise we have just consciousness, not *self*-consciousness. And it is necessary to rational conduct that the individual should thus take an objective, impersonal attitude toward himself, that he should become an object to himself. For the individual organism is obviously an essential and important fact or constituent element of the empirical situation in which it acts; and without taking objective account of itself as such, it cannot act intelligently, or rationally.

The individual experiences himself as such, not directly, but only indirectly, from the particular standpoints of other individual members of the same social group, or from the generalized standpoint of the social group as a whole to which he belongs. For he enters his own experience as a self or individual, not directly or immediately, not by becoming a subject to himself, but only in so far as he first becomes an object to himself just as other individuals are objects to him or in his experience; and he becomes an object to himself only by taking the attitudes of other individuals toward himself within a social environment or context of experience and behavior in which both he and they are involved.

The importance of what we term "communication" lies in the fact that it provides a form of behavior in which the organism or the individual may become an object to himself. It is that sort of communication which we have been discussing—not communication in the sense of the cluck of the hen to the chickens, or the bark of a wolf to the pack, or the lowing of a cow, but communication in the sense of significant symbols, communication which is directed not only to others but also to the individual himself. So far as that type of communication is a part of behavior it at least introduces a self. Of course, one may hear without listening; one may see things that he does not realize; do things that he is not really aware of. But it is where one does respond to that which he addresses to another and where that response of his own becomes a part of his conduct, where he not only hears himself but responds to himself, talks and replies to himself as truly as the other person replies to him, that we have behavior in which the individuals become objects to themselves.

The self, as that which can be an object to itself, is essentially a social structure, and it arises in social experience. After a self has arisen, it in a certain sense provides for itself its social experiences, and so we can conceive

of an absolutely solitary self. But it is impossible to conceive of a self arising outside of social experience. When it has arisen we can think of a person in solitary confinement for the rest of his life, but who still has himself as a companion, and is able to think and to converse with himself as he had communicated with others. That process to which I have just referred, of responding to one's self as another responds to it, taking part in one's own conversation with others, being aware of what one is saying and using that awareness of what one is saying to determine what one is going to say thereafter—that is a process with which we are all familiar. We are continually following up our own address to other persons by an understanding of what we are saying, and using that understanding in the direction of our continued speech. We are finding out what we are going to say, what we are going to do, by saying and doing, and in the process we are continually controlling the process itself. In the conversation of gestures what we say calls out a certain response in another and that in turn changes our own action, so that we shift from what we started to do because of the reply the other makes. The conversation of gestures is the beginning of communication. The individual comes to carry on a conversation of gestures with himself. He says something, and that calls out a certain reply in himself which makes him change what he was going to say. One starts to say something, we will presume an unpleasant something, but when he starts to say it he realizes it is cruel. The effect on himself of what he is saying checks him; there is here a conversation of gestures between the individual and himself. We mean by significant speech that the action is one that affects the individual himself, and that the effect upon the individual himself is part of the intelligent carrying-out of the conversation with others. Now we, so to speak, amputate that social phase and dispense with it for the time being, so that one is talking to one's self as one would talk to another person.[2]

This process of abstraction cannot be carried on indefinitely. One inevitably

[2]It is generally recognized that the specifically social expressions of intelligence, or the exercise of what is often called "social intelligence," depend upon the given individual's ability to take the rôles of, or "put himself in the place of," the other individuals implicated with him in given social situations; and upon his consequent sensitivity to their attitudes toward himself and toward one another. These specifically social expressions of intelligence, of course, acquire unique significance in terms of our view that the whole nature of intelligence is social to the very core—that this putting of one's self in the places of others, this taking by one's self of their rôles or attitudes, is not merely one of the various aspects or expressions of intelligence or of intelligent behavior, but is the very essence of its character. Spearman's "X factor" in intelligence—the unknown factor which, according to him, intelligence contains—is simply (if our social theory of intelligence is correct) this ability of the intelligent individual to take the attitude of the other, or the attitudes of others, thus realizing the significations or grasping the meanings of the symbols or gestures in terms of which thinking proceeds; and thus being able to carry on with himself the internal conversation with these symbols or gestures which thinking involves.

completion or resultant of the act it initiates (the meaning of the gesture being thus the response of the second organism to it as such, or as a gesture). What, as it were, takes the gesture out of the social act and isolates it as such—what makes it something more than just an early phase of an individual act—is the response of another organism, or of other organisms, to it. Such a response is its meaning, or gives it its meaning. The social situation and process of behavior are here presupposed by the acts of the individual organisms implicated therein. The gesture arises as a separable element in the social act, by virtue of the fact that it is selected out by the sensitivities of other organisms to it; it does not exist as a gesture merely in the experience of the single individual. The meaning of a gesture by one organism, to repeat, is found in the response of another organism to what would be the completion of the act of the first organism which that gesture initiates and indicates.

We sometimes speak as if a person could build up an entire argument in his mind, and then put it into words to convey it to someone else. Actually, our thinking always takes place by means of some sort of symbols. It is possible that one could have the meaning of "chair" in his experience without there being a symbol, but we would not be thinking about it in that case. We may sit down in a chair without thinking about what we are doing, that is, the approach to the chair is presumably already aroused in our experience, so that the meaning is there. But if one is thinking about the chair he must have some sort of a symbol for it. It may be the form of the chair, it may be the attitude that somebody else takes in sitting down, but it is more apt to be some language symbol that arouses this response. In a thought process there has to be some sort of a symbol that can refer to this meaning, that is, tend to call out this response, and also serve this purpose for other persons as well. It would not be a thought process if that were not the case.

Our symbols are all universal. You cannot say anything that is absolutely particular; anything you say that has any meaning at all is universal. You are saying something that calls out a specific response in anybody else provided that the symbol exists for him in his experience as it does for you. There is the language of speech and the language of hands, and there may be the language of the expression of the countenance. One can register grief or joy and call out certain responses. There are primitive people who can carry on elaborate conversations just by expressions of the countenance. Even in these cases the person who communicates is affected by that expression just as he expects somebody else to be affected. Thinking always implies a symbol which will call out the same response in another that it calls out in the thinker. Such a symbol is a universal of discourse; it is universal in its character. We always assume that the symbol we use is one which will call out in the other person the same response, provided it is a part of his mechanism of conduct. A person who is saying something is saying to himself what he says to others; otherwise he does not know what he is talking about.

Among primitive people, as I have said, the necessity of distinguishing the self and the organism was recognized in what we term the "double": the individual has a thing-like self that is affected by the individual as it affects other people and which is distinguished from the immediate organism in that it can leave the body and come back to it. This is the basis for the concept of the soul as a separate entity.

We find in children something that answers to this double, namely, the invisible, imaginary companions which a good many children produce in their own experience. They organize in this way the responses which they call out in other persons and call out also in themselves. Of course, this playing with an imaginary companion is only a peculiarly interesting phase of ordinary play. Play in this sense, especially the stage which precedes the organized games, is a play at something. A child plays at being a mother, at being a teacher, at being a policeman; that is, it is taking different rôles, as we say. We have something that suggests this in what we call the play of animals: a cat will play with her kittens, and dogs play with each other. Two dogs playing with each other will attack and defend, in a process which if carried through would amount to an actual fight. There is a combination of responses which checks the depth of the bite. But we do not have in such a situation the dogs taking a definite rôle in the sense that a child deliberately takes the rôle of another. This tendency on the part of the children is what we are working with in the kindergarten where the rôles which the children assume are made the basis for training. When a child does assume a rôle he has in himself the stimuli which call out that particular response or group of responses. He may, of course, run away when he is chased, as the dog does, or he may turn around and strike back just as the dog does in his play. But that is not the same as playing at something. Children get together to "play Indian." This means that the child has a certain set of stimuli which call out in itself the responses that they would call out in others, and which answer to an Indian. In the play period the child utilizes his own responses to these stimuli which he makes use of in building a self. The response which he has a tendency to make to these stimuli organizes them. He plays that he is, for instance, offering himself something, and he buys it; he gives a letter to himself and takes it away; he addresses himself as a parent, as a teacher; he arrests himself as a policeman. He has a set of stimuli which call out in himself the sort of responses they call out in others. He takes this group of responses and organizes them into a certain whole. Such is the simplest form of being another to one's self. It involves a temporal situation. The child says something in one character and responds in another character, and then his responding in another character is a stimulus to himself in the first character, and so the conversation goes on. A certain organized structure arises in him and in his other which replies to it, and these carry on the conversation of gestures between themselves.

If we contrast play with the situation in an organized game, we note the essential difference that the child who plays in a game must be ready to take the attitude of everyone else involved in that game, and that these different rôles must have a definite relationship to each other. Taking a very simple game such as hide-and-seek, everyone with the exception of the one who is hiding is a person who is hunting. A child does not require more than the person who is hunted and the one who is hunting. If a child is playing in the first sense he just goes on playing, but there is no basic organization gained. In that early stage he passes from one rôle to another just as a whim takes him. But in a game where a number of individuals are involved, then the child taking one rôle must be ready to take the rôle of everyone else. If he gets in a ball nine he must have the responses of each position involved in his own position. He must know what everyone else is going to do in order to carry out his own play. He has to take all of these roles. They do not all have to be present in consciousness at the same time, but at some moments he has to have three or four individuals present in his own attitude, such as the one who is going to throw the ball, the one who is going to catch it, and so on. These responses must be, in some degree, present in his own make-up. In the game, then, there is a set of responses of such others so organized that the attitude of one calls out the appropriate attitudes of the other.

This organization is put in the form of the rules of the game. Children take a great interest in rules. They make rules on the spot in order to help themselves out of difficulties. Part of the enjoyment of the game is to get these rules. Now, the rules are the set of responses which a particular attitude calls out. You can demand a certain response in others if you take a certain attitude. These responses are all in yourself as well. There you get an organized set of such responses as that to which I have referred, which is something more elaborate than the rôles found in play. Here there is just a set of responses that follow on each other indefinitely. At such a stage we speak of a child as not yet having a fully developed self. The child responds in a fairly intelligent fashion to the immediate stimuli that come to him, but they are not organized. He does not organize his life as we would like to have him do, namely, as a whole. There is just a set of responses of the type of play. The child reacts to a certain stimulus, and the reaction is in himself that is called out in others, but he is not a whole self. In his game he has to have an organization of these rôles; otherwise he cannot play the game. The game represents the passage in the life of the child from taking the rôle of others in play to the organized part that is essential to self-consciousness in the full sense of the term.

PLAY, THE GAME, AND THE GENERALIZED OTHER

The fundamental difference between the game and play is that in the latter the child must have the attitude of all the others involved in that game. The attitudes of the other players which the participant assumes organize into a sort of unit, and it is that organization which controls the response of the individual. The illustration used was of a person playing baseball. Each one of his own acts is determined by his assumption of the action of the others who are playing the game. What he does is controlled by his being everyone else on that team, at least in so far as those attitudes affect his own particular response. We get then an "other" which is an organization of the attitudes of those involved in the same process.

The organized community or social group which gives to the individual his unity of self may be called "the generalized other." The attitude of the generalized other is the attitude of the whole community. Thus, for example, in the case of such a social group as a ball team, the team is the generalized other in so far as it enters—as an organized process or social activity—into the experience of any one of the individual members of it.

If the given human individual is to develop a self in the fullest sense, it is not sufficient for him merely to take the attitudes of other human individuals toward himself and toward one another within the human social process, and to bring that social process as a whole into his individual experience merely in these terms: he must also, in the same way that he takes the attitudes of other individuals toward himself and toward one another, take their attitudes toward the various phases or aspects of the common social activity or set of social undertakings in which, as members of an organized society or social group, they are all engaged; and he must then, by generalizing these individual attitudes of that organized society or social group itself, as a whole, act toward different social projects which at any given time it is carrying out, or toward the various larger phases of the general social process which constitutes its life and of which these projects are specific manifestations. This getting of the broad activities of any given social whole or organized society as such within the experiential field of any one of the individuals involved or included in that whole is, in other words, the essential basis and prerequisite of the fullest development of that individual's self: only in so far as he takes the attitudes of the organized social group to which he belongs toward the organized, co-operative social activity or set of such activities in which that group as such is engaged, does he develop a complete self or possess the sort of complete self he has developed. And on the other hand, the complex co-operative processes and activities and institutional functionings of organized human society are also possible only in so far as every individual involved in them or belonging to that society can take the general attitudes of all other such individuals with reference to these processes and activities and institutional functionings, and to the organized social whole of experiential relations and interactions thereby constituted—and can direct his own behavior accordingly.

It is in the form of the generalized other that the social process influences the behavior of the individuals involved in it and carrying it on, that is, that the community exercises control over the conduct of its individual members; for it is in this form that the social process or community enters as a determining factor into the individual's thinking. In abstract thought the individual takes the attitude of the generalized other toward himself, without reference to its expression in any particular other individuals; and in concrete thought he takes that attitude in so far as it is expressed in the attitudes toward his behavior of those other individuals with whom he is involved in the given social situation or act. But only by taking the attitude of the generalized other toward himself, in one or another of these ways, can he think at all; for only thus can thinking—or the internalized conversation of gestures which constitutes thinking—occur. And only through the taking by individuals of the attitude or attitudes of the generalized other toward themselves is the existence of a universe of discourse, as that system of common or social meanings which thinking presupposes at its context, rendered possible.

I have pointed out, then, that there are two general stages in the full development of the self. At the first of these stages, the individual's self is constituted simply by an organization of the particular attitudes of other individuals toward himself and toward one another in the specific social acts in which he participates with them. But at the second stage in the full development of the individual's self that self is constituted not only by an organization of these particular individual attitudes, but also by an organization of the social attitudes of the generalized other or the social group as a whole to which he belongs. These social or group attitudes are brought within the individual's field of direct experience, and are included as elements in the structure or constitution of his self, in the same way that the attitudes of particular other individuals are; and the individual arrives at them, or succeeds in taking them, by means of further organizing, and then generalizing, the attitudes of particular other individuals in terms of their organized social bearings and implications. So the self reaches its full development by organizing these individual attitudes of others into the organized social or group attitudes, and by thus becoming an individual reflection of the general systematic pattern of social or group behavior in which it and the others are all involved—a pattern which enters as a whole into the individual's experience in terms of these organized group attitudes which, through the mechanism of his central nervous system, he takes toward himself, just as he takes the individual attitudes of others.

The game has a logic, so that such an organization of the self is rendered possible: there is a definite end to be obtained; the actions of the different individuals are all related to each other with reference to that end so that they do not conflict; one is not in conflict with himself in the attitude of another man on the team. If one has the attitude of the person throwing the ball he can also have the response of catching the ball. The two are related so that they further the purpose of the game itself. They are interrelated in a unitary, organic fashion. There is a definite unity, then, which is introduced into the organization of other selves when we reach such a stage as that of the game, as over against the situation of play where there is a simple succession of one rôle after another, a situation which is, of course, characteristic of the child's own personality. The child is one thing at one time and another at another, and what he is at one moment does not determine what he is at another. That is both the charm of childhood as well as its inadequacy. You cannot count on the child; you cannot assume that all the things he does are going to determine what he will do at any moment. He is not organized into a whole. The child has no definite character, no definite personality.

The game is then an illustration of the situation out of which an organized personality arises. In so far as the child does take the attitude of the other and allows that attitude of the other to determine the thing he is going to do with reference to a common end, he is becoming an organic member of society. He is taking over the morale of that society and is becoming an essential member of it. He belongs to it in so far as he does allow the attitude of the other that he takes to control his own immediate expression. What is involved here is some sort of an organized process. That which is expressed in terms of the game is, of course, being continually expressed in the social life of the child, but this wider process goes beyond the immediate experience of the child himself. The importance of the game is that it lies entirely inside of the child's own experience, and the importance of our modern type of education is that it is brought as far as possible within this realm. The different attitudes that a child assumes are so organized that they exercise a definite control over his response, as the attitudes in a game control his own immediate response. In the game we get an organized other, a generalized other, which is found in the nature of the child itself, and difficulty in recognizing as our own. The parts of the body are quite distinguishable from the self. We can lose parts of the body without any serious invasion of the self. The mere ability to experience different parts of the body is not different from the experience of a table. The table presents a different feel from what the hand does when one hand feels another, but it is an experience of something with which we come definitely into contact. The body does not experience itself as a whole, in the sense in which the self in some way enters into the experience of the self.

It is the characteristic of the self as an object to itself that I want to bring out. This characteristic is represented in the word "self," which is a reflexive, and indicates that which can be both subject and object. This type of object is essentially different from other objects, and in the past it has been distinguished as conscious, a term which indicates an experience with, an experience of, one's self. It was assumed that consciousness in some way carried this capacity of being an object to itself. In giving a behavioristic statement of consciousness we have to look for some sort of experience in which the physical organism can become an object to itself.[1]

When one is running to get away from someone who is chasing him, he is entirely occupied in this action, and his experience may be swallowed up in the objects about him, so that he has, at the time being, no consciousness of self at all. We must be, of course, very completely occupied to have that take place, but we can, I think, recognize that sort of a possible experience in which the self does not enter. . . . In such instances there is a contrast between an experience that is absolutely wound up in outside activity in which the self as an object does not enter, and an activity of memory and imagination in which the self is the principal object. The self is then entirely distinguishable from an organism that is surrounded by things and acts with reference to things, including parts of its own body. These latter may be objects like other objects, but they are just objects out there in the field, and they do not involve a self that is an object to the organism. This is, I think, frequently overlooked. It is that fact which makes our anthropomorphic reconstructions of animal life so fallacious. How can an individual get outside himself (experientially) in such a way as to become an object to himself? This is the essential psychological problem of selfhood or of self-consciousness; and its solution is to be found by referring to the process of social conduct or activity in which

[1]Man's behavior is such in his social group that he is able to become an object to himself, a fact which constitutes him a more advanced product of evolutionary development than are the lower animals. Fundamentally it is this social fact—and not his alleged possession of a soul or mind with which he, as an individual, has been mysteriously and supernaturally endowed, and with which the lower animals have not been endowed—that differentiates him from them.

the given person or individual is implicated. The apparatus of reason would not be complete unless it swept itself into its own analysis of the field of experience; or unless the individual brought himself into the same experiential field as that of the other individual selves in relation to whom he acts in any given social situation. Reason cannot become impersonal unless it takes an objective, non-affective attitude toward itself; otherwise we have just consciousness, not *self*-consciousness. And it is necessary to rational conduct that the individual should thus take an objective, impersonal attitude toward himself, that he should become an object to himself. For the individual organism is obviously an essential and important fact or constituent element of the empirical situation in which it acts; and without taking objective account of itself as such, it cannot act intelligently, or rationally.

The individual experiences himself as such, not directly, but only indirectly, from the particular standpoints of other individual members of the same social group, or from the generalized standpoint of the social group as a whole to which he belongs. For he enters his own experience as a self or individual, not directly or immediately, not by becoming a subject to himself, but only in so far as he first becomes an object to himself just as other individuals are objects to him or in his experience; and he becomes an object to himself only by taking the attitudes of other individuals toward himself within a social environment or context of experience and behavior in which both he and they are involved.

The importance of what we term "communication" lies in the fact that it provides a form of behavior in which the organism or the individual may become an object to himself. It is that sort of communication which we have been discussing—not communication in the sense of the cluck of the hen to the chickens, or the bark of a wolf to the pack, or the lowing of a cow, but communication in the sense of significant symbols, communication which is directed not only to others but also to the individual himself. So far as that type of communication is a part of behavior it at least introduces a self. Of course, one may hear without listening; one may see things that he does not realize; do things that he is not really aware of. But it is where one does respond to that which he addresses to another and where that response of his own becomes a part of his conduct, where he not only hears himself but responds to himself, talks and replies to himself as truly as the other person replies to him, that we have behavior in which the individuals become objects to themselves.

The self, as that which can be an object to itself, is essentially a social structure, and it arises in social experience. After a self has arisen, it in a certain sense provides for itself its social experiences, and so we can conceive of an absolutely solitary self. But it is impossible to conceive of a self aris, outside of social experience. When it has arisen we can think of a person solitary confinement for the rest of his life, but who still has himself as companion, and is able to think and to converse with himself as he had communicated with others. That process to which I have just referred, of responding to one's self as another responds to it, taking part in one's own conversation with others, being aware of what one is saying and using that awareness of what one is saying to determine what one is going to say thereafter—that is a process with which we are all familiar. We are continually following up our own address to other persons by an understanding of what we are saying, and using that understanding in the direction of our continued speech. We are finding out what we are going to say, what we are going to do, by saying and doing, and in the process we are continually controlling the process itself. In the conversation of gestures what we say calls out a certain response in another and that in turn changes our own action, so that we shift from what we started to do because of the reply the other makes. The conversation of gestures is the beginning of communication. The individual comes to carry on a conversation of gestures with himself. He says something, and that calls out a certain reply in himself which makes him change what he was going to say. One starts to say something, we will presume an unpleasant something, but when he starts to say it he realizes it is cruel. The effect on himself of what he is saying checks him; there is here a conversation of gestures between the individual and himself. We mean by significant speech that the action is one that affects the individual himself, and that the effect upon the individual himself is part of the intelligent carrying-out of the conversation with others. Now we, so to speak, amputate that social phase and dispense with it for the time being, so that one is talking to one's self as one would talk to another person.[2]

This process of abstraction cannot be carried on indefinitely. One inevitably

[2]It is generally recognized that the specifically social expressions of intelligence, or the exercise of what is often called "social intelligence," depend upon the given individual's ability to take the rôles of, or "put himself in the place of," the other individuals implicated with him in given social situations; and upon his consequent sensitivity to their attitudes toward himself and toward one another. These specifically social expressions of intelligence, of course, acquire unique significance in terms of our view that the whole nature of intelligence is social to the very core—that this putting of one's self in the places of others, this taking by one's self of their rôles or attitudes, is not merely one of the various aspects or expressions of intelligence or of intelligent behavior, but is the very essence of its character. Spearman's "X factor" in intelligence—the unknown factor which, according to him, intelligence contains—is simply (if our social theory of intelligence is correct) this ability of the intelligent individual to take the attitude of the other, or the attitudes of others, thus realizing the significations or grasping the meanings of the symbols or gestures in terms of which thinking proceeds; and thus being able to carry on with himself the internal conversation with these symbols or gestures which thinking involves.

seeks an audience, has to pour himself out to somebody. In reflective intelligence one thinks to act, and to act solely so that this action remains a part of a social process. Thinking becomes preparatory to social action. The very process of thinking is, of course, simply an inner conversation that goes on, but it is a conversation of gestures which in its completion implies the expression of that which one thinks to an audience. One separates the significance of what he is saying to others from the actual speech and gets it ready before saying it. He thinks it out, and perhaps writes it in the form of a book; but it is still a part of social intercourse in which one is addressing other persons and at the same time addressing one's self, and in which one controls the address to other persons by the response made to one's own gesture. That the person should be responding to himself is necessary to the self, and it is this sort of social conduct which provides behavior within which that self appears. I know of no other form of behavior than the linguistic in which the individual is an object to himself, and, so far as I can see, the individual is not a self in the reflexive sense unless he is an object to himself. It is this fact that gives a critical importance to communication, since this is a type of behavior in which the individual does so respond to himself.

We realize in everyday conduct and experience that an individual does not mean a great deal of what he is doing and saying. We frequently say that such an individual is not himself. We come away from an interview with a realization that we have left out important things, that there are parts of the self that did not get into what was said. What determines the amount of the self that gets into communication is the social experience itself. Of course, a good deal of the self does not need to get expression. We carry on a whole series of different relationships to different people. We are one thing to one man and another thing to another. There are parts of the self which exist only for the self in relationship to itself. We divide ourselves up in all sorts of different selves with reference to our acquaintances. We discuss politics with one and religion with another. There are all sorts of different selves answering to all sorts of different social reactions. It is the social process itself that is responsible for the appearance of the self; it is not there as a self apart from this type of experience.

The peculiar character possessed by our human social environment belongs to it by virtue of the peculiar character of human social activity; and that character, as we have seen, is to be found in the process of communication, and more particularly in the triadic relation on which the existence of meaning is based: the relation of the gesture of one organism to the adjustive response made to it by another organism, in its indicative capacity as pointing to the completion or resultant of the act it initiates (the meaning of the gesture being thus the response of the second organism to it as such, or as a gesture). What, as it were, takes the gesture out of the social act and isolates it as such—what makes it something more than just an early phase of an individual act—is the response of another organism, or of other organisms, to it. Such a response is its meaning, or gives it its meaning. The social situation and process of behavior are here presupposed by the acts of the individual organisms implicated therein. The gesture arises as a separable element in the social act, by virtue of the fact that it is selected out by the sensitivities of other organisms to it; it does not exist as a gesture merely in the experience of the single individual. The meaning of a gesture by one organism, to repeat, is found in the response of another organism to what would be the completion of the act of the first organism which that gesture initiates and indicates.

We sometimes speak as if a person could build up an entire argument in his mind, and then put it into words to convey it to someone else. Actually, our thinking always takes place by means of some sort of symbols. It is possible that one could have the meaning of "chair" in his experience without there being a symbol, but we would not be thinking about it in that case. We may sit down in a chair without thinking about what we are doing, that is, the approach to the chair is presumably already aroused in our experience, so that the meaning is there. But if one is thinking about the chair he must have some sort of a symbol for it. It may be the form of the chair, it may be the attitude that somebody else takes in sitting down, but it is more apt to be some language symbol that arouses this response. In a thought process there has to be some sort of a symbol that can refer to this meaning, that is, tend to call out this response, and also serve this purpose for other persons as well. It would not be a thought process if that were not the case.

Our symbols are all universal. You cannot say anything that is absolutely particular; anything you say that has any meaning at all is universal. You are saying something that calls out a specific response in anybody else provided that the symbol exists for him in his experience as it does for you. There is the language of speech and the language of hands, and there may be the language of the expression of the countenance. One can register grief or joy and call out certain responses. There are primitive people who can carry on elaborate conversations just by expressions of the countenance. Even in these cases the person who communicates is affected by that expression just as he expects somebody else to be affected. Thinking always implies a symbol which will call out the same response in another that it calls out in the thinker. Such a symbol is a universal of discourse; it is universal in its character. We always assume that the symbol we use is one which will call out in the other person the same response, provided it is a part of his mechanism of conduct. A person who is saying something is saying to himself what he says to others; otherwise he does not know what he is talking about.

Among primitive people, as I have said, the necessity of distinguishing the self and the organism was recognized in what we term the "double": the individual has a thing-like self that is affected by the individual as it affects other people and which is distinguished from the immediate organism in that it can leave the body and come back to it. This is the basis for the concept of the soul as a separate entity.

We find in children something that answers to this double, namely, the invisible, imaginary companions which a good many children produce in their own experience. They organize in this way the responses which they call out in other persons and call out also in themselves. Of course, this playing with an imaginary companion is only a peculiarly interesting phase of ordinary play. Play in this sense, especially the stage which precedes the organized games, is a play at something. A child plays at being a mother, at being a teacher, at being a policeman; that is, it is taking different rôles, as we say. We have something that suggests this in what we call the play of animals: a cat will play with her kittens, and dogs play with each other. Two dogs playing with each other will attack and defend, in a process which if carried through would amount to an actual fight. There is a combination of responses which checks the depth of the bite. But we do not have in such a situation the dogs taking a definite rôle in the sense that a child deliberately takes the rôle of another. This tendency on the part of the children is what we are working with in the kindergarten where the rôles which the children assume are made the basis for training. When a child does assume a rôle he has in himself the stimuli which call out that particular response or group of responses. He may, of course, run away when he is chased, as the dog does, or he may turn around and strike back just as the dog does in his play. But that is not the same as playing at something. Children get together to "play Indian." This means that the child has a certain set of stimuli which call out in itself the responses that they would call out in others, and which answer to an Indian. In the play period the child utilizes his own responses to these stimuli which he makes use of in building a self. The response which he has a tendency to make to these stimuli organizes them. He plays that he is, for instance, offering himself something, and he buys it; he gives a letter to himself and takes it away; he addresses himself as a parent, as a teacher; he arrests himself as a policeman. He has a set of stimuli which call out in himself the sort of responses they call out in others. He takes this group of responses and organizes them into a certain whole. Such is the simplest form of being another to one's self. It involves a temporal situation. The child says something in one character and responds in another character, and then his responding in another character is a stimulus to himself in the first character, and so the conversation goes on. A certain organized structure arises in him and in his other which replies to it, and these carry on the conversation of gestures between themselves.

If we contrast play with the situation in an organized game, we note the essential difference that the child who plays in a game must be ready to take the attitude of everyone else involved in that game, and that these different rôles must have a definite relationship to each other. Taking a very simple game such as hide-and-seek, everyone with the exception of the one who is hiding is a person who is hunting. A child does not require more than the person who is hunted and the one who is hunting. If a child is playing in the first sense he just goes on playing, but there is no basic organization gained. In that early stage he passes from one rôle to another just as a whim takes him. But in a game where a number of individuals are involved, then the child taking one rôle must be ready to take the rôle of everyone else. If he gets in a ball nine he must have the responses of each position involved in his own position. He must know what everyone else is going to do in order to carry out his own play. He has to take all of these rôles. They do not all have to be present in consciousness at the same time, but at some moments he has to have three or four individuals present in his own attitude, such as the one who is going to throw the ball, the one who is going to catch it, and so on. These responses must be, in some degree, present in his own make-up. In the game, then, there is a set of responses of such others so organized that the attitude of one calls out the appropriate attitudes of the other.

This organization is put in the form of the rules of the game. Children take a great interest in rules. They make rules on the spot in order to help themselves out of difficulties. Part of the enjoyment of the game is to get these rules. Now, the rules are the set of responses which a particular attitude calls out. You can demand a certain response in others if you take a certain attitude. These responses are all in yourself as well. There you get an organized set of such responses as that to which I have referred, which is something more elaborate than the rôles found in play. Here there is just a set of responses that follow on each other indefinitely. At such a stage we speak of a child as not yet having a fully developed self. The child responds in a fairly intelligent fashion to the immediate stimuli that come to him, but they are not organized. He does not organize his life as we would like to have him do, namely, as a whole. There is just a set of responses of the type of play. The child reacts to a certain stimulus, and the reaction is in himself that is called out in others, but he is not a whole self. In his game he has to have an organization of these rôles; otherwise he cannot play the game. The game represents the passage in the life of the child from taking the rôle of others in play to the organized part that is essential to self-consciousness in the full sense of the term.

PLAY, THE GAME, AND THE GENERALIZED OTHER

The fundamental difference between the game and play is that in the latter the child must have the attitude of all the others involved in that game. The attitudes of the other players which the participant assumes organize into a sort of unit, and it is that organization which controls the response of the individual. The illustration used was of a person playing baseball. Each one of his own acts is determined by his assumption of the action of the others who are playing the game. What he does is controlled by his being everyone else on that team, at least in so far as those attitudes affect his own particular response. We get then an "other" which is an organization of the attitudes of those involved in the same process.

The organized community or social group which gives to the individual his unity of self may be called "the generalized other." The attitude of the generalized other is the attitude of the whole community. Thus, for example, in the case of such a social group as a ball team, the team is the generalized other in so far as it enters—as an organized process or social activity—into the experience of any one of the individual members of it.

If the given human individual is to develop a self in the fullest sense, it is not sufficient for him merely to take the attitudes of other human individuals toward himself and toward one another within the human social process, and to bring that social process as a whole into his individual experience merely in these terms: he must also, in the same way that he takes the attitudes of other individuals toward himself and toward one another, take their attitudes toward the various phases or aspects of the common social activity or set of social undertakings in which, as members of an organized society or social group, they are all engaged; and he must then, by generalizing these individual attitudes of that organized society or social group itself, as a whole, act toward different social projects which at any given time it is carrying out, or toward the various larger phases of the general social process which constitutes its life and of which these projects are specific manifestations. This getting of the broad activities of any given social whole or organized society as such within the experiential field of any one of the individuals involved or included in that whole is, in other words, the essential basis and prerequisite of the fullest development of that individual's self: only in so far as he takes the attitudes of the organized social group to which he belongs toward the organized, co-operative social activity or set of such activities in which that group as such is engaged, does he develop a complete self or possess the sort of complete self he has developed. And on the other hand, the complex co-operative processes and activities and institutional functionings of organized human society are also possible only in so far as every individual involved in them or belonging to that society can take the general attitudes of all other such individuals with reference to these processes and activities and institutional functionings, and to the organized social whole of experiential relations and interactions thereby constituted—and can direct his own behavior accordingly.

It is in the form of the generalized other that the social process influences the behavior of the individuals involved in it and carrying it on, that is, that the community exercises control over the conduct of its individual members; for it is in this form that the social process or community enters as a determining factor into the individual's thinking. In abstract thought the individual takes the attitude of the generalized other toward himself, without reference to its expression in any particular other individuals; and in concrete thought he takes that attitude in so far as it is expressed in the attitudes toward his behavior of those other individuals with whom he is involved in the given social situation or act. But only by taking the attitude of the generalized other toward himself, in one or another of these ways, can he think at all; for only thus can thinking—or the internalized conversation of gestures which constitutes thinking—occur. And only through the taking by individuals of the attitude or attitudes of the generalized other toward themselves is the existence of a universe of discourse, as that system of common or social meanings which thinking presupposes at its context, rendered possible.

I have pointed out, then, that there are two general stages in the full development of the self. At the first of these stages, the individual's self is constituted simply by an organization of the particular attitudes of other individuals toward himself and toward one another in the specific social acts in which he participates with them. But at the second stage in the full development of the individual's self that self is constituted not only by an organization of these particular individual attitudes, but also by an organization of the social attitudes of the generalized other or the social group as a whole to which he belongs. These social or group attitudes are brought within the individual's field of direct experience, and are included as elements in the structure or constitution of his self, in the same way that the attitudes of particular other individuals are; and the individual arrives at them, or succeeds in taking them, by means of further organizing, and then generalizing, the attitudes of particular other individuals in terms of their organized social bearings and implications. So the self reaches its full development by organizing these individual attitudes of others into the organized social or group attitudes, and by thus becoming an individual reflection of the general systematic pattern of social or group behavior in which it and the others are all involved—a pattern which enters as a whole into the individual's experience in terms of these organized group attitudes which, through the mechanism of his central nervous system, he takes toward himself, just as he takes the individual attitudes of others.

The game has a logic, so that such an organization of the self is rendered possible: there is a definite end to be obtained; the actions of the different individuals are all related to each other with reference to that end so that they do not conflict; one is not in conflict with himself in the attitude of another man on the team. If one has the attitude of the person throwing the ball he can also have the response of catching the ball. The two are related so that they further the purpose of the game itself. They are interrelated in a unitary, organic fashion. There is a definite unity, then, which is introduced into the organization of other selves when we reach such a stage as that of the game, as over against the situation of play where there is a simple succession of one rôle after another, a situation which is, of course, characteristic of the child's own personality. The child is one thing at one time and another at another, and what he is at one moment does not determine what he is at another. That is both the charm of childhood as well as its inadequacy. You cannot count on the child; you cannot assume that all the things he does are going to determine what he will do at any moment. He is not organized into a whole. The child has no definite character, no definite personality.

The game is then an illustration of the situation out of which an organized personality arises. In so far as the child does take the attitude of the other and allows that attitude of the other to determine the thing he is going to do with reference to a common end, he is becoming an organic member of society. He is taking over the morale of that society and is becoming an essential member of it. He belongs to it in so far as he does allow the attitude of the other that he takes to control his own immediate expression. What is involved here is some sort of an organized process. That which is expressed in terms of the game is, of course, being continually expressed in the social life of the child, but this wider process goes beyond the immediate experience of the child himself. The importance of the game is that it lies entirely inside of the child's own experience, and the importance of our modern type of education is that it is brought as far as possible within this realm. The different attitudes that a child assumes are so organized that they exercise a definite control over his response, as the attitudes in a game control his own immediate response. In the game we get an organized other, a generalized other, which is found in the nature of the child itself, and finds its expression in the immediate experience of the child. And it is that organized activity in the child's own nature controlling the particular response which gives unity, and which builds up his own self.

Such is the process by which a personality arises. I have spoken of this as a process in which a child takes the rôle of the other, and said that it takes place essentially through the use of language. Language is predominantly based on the vocal gesture by means of which co-operative activities in a community are carried out. Language in its significant sense is that vocal gesture which tends to arouse in the individual the attitude which it arouses in others, and it is this perfecting of the self by the gesture which mediates the social activities that gives rise to the process of taking the rôle of the other. The latter phrase is a little unfortunate because it suggests an actor's attitude which is actually more sophisticated than that which is involved in our own experience. To this degree it does not correctly describe that which I have in mind. We see the process most definitely in a primitive form in those situations where the child's play takes different rôles. Here the very fact that he is ready to pay out money, for instance, arouses the attitude of the person who receives money; the very process is calling out in him the corresponding activities of the other person involved. The individual stimulates himself to the response which he is calling out in the other person, and then acts in some degree in response to that situation. In play the child does definitely act out the rôle which he himself has aroused in himself. It is that which gives, as I have said, a definite content in the individual which answers to the stimulus that affects him as it affects somebody else. The content of the other that enters into one personality is the response in the individual which his gesture calls out in the other.

We may illustrate our basic concept by a reference to the notion of property. If we say, "This is my property, I shall control it," that affirmation calls out a certain set of responses which must be the same in any community in which property exists. It involves an organized attitude with reference to property which is common to all the members of the community. One must have a definite attitude of control of his own property and respect for the property of others. Those attitudes (as organized sets of responses) must be there on the part of all, so that when one says such a thing he calls out in himself the response of the others. He is calling out the response of what I have called a generalized other. That which makes society possible is such common responses, such organized attitudes, with reference to what we term property, the cults of religion, the process of education, and the relations of the family. Of course, the wider the society the more definitely universal these objects must be. In any case there must be a definite set of responses, which we may speak of as abstract, and which can belong to a very large group. Property is in itself a very abstract concept. It is that which the individual himself can control and nobody else can control. The attitude is different from that of a dog toward a bone. A dog will fight any other dog trying to take the bone. The dog is not taking the attitude of the other dog. A man who says, "This is my property," is taking an attitude of the other person. The man is appealing to his rights because he is able to take the attitude which everybody else in the group has with reference to property, thus arousing in himself the attitude of others.

The "I" is the response of the organism to the attitudes of the others; the "me" is the organized set of attitudes of others which one himself assumes. The attitudes of the others constitute the organized "me," and then one reacts toward that as an "I." I now wish to examine these concepts in greater detail.

There is neither "I" nor "me" in the conversation of gestures; the whole act is not yet carried out, but the preparation takes place in this field of gesture. Now, in so far as the individual arouses in himself the attitudes of the others, there arises an organized group of responses. And it is due to the individual's ability to take the attitudes of these others in so far as they can be organized that he gets self-consciousness. The taking of all of those organized sets of attitudes gives him his "me"; that is the self he is aware of. He can throw the ball to some other member because of the demand made upon him from other members of the team. That is the self that immediately exists for him in his consciousness. He has their attitudes, knows what they want and what the consequence of any act of his will be, and he has assumed responsibility for the situation. Now, it is the presence of those organized sets of attitudes that constitutes that "me" to which he as an "I" is responding. But what that response will be he does not know and nobody else knows. Perhaps he will make a brilliant play or an error. The response to that situation as it appears in his immediate experience is uncertain, and it is that which constitutes the "I."

The "I" is his action over against that social situation within his own conduct, and it gets into his experience only after he has carried out the act. Then he is aware of it. He had to do such a thing and he did it. He fulfils his duty and he may look with pride at the throw which he made. The "me" arises to do that duty—that is the way in which it arises in his experience. He had in him all the attitudes of others, calling for a certain response; that was the "me" of that situation, and his response is the "I."

The "I," then, in this relation of the "I" and the "me," is something that is, so to speak, responding to a social situation which is within the experience of the individual. It is the answer which the individual makes to the attitude which others take toward him when he assumes an attitude toward them. Now, the attitudes he is taking toward them are present in his own experience, but his response to them will contain a novel element. The "I" gives the sense of freedom, of initiative. The situation is there for us to act in a self-conscious fashion. We are aware of ourselves, and of what the situation is, but exactly how we will act never gets into experience until after the action takes place.

Such is the basis for the fact that the "I" does not appear in the same sense in experience as does the "me." The "me" represents a definite organization of the community there in our own attitudes, and calling for a response, but the response that takes place is something that just happens. There is no certainty in regard to it. There is a moral necessity but no mechanical necessity for the act. When it does take place then we find what has been done. The above account gives us, I think, the relative position of the "I" and "me" in the situation, and the grounds for the separation of the two in behavior. The two are separated in the process but they belong together in the sense of being parts of a whole. They are separated and yet they belong together. The separation of the "I" and the "me" is not fictitious. They are not identical, for, as I have said, the "I" is something that is never entirely calculable. The "me" does call for a certain sort of an "I" in so far as we meet the obligations that are given in conduct itself, but the "I" is always something different from what the situation itself calls for. So there is always that distinction, if you like, between the "I" and the "me." The "I" both calls out the "me" and responds to it. Taken together they constitute a personality as it appears in social experience. The self is essentially a social process going on with these two distinguishable phases. If it did not have these two phases there could not be conscious responsibility, and there would be nothing novel in experience.

Symbolic Interactionism [1969]

HERBERT BLUMER

• *Herbert Blumer coined the term* symbolic interactionism *"in an offhand way in an article written in 1937." He calls it "a somewhat barbaric neologism," but "the term somehow caught on and is now in general use." Blumer's symbolic interactionism is built on Mead and Cooley, as well as on W. I. Thomas, John Dewey, and others. In Blumer's hands, it turned into a full-fledged dynamic sociology, as well as a militant intellectual movement critical of opposing approaches. In one of his later statements, Blumer sums up its principles.*

Symbolic interactionism rests in the last analysis on three simple premises. The first premise is that human beings act toward things on the basis of the meanings that the things have for them. Such things include everything that the human being may note in his world—physical objects, such as trees or chairs; other human beings, such as a mother or a store clerk; categories of human beings, such as friends or enemies; institutions, as a school or a government; guiding ideals, such as individual independence or honesty; activities of others, such as their commands or requests; and such situations as an individual encounters in his daily life. The second premise is that the meaning of such things is derived from, or arises out of, the social interaction that one has with one's fellows. The third premise is that these meanings are handled in, and modified through, an interpretative process used by the person in dealing with the things he encounters. I wish to discuss briefly each of these three fundamental premises.

It would seem that few scholars would see anything wrong with the first premise—that human beings act toward things on the basis of the meanings which these things have for them. Yet, oddly enough, this simple view is ignored or played down in practically all of the thought and work in contemporary social science and psychological science. Meaning is either taken for granted and thus pushed aside as unimportant or it is regarded as a mere neutral link between the factors responsible for human behavior and this behavior as the product of such factors. We can see this clearly in the predominant posture of psychological and social science today. Common to both of these fields is the tendency to treat human behavior as the product of various factors that play upon human beings; concern is with the behavior and with the factors regarded as producing them. Thus, psychologists turn to such factors as stimuli, attitudes, conscious or unconscious motives, various kinds of psychological inputs, perception and cognition, and various features of personal organization to account for given forms or instances of human conduct. In a similar fashion sociologists rely on such factors as social position, status demands, social roles, cultural prescriptions, norms and values, social pressures, and group affiliation to provide such explanations. In both such typical psychological and sociological explanations the meanings of things for the human beings who are acting are either bypassed or swallowed up in the factors used to account for their behavior. If one declares that the given kinds of behavior are the result of the particular factors regarded as producing them, there is no need to concern oneself with the meaning of the things toward which human beings act; one merely identifies the initiating factors and the resulting behavior. Or one may, if pressed, seek to accommodate the element of meaning by lodging it in the initiating factors or by regarding it as a neutral link intervening between the initiating factors and the behavior they are alleged to produce. In the first of these latter cases the meaning disappears by being merged into the initiating or causative factors; in the second case meaning becomes a mere transmission link that can be ignored in favor of the initiating factors.

The position of symbolic interactionism, in contrast, is that the meanings that things have for human beings are central in their own right. To ignore the meaning of the things toward which people act is seen as falsifying the behavior under study. To bypass the meaning in favor of factors alleged to produce the behavior is seen as a grievous neglect of the role of meaning in the formation of behavior.

The simple premise that human beings act toward things on the basis of the meaning of such things is much too simple in itself to differentiate symbolic interactionism—there are several other approaches that share this premise. A major line of difference between them and symbolic interactionism is set by the second premise, which refers to the source of meaning. There are two well-known traditional ways of accounting for the origin of meaning. One of them is to regard meaning as being intrinsic to the thing that has it, as being a natural part of the objective makeup of the thing. Thus, a chair is clearly a chair in itself, a cow a cow, a cloud a cloud, a rebellion a rebellion, and so forth. Being inherent in the thing that has it, meaning needs merely to be

disengaged by observing the objective thing that has the meaning. The meaning emanates, so to speak, from the thing and as such there is no process
involved in its formation; all that is necessary is to recognize the meaning that
is there in the thing. It should be immediately apparent that this view reflects
the traditional position of "realism" in philosophy—a position that is widely
held and deeply entrenched in the social and psychological sciences. The
other major traditional view regards "meaning" as a psychical accretion
brought to the thing by the person for whom the thing has meaning. This
psychical accretion is treated as being an expression of constituent elements of
the person's psyche, mind, or psychological organization. The constituent
elements are such things as sensations, feelings, ideas, memories, motives,
and attitudes. The meaning of a thing is but the expression of the given
psychological elements that are brought into play in connection with the
perception of the thing; thus one seeks to explain the meaning of a thing by
isolating the particular psychological elements that produce the meaning. One
sees this in the somewhat ancient and classical psychological practice of analyzing the meaning of an object by identifying the sensations that enter into
perception of that object; or in the contemporary practice of tracing the meaning of a thing, such as let us say prostitution, to the attitude of the person who
views it. This lodging of the meaning of things in psychological elements
limits the processes of the formation of meaning to whatever processes are
involved in arousing and bringing together the given psychological elements
that produce the meaning. Such processes are psychological in nature, and
include perception, cognition, repression, transfer of feelings, and association
of ideas.

Symbolic interactionism views meaning as having a different source than
those held by the two dominant views just considered. It does not regard
meaning as emanating from the intrinsic makeup of the thing that has meaning, nor does it see meaning as arising through a coalescence of psychological
elements in the person. Instead, it sees meaning as arising in the process of
interaction between people. The meaning of a thing for a person grows out of
the ways in which other persons act toward the person with regard to the
thing. Their actions operate to define the thing for the person. Thus, symbolic
interactionism sees meanings as social products, as creations that are formed
in and through the defining activities of people as they interact. This point of
view gives symbolic interactionism a very distinctive position, with profound
implications that will be discussed later.

The third premise mentioned above further differentiates symbolic interactionism. While the meaning of things is formed in the context of social
interaction and is derived by the person from that interaction, it is a mistake to

think that the use of meaning by a person is but an application of the meaning so derived. This mistake seriously mars the work of many scholars who otherwise follow the symbolic interactionist approach. They fail to see that the use of meanings by a person in his action involves an interpretative process. In this respect they are similar to the adherents of the two dominant views spoken of above—to those who lodge meaning in the objective makeup of the thing that has it and those who regard it as an expression of psychological elements. All three are alike in viewing the use of meaning by the human being in his action as being no more than an arousing and application of already established meanings. As such, all three fail to see that the use of meanings by the actor occurs through *a process of interpretation.* This process has two distinct steps. First, the actor indicates to himself the things toward which he is acting; he has to point out to himself the things that have meaning. The making of such indications is an internalized social process in that the actor is interacting with himself. This interaction with himself is something other than an interplay of psychological elements; it is an instance of the person engaging in a process of communication with himself. Second, by virtue of this process of communicating with himself, interpretation becomes a matter of handling meanings. The actor selects, checks, suspends, regroups, and transforms the meanings in the light of the situation in which he is placed and the direction of his action. Accordingly, interpretation should not be regarded as a mere automatic application of established meanings but as a formative process in which meanings are used and revised as instruments for the guidance and formation of action. It is necessary to see that meanings play their part in action through a process of self-interaction.

It is not my purpose to discuss at this point the merits of the three views that lodge meaning respectively in the thing, in the psyche, and in social action, nor to elaborate on the contention that meanings are handled flexibly by the actor in the course of forming his action. Instead, I wish merely to note that by being based on these three premises, symbolic interaction is necessarily led to develop an analytical scheme of human society and human conduct that is quite distinctive. It is this scheme that I now propose to outline.

Symbolic interactionism is grounded on a number of basic ideas, or "root images," as I prefer to call them. These root images refer to and depict the nature of the following matters: human groups or societies, social interaction, objects, the human being as an actor, human action, and the interconnection of the lines of action. Taken together, these root images represent the way in which symbolic interactionism views human society and conduct. They constitute the framework of study and analysis. Let me describe briefly each of these root images.

NATURE OF HUMAN SOCIETY OR HUMAN GROUP LIFE

Human groups are seen as consisting of human beings who are engaging in action. The action consists of the multitudinous activities that the individuals perform in their life as they encounter one another and as they deal with the succession of situations confronting them. The individuals may act singly, they may act collectively, and they may act on behalf of, or as representatives of, some organization or group of others. The activities belong to the acting individuals and are carried on by them always with regard to the situations in which they have to act. The import of this simple and essentially redundant characterization is that fundamentally human groups or society *exists in action* and must be seen in terms of action. This picture of human society as action must be the starting point (and the point of return) for any scheme that purports to treat and analyze human society empirically. Conceptual schemes that depict society in some other fashion can only be derivations from the complex of ongoing activity that constitutes group life. This is true of the two dominant conceptions of society in contemporary sociology—that of culture and that of social structure. Culture as a conception, whether defined as custom, tradition, norm, value, rules, or such like, is clearly derived from what people do. Similarly, social structure in any of its aspects, as represented by such terms as social position, status, role, authority, and prestige, refers to relationships derived from how people act toward each other. The life of any human society consists necessarily of an ongoing process of fitting together the activities of its members. It is this complex of ongoing activity that establishes and portrays structure or organization. A cardinal principle of symbolic interactionism is that any empirically oriented scheme of human society, however derived, must respect the fact that in the first and last instances human society consists of people engaging in action. To be empirically valid the scheme must be consistent with the nature of the social action of human beings.

NATURE OF SOCIAL INTERACTION

Group life necessarily presupposes interaction between the group members; or, put otherwise, a society consists of individuals interacting with one another. The activities of the members occur predominantly in response to one another or in relation to one another. Even though this is recognized almost universally in definitions of human society, social interaction is usually taken for granted and treated as having little, if any, significance in its own right. This is evident in typical sociological and psychological schemes—they treat social interaction as merely a medium through which the determinants of behavior pass to produce the behavior. Thus, the typical sociological scheme ascribes behavior to such factors as status position, cultural prescriptions, norms, values, sanctions, role demands, and social system requirements; explanation in terms of such factors suffices without paying attention to the social interaction that their play necessarily presupposes. Similarly, in the typical psychological scheme such factors as motives, attitudes, hidden complexes, elements of psychological organization, and psychological processes are used to account for behavior without any need of considering social interaction. One jumps from such causative factors to the behavior they are supposed to produce. Social interaction becomes a mere forum through which sociological or psychological determinants move to bring about given forms of human behavior. I may add that this ignoring of social interaction is not corrected by speaking of an interaction of societal elements (as when a sociologist speaks of an interaction of social roles or an interaction between the components of a social system) or an interaction of psychological elements (as when a psychologist speaks of an interaction between the attitudes held by different people). Social interaction is an interaction between actors and not between factors imputed to them.

Symbolic interactionism does not merely give a ceremonious nod to social interaction. It recognizes social interaction to be of vital importance in its own right. This importance lies in the fact that social interaction is a process that *forms* human conduct instead of being merely a means or a setting for the expression or release of human conduct. Put simply, human beings in interacting with one another have to take account of what each other is doing or is about to do; they are forced to direct their own conduct or handle their situations in terms of what they take into account. Thus, the activities of others enter as positive factors in the formation of their own conduct; in the face of the actions of others one may abandon an intention or purpose, revise it, check or suspend it, intensify it, or replace it. The actions of others enter to set what one plans to do, may oppose or prevent such plans, may require a revision of such plans, and may demand a very different set of such plans. One has to *fit* one's own line of activity in some manner to the actions of others. The actions of others have to be taken into account and cannot be regarded as merely an arena for the expression of what one is disposed to do or sets out to do.

We are indebted to George Herbert Mead for the most penetrating analysis of social interaction—an analysis that squares with the realistic account just given. Mead identifies two forms or levels of social interaction in human society. He refers to them respectively as "the conversation of gestures" and "the use of significant symbols"; I shall term them respectively "non-symbolic interaction" and "symbolic interaction." Non-symbolic interaction takes place when one responds directly to the action of another without interpreting that action; symbolic interaction involves interpretation of the action. Non-symbolic interaction is most readily apparent in reflex responses, as in the case of a boxer who automatically raises his arms to parry a blow. However, if the boxer were reflectively to identify the forthcoming blow from his opponent as a feint designed to trap him, he would be engaging in symbolic interaction. In this case, he would endeavor to ascertain the meaning of the blow—that is, what the blow signifies as to his opponent's plan. In their association human beings engage plentifully in non-symbolic interaction as they respond immediately and unreflectively to each other's bodily movements, expressions, and tones of voice, but their characteristic mode of interaction is on the symbolic level, as they seek to understand the meaning of each other's action.

Mead's analysis of symbolic interaction is highly important. He sees it as a presentation of gestures and a response to the meaning of those gestures. A gesture is any part or aspect of an ongoing action that signifies the larger act of which it is a part—for example, the shaking of a fist as an indication of a possible attack, or the declaration of war by a nation as an indication of a posture and line of action of that nation. Such things as requests, orders, commands, cues, and declarations are gestures that convey to the person who recognizes them an idea of the intention and plan of forthcoming action of the individual who presents them. The person who responds organizes his response on the basis of what the gestures mean to him; the person who presents the gestures advances them as indications or signs of what he is planning to do as well as of what he wants the respondent to do or understand. Thus, the gesture has meaning for both the person who makes it and for the person to whom it is directed. When the gesture has the same meaning for both, the two parties understand each other. From this brief account it can be seen that the meaning of the gesture flows out along three lines (Mead's triadic nature of meaning): It signifies what the person to whom it is directed is to do; it signifies what the person who is making the gesture plans to do; and it signifies the joint action that is to arise by the articulation of the acts of both. Thus, for illustration, a robber's command to his victim to put up his hands is (a) an indication of what the victim is to do; (b) an indication of what the robber plans to do, that is, relieve the victim of his money; and (c) an indication of the joint act being formed, in this case a holdup. If there is confusion or misunderstanding along any one of these three lines of meaning, communication is ineffective, interaction is impeded, and the formation of joint action is blocked.

One additional feature should be added to round out Mead's analysis of symbolic interaction, namely, that the parties to such interaction must necessarily take each other's roles. To indicate to another what he is to do, one has to make the indication from the standpoint of that other; to order the victim to put up his hands the robber has to see this response in terms of the victim making it. Correspondingly, the victim has to see the command from the standpoint of the robber who gives the command; he has to grasp the intention and forthcoming action of the robber. Such mutual role-taking is the *sine qua non* of communication and effective symbolic interaction.

The central place and importance of symbolic interaction in human group life and conduct should be apparent. A human society or group consists of people in association. Such association exists necessarily in the form of people acting toward one another and thus engaging in social interaction. Such interaction in human society is characteristically and predominantly on the symbolic level; as individuals acting individually, collectively, or as agents of some organization encounter one another they are necessarily required to take account of the actions of one another as they form their own action. They do this by a dual process of indicating to others how to act and of interpreting the indications made by others. Human group life is a vast process of such defining to others what to do and of interpreting their definitions; through this process people come to fit their activities to one another and to form their own individual conduct. Both such joint activity and individual conduct are formed *in* and *through* this ongoing process; they are not mere expressions or products of what people bring to their interaction or of conditions that are antecedent to their interaction. The failure to accommodate to this vital point constitutes the fundamental deficiency of schemes that seek to account for human society in terms of social organization or psychological factors, or of any combination of the two. By virtue of symbolic interaction, human group life is necessarily a formative process and not a mere arena for the expression of pre-existing factors.

NATURE OF OBJECTS

The position of symbolic interactionism is that the "worlds" that exist for human beings and for their groups are composed of "objects" and that these objects are the product of symbolic interaction. An object is anything that can be indicated, anything that is pointed to or referred to—a cloud, a book, a legislature, a banker, a religious doctrine, a ghost, and so forth. For purposes of convenience one can classify objects in three categories: (a) physical objects, such as chairs, trees, or bicycles; (b) social objects, such as students, priests, a president, a mother, or a friend; and (c) abstract objects, such as moral principles, philosophical doctrines, or ideas such as justice, exploitation, or compassion. I repeat that an object is anything that can be indicated or referred to. The nature of an object—of any and every object—consists of the meaning that it has for the person for whom it is an object. This meaning sets the way in which he sees the object, the way in which he is prepared to act toward it, and the way in which he is ready to talk about it. An object may have a different meaning for different individuals: a tree will be a different object to a botanist, a lumberman, a poet, and a home gardener; the President of the United States can be a very different object to a devoted member of his political party than to a member of the opposition; the members of an ethnic group may be seen as a different kind of object by members of other groups. The meaning of objects for a person arises fundamentally out of the way they are defined to him by others with whom he interacts. Thus, we come to learn through the indications of others that a chair is a chair, that doctors are a certain kind of professional, that the United States Constitution is a given kind of legal document, and so forth. Out of a process of mutual indications common objects emerge—objects that have the same meaning for a given set of people and are seen in the same manner by them.

Several noteworthy consequences follow from the foregoing discussion of objects. First, it gives us a different picture of the environment or milieu of human beings. From their standpoint the environment consists *only* of the objects that the given human beings recognize and know. The nature of this environment is set by the meaning that the objects composing it have for those human beings. Individuals, also groups, occupying or living in the same spatial location may have, accordingly, very different environments; as we say, people may be living side by side yet be living in different worlds. Indeed, the term "world" is more suitable than the word "environment" to designate the setting, the surroundings, and the texture of things that confront them. It is the world of their objects with which people have to deal and toward which they develop their actions. It follows that in order to understand the action of people it is necessary to identify their world of objects—an important point that will be elaborated later.

Second, objects (in the sense of their meaning) must be seen as social creations—as being formed in and arising out of the process of definition and interpretation as this process takes place in the interaction of people. The meaning of anything and everything has to be formed, learned, and transmitted through a process of indication—a process that is necessarily a social process. Human group life on the level of symbolic interaction is a vast process in which people are forming, sustaining, and transforming the objects of their world as they come to give meaning to objects. Objects have no fixed status except as their meaning is sustained through indications and definitions that people make of the objects. Nothing is more apparent than that objects in all categories can undergo change in their meaning. A star in the sky is a very different object to a modern astrophysicist than it was to a sheepherder of biblical times; marriage was a different object to later Romans than to earlier Romans; the president of a nation who fails to act successfully through critical times may become a very different object to the citizens of his land. In short, from the standpoint of symbolic interactionism human group life is a process in which objects are being created, affirmed, transformed, and cast aside. The life and action of people necessarily change in line with the changes taking place in their world of objects.

THE HUMAN BEING AS AN ACTING ORGANISM

Symbolic interactionism recognizes that human beings must have a makeup that fits the nature of social interaction. The human being is seen as an organism that not only responds to others on the non-symbolic but as one that makes indications to others and interprets their indications. He can do this, as Mead has shown so emphatically, only by virtue of possessing a "self." Nothing esoteric is meant by this expression. It means merely that a human being can be an object of his own action. Thus, he can recognize himself, for instance, as being a man, young in age, a student, in debt, trying to become a doctor, coming from an undistinguished family and so forth. In all such instances he is an object to himself; and he acts toward himself and guides himself in his actions toward others on the basis of the kind of object he is to himself. This notion of oneself as an object fits into the earlier discussion of objects. Like other objects, the self-object emerges from the process of social interaction in which other people are defining a person to himself. Mead has traced the way in which this occurs in his discussion of role-taking. He points out that in order to become an object to himself a person has to see himself from the outside. One can do this only by placing himself in the position of others and viewing himself or acting toward himself from that position. The roles the person takes range from that of discrete individuals (the "play stage"), through that of discrete organized groups (the "game stage") to that of the abstract community (the "generalized other"). In taking such roles the person is in a position to address or approach himself—as in the case of a young girl who in "playing mother" talks to herself as her mother would do, or in the case of a young priest who sees himself through the eyes of the priesthood. We form our objects of ourselves through such a process of role-taking. It follows that we see ourselves through the way in which others see or define us—or,

more precisely, we see ourselves by taking one of the three types of roles of
others that have been mentioned. That one forms an object of himself
through the ways in which others define one to himself is recognized fairly
well in the literature today, so despite its great significance I shall not comment on it further.

There is an even more important matter that stems from the fact that the
human being has a self, namely that this enables him to interact with himself.
This interaction is not in the form of interaction between two or more parts of
a psychological system, as between needs, or between emotions, or between
ideas, or between the id and the ego in the Freudian scheme. Instead, the
interaction is social—a form of communication, with the person addressing
himself as a person and responding thereto. We can clearly recognize such
interaction in ourselves as each of us notes that he is angry with himself, or
that he has to spur himself on in his tasks, or that he reminds himself to do
this or that, or that he is talking to himself in working out some plan of action.
As such instances suggest, self-interaction exists fundamentally as a process of
making indications to oneself. This process is in play continuously during
one's waking life, as one notes and considers one or another matter, or observes this or that happening. Indeed, for the human being to be conscious or
aware of anything is equivalent to his indicating the thing to himself—he is
identifying it as a given kind of object and considering its relevance or importance to his line of action. One's waking life consists of a series of such
indications that the person is making to himself, indications that he uses to
direct his action.

We have, then, a picture of the human being as an organism that interacts
with itself through a social process of making indications to itself. This is a
radically different view of the human being from that which dominates contemporary social and psychological science. The dominant prevailing view
sees the human being as a complex organism whose behavior is a response to
factors playing on the organization of the organism. Schools of thought in the
social and psychological sciences differ enormously in which of such factors
they regard as significant, as is shown in such a diverse array as stimuli,
organic drives, need-dispositions, conscious motives, unconscious motives,
emotions, attitudes, ideas, cultural prescriptions, norms, values, status demands, social roles, reference group affiliations, and institutional pressures.
Schools of thought differ also in how they view the organization of the human
being, whether as a kind of biological organization, a kind of psychological
organization, or a kind of imported societal organization incorporated from
the social structure of one's group. Nevertheless, these schools of thought are
alike in seeing the human being as a responding organism, with its behavior

being a product of the factors playing on its organization or an expression of the interplay of parts of its organization. Under this widely shared view the human being is "social" only in the sense of either being a member of social species, or of responding to others (social stimuli), or of having incorporated within it the organization of his group.

The view of the human being held in symbolic interactionism is fundamentally different. The human being is seen as "social" in a much more profound sense—in the sense of an organism that engages in social interaction with itself by making indications to itself and responding to such indications. By virtue of engaging in self-interaction the human being stands in a markedly different relation to his environment than is presupposed by the widespread conventional view described above. Instead of being merely an organism that responds to the play of factors on or through it, the human being is seen as an organism that has to deal with what it notes. It meets what it so notes by engaging in a process of self-indication in which it makes an object of what it notes, gives it a meaning, and uses the meaning as the basis for directing its action. Its behavior with regard to what it notes is not a response called forth by the presentation of what it notes but instead is an action that arises out of the interpretation made through the process of self-indication. In this sense, the human being who is engaging in self-interaction is not a mere responding organism but an acting organism—an organism that has to mold a line of action on the basis of what it takes into account instead of merely releasing a response to the play of some factor on its organization.

NATURE OF HUMAN ACTION

The capacity of the human being to make indications to himself gives a distinctive character to human action. It means that the human individual confronts a world that he must interpret in order to act instead of an environment to which he responds because of his organization. He has to cope with the situations in which he is called on to act, ascertaining the meaning of the actions of others and mapping out his own line of action in the light of such interpretation. He has to construct and guide his action instead of merely releasing it in response to factors playing on him or operating through him. He may do a miserable job in constructing his action, but he has to construct it.

This view of the human being directing his action by making indications to himself stands sharply in contrast to the view of human action that dominates current psychological and social science. This dominant view, as already implied, ascribes human action to an initiating factor or a combination of such factors. Action is traced back to such matters as motives, attitudes, need-dispositions, unconscious complexes, stimuli configurations, status demands, role requirements, and situational demands. To link the action to one or more of such initiating agents is regarded as fulfilling the scientific task. Yet, such an approach ignores and makes no place for the process of self-interaction through which the individual handles his world and constructs his action. The door is closed to the vital process of interpretation in which the individual notes and assesses what is presented to him and through which he maps out lines of overt behavior prior to their execution.

Fundamentally, action on the part of a human being consists of taking account of various things that he notes and forging a line of conduct on the basis of how he interprets them. The things taken into account cover such matters as his wishes and wants, his objectives, the available means for their achievement, the actions and anticipated actions of others, his image of himself, and the likely result of a given line of action. His conduct is formed and guided through such a process of indication and interpretation. In this process, given lines of action may be started or stopped, they may be abandoned or postponed, they may be confined to mere planning or to an inner life of reverie, or if initiated, they may be transformed. My purpose is not to analyze this process but to call attention to its presence and operation in the formation of human action. We must recognize that the activity of human beings consists of meeting a flow of situations in which they have to act and that their action is built on the basis of what they note, how they assess and interpret what they note, and what kind of projected lines of action they map out. This process is not caught by ascribing action to some kind of factor (for example, motives, need-dispositions, role requirements, social expectations, or social rules) that is thought to initiate the action and propel it to its conclusion; such a factor, or some expression of it, is a matter the human actor takes into account in mapping his line of action. The initiating factor does not embrace or explain how it and other matters are taken into account in the situation that calls for action. One has to get inside of the defining process of the actor in order to understand his action.

This view of human action applies equally well to joint or collective action in which numbers of individuals are implicated. Joint or collective action constitutes the domain of sociological concern, as exemplified in the behavior of groups, institutions, organizations, and social classes. Such instances of societal behavior, whatever they may be, consist of individuals fitting their lines of action to one another. It is both proper and possible to view and study such behavior in its joint or collective character instead of in its individual components. Such joint behavior does not lose its character of being constructed through an interpretative process in meeting the situations in which the collectivity is called on to act. Whether the collectivity be an army engaged in a campaign, a corporation seeking to expand its operations, or a nation trying to correct an unfavorable balance of trade, it needs to construct its action through an interpretation of what is happening in its area of operation. The interpretative process takes place by participants making indications to one another, not merely each to himself. Joint or collective action is an outcome of such a process of interpretative interaction.

INTERLINKAGE OF ACTION

As stated earlier, human group life consists of, and exists in, the fitting of lines of action to each other by the members of the group. Such articulation of lines of action gives rise to and constitutes "joint action"—a societal organization of conduct of different acts of diverse participants. A joint action, while made up of diverse component acts that enter into its formation, is different from any one of them and from their mere aggregation. The joint action has a distinctive character in its own right, a character that lies in the articulation or linkage as apart from what may be articulated or linked. Thus, the joint action may be identified as such and may be spoken of and handled without having to break it down into the separate acts that comprise it. This is what we do when we speak of such things as marriage, a trading transaction, war, a parliamentary discussion, or a church service. Similarly, we can speak of the collectivity that engages in joint action without having to identify the individual members of that collectivity, as we do in speaking of a family, a business corporation, a church, a university, or a nation. It is evident that the domain of the social scientist is constituted precisely by the study of joint action and of the collectivities that engage in joint action.

In dealing with collectivities and with joint action one can easily be trapped in an erroneous position by failing to recognize that the joint action of the collectivity is an interlinkage of the separate acts of the participants. This failure leads one to overlook the fact that a joint action always has to undergo a process of formation; even though it may be a well-established and repetitive form of social action, each instance of it has to be formed anew. Further, this career of formation through which it comes into being necessarily takes place through the dual process of designation and interpretation that was discussed above. The participants still have to guide their respective acts by forming and using meanings.

With these remarks as a background I wish to make three observations on the implications of the interlinkage that constitutes joint action. I wish to consider first those instances of joint action that are repetitive and stable. The preponderant portion of social action in a human society, particularly in a settled society, exists in the form of recurrent patterns of joint action. In most situations in which people act toward one another they have in advance a firm understanding of how to act and of how other people will act. They share common and pre-established meanings of what is expected in the action of the participants, and accordingly each participant is able to guide his own behavior by such meanings. Instances of repetitive and pre-established forms of joint action are so frequent and common that it is easy to understand why scholars have viewed them as the essence or natural form of human group life. Such a view is especially apparent in the concepts of "culture" and "social order" that are so dominant in social science literature. Most sociological schemes rest on the belief that a human society exists in the form of an established order of living, with that order resolvable into adherence to sets of rules, norms, values, and sanctions that specify to people how they are to act in their different situations.

Several comments are in order with regard to this neat scheme. First, it is just not true that the full expanse of life in a human society, in any human society, is but an expression of pre-established forms of joint action. New situations are constantly arising within the scope of group life that are problematic and for which existing rules are inadequate. I have never heard of any society that was free of problems nor any society in which members did not have to engage in discussion to work out ways of action. Such areas of unprescribed conduct are just as natural, indigenous, and recurrent in human group life as are those areas covered by pre-established and faithfully followed prescriptions of joint action. Second, we have to recognize that even in the case of pre-established and repetitive joint action each instance of such joint action has to be formed anew. The participants still have to build up their lines of action and fit them to one another through the dual process of designation and interpretation. They do this in the case of repetitive joint action, of course, by using the same recurrent and constant meanings. If we recognize this, we are forced to realize that the play and fate of meanings are what is important, not the joint action in its established form. Repetitive and stable joint action is just as much a result of an interpretative process as is a new form of joint action that is being developed for the first time. This is not an idle or pedantic point; the meanings that underlie established and recurrent joint action are themselves subject to pressure as well as to reinforcement, to incipient dissatisfaction as well as to indifference; they may be challenged as well as affirmed, allowed to slip along without concern as well as subjected to infusions of new vigor. Behind the facade of the objectively perceived joint action the set of meanings that sustains that joint action has a life that the social scientists can ill afford to ignore. A gratuitous acceptance of the concepts of norms, values, social rules, and the like should not blind the social scientist to the fact that any one of them is subtended by a process of social interaction—a process that is necessary not only for their change but equally well for their retention in a fixed form. It is the social process in group life that creates and upholds the rules, not the rules that create and uphold group life.

The second observation on the interlinkage that constitutes joint action refers to the extended connection of actions that make up so much of human group life. We are familiar with these large complex networks of action involving an interlinkage and interdependency of diverse actions of diverse people— as in the division of labor extending from the growing of grain by the farmer to an eventual sale of bread in a store, or in the elaborate chain extending from the arrest of a suspect to his eventual release from a penitentiary. These networks with their regularized participation of diverse people by diverse action at diverse points yields a picture of institutions that have been appropriately a major concern of sociologists. They also give substance to the idea that human group life has the character of a system. In seeing such a large complex of diversified activities, all hanging together in a regularized operation, and in seeing the complementary organization of participants in well-knit interdependent relationships, it is easy to understand why so many scholars view such networks or institutions as self-operating entities, following their own dynamics and not requiring that attention be given to the participants within the network. Most of the sociological analyses of institutions and social organization adhere to this view. Such adherence, in my judgment, is a serious mistake. One should recognize what is true, namely, that the diverse array of participants occupying different points in the network engage in their actions at those points on the basis of using given sets of meanings. A network or an institution does not function automatically because of some inner dynamics or system requirements; it functions because people at different points do something, and what they do is a result of how they define the situation in which they are called on to act. A limited appreciation of this point is reflected today in some of the work on decision-making, but on the whole the point is grossly ignored. It is necessary to recognize that the sets of meanings that lead participants to act as they do at their stationed points in the network have their own setting in a localized process of social interaction—and that these meanings are formed, sustained, weakened, strengthened, or transformed, as the case may be, through a socially defining process. Both the functioning and the fate of institutions are set by this process of interpretation as it takes place among the diverse sets of participants.

A third important observation needs to be made, namely, that any instance of joint action, whether newly formed or long established, has necessarily arisen out of a background of previous actions of the participants. A new kind of joint action never comes into existence apart from such a background. The participants involved in the formation of the new joint action always bring to that formation the world of objects, the sets of meanings, and the schemes of interpretation that they already possess. Thus, the new form of joint action always emerges out of and is connected with a context of previous joint action. It cannot be understood apart from that context; one has to bring into one's consideration this linkage with preceding forms of joint action. One is on treacherous and empirically invalid grounds if he thinks that any given form of joint action can be sliced off from its historical linkage, as if its makeup and character arose out of the air through spontaneous generation instead of growing out of what went before. In the face of radically different and stressful situations people may be led to develop new forms of joint action that are markedly different from those in which they have previously engaged, yet even in such cases there is always some connection and continuity with what went on before. One cannot understand the new form without incorporating knowledge of this continuity into one's analysis of the new form. Joint action not only represents a horizontal linkage, so to speak, of the activities of the participants, but also a vertical linkage with previous joint action.

SUMMARY REMARKS

The general perspective of symbolic interactionism should be clear from our brief sketch of its root images. This approach sees a human society as people engaged in living. Such living is a process of ongoing activity in which participants are developing lines of action in the multitudinous situations they encounter. They are caught up in a vast process of interaction in which they have to fit their developing actions to one another. This process of interaction consists in making indications to others of what to do and in interpreting the indications as made by others. They live in worlds of objects and are guided in their orientation and action by the meaning of these objects. Their objects, including objects of themselves, are formed, sustained, weakened, and transformed in their interaction with one another. This general process should be seen, of course, in the differentiated character which it necessarily has by virtue of the fact that people cluster in different groups, belong to different associations, and occupy different positions. They accordingly approach each other differently, live in different worlds, and guide themselves by different sets of meanings. Nevertheless, whether one is dealing with a family, a boy's gang, an industrial corporation, or a political party, one must see the activities of the collectivity as being formed through a process of designation and interpretation.

CONCLUSION

My conclusion . . . is indeed brief. It can be expressed as a simple injunction: Respect the nature of the empirical world and organize a methodological stance to reflect that respect. This is what I think symbolic interactionism strives to do.

The Ethnomethodology of the Human Reality Constructor [1975]

HUGH MEHAN AND HOUSTON WOOD

• *Ethnomethodology is notoriously difficult material for outsiders to get a feeling for, and that is especially true of the writings of its inspirational center, Harold Garfinkel. Ethnomethodology is in many ways more of an oral, face-to-face, intellectual analysis than it is a written discipline; given the nature of its insights into the social process of reality-constructing, perhaps that is not surprising. "Signed objects" (objects that have been turned into social symbols and signs, like language) have always irretrievably lost something of the qualities of "lebenswelt objects" of ordinary, unreflective experience. Ethnomethodology investigates the laws of that transformation. The word itself alludes to its mission: "ethno"—the ethnographic description of—"methodology," the folk-methods people use in their everyday, practical reasoning, conversation, and work. The following selection, by Hugh Mehan and Houston Wood, is an unusually lucid résumé of ethnomethodology's central discoveries and of the famous "breaching experiments" Garfinkel used to point up some of them.*

Much ethnomethodological theorizing has explored the work entailed in achieving the object constancy belief and other fundamental propositions of daily life. The ethnomethodologist finds that persons are constructing social structures without being aware of this work. This reality work is explicated by the construction of a "model of the actor."

In the normative model, rules, actors, and situations are assumed to be independent entities. In the ethnomethodological model, persons are treated as reality constructors. Rules are dependent upon the ceaseless, ongoing activities of persons within social situations. The ethnomethodological model is a characteristization of the way persons *create* situations and rules, and so at once create themselves and their social realities.[1]

From Hugh Mehan and Houston Wood, *The Reality of Ethnomethodology*, pp. 98–114. Copyright 1975, John Wiley and Sons. Reprinted by permission of John Wiley and Sons, Inc.

[1] Ethnomethodologists adopted this research program from Schutz (1962, 1964), who spoke of the construction of "homunculi" and "puppets" as the theorists' solution of theoretical problems. Trading off a more recent metaphor, Crowle (1971) has suggested that the model is analogous to an android, that is, an automated simulated human (cf. Sacks, 1963).

A CONSTRUCTION OF A REALITY CONSTRUCTOR

I will now attribute some minimal requisites for social interaction to a model of the actor. The attributions are *constitutive*. They both create interaction and the possibility of interaction. These features have been culled from the writings of Schutz (1962, 1964, 1966, 1967, 1970a), from Garfinkel's (1963, 1967a) distillation of these writings, and from Cicourel's (1973a) further elaboration of this work.[2] My purpose is not to provide an accurate historical sequence in the development of the model. It is rather to provide a single, unified formulation so that the use of this device can be better understood.

This model of the reality constructor is composed of (1) social knowledge and (2) interpretive procedures that operate on that social knowledge.

Social Knowledge

The properties of social knowledge can be summarized as follows:

1. Social knowledge provides *a practical interest* in the world. Garfinkel describes this feature as follows:

> Events, their relationships, their causal texture are not for [the person] matters of theoretic interest. He does not sanction the notion that in dealing with them it is correct to address them with the interpretive rule that he knows nothing, or that he can assume that he knows nothing "just to see where it leads." In everyday situations what he knows is an integral feature of his social competence (1967a:273).

That is, as people conduct the affairs of their daily life, they are *not* constrained by the canons of the "scientific rationalities" (Garfinkel, 1967a:262–283). They are *not* concerned with semantic or conceptual clarity for its own sake, or insuring that their actions conform to the demands of formal logic.

---

[2] Garfinkel has on numerous occasions attempted to codify and systematize Schutz's various discussions of the attitude of everyday life. His first attempt at this synthesis appears in his dissertation (Garfinkel, 1952). In his "Documentary Method" paper (Garfinkel, 1967a:89–94), he speaks in terms of the "findings" of an experiment reported there. In his 1960 paper on the "Rationalities" (1967a:272–279), he offers another summary of the "presuppositions of everyday life." A far more complex listing appears in his "Trust" paper (1963), where 8 presuppositions are listed and described. This list is repeated again as 11 presuppositions in the 1964 "Routine Grounds" paper (1967a:55–56).

Cicourel's treatment of the "interpretive procedures" has a similar history. His first writing (1968, in 1973a:42–73) made a strong analogy to linguistics; six interpretive procedures were "deep" rules to normative "surface rules." A discussion of "role theory" (1970, in 1973a:11–41) distributes the interpretive procedures into three "basic rules." Still another formulation (1969, in 1973a:74–98) produces four interpretive procedures.

2. Social knowledge is *socially distributed*. Garfinkel describes this feature as follows:

> There corresponds, thereby, to the common intersubjective world of communication, unpublicized knowledge which in the eyes of the actor is distributed among persons as grounds of their actions, that is, of their motives or, in the radical sense of the term, their "interests," as constituent features of the social relationships of interaction. He assumes that there are matters that one person knows that he assumes others do not know. The ignorance of one party consists in what another knows that is motivationally relevant to the first. Thereby matters that are known in common are informed in their sense by the personal reservations, the matters that are selectively withheld. Thus the events of everyday situations are informed by this integral background of "meanings held in reserve," of matters known about self and others that are none of somebody else's business; in a word, the private life (Ibid.:276).

This feature of social knowledge provides that some people know some things, but not everybody knows all things. Interactants recognize this. Nonetheless, biographically specific meanings are treated as irrelevant for the purposes of communicating the here-and-now event to others.

3. Social knowledge is *tacit*. Garfinkel points out that any "event means for both the witness and the other more than the witness can say" (Ibid.:56). This feature of social knowledge provides that what both persons know in common cannot be said in so many words. This common, tacit knowing is used by people to build interaction.

4. Social knowledge *takes the world for granted*. Garfinkel writes:

> a relationship of undoubted correspondence is the sanctioned relationship between the-presented-appearance-of-the-object and the-intended-object-that-presents-itself-in-the-perspective-of-the-particular-appearance (Ibid.:55).

And he writes elsewhere:

> Schutz finds that in everyday situations the "practical theorist" achieves an ordering of events while seeking to retain and sanction the presupposition that the objects of the world are as they appear. The person coping with everyday affairs seeks an interpretation of these affairs while holding a line of "official neutrality" towards the interpretive rule that one may doubt the objects of the world as they appear. The actor's assumption consists in the expectation that a relationship of

undoubted correspondence exists between the particular appearances of an object and the intended-object-that-appears-in-this-particular-fashion (Ibid.:272).

That is, people expect the world beyond to be accurately pictured by their way of looking at it. This feature of social knowledge makes it possible for objects to be accepted for what they appear to be on the surface.

This discussion establishes that the reality constructor has social knowledge, but this conception is static. People do not use all their knowledge in every situation. They do not apply all that they (tacitly) know at once. Therefore, our model must have a mechanism that activates the situationally relevant aspects of this constantly changing stock of knowledge.

Borrowing from Schutz, this feature has been talked about in various ways: as "constitutive rules" (Garfinkel, 1963), as "interpretive rules" (Garfinkel, 1967a), as "interpretive procedures" or "basic rules" (Cicourel, 1973a).[3] I will use the term "procedure," because it best conveys the sense that these are descriptions of interactional activities that are *done* by people in interaction.

Interpretive Procedures

Three interpretive procedures have been described by the ethnomethodologist:

1. *Searching for a normal form.* Cicourel (1973a:86) describes this interpretive procedure as follows:

> when discrepancies or ambiguities appear, speakers will attempt to normalize the presumed discrepancies . . . this commonsense principle provides each member with instructions for unwittingly (and sometimes deliberately) evaluating and striving for a reciprocally assumed normal form judgment of his utterances and perceptions.

2. *Doing a reciprocity of perspectives.* Cicourel (Ibid.:85–86) describes the reciprocity of perspectives as doing the work of sustaining the assumption that:

> (i) each would have the same experiences if they were to change places, and (ii) that until further notice they can disregard any differences that might arise from their respective personal ways of assigning meaning to objects and events.

[3]In this talk, these theorists continually refer to the assumptions that the actor makes in interaction. They do *not* mean that the actor is consciously making choices prior to doing things. Postulating "assumptions" is one way the ethnomethodologist has for talking about the necessary aspects of interaction. There is no necessary commitment to a cognitive formulation.

3. *Employing the et cetera principle.* Cicourel (Ibid.:87) describes this interpretive procedure as follows:

> The participants to a conversation must "fill in" meanings throughout the exchange and after the exchange when attempting to recall or reconstruct what happened because of the inadequacies of oral and non-oral communication, and the routine practice of leaving many intentions unstated (Garfinkel, 1964). Vague or ambiguous or truncated expressions are located by members, given meaning contextually and across contexts, by their retrospective-prospective sense of occurrence. Present utterances or descriptive accounts that contain ambiguous or promissory overtones can be examined prospectively by the speaker-hearer for their possible meaning in some future sense under the assumption of filling in meanings now and imagining the kinds of intentions that can be expected later. Or, past remarks can now be seen as clarifying present utterances.

Hence, the et cetera principle has three interrelated parts. In some versions of the model, these features are treated as separate entities.

a. Unclear information is allowed to pass while clarifying information is sought.

b. Contextual information is sought over time to fill in the ambiguity of indexical expressions.

c. The filling in is accomplished by retrospective-prospective means. When vague, ambiguous, or unclear utterances occur, the vagueness is not immediately challenged or questioned. The hearer allows the unclear utterance to pass. He assumes that subsequent events will clarify the present ambiguity. If and when subsequent information becomes available, that present information is used to clarify the previously unclear events.

DISPLAYING THE REALITY CONSTRUCTOR

The model of the reality constructor can be used as an analytic tool. I will illustrate this by providing a hypothetical account of an everyday event. A man driving to work sees a fuzzy object. After several minutes during which the object's appearance baffles him, he determines that it is a freeway sign. To account for this occurrence, I will attribute to the model of a freeway driver some of the elements necessary for driving the freeway in an acceptable manner.

Before this man can begin driving his car, in fact, even before he can leave his bed in the morning, put on his clothes, or drink his coffee, he must assume that objects are what they appear to be on the surface. If the motorist had scientifically rational doubts about the nature of objects appearing before him, he would not be able to act at all. If the motorist doubts that the floor under his bed is a floor, he will be unable to stand on that floor. If our motorist does not see the long ribbon of black ooze as a "freeway," the brightly colored mass hurtling toward him as a "car" with a competent driver who will drive past, not at him, he may be unable to negotiate the roadway.[4] These suggest the taken-for-granted features of social knowledge I summarized above.

As the motorist drives the freeway, he is confronted by swirls of colors and sounds. Our motorist must transform these stimuli into meaningful wholes. This is the interpretive procedure "searching for a normal form." As an individual goes through a social situation (as the motorist drives his car), the individual searches for and selects features of the world which can be placed in a familiar schemata. Casting for coherent forms is an interpretive procedure performed on all knowledge systems.

When first confronted by swirling colors, the motorist sensed the presence of a "something," but its specific form, content, and dimensions were unknown. The assumed presence of "some object there" enabled the motorist to continue to look for features that would help him identify "the something" as a specific thing. In the language of the interpretive procedures discussed above, the motorist allowed unclear events to pass while seeking clarification. He waited to see what the object would mean then.

Although an object may not have a specific meaning at the time that it is initially apprehended, it has some meaning. For example, it is "an unclear object." Its specific meaning may become clear with subsequent events. After these events occur, the motorist is able to see in retrospect what the object was "all along." This retrospective filling in is an aspect of the interpretive procedure: employing the et cetera principle.

Of course, this now specific, clear meaning is also subject to subsequent reinterpretation. The object may not be a freeway sign, but a scaffold, or a truck; any subsequent determination will modify previous ones. "What it is now" will be "what it was all along."

The meaning of an object, event, or utterance is also "prospective." When a person does not immediately know the normal form meaning of an object,

---

[4] I cannot help but reflect on how difficult it is to talk about "meaninglessness." The very words we use to talk about "meaninglessness" are themselves meaningful. The expression "black ooze" does not refer to a meaningless object. Although the expression does not carry a noun as specific as "asphalt," "black ooze" nevertheless is meaningful.

It may in fact be impossible to suspend or "get behind" the meanings provided to us by language and culture to "pure sensation." Layers of meaning may be stripped off (so that "freeway sign" becomes "bright shiny object," then "green flashes"), but each successive account requires a tie to a meaningful category to be processed. As Merleau-Ponty said: "We are condemned to meaning."

he assumes that its meaning will become clear later. The practice of "waiting until later to see what was intended now" is the "prospective" interpretive procedure.

The motorist knows this swirling object was a sign all along. He also knows that this object will be the same object the next time he confronts it. It will be the same object on all subsequent occasions. It will be the same object to any and all others who look at it. He maintains this knowledge by employing the "reciprocity of perspectives" interpretive procedure.

Now suppose our motorist needs to go from one part of the city to another. He might ask a gas station attendant for directions:

How do I get to Jack-in-the-Box from here?

The gas station attendant might give the following directions: "See this street here? That takes you to the freeway. Stay on the freeway until you see the sign for Mazeville Road. Get off there. Jack-in-the-Box will be on your right, a few blocks down."

In order for the gas station attendant to tell our motorist this, the attendant must treat the freeway sign as a constant object. That is, the gas station attendant must also employ the reciprocity of perspectives interpretive procedure, which provides that the meaning of the objects, utterances, or events that he has encountered are the same that others have encountered. And, in order for the motorist to follow those directions, he must treat the signs, streets, and buildings he encounters and calls by certain names, as the same objects the gas station attendant or anybody else names in the same way.

Now, the motorist who follows these instructions may have had peculiar experiences with that particular street exit. For example, he may once have had a flat tire or an accident there. The gas station attendant may be having "a bad day," or he may have just won money at the racetrack. But the motorist is not interested in these biographical features. He is interested in getting to Jack-in-the-Box. If the gas station attendant were to begin to provide the motorist with the details about his declining business, the rising prices of his products, or what he will do with his winnings, the motorist would see that as strange. Likewise, the gas station attendant is not interested in *why* the motorist wants to go to Jack-in-the-Box. It is irrelevant for his purpose of giving instructions whether the motorist is going to Jack-in-the-Box to make a purchase, to meet someone, or to rob it. Both the motorist and the gas station attendant must treat any such biographically specific meanings as irrelevant for the purposes at hand. They must employ the socially distributed aspect of social knowledge.

The motorist who asks the gas station attendant for directions has a "practical interest in the world" (see the first property of social knowledge, above). He wants to go from one place to another. That practical problem occupies his time. He is not interested in theoretical matters about the journey, the freeway, or the sign, such as the laws of physics that explain how the sign is able to stand in high winds, or the principle that explains how the asphalt is able to support the weight of cars on it, or the kinetic theory that explains why the sign "lights up" when headlights shine on the sign at night. Theoretical reflection and practical problem-solving are separate activities. It is difficult to engage in both simultaneously. On another occasion, at another time, say, when the motorist and a friend are sipping coffee after dinner, they might engage in a discussion of the physical principles of light reflection. But at the moment when the motorist is trying to navigate unfamiliar streets and heavy traffic, he is hardly interested in such theoretical matters.

The motorist is able to concentrate on his practical concerns of finding streets and signs and does not need to worry about asphalt strength and principles of light reflection because he "knows" that other people have these theoretical matters as *their* practical concerns. This is another facet of the social distribution of social knowledge. No member of society need know all society's knowledge in order to interact. But in order to function in everyday life, each must rely on the fact that some people have some knowledge of the world, and that others have other knowledge.

Likewise, no person need have a *formal* acquaintance with any of that knowledge. Just as a speaker of a language need not know the rules of grammar to speak that language (Chomsky, 1965), a person need not be able to list the rules of society to act in it. This illumines the meaning of the "tacit" feature of social knowledge.

Now let us examine the conversation between the motorist and the gas station attendant, especially the instruction the gas station attendant gave to the motorist so that he could go from one part of town to another.

Motorist:	How do I get to Jack-in-the-Box from here?
Gas station attendant:	See this street here? That takes you to the freeway. Stay on the freeway until you see the sign for Mazeville Road. Get off there. Jack-in-the-Box will be on your right, a few blocks down.

To ask the gas station attendant for directions, the motorist would need to know at least the following about socially distributed social knowledge: that there are people who can legitimately be asked for directions; that there are places where directions can be legitimately asked; and that there are times when such questions can legitimately be asked. If a priest hearing confession were asked for directions to Jack-in-the-Box, the person asking the question might be considered bizarre, a stranger, or incompetent. Knowing that there are people who can and cannot be asked for instructions, and knowing that there are those who *can* legitimately be asked for directions, and knowing that such a person has certain obligations to respond is presumably knowledge that "everyone (who is a competent member of society) knows."

The ethnomethodologist is not interested in compiling a list of the "background" knowledge required for successful interaction. The list I have begun above for the motorist merely scratches the surface of what he would have to know to ask that question. As I explain in a later section of this chapter, it seems unlikely that a complete list could ever be constructed.

To ask for directions, the motorist must consult his normal forms, which guide his selection of a person who would be likely to help him. The initial selection is prospective, for the person selected for instructions may be a stranger, a pathological liar, or a robber. Subsequent events will retrospectively inform the motorist if his initial prospective selection was accurate.

What does the gas station attendant's instruction tell the motorist? It seems to tell him everything that he needs to know. It tells him to turn at a certain street of a certain freeway. But notice that far more is implied by the utterance than is stated in words. The utterance assumes that the hearer can supply contextual information (see interpretive procedure 3b)—for example, that he knows the meaning of "freeway" and can recognize one when he sees one, and that he knows what a car is and can use one. It assumes that the person knows about making turns, and can make one, et cetera.

The instruction refers to a few landmarks, a freeway, and a particular sign. It does not provide a detailed map on which every building and street is identified with its dimensions, age, and number of dollars spent in its construction. The hearer must go beyond the information given in the instruction itself and fill in with particulars from his own past experience, and with normal forms that he gains along the way. Thus, the instructions . . . are incomplete. The operation of interpretive procedures on social knowledge show how such symbolic forms are managed by the actor.

EXPLORING THE MODEL THROUGH ETHNOGRAPHIES

No studies describing the use of social knowledge and interpretive procedures in actual settings have been conducted. However, the model of the reality constructor need not be restricted to free inventions. It is a schemata that enables actual social scenes to be examined at a greater depth than is usual in sociological field studies. It suggests a way of investigating particular scenes in order to *see general* features. Sociology presently searches particular scenes for *particular* features.

Consider, for example, the works of Becker, Whyte, and Goffman, acknowledged masters of the field study technique. Becker's (1953) analysis of marijuana users is typical. He describes how jazz musicians use "the smoke" to get "high" and improve their performance. Becker's (1968) later analysis of LSD use also describes how particular activities get done. He is not interested in using those particular activities as a vehicle for exploring the general features of all activities. Whyte (1955) provides descriptions of how gang members behave on street corners. Goffman's (1959, 1961, 1969) work reaches toward a deeper level, but it does not to seek features that appear in all situations.[5]

The model of the reality constructor, like Goffman's model, is "only" a schemata. However, it differs from Goffman, Becker and Whyte in directing the researcher's attention to transsituational features of particular situations. It provides a method for attempting ethnographies of the general problem of social order.

The choice between these alternative approaches must be made on extra-theoretical grounds. The model of the reality constructor is *not* a higher ontological truth. (I return to this ontological issue at the end of this chapter.) For those interested in the particular features of particular scenes, traditional field work schemata are efficacious. For those interested in the general problem of social order, a model like the reality constructor is indicated.

EXPLORING THE MODEL THROUGH BREACHING

Field work studies are only one method of refining the reality constructor model. A second method is the use of "incongruity" or "breaching" procedures . . . The logic of the procedures derives from the claim that social structures are created by social structuring activities, work that is not apparent under normal circumstances. A corollary of this suggests that suppressing any of the models' features should "produce anomic effects and increase disorga-

[5]Garfinkel (1967a:116–185) . . . explored some differences between situated "passing" practices and Goffman's "management" practices in his "Agnes" study (see especially Garfinkel, 1967a: 164–185). Garfinkel argues that Goffman's dramaturgical model presupposes a world of constant objects. Goffman does not describe how such objects are ceaselessly created. Garfinkel shows that no amount of "staging" or strategic planning before social scenes was sufficient to account for Agnes's creation of her female sexuality.

nization" (Garfinkel, 1963:215). I will adapt Garfinkel's breaching procedures to illustrate the necessity of the features of social knowledge, and interpretive procedures.

Breaching Social Knowledge

One of the features of everyday knowledge is that it provides a practical interest in the world . . . Garfinkel (1964, in 1967a:41–44) instructed a number of persons to converse while repressing this feature. He told them to adopt a *theoretic* interest in the conversation. This entailed seeking meanings "for their own sake," "just to see where it might lead." They were to show no regard for the practical circumstances surrounding the conversation.

The people who followed this procedure typically found that social order halted. This is the report of one person (*E*) who attempted to suppress the practical interest feature of social knowledge:

> E: My friend and I were talking about a man whose overbearing attitude annoyed us. My friend expressed his feeling:
> S: I'm sick of him.
> E: Would you explain what is wrong with you that you are sick?
> S: Are you kidding me? You know what I mean.
> E: Please explain your ailment.
> S: (He listened to me with a puzzled look.) What came over you? We never talk this way, do we? (Ibid.:44).

The experimenter is not allowing what he knows to be "an integral feature" (Ibid.:273) of the scene. As a result, the ongoing interaction is swiftly disrupted. The subject demands to know "what came over" the experimenter, and points out that "We never talk this way." The repression of this feature of social knowledge breaches the subject's sense of normality, indicating that this feature is vital for the construction of everyday scenes.

A second feature of social knowledge is that it is socially distributed . . . Persons recognize that some persons know some things that others do not. These *personal* disparities in knowledge are supposed to be irrelevant in everyday interaction. Where they are not, it is assumed that the party with relevant personal knowledge will inform the other.

Garfinkel (Ibid.:75) demonstrated the importance of this feature by using the following procedure:

> the experimenter engaged others in conversation while he had a wire recorder hidden under his coat. In the course of the conversation the

experimenter opened his jacket to reveal the recorder saying, "See what I have?" An initial pause was almost invariably followed by the question, "What are you doing with it?" . . . The fact that the conversation was revealed to have been recorded motivated new possibilities which the parties then sought to bring under the jurisdiction of an agreement that they had never specifically mentioned and that indeed did not previously exist.

The subjects knew that the experimenter knew things they did not, just as they knew they had knowledge the experimenter did not. But the subjects assumed as well that these disparities in knowledge were irrelevant to the interaction at hand. The appearance of the tape recorder made this taken-for-granted feature visible. By breaching it, Garfinkel demonstrated its importance to everyday interactions where it exists but is unnoticed. (For allied procedures breaching this feature, see Garfinkel, 1963:201–206; 1967a:71–73.)

The third feature of social knowledge I described above (p. 100) is its tacitness. Social knowledge is assumed to be shared by parties to an interaction. Though this shared knowledge is never exhaustively articulated, persons assume that they know a single world in common.

Garfinkel (1967a:51) designed a procedure to reveal the importance of this feature of social knowledge:

> Students were instructed to engage someone in conversation and to imagine and act on the assumption that what the other person was saying was directed by hidden motives which were his real ones.

In other words, students were asked to suspend the assumption that a body of knowledge was being tacitly held in common. The other person was seen as having a hidden body of knowledge ("motives") which were coloring all that person was doing.

Reviewing 35 instances of the implementation of this breaching procedure, Garfinkel concludes:

> The attitude was difficult to sustain and carry through. Students reported acute awareness of being "in an artificial game," of being unable to "live the part," and of frequently being "at a loss as to what to do next." . . . One student spoke for several when she said she was unable to get any results because so much of her effort was directed to maintaining an attitude of distrust that she was unable to follow the conversation. She said she was unable to imagine how her fellow conversationalist might be deceiving her because they were talking about such inconsequential matters (Ibid.).

In sum, students found that they could not suppress the belief that they held a corpus of knowledge in common with the other. Even attempting to breach this feature disrupted the interaction. Common tacit knowledge is thus indicated to be essential to social scenes.

A fourth and final feature of social knowledge is that it takes the world for granted . . . A real world exists independent of the knowledge of the world. This world is in direct correspondence with the knowledge. Knowledge and world picture each other (cf. Wittgenstein; 1921).

Garfinkel (Ibid.:46) breached this feature by asking subjects to enter their homes with the attitude of a boarder. The home was a familiar world. The attitude of a boarder required the use of unfamiliar knowledge. The procedure was designed to explore the clash of foreign knowledge and a familiar world.

Some of the students were instructed only to observe their homes as a boarder. They were not to act on this attitude:

> Many reported that the attitude was difficult to sustain because with it quarreling, bickering, and hostile motivations became discomfitingly visible. Frequently an account that recited newly visible troubles was accompanied by the student's assertion that his account of family problems was not a "true" picture; the family was *really* a very happy one. Students were convinced that the view from the boarder's attitude was not their real home environment (Ibid.).

The fourth feature of knowledge maintains that there is an undoubted correspondence between knowledge and world. Thus, students found that if they adopted a boarder's knowledge, they experienced a boarder's world. They were anxious to assure themselves that the world that appeared under the aegis of the different knowledge was not the "real" world. That new world offered troubles that were not visible through a family member's knowledge.

Garfinkel's procedure does not suggest that one or the other of these experiences of the home is true. It suggests instead that any knowledge will produce the experience of a world that corresponds with that knowledge. An omnipresent feature of all social knowledge is that it matches a real and external reality.

Breaching Interpretive Procedures

The first of three interpretive procedures I described was "searching for a normal form" . . . This refers to the work people do to transform discrepancies and ambiguities into similar patterns. I have adapted another of Garfinkel's (1963:229–235; 1967a:59–67) procedures to illustrate the results of frustrating normal forming.

Garfinkel's subjects were 28 premedical students. They were separately introduced to a purported expert on medical school admissions, who said he was interested in decreasing student anxiety over medical school admissions interviews. He solicited the student's opinion on how this might be done.

After a casual hour's discussion, the interviewer asked the students if they would like to hear a recording of an actual admissions interview. All of the students had such interviews in their future and leaped at the opportunity as a possible means of increasing their chances of admission.

The applicant the students heard was excessively boorish. He used poor grammar and was stupid. He was pushy and abrasive, contradicting the interviewer when not being evasive. He degraded other schools and professions. On top of it all, he demanded to be told at the end of the interview how he had done. At this point the recording ended.

The students were asked to write a detailed assessment of this tape-recorded applicant's performance. They described him much as I did above. This was, then, a first and initially successful attempt at normal forming. The interviewer-experimenter then breached this procedure. He presented the subject with the fake applicant's "official records," which showed superior grades and recommendations. Before the subjects could begin to attempt to normalize this information, they were inundated with more. They were handed the fake interviewer's assessment, which showed that the interviewer had rated the applicant highly. Subjects were given the opinions of a "panel of psychiatrists," who, along with other premedical students, were alleged to have also listened to the recording. These materials, which were individually arranged, contradicted almost adjective by adjective the assessment the subjects had originally offered.

The procedures of normal forming were thus rendered inoperative. Three of the 28 subjects resolved the situation by deciding it was all "a joke" or "merely an experiment." But for the majority who were unable to normalize in these ways, the world became "specifically senseless" (Garfinkel, 1963:189). They were bewildered. They exhibited great anxiety and discomfort. Some wondered if they had "gone crazy." It was as if once the normal forming procedures were rendered unsuccessful, they found themselves with "an amnesia for social structure" (Ibid.).

Garfinkel (Ibid.:223–226) designed another procedure that illustrates the importance of the interpretive procedure that I have labeled "doing a reciprocity of perspectives" . . . This procedure indicates that persons normally act to maintain that they share the same worlds and knowledge. To make this procedure fail:

> students were asked to enter a store, to select a customer, and to treat the customer as a clerk while giving no recognition that the subject was any other person than the experimenter took him to be and without giving any indication that the experimenter's treatment was anything other than perfectly reasonable and legitimate (Ibid.:223).

. . . The other results offered by Garfinkel display the anomia exhibited [in another experiment]. A physics professor, it will be remembered, becomes the unsuspecting subject of an experimenter, who "mistakes" him for a maître d' and persists in her error despite his attempts to create a reciprocity of perspectives. He tells her afterward "I haven't been so shaken since————denounced my theory of————in 19—" (Ibid.: 226). These studies indicate that if the reciprocity of perspectives is not accepted by other interactants, social scenes are severely disrupted.

I labeled the third interpretive procedure "employing the et cetera principle" (see p. 304 above). Although this procedure has three subfeatures, the breaching experiment I use as an example seems to explore the importance of only one of them. This feature suggests that normal interactants must permit unclear information to pass while waiting for later clarifying information. Garfinkel (Ibid.:221–223) instructed students to converse without letting any statements pass that they did not immediately feel they understood. Here is one of the cases that resulted from this procedure:

> Case 4. During a conversation (with the E's fiancée) the E questioned the meaning of various words used by the subject. For the first minute and a half the subject responded to the questions as if they were legitimate inquiries. Then she responded with "Why are you asking me these questions?" . . . She became nervous and jittery, her face and hand movements . . . uncontrolled. She appeared bewildered and complained that I was making her nervous and demanded that I "Stop it!"

The fiancée at last covered her face with a magazine and refused to talk. Their orderly relations had been temporarily anomicized by the experimenter's refusal to employ one of the et cetera procedures. His refusal forced the other interactant into simulating schizophrenia.

The Empirical Status of the Breaching Studies

Breaching procedures such as these are not experiments. Instead, Garfinkel (1967a:65) has suggested that they be called *demonstrations*, to emphasize their "results do no more than illustrate what I am talking about" (italics omitted). The linkage between any specific incongruity demonstration and a feature of social knowledge or interpretive procedure is obscure. The logic of the demonstrations does not follow from the theory in any determinate way. One must not look to these breaching studies as a way of building a theory of the reality constructor that will be comparable to the theories of the truly experimental sciences.

The value of such demonstrations is great nonetheless. Deep disruptions of the social order are possible at any moment, in any scene. These demonstrations strongly suggest that ceaseless reality work is necessary for social order to persist.

A serious problem with the breaching procedures is that they became too potent . . . Refinements on several of the techniques I mentioned led to anomia that threatened to linger for days. *Interested persons are strongly advised not to undertake any new breaching studies.* It is immoral to inflict them on others. However, there are ways that one can breach one's own sense of social order. This is not immoral, though it may be foolish. . . .

THE REALITY CONSTRUCTOR

Objective and constraining social structures are constructed by social structuring activities. To determine the nature of this reality work, the ethnomethodologist constructs a "model of the actor." The procedures he attributes to the model are descriptions of activities that display the objective and constraining social structures.

Thus the ethnomethodological theory of the reality constructor is about the *procedures* that accomplish reality. It is not about any specific reality. Social scientists often adopt a privileged position about their pursuits. They claim that their findings are about the reality they study. Making connections between social class and occupation, for example, social scientists propose that social class is actually the reason a person has a certain job.

My ethnomethodology makes no such claim. I do not assume a correspondence between my theory and particular realities. The reality constructor is not a picture of actual persons. Jennings (personal communication) once proposed that the ultimate model of the reality constructor would be a machine that could engage in interaction with humans without detection. If the technological problems of such an operation could be overcome, and the ethnomethodologist was actually able to "plug in" the social knowledge and interpretive procedures sufficient for the machine to "pass," there would be no claim that the way the machine engages in interaction is the way a person engages in interaction.

Ethnomethodology is not a method of pursuing the truth about the world. Rather, it examines the many versions, including its own, of the way the world is assembled. Ethnomethodology is not concerned with the truth value of statements about the world except as phenomena. It tries to determine the practices that make any statement true.

To this point we have discussed two kinds of "rules": normative rules (including legal, linguistic, and social science rules . . .), and interpretive rules or procedures. Interpretive rules can be used as a theoretical device for understanding normative rule use. Interpretive procedures "fill in" the essential incompleteness of normative rules. Though interpretive procedures can be used in this way, it would be inconsistent to conclude that they are immune from the feature of incompleteness found in normative rules. In fact, each interpretive procedure exhibits the same feature of incompleteness.

The specter of incompleteness neither jeopardizes the enterprise nor spells its end. It is a source of mystery and wonder.

Looked at this way, constructing a list of interpretive procedures, or constructing any finite model is like fashioning a ladder, a tool to carry us upward. At some point, the ladder can be tossed away, as we will no longer depend on it for our climb (Wittgenstein, 1921).

REFERENCES

Becker, Howard
    1953   *Outsiders—Studies in the Sociology of Deviance*. New York: The Free Press.
    1968   History, Culture and Subjective Experience: An Exploration of the Social Bases of Drug-Induced Experiences. *Journal of Health and Human Behavior* 8:961–968.
Chomsky, Noam
    1965   *Aspects of the Theory of Syntax*. Cambridge: The M.I.T. Press.
Cicourel, Aaron V.
    1964   *Method and Measurement in Sociology*. New York: The Free Press.
    1968   *The Social Organization of Juvenile Justice*. New York: John Wiley & Sons.
    1970   Language as a Variable in Social Research. *Sociological Focus* 3:2.

1972   Cross Modal Communication. Paper presented at the 23rd Annual Soci-
         olinguistics Roundtable: Language and Linguistics, Georgetown Univer-
         sity, March 16–18, 1972. In Roger Shuy (ed.), *Monograph 25, Linguis-
         tics and Language Science.* Washington, D.C.: Georgetown University
         Press, 1973.
1973a   *Cognitive Sociology.* London: Macmillan & Co.

Crowle, Anthony
1971   Post Experimental Interviews: An Experiment and a Sociolinguistic
         Analysis. Unpublished Ph.D. dissertation. University of California, Santa
         Barbara.

Goffman, Erving
1959   *The Presentation of Self in Everyday Life.* Garden City; N.Y.: Doubleday
         & Company; Anchor Books.
1961   *Encounters.* Indianapolis: The Bobbs-Merrill Co.
1969   *Strategic Interaction.* Philadelphia: University of Pennsylvania Press.

Garfinkel, Harold
1952   Perception of the Other. Unpublished Ph.D. dissertation. Harvard Uni-
         versity.
1956a   Conditions of Successful Degradation Ceremonies. *American Journal of
         Sociology* 61:420–424.
1956b   Some Sociological Concepts of Methods for Psychiatrists. *Psychiatric Re-
         search Reports* 6:181–195.
1959   Aspects of the Problem of Common Sense Knowledge of Social Struc-
         tures. *Transactions of the Fourth World Congress of Sociology,* 4:51–65.
         Milan: Stressa.
1960   The Rational Properties of Scientific and Common Sense Activities. *Be-
         havioral Science* 5:72–83. (Chapter 8 in Garfinkel, 1967a.)
1962   Common Sense Knowledge of Social Structures: The Documentary
         Method of Interpretation. In Jordan M. Scher (ed.), *Theories of the Mind.*
         New York: The Free Press.
1963   A Conception of and Experiments with "Trust" as a Condition of Con-
         certed Stable Actions. In O.J. Harvey (ed.), *Motivation and Social Inter-
         action.* New York: The Ronald Press Company.
1964   Studies of the Routine Grounds of Everyday Activities. *Social Problems*
         11:225–250 (Chapter 2 in Garfinkel, 1967a.)
1967a   *Studies in Ethnomethodology.* New York: Prentice-Hall.

Sacks, Harvey
1963   Sociological Description. *Berkeley Journal of Sociology* 8:1–17.
1965–
1968   Unpublished lectures at University of California, Los Angeles and Irvine.
1966   The Search for Help: No One to Turn to. Unpublished Ph.D. disserta-
         tion. University of California, Berkeley.

Schutz, Alfred
1962   *Collected Papers I: The Problem of Social Reality.* The Hague: Martinus
         Nijhoff.
1964   *Collected Papers II: Studies in Social Theory.* The Hague: Martinus
         Nijhoff.

1966   *Collected Papers III: Studies in Phenomenological Philosophy*. The Hague: Martinus Nijhoff.

1967   *The Phenomenology of the Social World*. Evanston, Ill.: Northwestern University Press.

1970a   *On Phenomenology and Social Relations*. Chicago: University of Chicago Press.

Whyte, W. H.

1955   *Street Corner Society*. Chicago: University of Chicago Press.

Wittgenstein, Ludwig

[1921]

1961   *Tractatus Logico-Philosphicus*. London: Basil Blackwell, & Mott.

Frame Analysis [1974]

ERVING GOFFMAN

> • *Goffman, as we have seen (pp. 244–261 above), began as a Durkheimian anthropologist, donning his pith helmet to investigate the rituals of modern everyday life. Never very friendly to the situationalism and mental constructionism of the symbolic interactionists (who lack the emphasis of the ritualists on the emotional and moral aspect of society), Goffman reacted more sharply when the ethnomethodologists arose in the 1960s and invaded his turf with a more extreme Husserlian phenomenology. Frame Analysis is Goffman's counterattack. Intellectually strong, it also shows Goffman's command of writing style, a theatrical performance by the master of sociological staging at the height of his powers.*

There is a venerable tradition in philosophy that argues that what the reader assumes to be real is but a shadow, and that by attending to what the writer says about perception, thought, the brain, language, culture, a new methodology, or novel social forces, the veil can be lifted. That sort of line, of course, gives as much a role to the writer and his writings as is possible to imagine and for that reason is pathetic. (What can better push a book than the claim that it will change what the reader thinks is going on?) A current example of this tradition can be found in some of the doctrines of social psychology and the W. I. Thomas dictum: "If men define situations as real, they are real in their consequences." This statement is true as it reads but false as it is taken. Defining situations as real certainly has consequences, but these may contribute very marginally to the events in progress: in some cases only a slight embarrassment flits across the scene in mild concern for those who tried to define the situation wrongly. All the world is not a stage—certainly the theater isn't entirely. (Whether you organize a theater or an aircraft factory, you need to find places for cars to park and coats to be checked, and these had better be real places, which, incidentally, had better carry real insurance against theft.) Presumably, a "definition of the situation" is almost always to be found, but

Erving Goffman, *Frame Analysis* (New York: Harper & Row, 1974), pp. 1–20. Reprinted by permission of the executrix of Erving Goffman's estate.

those who are in the situation ordinarily do not *create* this definition, even though their society often can be said to do so; ordinarily, all they do is to assess correctly what the situation ought to be for them and then act accordingly. True, we personally negotiate aspects of all the arrangements under which we live, but often once these are negotiated, we continue on mechanically as though the matter had always been settled. So, too, there are occasions when we must wait until things are almost over before discovering what has been occurring and occasions of our own activity when we can considerably put off deciding what to claim we have been doing. But surely these are not the only principles of organization. Social life is dubious enough and ludicrous enough without having to wish it further into unreality.

Within the terms, then, of the bad name that the analysis of social reality has, this book presents another analysis of social reality. I try to follow a tradition established by William James in his famous chapter "The Perception of Reality,"[1] first published as an article in *Mind* in 1869. Instead of asking what reality is, he gave matters a subversive phenomenological twist, italicizing the following question: *Under what circumstances do we think things are real?* The important thing about reality, he implied, is our sense of its realness in contrast to our feeling that some things lack this quality. One can then ask under what conditions such a feeling is generated, and this question speaks to a small, manageable problem having to do with the camera and not what it is the camera takes pictures of.

In his answer, James stressed the factors of selective attention, intimate involvement and noncontradiction by what is otherwise known. More important, he made a stab at differentiating the several different "worlds" that our attention and interest can make real for us, the possible subuniverses, the "orders of existence" (to use Aron Gurwitsch's phrase), in each of which an object of a given kind can have its proper being: the world of the senses, the world of scientific objects, the world of abstract philosophical truths, the worlds of myth and supernatural beliefs, the madman's world, etc. Each of these subworlds, according to James, has "its own special and separate style of existence,"[2] and "each world, *whilst it is attended to*, is real after its own fashion; only the reality lapses with the attention."[3] Then, after taking this radical stand, James copped out; he allowed that the world of the senses has a special status, being the one we judge to be the realest reality, the one that retains our liveliest belief, the one before which the other worlds must give

---

[1]William James, *Principles of Psychology*, vol. 2 (New York: Dover Publications, 1950), chap. 21, pp. 283–324. Here, as throughout, italics in quoted materials are as in the original.
[2]*Ibid.*, p. 291.
[3]*Ibid.*, p. 293.

way.[4] James in all this agreed with Husserl's teacher, Brentano, and implied, as phenomenology came to do, the need to distinguish between the content of a current perception and the reality status we give to what is thus enclosed or bracketed within perception.[5]

James' crucial device, of course, was a rather scandalous play on the word "world" (or "reality"). What he meant was not *the* world but a particular person's current world—and, in fact, as will be argued, not even that. There was no good reason to use such billowy words. James opened a door; it let in wind as well as light.

In 1945 Alfred Schutz took up James' theme again in a paper called "On Multiple Realities."[6] His argument followed James' surprisingly closely, but more attention was given to the possibility of uncovering the conditions that must be fulfilled if we are to generate one realm of "reality," one "finite province of meaning," as opposed to another. Schutz added the notion, interesting but not entirely convincing, that we experience a special kind of "shock" when suddenly thrust from one "world," say, that of dreams, to another, such as that of the theater:

> There are as many innumerable kinds of different shock experiences as there are different finite provinces of meaning upon which I may bestow the accent of reality. Some instances are: the shock of falling asleep as the leap into the world of dreams; the inner transformation we endure if the curtain in the theater rises as the transition into the world of the stageplay; the radical change in our attitude if, before a painting, we permit our visual field to be limited by what is within the frame as the passage into the pictorial world; our quandary, relaxing into laughter, if, in listening to a joke, we are for a short time ready to

[4]James' interest in the varieties-of-worlds problem was not fleeting. In his *Varieties of Religious Experience* (New York: Longmans, Green & Co., 1902) he approached the same question but through a different route.

[5]"But who does not see that in a disbelieved or doubted or interrogative or conditional proposition, the ideas are combined in the same identical way in which they are in a proposition which is solidly believed" (James, *Principles of Psychology*, 2:286). Aron Gurwitsch in his *The Field of Consciousness* (Pittsburgh: Duquesne University Press, 1964) makes a similar comment in a discussion of Husserl:

> Among such characters we mentioned those concerning modes of presentation, as when a thing is one time perceived, another time remembered or merely imagined, or when a certain state of affairs (the identical matter of a proposition) is asserted or denied, doubted, questioned, or deemed probable. [p. 327]

[6]First appearing in *Philosophy and Phenomenological Research*, V (1945): 533–576; reprinted in his *Collected Papers*, 3 vols. (The Hague: Martinus Nijhoff, 1962), 1:207–259.) A later version is "The Stratification of the Life-World," in Alfred Schutz and Thomas Luckmann, *The Structures of the Life-World*, trans. Richard M. Zaner and H. Tristram Engelhardt, Jr. (Evanston, Ill.: Northwestern University Press, 1973), pp. 21–98. An influential treatment of Schutz's ideas is Peter L. Berger and Thomas Luckmann, *The Social Construction of Reality* (Garden City, N.Y.: Doubleday & Company, Anchor Books, 1966).

accept the fictitious world of the jest as a reality in relation to which the world of our daily life takes on the character of foolishness; the child's turning toward his toy as the transition into the play-world; and so on. But also the religious experiences in all their varieties—for instance, Kierkegaard's experience of the "instant" as the leap into the religious sphere—are examples of such a shock, as well as the decision of the scientist to replace all passionate participation in the affairs of "this world" by a disinterested contemplative attitude.[7]

And although, like James, he assumed that one realm—the "working world"—had a preferential status, he was apparently more reserved than James about its objective character:

> We speak of provinces of *meaning* and not of subuniverses because it is the meaning of our experience and not the ontological structure of the objects which constitute reality,[8]

attributing its priority to ourselves, not the world:

> For we will find that the world of everyday life, the common-sense world, has a paramount position among the various provinces of reality, since only within it does communication with our fellow-men become possible. But the common-sense world is from the outset a sociocultural world, and the many questions connected with the intersubjectivity of the symbolic relations originate within it, are determined by it, and find their solution within it.[9]

and to the fact that our bodies always participate in the everyday world whatever our interest at the time, this participation implying a capacity to affect and be affected by the everyday world.[10] So instead of saying of a subuniverse that it is generated in accordance with certain structural principles, one says it has a certain "cognitive style."

Schutz's paper (and Schutz in general) was brought to the attention of ethnographic sociologists by Harold Garfinkel, who further extended the argument about multiple realities by going on (at least in his early comments) to look for rules which, when followed, allow us to generate a "world" of a given kind. Presumably a machine designed according to the proper specifications

---

[7]Schutz, *Collected Papers*, 1:231.

[8]*Ibid.*, p. 230. See also Alfred Schutz, *Reflections on the Problem of Relevance*, ed. Richard M. Zaner (New Haven, Conn.: Yale University Press, 1970), p. 125. On matters Schutzian I am indebted to Richard Grathoff.

[9]From "Symbol, Reality, and Society," Schutz, *Collected Papers*, 1:294.

[10]*Ibid.*, p. 342.

could grind out the reality of our choice. The conceptual attraction here is obvious. A game such as chess generates a habitable universe for those who can follow it, a plane of being, a cast of characters with a seemingly unlimited number of different situations and acts through which to realize their natures and destinies. Yet much of this is reducible to a small set of interdependent rules and practices. If the meaningfulness of everyday activity is similarly dependent on a closed, finite set of rules, then explication of them would give one a powerful means of analyzing social life. For example, one could then see (following Garfinkel) that the significance of certain deviant acts is that they undermine the intelligibility of everything else we had thought was going on around us, including all next acts, thus generating diffuse disorder. To uncover the informing, constitutive rules of everyday behavior would be to perform the sociologist's alchemy—the transmutation of any patch of ordinary social activity into an illuminating publication. It might be added that although James and Schutz are convincing in arguing that something like the "world" of dreams is differently organized from the world of everyday experience, they are quite unconvincing in providing any kind of account as to how many different "worlds" there are and whether everyday, wide-awake life can actually be seen as but one rule-produced plane of being, if so seen at all. Nor has there been much success in describing constitutive rules of everyday activity.[11] One is faced with the embarrassing methodological fact that the announcement of constitutive rules seems an open-ended game that any number can play forever. Players usually come up with five or ten rules (as I will), but there are no grounds for thinking that a thousand additional assumptions might not be listed by others. Moreover, these students neglect to make clear that what they are often concerned with is not an individual's sense of what is

---

[11]Schutz's various pronouncements seem to have hypnotized some students into treating them as definitive rather than suggestive. His version of the "cognitive style" of everyday life he states as follows:

1. a specific tension of consciousness, namely, wide-awakeness, originating in full attention to life;
2. a specific *epoché*, namely suspension of doubt;
3. a prevalent form of spontaneity, namely working (a meaningful spontaneity based upon a project and characterized by the intention of bringing about the projected state of affairs by bodily movements gearing into the outer world);
4. a specific form of experiencing one's self (the working self as the total self);
5. a specific form of sociality (the common intersubjective world of communication and social action);
6. a specific time-perspective (the standard time originating in an interaction between *durée* and cosmic time as the universal temporal structure of the intersubjective world).

These are at least some of the features of the cognitive style belonging to this particular province of meaning. As long as our experiences of this world—the valid as well as the invalidated ones—partake of this style we may consider this province of meaning as real, we may bestow upon it the accent of reality. [*Ibid.*, pp. 230–231.]

real, but rather what it is he can get caught up in, engrossed in, carried away by; and this can be something he can claim is really going on and yet claim is not real. One is left, then, with the structural similarity between everyday life—neglecting for a moment the possibility that no satisfactory catalog might be possible of what to include therein—and the various "worlds" of make-believe but no way of knowing how this relationship should modify our view of everyday life.

Interest in the James-Schutz line of thought has become active recently among persons whose initial stimulus came from sources not much connected historically with the phenomenological tradition: The work of those who created what has come to be called "the theater of the absurd," most fully exhibited in the analytical dramas of Luigi Pirandello. The very useful paper by Gregory Bateson, "A Theory of Play and Phantasy,"[12] in which he directly raised the question of unseriousness and seriousness, allowing us to see what a startling thing experience is, such that a bit of serious activity can be used as a model for putting together unserious versions of the same activity, and that, on occasion, we may not know whether it is play or the real thing that is occurring. (Bateson introduced his own version of the notion of "bracketing," a usable one, and also the argument that individuals can intentionally produce framing confusion in those with whom they are dealing; it is in Bateson's paper that the term "frame" was proposed in roughly the sense in which I want to employ it.)[13] The work of John Austin, who, following Wittgenstein,[14] suggested again that what we mean by "really happening" is complicated, and that although an individual may dream unrealities, it is still proper to say of him on that occasion that he is really dreaming.[15] (I have also drawn on the work of a student of Austin, D. S. Schwayder, and his fine book, *The Stratification of Behavior*.)[16] The efforts of those who study (or at least publish on) fraud, deceit, misidentification, and other "optical" effects, and the work of those who study "strategic interaction," including the way in which concealing and revealing bear upon definitions of the situation. The useful paper by Barney Glaser and Anselm Strauss, "Awareness Contexts and Social Inter-

[12]*Psychiatric Research Reports* 2, American Psychiatric Association (December 1955), pp. 39–51. Now reprinted in his *Steps to an Ecology of Mind* (New York: Ballantine Books, 1972), pp. 177–193. A useful exegesis is William F. Fry, Jr., *Sweet Madness: A Study of Humor* (Palo Alto, Calif.: Pacific Books, 1968).

[13]Edward T. Cone, in the first chapter of his *Musical Form and Musical Performance* (New York: W. W. Norton & Company, 1968), quite explicitly uses the term "frame" in much the same way that Bateson does and suggests some of the same lines of inquiry, but I think quite independently.

[14]See, for example, Ludwig Wittgenstein, *Philosophical Investigations*, trans. G. E. M. Anscombe (Oxford: Basil Blackwell, 1958), pt. 2, sec. 7.

[15]See, for example, chap. 7 in his *Sense and Sensibilia* (Oxford: Oxford University Press, 1962).

[16]London: Routledge & Kegan Paul, 1965.

action."[17] Finally, the modern effort in linguistically oriented disciplines to employ the notion of a "code" as a device which informs and patterns all events that fall within the boundaries of its application.

I have borrowed extensively from all these sources, claiming really only the bringing of them together. My perspective is situational, meaning here a concern for what one individual can be alive to at a particular moment, this often involving a few other particular individuals and not necessarily restricted to the mutually monitored arena of a face-to-face gathering. I assume that when individuals attend to any current situation, they face the question: "What is it that's going on here?" Whether asked explicitly, as in times of confusion and doubt, or tacitly, during occasions of usual certitude, the question is put and the answer to it is presumed by the way the individuals then proceed to get on with the affairs at hand. Starting, then, with that question, this volume attempts to limn out a framework that could be appealed to for the answer.

Let me say at once that the question "What is it that's going on here?" is considerably suspect. Any event can be described in terms of a focus that includes a wide swath or a narrow one and—as a related but not identical matter—in terms of a focus that is close-up or distant. And no one has a theory as to what particular span and level will come to be the ones employed. To begin with, I must be allowed to proceed by picking my span and level arbitrarily, without special justification.[18]

A similar issue is found in connection with perspective. When participant roles in an activity are differentiated—a common circumstance—the view that one person has of what is going on is likely to be quite different from that of another. There is a sense in which what is play for the golfer is work for the caddy. Different interests will—in Schutz's phrasing—generate different motivational relevances. (Moreover, variability is complicated here by the fact that those who bring different perspectives to the "same" events are likely to employ different spans and levels of focus.) Of course, in many cases some of those who are committed to differing points of view and focus may still be willing to acknowledge that theirs is not the official or "real" one. Caddies work at golf, as do instructors, but both appreciate that their job is special, since it has to do with servicing persons engaged in play. In any case, again I will initially assume the right to pick my point of view, my motivational relevancies, only limiting this choice of perspective to one that participants would easily recognize to be valid.

[17]*American Sociological Review*, XXIX (1964): 669–679.

[18]See the discussion by Emanuel A. Schegloff, "Notes on a Conversational Practice: Formulating Place," in David Sudnow, ed., *Studies in Social Interaction* (New York: The Free Press, 1972), pp. 75–119. There is a standard criticism of "role" as a concept which presents the same argument.

Further, it is obvious that in most "situations" many different things are happening simultaneously—things that are likely to have begun at different moments and may terminate dissynchronously.[19] To ask the question "What is *it* that's going on here?" biases matters in the direction of unitary exposition and simplicity. This bias, too, I must be temporarily allowed.

So, too, to speak of the "current" situation (just as to speak of something going on "here") is to allow reader and writer to continue along easily in their impression that they clearly know and agree on what they are thinking about. The amount of time covered by "current" (just as the amount of space covered by "here") obviously can vary greatly from one occasion to the next and from one participant to another; and the fact that participants seem to have no trouble in quickly coming to the same apparent understanding in this matter does not deny the intellectual importance of our trying to find out what this apparent consensus consists of and how it is established. To speak of something happening before the eyes of observers is to be on firmer ground than usual in the social sciences; but the ground is still shaky, and the crucial question of how a seeming agreement was reached concerning the identity of the "something" and the inclusiveness of "before the eyes" still remains.

Finally, it is plain that retrospective characterization of the "same" event or social occasion may differ very widely, that an individual's role in an undertaking can provide him with a distinctive evaluative assessment of what sort of an instance of the type the particular undertaking was. In that sense it has been argued, for example, that opposing rooters at a football game do not experience the "same" game,[20] and that what makes a party a good one for a participant who is made much of is just what makes it a bad one for a participant who thereby is made little of.

All of which suggests that one should even be uneasy about the easy way in which it is assumed that participants in an activity can be terminologically identified and referred to without issue. For surely, a "couple" kissing can also be a "man" greeting his "wife" or "John" being careful with "Mary's" makeup.

I only want to claim that although these questions are very important, they are not the only ones, and that their treatment is not necessarily required before one can proceed. So here, too, I will let sleeping sentences lie.

My aim is to try to isolate some of the basic frameworks of understanding available in our society for making sense out of events and to analyze the

---

[19]Nicely described by Roger G. Barker and Herbert F. Wright, *Midwest and Its Children* (Evanston, Ill.: Row, Peterson & Company, 1964), chap. 7, "Dividing the Behavior Stream," pp. 225–273.
[20]Presented perhaps overstrongly in a well-known early paper by Albert H. Hastorf and Hadley Cantril, "They Saw a Game: A Case Study," *Journal of Abnormal and Social Psychology*, XLIX (1954): 129–234.

special vulnerabilities to which these frames of reference are subject. I start with the fact that from an individual's particular point of view, while one thing may momentarily appear to be what is really going on, in fact what is actually happening is plainly a joke, or a dream, or an accident, or a mistake, or a misunderstanding, or a deception, or a theatrical performance, and so forth. And attention will be directed to what it is about our sense of what is going on that makes it so vulnerable to the need for these various rereadings.

Elementary terms required by the subject matter to be dealt with are provided first. My treatment of these initial terms is abstract, and I am afraid the formulations provided are crude indeed by the standards of modern philosophy. The reader must initially bestow the benefit of mere doubt in order for us both to get to matters that (I feel) are less dubious.

The term "strip" will be used to refer to any arbitrary slice or cut from the stream of ongoing activity, including here sequences of happenings, real or fictive, as seen from the perspective of those subjectively involved in sustaining an interest in them. A strip is not meant to reflect a natural division made by the subjects of inquiry or an analytical division made by students who inquire; it will be used only to refer to any raw batch of occurrences (of whatever status in reality) that one wants to draw attention to as a starting point for analysis.

And of course much use will be made of Bateson's use of the term "frame." I assume that definitions of a situation are built up in accordance with principles of organization which govern events—at least social ones—and our subjective involvement in them; frame is the word I use to refer to such of these basic elements as I am able to identify. That is my definition of frame. My phrase "frame analysis" is a slogan to refer to the examination in these terms of the organization of experience.

In dealing with conventional topics, it is usually practical to develop concepts and themes in some sort of logical sequence: nothing coming earlier depends on something coming later, and, hopefully, terms developed at any one point are actually used in what comes thereafter. Often the complaint of the writer is that linear presentation constrains what is actually a circular affair, ideally requiring simultaneous introduction of terms, and the complaint of the reader is that concepts elaborately defined are not much used beyond the point at which the fuss is made about their meaning. In the analysis of frames, linear presentation is no great embarrassment. Nor is the defining of terms not used thereafter. The problem, in fact, is that once a term is introduced (this occurring at the point at which it is first needed), it begins to have too much bearing, not merely applying to what comes later, but reapplying in each chapter to what it has already applied to. Thus each succeeding section of the study becomes more entangled, until a step can hardly be made because of what must be carried along with it. The process closely follows the horrors of repetition songs, as if—in the case of frame analysis—what Old MacDonald had on his farm were partridge and juniper trees.

Discussions about frame inevitably lead to questions concerning the status of the discussion itself, because here terms applying to what is analyzed ought to apply to the analysis also. I proceed on the commonsense assumption that ordinary language and ordinary writing practices are sufficiently flexible to allow anything that one wants to express to get expressed.[21] Here I follow Carnap's position:

> The sentences, definitions, and rules of the syntax of a language are concerned with the forms of that language. But, now, how are these sentences, definitions, and rules themselves to be correctly expressed? Is a kind of super-language necessary for the purpose? And, again, a third language to explain the syntax of this superlanguage, and so on to infinity? Or is it possible to formulate the syntax of a language within that language itself? The obvious fear will arise that in the latter case, owing to certain reflexive definitions, contradictions of a nature seemingly similar to those which are familiar both in Cantor's theory of transfinite aggregates and in the pre-Russellian logic might make their appearance. But we shall see later that without any danger of contradictions or antinomies emerging it is possible to express the syntax of a language in that language itself, to an extent which is conditioned by the wealth of means of expression of the language in question.[22]

Thus, even if one took as one's task the examination of the use made in the humanities and the less robust sciences of "examples," "illustrations," and "cases in point," the object being to uncover the folk theories of evidence which underlie resort to these devices, it would still be the case that examples and illustrations would probably have to be used, and they probably could be without entirely vitiating the analysis.

In turning to the issue of reflexivity and in arguing that ordinary language is an adequate resource for discussing it, I do not mean that these particular linguistic matters should block all other concerns. Methodological self-consciousness that is full, immediate, and persistent sets aside all study and analysis except that of the reflexive problem itself, thereby displacing fields of inquiry instead of contributing to them. Thus, I will throughout use quota-

---

[21]*Wovan man nicht sprechen kann, ist nicht der satz, "Wovan man nicht sprechen kann, darüber muss man schweigen."* [Of that which one cannot speak, it is *not* the case: "of that which one cannot speak, one must keep silent."—Ed.]

[22]Rudolf Carnap, *The Logical Syntax of Language*, trans. Amethe Smeaton (London: Kegan Paul, Trench, Trubner & Co., 1937), p. 3.

tion marks to suggest a special sense of the word so marked and not concern myself systematically with the fact that this device is routinely used in a variety of quite different ways,[23] that these seem to bear closely on the question of frame, and that I must assume that the context of use will automatically lead my readers and me to have the same understanding, although neither I nor they might be able to explicate the matter further. So, too, with the warning and the lead that ordinary language philosophers have given us. I know that the crucial term "real" may have been permanently Wittgensteined into a blur of slightly different uses, but proceed on the assumption that carefulness can gradually bring us to an understanding of basic themes informing diversity, a diversity which carefulness itself initially establishes, and that what is taken for granted concerning the meaning of this word can safely so be done until it is convenient to attend to what one has been doing.

A further caveat. There are lots of good grounds for doubting the kind of analysis about to be presented. I would do so myself if it weren't my own. It is too bookish, too general, too removed from fieldwork to have a good chance of being anything more than another mentalistic adumbration. And, as will be noted throughout, there are certainly things that cannot be nicely dealt with in the arguments that follow. (I coin a series of terms—some "basic"; but writers have been doing that to not much avail for years.) Nonetheless, some of the things in this world seem to urge the analysis I am here attempting, and the compulsion is strong to try to outline the framework that will perform this job, even if this means some other tasks get handled badly.

Another disclaimer. This book is about the organization of experience—something that an individual actor can take into his mind—and not the organization of society. I make no claim whatsoever to be talking about the core matters of sociology—social organization and social structure. Those matters have been and can continue to be quite nicely studied without refer-

---

[23]I. A. Richards, for example, has a version in his *How to Read a Page* (New York: W.W. Norton & Company, 1942):

We all recognize—more or less unsystematically—that quotation marks serve varied purposes:
1. Sometimes they show merely that we are quoting and where our quotation begins and ends.
2. Sometimes they imply that the word or words within them are in some way open to question and are only to be taken in some special sense with reference to some special definition.
3. Sometimes they suggest further that what is quoted is nonsense or that there is really no such thing as the thing they profess to name.
4. Sometimes they suggest that the words are improperly used. The quotation marks are equivalent to *the so-called*.
5. Sometimes they only indicate that we are talking of the words as distinguished from their meanings. "Is" and "at" are shorter than "above." "Chien" means what "dog" means, and so forth.

There are many other uses. . . . . [p. 66]

ence to frame at all. I am not addressing the structure of social life but the structure of experience individuals have at any moment of their social lives. I personally hold society to be first in every way and any individual's current involvements to be second; this report deals only with matters that are second. This book will have weaknesses enough in the areas it claims to deal with; there is no need to find limitations in regard to what it does not set about to cover. Of course, it can be argued that to focus on the nature of personal experiencing—with the implication this can have for giving equally serious consideration to all matters that might momentarily concern the individual—is itself a standpoint with marked political implications, and that these are conservative ones. The analysis developed does not catch at the differences between the advantaged and disadvantaged classes and can be said to direct attention away from such matters. I think that is true. I can only suggest that he who would combat false consciousness and awaken people to their true interests has much to do, because the sleep is very deep. And I do not intend here to provide a lullaby but merely to sneak in and watch the way the people snore.

Finally, a note about the materials used. First, there is the fact that I deal again in this book with what I have dealt with in others—another go at analyzing fraud, deceit, con games, shows of various kinds, and the like. There are many footnotes to and much repetition of other things I've written.[24] I am trying to order my thoughts on these topics, trying to construct a general statement. That is the excuse.

Second, throughout the book very considerable use is made of anecdotes cited from the press and from popular books in the biographical genre.[25] There could hardly be data with less face value. Obviously, passing events that are typical or representative don't make news just for that reason; only extraordinary ones do, and even these are subject to the editorial violence routinely employed by gentle writers. Our understanding of the world precedes these stories, determining which ones reporters will select and how the ones that are selected will be told. Human interest stories are a caricature of evidence in the very degree of their interest, providing a unity, coherence, pointedness, self-completeness, and drama only crudely sustained, if at all, by everyday living. Each is a cross between an *experimentum crucim* and a sideshow. That is their point. The design of these reported events is fully responsive to our demands—which are not for facts but for typifications. Their telling demon-

---

[24]So much so that I use source abbreviations, a list of which can be found on p. xi.

[25]An analysis of incidentally published stories—"fillers"—is provided by Roland Barthes along with an exhibition of literary license in "Structure of *Fait-Divers*," in his *Critical Essays*, trans. Richard Howard (Evanston, Ill.: Northwestern University Press, 1972), pp. 185–195.

strates the power of our conventional understandings to cope with the bizarre potentials of social life, the furthest reaches of experience. What appears, then, to be a threat to our way of making sense of the world turns out to be an ingeniously selected defense of it. We press these stories to the wind; they keep the world from unsettling us. By and large, I do not present these anecdotes, therefore, as evidence or proof, but as clarifying depictions, as frame fantasies which manage, through the hundred liberties taken by their tellers, to celebrate our beliefs about the workings of the world. What was put into these tales is thus what I would like to get out of them.

These data have another weakness. I have culled them over the years on a hit-or-miss basis using principles of selection mysterious to me which, furthermore, changed from year to year and which I could not recover if I wanted to. Here, too, a caricature of systematic sampling is involved.

In addition to clippings as a source of materials, I draw on another, one as questionable as the first. Since this study attempts to deal with the organization of experience as such, whether "actual" or of the other kinds, I will have recourse to the following: cartoons, comics, novels, the cinema, and especially, it turns out, the legitimate stage. I am here involved in no horrors of bias different from the ones already exhibited in the selection of bits of human interest news. But I am led to draw on materials that writers in other traditions use, whether in literary and dramatic criticism of current "high" culture or in the sort of sociological journalism which attempts to read from surface changes in commercially available vicarious experience to the nature of our society at large. In consequence, many of the things I have to say about these materials will have already been said many times and better by fashionable writers. My excuse for brazenly dipping into this preempted domain is that I have a special interest, one that does not recognize a difference in value between a good novel and a bad one, a contemporary play or an ancient one, a comic strip or an opera. All are equally useful in explicating the character of strips of experienced activity. I end up quoting from well-known works recognized as setting standards, and from minor works current at the time of writing, but not because I think these examples of their genre have special cultural worth and warrant endorsement. Critics and reviewers cite the classics of a genre in dealing with current works in order to explicate what if anything is significant and artful in them. I draw clumsily on the same materials—as well as critiques of them—simply because that is what is easy to hand. Indeed, these materials are easy to everyone's hand, providing something of a common fund of familiar experience, something that writers can assume readers know about.

* * * * * *

That is the introduction. Writing one allows a writer to try to set the terms of what he will write about. Accounts, excuses, apologies designed to reframe what follows after them, designed to draw a line between deficiencies in what the author writes and deficiencies in himself, leaving him, he hopes, a little better defended than he might otherwise be.[26] This sort of ritual work can certainly disconnect a hurried pedestrian from a minor inconvenience he might cause a passing stranger. Just as certainly, such efforts are optimistic when their purpose is to recast the way in which a long book is to be taken. (And more optimistic still in the case of a second edition's preface to an already prefaced edition, this being an attempt to recast a recasting.)

* * * * * *

But what about comments on prefaces? Where does such a topic taken up at such a point leave the writer and the reader (or a speaker and an audience)? Does that sort of talk strike at the inclination of the reader to discount or

---

[26]There is a useful article by Jacob Brackman called "The Put-On" (*The New Yorker*, June 24, 1967, pp. 34–73). In his twelve-page introduction to the paperback edition he writes:

> Updating. If "updating" this essay were to mean exchanging more current jokes and performers for ones since disappeared, and appending how there came to be "put-on" head boutiques, and TV game shows, and a Sears Put-On clothing shop, and publishers crowing "This is the novel that makes you ask: *Is the author putting me on?*", and thousands of winkful commercials that seemed to say, "I know that you know that I'm trying to sell you. Let's you and me both goof on the product together."—if I were to "update" along these lines, and if I were to add little exegeses of Tiny Tim's wedding, Paul Morrissey's movies, Paul McCartney's death, then the piece would begin to stink of inauthenticity.
>
> I think you must let a piece like this stand—not in its syntax, necessarily, but within the limits of its original awareness—as a fragment of cultural history. It may have been valid to the precise present for a matter of months, or days; who will quibble now that time is so short? Once the vision's devoured, mulched and incorporated, unless it has been frozen somewhere, its moment—when only so much had happened, when only so much had been revealed—is lost forever. All we have left are "updated" reports, grotesquely stretched, debased and freshened up, as what played itself out between haircuts is made to seem the rage of a decade. If I were to do this piece today (which would itself be impossible) hardly anything in it would stay the same. Of things in the real world about which one can try to write, sensibility may be the slipperiest. If I won't write the new piece now, how can I go back and meddle with the old one? [*The Put-On* (New York: Bantam Books, 1972), pp. 10–11.]

Brackman also argues that current items of cultural interest date very rapidly and fully, and, by implication, that writings concerned with these items will date quickly, too. He also suggests that the point of such writings is to bring the not quite consciously appreciated to awareness, and to do this first, and that once again a restatement or republication will sound stale. All of this I think has some truth and correctly describes the contingencies of that kind of subject matter, there being inevitably an unstated element of the reader's interest that derives from the current interest of the item. This element will decline rather quickly, leaving the writer having written something that can no longer be read with interest. In fact, every analyst of jokes has faced this problem, since the current version of a basic joke which he writes about today will sound very dated tomorrow. But given what Brackman is stuck with reprinting, his introduction does the framing work that introductions can do to segregate the producer from his product, in this case arguing that the piece was an expression of his sensibility *then*, not now.

criticize prefacing as an activity? And if it turns out that the preface was written in bad faith, tailored from the beginning to exemplify this use that will have come to be made of it? Will the preface then be retrospectively reframed by the reader into something that really isn't a preface at all but an inappropriately inserted illustration of one? Or if an admission of bad faith is made unconvincingly, leaving open the possibility that the disclosure was an afterthought? What then?

*   *   *   *   *   *

And does the last comment excuse me in any degree from having been puerile and obvious in commenting on prefaces, as when, in a book analyzing jokes, the writer is excused the badness of the cited jokes but not the badness of the analysis of them? (A novelist who nowadays injects direct address in the body of his work—"Dear Reader, if you've gone this far, you'll know I hate that character . . ."—easily fails to change the footing we allow him; but what if he writes that he would like to succeed in such a device but knows we will not let him?)

*   *   *   *   *   *

And what about discussions about being puerile and obvious? A word incorrectly spelled can, I think, be successfully used by the misspeller as an illustration of incorrect spelling and analyzed as such. But can a writer posture in his writing and then effectively claim that all along he was only providing an illustration of bad taste and lack of sophistication? Would it be necessary for him to show, and if so, how would he, that his claims were not merely a device hit upon after the fact to make the best out of what he was not able to prevent from being a bad thing?

*   *   *   *   *   *

And if in the first pages after acknowledging colleagues who had helped, I had said: "Richard C. Jeffrey, on the other hand, did not help." And if I had gone on here (in these later pages) to suggest that the aim had been to make a little joke and incidentally bring awareness to a tacit constraint on acknowledgment writing? Then the explication of this aim could be seen as bad faith— either a post-hoc effort to hedge on having tried to be witty or an admission of having entrapped the reader into accepting a plant, that is, a statement whose reason for inclusion would later be shown to have not been apparent. But if, as is in fact the case, the whole matter is enclosed as a question within a section of the introduction dealing with a consideration of introductions and is therefore not to be seen as having an initial character as a simple, straightforward introduction, what then?

And after all of this, can I get the point across that Richard C. Jeffrey in fact didn't help? Does this last sentence do it? And if so, had a conditional been used, as in: "And after all of this, could I get the point across . . . etc." What then? And would this last comment transform an assertion into an illustration and so once again cast the matter of Richard C. Jeffrey in doubt?

*   *   *   *   *   *

And if the preface and the comments on the preface and the comments on the comments on the preface are put in question, what about the asterisks which divide up and divide off the various sections in which this is managed? And if the orthography had still been intact, would this last question itself have undermined these framing devices, including the ones which bracket this sentence with the prior one?

*   *   *   *   *   *

And if above I had said: "What about the * * * * * *which divide up and divide off . . ."; would this be a proper use of print, and can an easy rule be formulated? Given the motivational relevancies of orthographers, a book on orthography can properly use a batch of print to illustrate print, to the neglect of saying something with its meaning. Similarly, a geography book can properly switch from words to maps. But when a mystery writer has his hero find a coded message on a torn bit of paper and then shows the clue to the reader by insetting it in the center of the page as though it were a map in a geography book, so that the reader sees the tear as well as the message, what sort of shift to a nonfictional frame has the writer asked the reader to make, and was he quite within his rights to ask it? Is it overly cute for an anthropologist reporting on the role of metaphor (with special reference to animal sources) to write, "One always feels a bit sheepish, of course, about bringing the metaphor concept into the social sciences and perhaps that is because one always feels there is something soft and wooly about it"?[27] Similarly, if I try to get dodgy with prefaces, is this not different from writing about tricks done with prefaces (which characteristically need not be undertaken at the beginning of a study)? Is this not the difference between doing and writing about the doing? And in considering all of these matters, can I properly draw on my own text ("And if above I had said: 'What about the * * * * * * that divide up and divide off . . .'; would this be . . .") as an illustration? And in this last sentence has not all need to be hesitant about the right to use actual asterisks disappeared, for after all, a doubtful usage cited as an example of doubtful usage ceases to be something that is doubtful to print?

[27]James W. Fernandez, "Persuasions and Performances: Of the Beast in Every Body . . . And the Metaphors of Everyman," *Daedalus*, Winter 1972, p. 41.

*   *   *   *   *   *

And if I wanted to comment on the next to last sentence, the one containing a parenthesized quoted sentence and questionably real asterisks, could I quote *that* sentence effectively, that is, employ the apparently required punctuation marks and yet allow the reader an easy comprehension of what was being said about what? Would the limits of doing things in print have been reached?

*   *   *   *   *   *

That is what frame analysis is about.